JEWISH AMERICAN POETRY

JEWISH
AMERICAN
POETRY

Poems, Commentary, and Reflections

Edited by

Jonathan N. Barron *and*

Eric Murphy Selinger

Brandeis University Press

Published by University Press of New England

Hanover and London

Brandeis University Press

Published by University Press of New England, Hanover, NH 03755

© 2000 by Brandeis University Press

Printed in the United States of America

5 4 3 2 1

Library of Congress Cataloging-in-Publication Data

Jewish American poetry: poems, commentary, and reflections / edited by Jonathan N. Barron and Eric Murphy Selinger.
    p. cm.—(Brandeis series in American Jewish history, culture, and life)
    ISBN 1–58465–042–7 (cloth: alk. paper)— ISBN 1–58465–043–5 (pbk. : alk. paper)
    1. American poetry—Jewish authors. 2. Jewish religious poetry, American. 3. American poetry—20th century. 4. American poetry—Jewish authors—History and criticism. I. Barron, Jonathan N. II. Selinger, Eric Murphy. III. Series.
PS591.J4 J42   2000
811'.50808924—dc21   00–025283

Copyright to poems in this volume is held by the individual authors, with a few exceptions, as noted below. The editors gratefully acknowledge permission from the poets and/or their publishers to reprint the poems and essays in this collection. Every effort has been made to obtain permission for poems in this volume.

A Faculty Research Grant from the University of Southern Mississippi and the DePaul University Research Council funded these permissions and other expenses in the preparation of this book. We are grateful for their support.

"First Set" and "I Had Thought of Writing a Play Based on the Following Facts" are from Ammiel Alcalay's *the cairo notebooks* (Singing Horse Press, 1994). Copyright © 1994 by Ammiel Alcalay. Used with the permission of the poet.

Vicki Angel, "From the Other Side of the Nile," appeared in *Seattle Review* 18 under the title "Falling in Line." Used with permission of the poet.

"Peter Pan" from *All-American Girl,* by Robin Becker, © 1996. Reprinted by permission of the University of Pittsburgh Press.

Charles Bernstein's "Solidarity Is the Name We Give to What We Cannot Hold" is from *My Way: Speeches and Poems* (Chicago: University of Chicago Press, 1999). Copyright © 1999 by Charles Bernstein. Used with the permission of the poet.

Reprinted with the poet's permission are excerpts from Chana Bloch's "Don't Tell the Children" and "Esperanto" from *Mrs. Dumpty* (Madison: University of Wisconsin Press, 1998); "Brothers," "The Converts," "The Flood," "Furniture," and "The Sacrifice" from *The Secrets of the Tribe* (New York: The Sheep Meadow Press, 1981); and "Goodbye" and "White Petticoats" from *The Past Keeps Changing* (New York: The Sheep Meadow Press, 1992). "Spell," previously unpublished, is copyright © 1999 by Chana Bloch.

"Poem to Gentiles." Copyright © 1944 by Maxwell Bodenheim from *Seven Poets in Search of an Answer*, edited by Thomas Yoseloff, published by B. Ackerman. Reprinted by permission of Jack B. Moore.

Michael Castro's "The Grandparent Poems: Self-Reflections in a Smoky Mirror" are reprinted with the permission of the poet. "La America" and "Stella's Story" appeared in *The Sagarin Review* (1991). "Grandfathers" appeared in *Voices Within the Ark: The Modern Jewish Poets* (Avon, 1980), copyright © 1980 by Michael Castro. All are reprinted with the permission of the poet.

Robert Creeley, "Ever Since Hitler," *Selected Poems*. University of California Press, 1991. © The Regents of the University of California. Reprinted by permission of the University of California Press.

Continued on page 345

Brandeis Series in American Jewish History, Culture, and Life

Jonathan D. Sarna, Editor

Sylvia Barack Fishman, Associate Editor

Leon A. Jick, 1992
The Americanization of the Synagogue, 1820–1870

Sylvia Barack Fishman, editor, 1992
Follow My Footprints: Changing Images of Women in American Jewish Fiction

Gerald Tulchinsky, 1993
Taking Root: The Origins of the Canadian Jewish Community

Shalom Goldman, editor, 1993
Hebrew and the Bible in America: The First Two Centuries

Marshall Sklare, 1993
Observing America's Jews

Reena Sigman Friedman, 1994
These Are Our Children: Jewish Orphanages in the United States, 1880–1925

Alan Silverstein, 1994
Alternatives to Assimilation: The Response of Reform Judaism to American Culture, 1840–1930

Jack Wertheimer, editor, 1995
The American Synagogue: A Sanctuary Transformed

Sylvia Barack Fishman, 1995
A Breath of Life: Feminism in the American Jewish Community

Diane Matza, editor, 1996
Sephardic-American Voices: Two Hundred Years of a Literary Legacy

Joyce Antler, editor, 1997
Talking Back: Images of Jewish Women in American Popular Culture

Jack Wertheimer, 1997
A People Divided: Judaism in Contemporary America

Beth S. Wenger and Jeffrey Shandler, editors, 1998
Encounters with the "Holy Land": Place, Past and Future in American Jewish Culture

David Kaufman, 1998
Shul with a Pool: The "Synagogue-Center" in American Jewish History

Roberta Rosenberg Farber and Chaim I. Waxman, 1999
Jews in America: A Contemporary Reader

Murray Friedman and Albert D. Chernin, 1999
A Second Exodus: The American Movement to Free Soviet Jews

Stephen J. Whitfield, 1999
In Search of American Jewish Culture

Naomi W. Cohen, 1999
Jacob H. Schiff: A Study in American Jewish Leadership

Barbara Kessel, 2000
Suddenly Jewish: Jews Raised as Gentiles

Jonathan N. Barron and Eric Murphy Selinger, editors, 2000
Jewish American Poetry: Poems, Commentary, and Reflections

To our parents, who introduced us as children,

And for our children, who have yet to meet.

Contents

PART II: REFLECTIONS   173

Acknowledgments

I would like to thank the University of Southern Mississippi for a research grant, and my department for a course release and for providing me with re-search assistants. I particularly thank Nyleva Corley, who made the hard work far smoother than would otherwise have been possible. I thank Phyllis Deutsch of the University Press of New England; encouraging always, and cajoling where necessary, she made this project possible. Jennifer Thomas, Permissions Editor, also deserves high praise for her heroic efforts on our behalf. I also extend a warm "thank you" to my coeditor and rediscovered friend, Eric. I thank my parents for their support and for their eagle-eyed reading. Above all, I thank my wife, Ellen Weinauer, colleague, first reader, best friend. She has given more, sacrificed more, and helped more than any acknowledgment can say. I thank her and my children, Liana and Raphael, who mean the world to me. The Talmud tells us that "the World is a Wedding." To this world, this wedding, my family, I dedicate this book. No wedding should be without poetry.

Jonathan N. Barron

My interest in Jewish American poetry was sparked some years ago by conversations with Norman Finkelstein and Maeera Shreiber. I am pleased to include them in this book. Many friends have supplied me with texts to study and questions to address, notably Elizabeth Feldman of Havurah Lomdim, whose bookshelves I browsed with great success during my research on "Shekhinah in America."(Summer funding from the DePaul University Research Council made this essay possible, and I thank my colleagues at DePaul for their enthusiastic support.) My thanks to Phyllis Deutsch for her faith in this project, and to my coeditor, Jonathan, not least for his organizational skills and his patience with my lack thereof. Finally, I too wish to thank family: my parents, for keeping me in touch with Jonathan; my children, Nathan and Margaret; and my wife, Rosalie Murphy, for her love and advice once more. This book is for my grandparents, Manny and Shirley, whose love of Kipling, Joyce, and one another has taught me more than they know.

Eric Murphy Selinger

Note on Transliteration

In the poems, commentaries, and reflections that follow, authors have had occasion to transliterate from Yiddish, Ladino, and Hebrew. We have left the style and spelling of this transliteration up to each individual author.

JEWISH AMERICAN POETRY

Emma Lazarus

The New Colossus

Not like the brazen giant of Greek fame,
With conquering limbs astride from land to land;
Here at our sea-washed, sunset gates shall stand
A mighty woman with a torch, whose flame
Is the imprisoned lightning, and her name
Mother of Exiles. From her beacon-hand
Glows world-wide welcome; her mild eyes command
The air-bridged harbor that twin cities frame.
"Keep ancient lands, your storied pomp!" cries she
With silent lips. "Give me your tired, your poor,
Your huddled masses yearning to breathe free,
The wretched refuse of your teeming shore.
Send these, the homeless, tempest-tost to me,
I lift my lamp beside the golden door!"

Emma Lazarus was born in New York City in 1849. When she was only eighteen, her well-off father privately published her first book, *Poems and Translations*. The following year she found a mentor in the great Transcendentalist Ralph Waldo Emerson. Later, as an established author, Lazarus wrote essays and poems on behalf of the Jewish immigrants who came to America after the devasting Russian pogroms of 1881. Her most famous poem is undoubtedly "The New Colossus" (1885), the sonnet whose last five lines are engraved on the pedestal of the Statue of Liberty.

Introduction

Jewish American poets have long been a presence in American poetry. Only in recent years, however, has one seen the rise of a distinct phenomenon that one might call "Jewish American Poetry." This change in the landscape of contemporary poetry invites us to look back at everything that came before it from a new perspective. What once seemed a group of isolated voices now seems like the stirrings of a distinct, although not necessarily discrete, American poetic tradition. And with its Jewish presence brought back into focus, the whole of American poetry begins to look slightly different. Including the voice of American Jewish poets in a consideration of American poetry exposes the explicitly and implicitly Christian assumptions in the most famous American poems and poetic movements. Once these assumptions are made visible, they no longer define American poetry, but are simply one thematic aspect of it. With this shift in thematic emphasis, other doors of possibility begin to open.

Once the idea of a singular story, a singular theme for American poetry is put to rest, one can see American poetry as a house with many entrances, many doors. One finds, for example, a way into this house through Native American poetry, African American poetry, Hispanic-Latino-Chicano poetry. In short, American poetry is and always has been an inclusive genre.

In this book, we enter that house through the door of Jewish American poetry, a tradition with a nearly two-hundred-year history. In order to see the world of American poetry that this door welcomes us into we begin by briefly retelling the story of American poetry as a whole. For those familiar with Jewish history, the first part of this story can sound strangely familiar. If one begins with the first poets to inhabit these shores, those of the hundreds of Native American nations, then one finds a mix of praise-songs, name-songs, incantations, chronicles and boasts, lessons in conduct, and records of vision that calls to mind the oldest strata of Hebrew poetry, oral texts still audible here and there in the written Torah. Like Jewish poetry before the rabbinic period, when the holy and poetic start to split, the first American poetry was inseparable from the sacred: a technique for both attaining and expressing the deepest spiritual truths. Several recent Jewish American poets, notably Jerome Rothenberg and Michael Castro, have turned to Native American poetics as a way to rediscover their own ancestral traditions and be rejuvenated by them. As one Zuni creation poem says, "My father picked up the prayer plume, / And with the precious prayer plume / Me he appointed."

The echoes of Jewish culture are even stronger when one turns to the first English-language poetry in what would become the United States, that of the seventeenth-century New England Puritans. Steeped in the Bible, the Puritan colonists believed themselves to be new Israelites in what they called a New

Canaan—a pagan world where they expected to build their New Jerusalem. Puritan poets like Anne Bradstreet, Edward Taylor, Michael Wigglesworth, and the authors of the Bay State Hymn Book looked to the Bible for compositional models. They translated psalms, wrote liturgical and didactic verse, and, in their more intimate lyrics, took richly allusive stock of their own souls' wrestling with Puritan doctrine and the experience of the divine. Insisting that one could literally read the signs and symbols of the Bible in the American landscape, what they called "typology," the Puritans began a moral, prophetic, idealistic tradition that informs American poetry to this day. One might say that they, too, wrote poetry with a "precious prayer plume"—but unlike the Native Americans, and often directly opposed to them, Puritan poets insisted that the American experience be read as a version of the three-part Christian story: the Fall, Grace, and Redemption.

An American Incarnation: Transcendentalism

By the early nineteenth century, this Christian story had become a familiar feature of much American poetry, particularly in New England. But as New England became more and more secular, a group of poets began to remove the Christian particulars from the underlying narrative that moved from sin to grace. Rather than view America as a New Canaan, they returned to an even earlier Biblical figure: Eden. Rather than read American history as a triumph of Jerusalem over Canaan, poets like William Cullen Bryant, Ralph Waldo Emerson, and Walt Whitman, to name just three, hymned an incarnate holiness, an immanence, an Edenic optimism and possibility latent in the American landscape, in the American language, and in the American people.

For these poets of what is now called American Romanticism, the Bible no longer mediated between poetry and place. Instead, they insisted that nature, as a correspondent symbol of the spirit, could speak directly to individuals who were, themselves, already invested with sparks of the Divine. In his great essay "Nature" (1836), Emerson went so far as to establish the connections between the spirit, language, and nature as a simple sequence of declarations: "1. Words are signs of natural facts. 2. Particular natural facts are symbols of particular spiritual facts. 3. Nature is the symbol of spirit" (20). In "The Poet," he took this argument to its natural conclusions: Americans ought to write their own scripture. Said Emerson, it is time to be free of the stale past of Hebrew history, or, as Thoreau put it: "The good Hebrew Revelation takes no cognizance of all this cheerful snow" ("A Winter Walk," [75] 1847). Freed from both the Old and New Testament particulars, Americans like Thoreau and Whitman aspired to create a new Bible, and each did, in a sense, with Thoreau's *Walden* and Whitman's epochal *Leaves of Grass*.

This turn to the transcendental, an "American Incarnation," has since become the most well known, most studied poetry of the American nineteenth century, and with good reason. It gives rise to two founding figures of later American poetry, Walt Whitman and Emily Dickinson—unpublished until after her death, but arguably the most subtle and searching writer of her time. There were also at the time, however, several competing poetries alongside this Romanticism. To understand the origins and shaping tensions of Jewish American poetry, one needs to keep them in mind as well.

Other Nineteenth-Century Poetries

On the one hand, literary historians describe a flourishing "performance culture" in the antebellum world: recitation pieces, didactic and narrative verse, and poems on political topics of the day. (Rowdy, unpolished, democratic, such performance poems are the great-great-grandparents of the open mikes and poetry slams of the 1990s, where poets compete for audience approval.) At the same time, the topical, political poetry written by such New Englanders as John Greenleaf Whittier and the other "Fireside Poets" depicted an impassioned abolitionism and celebrated working-class life. A third kind of poetry, by the Southerner Edgar Allan Poe, scorned both realism and the performance style as betrayals of poetry's commitment to Beauty. Poe also implicitly and directly mocked the Transcendentalists' optimism by exploring the darker, amoral, even decadent corners of the soul.

Finally, at the center of the literary world, one found Henry Wadsworth Longfellow: a poet-professor whose command of European and English literary tradition was unrivaled, whose literary authority helped shape the Harvard curriculum for decades, and whose lyrics, translations, and narrative poems were not only confident and masterful, but immensely popular, both here and abroad. "Baudelaire adapted part of *The Song of Hiawatha* into the rhymed alexandrines of '*Le Calumet de Paix*,'" the poet Dana Gioia reminds us; "Franz Liszt set the 'Prologue' of *The Golden Legend* to music," and "in England he eventually outsold Tennyson and Browning" (65). No American poet would have such international impact until the arrival of Longfellow's grand-nephew, Ezra Pound, and Pound's comrade-in-avant-garde-arms, the Harvard-schooled and tradition-minded T. S. Eliot. And no American poet would so confidently bridge the gap between populist and high art poetries—even Poe acknowledged Longfellow's accomplishment—until Robert Frost, who declared: "You can damn all you want to . . . [William Cullen] Bryant, [James Russell] Lowell, [Oliver Wendell] Holmes, and [James Greenleaf] Whittier, but keep hands off of Longfellow" (Monteiro 17).

By the end of the Civil War, of all these kinds of poetry, the realist, pragmatic kind represented by Longfellow had become the most beloved. Like Poe, Longfellow was as likely to oppose the Romantic tradition of incarnate spirituality as he was to represent it. And like Poe, when he did represent it, one often found a bleak terror in the spiritual world rather than a benign presence. But perhaps Longfellow's most important contribution to American poetry was his insistence that America was, from the outset, a multiculture. His work depicted the lives of Native Americans (*Hiawatha*), transplanted Acadians (*Evangeline*), and even the Jews.

Emma Lazarus: Nineteenth-Century Jewish American Poet

With Longfellow's representation of the Jews, the story of the Jewish presence in American poetry properly begins. In his famous "The Jewish Cemetery at Newport," Longfellow tells his readers that the Jews are already an ancient, all-but-vanished tribe: "Closed are the portals of their Synagogue, / No Psalms of David now the silence break, / No Rabbi reads the ancient Decalogue / In the grand dialect the Prophets spake." He concludes with the melancholy observation that "the dead nations never rise again." But even as he said this, a Jewish American poet, Emma Lazarus, whom none other than Emerson himself referred to as "the great Hebrew Poetess," began her career.

Born in New York City to a well-established family of mixed Sephardi (Spanish Jewish) and Ashkenazi (German Jewish) ancestry, Lazarus gained early fame for a poetry that was as thoroughly assimilated and as uninterested in things Jewish as she was. The devastating Russian pogroms of 1881, however, and the subsequent arrival of Eastern European Jewish refugees shocked Lazarus into a new sense of Jewish identity—as did, the story has it, reading George Eliot's novel *Daniel Deronda*, with its romantic Jewish hero. Still quite secular, Lazarus began educating herself about Jewish history and tradition. She had already translated Jewish poets (notably the German poet Heinrich Heine); now she began publishing a series of essays in *The American Hebrew* ("An Epistle to the Hebrews," they were called); also she grew politically active in immigration issues, and in her last two books, she wrote of Jewish immigrants to Texas and experimented with the then-new prose poem form in order to write about the dangers of exile and foster a Zionist hope.

Although Emma Lazarus was not the first Jewish American poet—that honor belongs to Penina Moise—Lazarus does mark the first example of the way Jewish American poets construct an ethnic identity through voluntary association and through what David Bleich, in his essay for this volume, calls "Learning, Learning, Learning." She also exhibits what has become a central characteristic of Jewish American poetry: a poetics of commentary. Her early poem "In the Jewish Synagogue at Newport" (1867) implicitly comments on Longfellow's view of the Jews. At first, she seems to agree with Longfellow: "No signs of life are here." Steve Rubin, in his essay for this volume, takes this line as the poet's own conclusion. We, however, read the poem somewhat differently. In the America that her poem calls "this new world of light," we believe that Lazarus takes it as her task to make that past live again. Rather than reject the past in favor of a return to the innocence of Eden, that is to say, or confidently look forward to a Messianic restoration, Lazarus transforms the abandoned Jewish synagogue into a place where the past may shape the present, not least because of the continuing presence there of a Biblically-inflected sense of the Divine. Where Longfellow saw only death and fate, she sees another Presence as well: "Take off your shoes as by the burning bush," she concludes the poem, "Before the mystery of death *and God.*" (The italics are ours.) Placing the reader in the position of Moses, about to receive his commission, Lazarus sees the synagogue as no more dead a place than the desert of Midian—and as likely a spot for the chance of renewal.

With her poetry of textual commentary, ethnic identity, and stubbornly vital spiritual force, Lazarus stepped into the gap between the incarnate spirituality of Emerson and the romantics, and the social, material, multicultural realism of Longfellow and Whittier. Her new work troubled Emerson, her early mentor—perhaps, as the literary critic Maeera Shreiber suggests, because it insisted on the continuing importance of a merely "local" or "particular" history that he felt ought to be subsumed in the new American present. Indeed, to her anger and chagrin, Emerson left Lazarus out of his own anthology of American poetry. By way of recompense we have included her most famous poem, "The New Colossus," as our own first offering.

1900: Lyric Poetry as Refuge and Relief

No matter how influential or serious American Romantic poetry became in the nineteenth century, Lazarus, like most late-nineteenth-century American poets, also wrote in the shadow of what had clearly become the great American genre: Realist fiction. By 1900, poets had to ask: How should their art respond to fiction's challenge? One answer came in the form of Edmund Clarence Stedman's *An American Anthology, 1787–1900* (1901). There, collected in over 800 pages, one finds an American lyric tradition spanning the centuries from the Puritans to the dawn of the twentieth century. It included each of the kinds of poetry we have so far described. But it emphasized the American multiculture in particular by including such late-nineteenth-century dialect poets as the "great Hoosier poet" James Whitcomb Riley, the African American Paul Laurence Dunbar, the Catholic Imogen Louise Guiney, and Emma Lazarus herself. If the Realist novelists sought to "widen the bounds of sympathy" and demonstrate that "nothing that God made is contemptible," as William Dean Howells insisted, so did these poets—and, indeed, Howells wrote enthusiastic introductions both for Dunbar's *Lyrics of Lowly Life* and for the translated *Songs of the Ghetto* by the first major Yiddish poet in America, the immigrant tailor and "Sweatshop Poet," Morris Rosenfeld.

Despite the raucous energy of these vernacular poetries, the Stedman anthology, with its careful selections, presented American poetry primarily as a largely genteel and lyric tradition: Poetry, it appeared, would offer readers refuge from the new urban reality of the twentieth century. Eventually Stedman's view came to dominate, and poetry came to mean only lyric poetry, only the music of language: metrical, chiming melodiousness. Gone was the "barbaric yawp" of common speech and common life.

Poetic Modernism: The First Wave

It was precisely this lyric emphasis on the refuge and solace of music that provoked the first English-language rebellions now collectively referred to as Modernism. Robert Frost brought what he called "the sound of sense"—an emphasis not on musical rhythms for their own sake but rather on speech patterns set in counterpoint to traditional forms and meter. Meanwhile, poetry ought to be at least "as well-written as prose," declared the Idaho-born Ezra Pound from his new home in London. He argued for a ruthless pruning away of vague but luxurious euphony, "emotional slither," and above all, metrical filler. Replace such "cream puffs," he said, with the crisp articulations common to the poetry of ancient Greece, the Troubadours, China, and Japan. The three-part credo of the "Imagists," the short-lived but still-influential movement Pound promoted with the work of, among others, the American Hilda Doolittle (H.D.), flung down the gauntlet. "Use absolutely no word that does not contribute to the presentation," it demanded. "Compose in the sequence of the musical phrase, not in the sequence of the metronome" (*Poetry* [1913] 198–206).

This impulse to change the very fabric and identity of poetry made the first decades of the twentieth century an age of competing "-isms," heady with the ferment of "the New." The various New Poetries of Modernism both echoed and advanced the many other radicalisms of the time: the "New Art" of cubism, expressionism, Dada, and collage; the "New Woman" and her struggles for political and sexual freedom; the "New Politics" of both the revolutionary left and the reactionary right; the "New Physics" of relativity (however rarely understood); and the "New Psychology" of Freud and Jung.

Of the "first wave" of American Modernist poets—Marianne Moore, T. S. Eliot, Wallace Stevens, William Carlos Williams, Gertrude Stein, Ezra Pound, H.D., Robert Frost, to name some of the most enduring—one, Gertrude Stein, deserves particular mention. After Emma Lazarus, Stein was the second great Jewish poet in the pantheon of American poetry. Born and raised in an immigrant German Jewish family, she was already a well-known—even infamous

—writer of experimental fiction when she wrote her first of many important poetic experiments, the prose poems of *Tender Buttons* (1914). Here one finds many of the features familiar to students of the avant-garde, and of Modernism more generally: radical juxtaposition, verbal and visual puns, and an intense focus on the slippery materiality of language—words' endlessly productive division into sound and sense. Stein's ability to conjure subtle effects in time and mood with the simplest of words, "the language of dishes and daylight," was enormously influential on other modern novelists and poets, notably Ernest Hemingway, William Carlos Williams, and Mina Loy, and in 1926 she was invited to lecture on her theories of language, literature, and punctuation at Oxford and Cambridge universities. How much Stein identified herself as a Jew is the subject of some debate, not least because she was just as radical in her ideas of selfhood as she was in her theories about art. But recent Jewish American writers, notably Charles Bernstein, have found something quite Jewish in Stein's wariness of imposed ethnic or religious identity, even as her playful, rigorous writings continue to tease and inspire.

Modernism: The Second Wave

Despite Stein's importance to the story of Jewish American poetry and to a distinctly avant-garde modernism, T. S. Eliot, at first, had the most dramatic impact of all of the first wave of modernist poets. Between 1922 (when *The Waste Land* was published) and the early 1960s, Eliot's poetic achievement—and, perhaps still more, his stern dicta as a critic—haunted younger generations of poets. The source of a host of new literary-critical terms, including the poem's "impersonality," the "mythic method," the "objective correlative," and the need for modern poetry to be "difficult," Eliot's work embodied a deeply conservative cultural politics, at times even a veritable culture war to defend the declining West against a number of threatening Others: among them, the Jews. Other poets found themselves drawn (or forced) to define themselves in and against this cultural politics. Some were sympathetic, like the Southern poets called the Fugitives (John Crowe Ransom, Allen Tate, the young Robert Penn Warren), who insisted that modern poetry return to the use of traditional rhyming and metrical forms, as well as to a pastoral or agrarian and often Christian sensibility. Others tried to put Eliotic techniques—allusion, collage, and so on—to more optimistic or even romantic use, notably Hart Crane (in *The Bridge*).

A Jewish Modernism? Rukeyser, Zukofsky, and the Objectivists

By the late 1930s, two distinctly Jewish voices announced themselves using the language and forms of Modernism. Muriel Rukeyser, a third great Jewish

American poet, began publishing a poetry at once personal and allusive, Eliotic yet also staunchly progressive in its politics. In her early "Poem out of Childhood," she weighed the attraction of the Classical past against reflections on the most pressing current issues of social justice. "Not Sappho, Sacco," she pointedly decided, referring to the trial and execution of the Italian American anarchists Sacco and Vanzetti, but Rukeyser was not a poet to leave any resource unused. After traveling to Gauley Bridge, West Virginia, in 1936 to research a nationally infamous mining disaster, for example, she wrote "The Book of the Dead," a long poem that effortlessly incorporates prose excerpts from legal testimony and medical records with lyrical pentameter verse and echoes of such canonical texts as Dante's *Inferno*, the Bible, and *Paradise Lost*.

While Rukeyser came from a well-off and long-established Reform Jewish family, a second Jewish modernist of the 1920s and 1930s, Louis Zukofsky, was born to immigrant parents on the Lower East Side, where he first encountered the works of Shakespeare and Longfellow in Yiddish, his native tongue. As an adult, Zukofsky returned to Emma Lazarus's mode of poetry-as-commentary to write his first major piece, "Poem Beginning 'The,'" as among other things a commentary on *The Waste Land*, complete with line numbers, touchstone allusions, and scholarly notes. This time, however, the references were not only to Eliot's Classical and Christian "mind of Europe" but also to the Yiddish poet Yehoash (Solomon Blumgarten), the Russian revolution, and the poet's own mother ("Symbol of our Relatively Most Permanent Self, Origin, and Destiny," as he calls her, with an Oedipal wink).

With this poem and others like it, Zukofsky ultimately launched, with four other Jewish American poets, a new poetic movement that had far more in common with the Imagism of Pound and Williams and the language play of Gertrude Stein than it did with the work of Eliot. This movement, Objectivism, centered on Zukofsky, Charles Reznikoff, George Oppen, and Carl Rakosi. These poets rejected Eliot's fascination with symbol and myth in favor of a more realist sensibility that Zukofsky called "thinking with the things as they exist" (12). According to the second-generation Objectivist poet Michael Heller, who contributes an essay to the second part of this collection, Objectivism is best understood as an ethics as well as a poetics, a surrogate moral code akin to the set of Jewish laws, the *halacha*. Says Heller, in the history of American poetry "the Objectivists stand out as a salutary force, a flying poetic truth squad" (7).

While all but unknown in the 1930s, this group of poets would prove increasingly influential in the 1960s, as was the rediscovered Rukeyser. The ethical force of their works particularly appealed to the postwar generation of poets, as well as their reflections, in form and content, on the crucial question: What should the relationship be between poetry and politics? How closely tied were the struggles of the writer and the struggles of the age? After 1945, these questions grew ever more pressing as Modernism, associated with difficult poetry dense in allusion and free verse, gave rise to a series of antimodernisms and postmodernisms. Should Modernist experiments in language be abandoned, subsequent writers wondered? Or should poets be even more obliged to press forward with the Modernist "revolution of the word"?

American Poetry After Modernism: Traditional, Popular, Experimental

After World War II there followed a succession of poetry movements: Beat, Black Mountain, New York School, Confessional, Deep Image, Naked Poetry, Black Arts Poetry, Feminist Poetry, and more. Each of these movements claimed to address the pressing questions of poetic theme and form raised by both waves of Modernism. Also, in each of these postwar movements Jewish poets have played a significant role. Instead of providing an overview of these movements, and instead of contrasting them with the various strains of Modernism that preceded them, it is simply worth noting that in this postwar period right through to today, American poetry divides itself at least three ways. Each of the movements just named emphasizes to varying degrees either a traditional, popular, or experimental poetic tradition.

Initially, in the postwar period, the traditionalists favored a difficult, serious, highly allusive, intricately patterned poetry in the tradition of the later T. S. Eliot or the Fugitives. As Karl Shapiro, writing in 1958, put it, Eliot had become as central to this kind of poetry as the Book of Revelations: "still / Eliot and John are always there / To tempt our admirari nil" ("Recapitulations"). Shapiro did not mean these lines to be complimentary. In fact, he proved to be the first prominent critic of such ornate, thick, and densely packed intellectual poetry. If Shapiro became one of the first poets to critique the Modernism of Eliot, then another Jewish American poet, Delmore Schwartz, born like Shapiro in 1913, was one of the first to make it palatable to a new generation. A member of a circle of intellectuals known as the New York Intellectuals who were associated with the magazine *Partisan Review*, Schwartz managed to bridge the intellectual, symbolic, and densely textured poetry of T. S. Eliot with a new world of popular culture and youth. He accomplished this feat at the age of twenty-five with the publication of *In Dreams Begin Responsibilities* (1938), a combination of stories, memoir, and the kind of poetry familiar to readers of Eliot but shocking to those who did not expect to find positive references both to Jews and to popular culture in its pages. This eclectic book made symbolic use of such popular cultural themes as contemporary movies, Tin-Pan Alley songs, and billboards. It also introduced in a straightforward, non-apologetic way a variety of Jewish American themes.

In 1959, Schwartz won the prestigious Bollingen Prize in Poetry—but this was, ultimately, recognition of his early promise more than anything else. In fact, his later years were spent combatting mental illness as he struggled to maintain his position as a professor at Syracuse University. One bright moment in these last years: He taught poetry to Lou Reed, later the founder of the influential rock band the Velvet Underground. Even today Reed thinks of Schwartz as his "spiritual godfather." Reed, however, is an unlikely inheritor of Schwartz's mantle, for in the end, Schwartz's incorporation of the popular into Eliot's ideal of poetry was never designed to make the lowly into high art, nor did it seek out the popular by appeasing or being less difficult. (Perhaps that is why Reed's rock homage to Delmore Schwartz, "European Son," has so few words.) In the end, Schwartz became a grim warning, even a martyr to the idea that a poet could be at once difficult, serious, allusive, symbolic, and widely read.

By contrast, in the camp of "the popular," there did thrive a more accessible, more urbane sort of lyric in the style of Robert Frost and of the English poet W. H. Auden, who had by then obtained American citizenship. This kind of poetry was particularly championed by Karl Shapiro. Not only did Shapiro condemn Eliot and praise Frost in a series of widely read articles published in the mainstream press, but he also ensured such work would get published as editor from 1950 to 1956 of the prestigious magazine *Poetry*. Like Schwartz, he too brought his Jewishness into his work, particularly in his collection *Poems of a Jew* (1958), which introduced Jewish concerns to readers at a time when such appeals to one's ethnicity were held in disdain by the poetry establishment.

Meanwhile, Auden himself, throughout the 1950s, selected and wrote the introductions to the annual and influential Yale Series of Younger Poets. And in 1957, Robert Frost, by then in his eighties, wrote the introduction to the defining anthology of the newer generation of post World War II American poets: *New Poets of England and America*. Between them, then, Shapiro, Auden, and Frost helped guide into prominence a wide variety of poets: among them Robert Lowell, John Berryman, Richard Wilbur, Elizabeth Bishop, John Logan, James Merrill, W. S. Merwin, Frank O'Hara, Galway Kinnell, Adrienne Rich, Gwendolyn Brooks, and Robert Hayden.

At the same time, an alternative world of poetic experimentation also thrived. Originally lumped together as "Beats" by the media and by themselves, the poets of this world embraced many different poetic movements and schools. Today, it is most accurate to use the name of the famous anthology that introduced them to the literary world, an anthology designed to challenge the kind of work one found in *New Poets of England and America*, *The New American Poets* (1960). Determined to put an end to what even the more traditional Delmore Schwartz in a famous essay had called "The Literary Dictatorship of T. S. Eliot" (1947), they were eager to bring their own personal, ethnic, religious, and sexual lives into the work of poetry. Ready to engage in direct social and political critique, even wild satire, in the name of freedom, they were also, to a poet, committed to free verse.

Among the New American Poets, we call attention particularly to Allen Ginsberg. Not only did Ginsberg gain the most attention of all of these younger writers, but he also became a media icon, thanks first to the obscenity trial of his early poem "Howl," and then to his central role in the new youth culture of the 1960s. Ginsberg read and chanted at antiwar rallies, hung out with Bob Dylan, the Beatles, and the Rolling Stones, jammed with The Band, and was elected Kral Majales, King of the May, by students in Prague in 1965, shortly before being expelled for subversive behavior. Ginsberg's fame has often blinded readers to just how remarkable a poet he could be, but his work combines the devotion to detail of the Objectivists (he particularly admired Reznikoff) with the grand Romantic sweep he learned from Whitman, Shelley, and William Blake, and adds a tenderness and tragicomic humor all its own. Although "Howl" remains his best-known work, his finest poem is also his most profoundly Jewish one: "Kaddish," an elegy for Ginsberg's mother, Naomi. With its willingness to tell what Ginsberg called "the whole secret family-self tale," and with its ability to take even the most harrowing (and ethnically particular) details of his mother's descent into madness and death and shape them into archetype and lasting art, "Kaddish" marked a turning point in American poetry.

American Poetry after Modernism: Confessional Poetry, Deep Image Poetry, and the Return of the Multicultural

By the late 1960s, then, even the poets who had once written exclusively metrical verse rich in dense allusive symbols, the poets one would have found in the 1957 *New Poets* anthology, wrote free verse often depicting their own private, personal experience. Poets previously committed to an art of meter, traditional forms, literary allusion, and "high" diction—Robert Lowell most notably, but also James Merrill and Adrienne Rich—began to change their ways. By the mid 1960s, most had turned their attention, at least at times, both to free verse and to their own personal and political views as subjects fit for poetry. Two groups that gained particular attention in the 1960s, the Confessionals (Robert Lowell, Sylvia Plath, Anne Sexton, John Berryman) and the Deep Image poets (James Wright, Robert Bly, Louis Simpson, W. S. Merwin), are particularly introspective, personal, and committed to exploring connections between the outer world of politics—including gender politics—and the inner world of the (respectively) Freudian or Jungian unconscious.

Serious omissions no doubt will strike those reading this rather traditional account of the story of American poetry. Particularly egregious is the woefully underrepresented presence of African Americans, women, and other minorities.

In the late 1960s this underrepresentation struck such poets this way as well. Tired of learning about a poetry that excluded them, African Americans were among the first groups of poets to insist on their inclusion on their own terms in the story of American poetry. The Black Arts Poets were the first contemporary group to reject both terms of the postmodern American debate. Seeing little room for their work in either "New American Poets" or "the New Poets," the Black Arts Poets of the 1960s espoused a particularly Black Aesthetic, at once politically and formally radical, composed, by and large, for oral performance. "The poet must become a performer the way James Brown is a performer—loud, gaudy, and racy," declared the Black Arts poet Larry Neal in 1968; "He must take his work where his people are."

At the same time that the Black Arts poets investigated a Black Aesthetic, and in large part following from their example, women of every race began to search out a specifically female and feminist poetics. "What would happen if a woman spoke the truth about her life?" Muriel Rukeyser asked in "Käthe Kollwitz," a poem from her 1968 collection *The Speed of Darkness.* Her answer: "The world would split open." In the hands of Rukeyser, Adrienne Rich, Judy Grahn, Audre Lorde, Irena Klepfisz, and the many other women of the Feminist Poetry movement, poetry indeed became a force to "split open" and reconceive both the literary and the political world. In her poem "Prospective Immigrants Please Take Note" Adrienne Rich, for example, "split open" the shining promise of Emma Lazarus's poem "The New Colossus." Where Lazarus's sonnet ends in a note of unadulterated hope—"I lift my lamp beside the golden door!"—Rich's poem concludes simply: "The door itself / makes no promises. / It is only a door."

Throughout the 1970s, other groups also defined, again for themselves, their own poetic traditions: Chicanismo and Chicano poetry, Nuyorican poetry, Native American poetry, and others. As part of the broadly defined "ethnopoetics" movement—less a movement, perhaps, than a creative dialogue among anthropologists, performers, and poets—one found many Jewish writers, among them David Meltzer, Nathaniel Tarn, and Jerome Rothenberg. Liberated and provoked by this dialogue, these poets returned to the worlds of Jewish ritual, mysticism, and folk culture and soon began writing and performing their own "ancestral poems" as well.

The Reign of the Free Verse Lyric, and Two Responses to It

For all the many kinds of poetry that had flourished in the wake of Modernism, by the mid 1970s one kind of poem had come to dominate the major American literary institutions: a personal anecdote charged with emotion in plain language and in free verse. Some poet-critics, notably Charles Bernstein (who appears in this anthology), have labeled such poetry our "official verse culture." Against its dominance in literary circles, two new movements arose, New Formalism and Language Poetry. The first—whom some prefer to call the Expansive Poets—staged a populist recovery of pleasures that few readers had ever wanted to give up: metrical form, rhyme, the beauty of sentence sounds, and of story. Although often read as entirely of the political right, such poetry also includes the work of passionate liberals, progressives, and leftists Julia Alvarez, Raphael Campo, and Marilyn Hacker, whom we also include here.

Another reaction to the free verse personal lyric came from the so-called "Language Poets," named for one of their early journals, $L=A=N=G=U=A=G=E$. Building on the formally experimental work of Stein, Zukofsky, William Carlos Williams, and the poet-composer John Cage, the Language Poets rarely strive to capture "authentic" selfhood. Instead, they write a poetry that investigates the way concepts like authenticity and selfhood turn out, on inspection, to be shaped by the language we use—and, in a sense, the language that uses us, giving us the terms and habits of thought that we live by. This may sound abstract, even grim. But these poetic investigations can be remarkably playful, and their admirers see these poets as offering a wider range of pleasures in their work than can be found in the "official verse culture" ideal of the free verse, first-person lyric: language that is teasing, free-wheeling, associative, and above all, surprising. As Charles Bernstein puts it in a much-quoted Language poem, "The Klupzy Girl," "Poetry is like a swoon, with this difference: / it brings you to your senses." Aside from Bernstein, another particularly engaging Language Poet, Bob Perelman, also appears in this anthology.

What Is Jewish American Poetry?

Evidently, then, in the story of American poetry the Jewish presence has been notable. But is there, in fact, a specifically Jewish American poetry? As a singular definition of American poetry breaks down, it is quite clear that in America there are now multiple poetries. Is there a Jewish American poetry among them? What would it be? What can it be? Should there even be a discrete category of Jewish American poetry?

In order to answer these questions, we sought contributions from a wide range of Jewish American poets. We do not in any sense intend to be inclusive of all the fine Jewish American poets currently writing. But we did want to bring together the various American poetries currently circulating in which Jews participate. Among those postwar poets who inherited the traditions of radical Modernism and the New American Poets of the 1960s, one finds here poets like Ammiel Alcalay, Charles Bernstein, Bob Perelman, and the popular dead-pan performance poet Hal Sirowitz from the downtown poetry scene of

New York City, the world of poetry slams. Also here one finds Jerome Rothenberg, a leading poet and theorist of the ethnopoetics movement. We should also mention that part of Alcalay's poetic allure is that his poetic experiments, which return to the prose poetry of William Carlos Williams and Gertrude Stein, also invoke (more distantly) Emma Lazarus, as he brings a self-consciously Sephardi experience into a predominantly Ashkenazi Jewish America.

Meanwhile, we also include, at the other end of this spectrum, the continuing poetic tradition that follows from Frost and Auden, among others. In the poetry of Anthony Hecht, John Hollander, Marilyn Hacker, and Allen Grossman one finds poets whose commitment to the traditions of the Romantic lyric remains firm despite the various challenges put to those forms by the various movements of the past hundred years.

Meanwhile, in between these two experimental and traditional poles, we also print recognized and established figures of the predominantly free verse lyric tradition (although many of them have written in and continue to write in traditional forms): Philip Levine, Maxine Kumin, Gerald Stern, Marge Piercy, Alicia Ostriker, Albert Goldbarth, and C. K. Williams. Two of these poets, Piercy and Ostriker, along with Irena Klepfisz and Marilyn Hacker, have also been instrumental in establishing a particular feminist poetry. In this same broad central category, we also print the work of younger poets, many of whom are only in the middle of promising careers: Chana Bloch, Michael Castro, Norman Finkelstein, Jacqueline Osherow, Hilda Raz, Howard Schwartz, Alan Shapiro.

Recent years have also been kind to one of the oldest genres of Jewish poetry, the liturgical poem, verse meant specifically for use in and as prayer. While both Anthony Hecht and Marge Piercy have written such work, Marcia Falk, whom we also include, has made this kind of poetry (along with translation) a focus of her literary career. She is most recently the author of an entirely new Jewish prayer book, *The Book of Blessings*, composed in Hebrew and English with in-depth commentaries on each prayer and poem. We are happy to include her here as well.

Principal Themes in Jewish American Poetry

By including Jewish American poets who write in such a wide variety of forms, we mean to raise more questions than we answer. Are Jewish American poets merely participants or are they indicative of a new thing: a Jewish American poem? Rather than answer that question ourselves, we put it to the poets, inviting them to address it in a format rich in Jewish tradition: text and commentary. But we gave this tradition an American twist, since rather than comment on traditional Jewish texts from the Bible, Talmud, and *midrash*, we asked each of the twenty-six poets to select and comment on one of their own poems, from whatever angle they might choose. We asked women and men, from the deeply religious and the adamantly secular, from traditions as varied as Sephardi and Yiddish and that new postmodern hybrid, the American. We include poets who write by the waters of Manhattan (as Charles Reznikoff did), as well as by the Great Salt Lake, the Gulf Coast, and even the Seine. They work in styles from the most experimental Language Poetry to those most traditional of lyric genres, the sonnet and the sestina. Collectively, this first part of our book now opens twenty-six different doors, each into new terrain.

That said, however, we did discover in the poems and commentaries three distinct themes that confirm that Jewish American literature has entered a new period, and that cross the great divides of gender, of background, and of style.

1. *Return to sources.* The poets we print return, and not always in obvious ways, both to Jewish traditional texts from the Bible and Talmud and *siddur* (prayerbook) and to those aspects of Jewish culture that have long been themselves marginalized: from the Kabbalistic *Zohar* to legends, characters, and scenes from alternative Jewish traditions. In this return, many of the poets we collect here find a new source for contemporary language play. As Jacqueline Osherow puts it, her favorite footnote in the Bible is "Meaning of the Hebrew uncertain" because it marks an "invitation to poetry."

2. *Multiple identities.* Unlike so much Jewish American literature of the first half of this century, the poets here do not describe a singular Jewish or American experience. The poets find Judaism as much a religious identity as an ethnic one, although the divide between culture and religion is not easily marked. For some of the poets, religious identity is specific to Jewish law (*halacha*). Others trace religious identity not in the familiar ground of orthodoxy but rather in the new earth of a specifically American landscape. The cultural meaning of Jewish experience in America multiplies for the poets as well. They write from both Ashkenazi and Sephardi traditions, as well as from a perspective that belongs to neither of those two dominant experiences. Many of the poets here write of a Jewish America that is, itself, a new Jewish experience altogether. As Alan Shapiro says in his commentary, "The Jew was the first American long before America existed."

Meanwhile, the often vexed relationship between American and Israeli Jews constantly disrupts each of these identities. Many of the poets we print here—some living in the United States, some writing from the heart of Jerusalem—address issues of identity through a deeply felt exploration of American-Israeli and Israeli-Palestinian relations.

These new developments question, in striking ways, what once might have been assumed to be a stable identity. Just as striking, perhaps even more so, is the relentless focus on gender common to the poems gathered here. Fundamental questions about Jewishness are now raised in terms of the gender assumptions that seem, now, to have been implicit in the term.

This is not to say that older contexts for identity common to Jewish American literature have now vanished. Like so many Jewish American poets of the last half-century, the poems here also situate themselves in terms of family. But even this has a new twist, as now grandparents are more common than parents. Also, like the poets who precede them, the poets here manifest a healthy interest in political matters, the life of the polis. The social concern so often associated with Jewish American literature still makes itself known in the works of today's writers. It, too, has become a way to complicate, settle, or simply explore the meanings of "Jewish," "American," and even "poetic" identity.

3. *Questions of poetics*. The art of poetry itself turned out to be another recurrent concern. Many of the poets here savored the opportunity to meditate on questions of Jewishness by asking basic questions about poetry as well. One result of such meditations is that readers will gain new insights into the history of the past fifty years of American poetry. Here, for example, Maxine Kumin recalls her friendship with Anne Sexton, Anthony Hecht discusses his experiences as a poet after World War II, and Philip Levine invokes his friendship with the poet Charles Wright. But more than just a new look at American poetic history, these poets also invite readers to consider fundamental questions: What is a poem? How should a poet write it in the contemporary era? And, in a question specific not only to Jews but to all poets of conscience, how should, how *dare* one write poetry after the Holocaust? When the poets here ask what their aesthetic choices of language and pattern say about history, culture, and art, they do not necessarily mean Jewish history, culture, and art. But for some, on the other hand, this is exactly what is meant. They cast a wary, witty eye on just how deeply their own writing and thinking have been Christianized, if only (for most) because of the habits of American English. Or they put that English through its paces, delighting in the way this polyglot language can approximate—if never quite match—the lost or only distantly recoverable resources of Yiddish. Many, like Allen Grossman, C. K. Williams, and Albert Goldbarth, find themselves returning to the foundational, mythic split between Athens and Jerusalem, the Greek and Jewish origins of the West. In late-century America, it seems, this once-anxious tension can look more like the muscle-building "Dynamic Tension" trumpeted in those old Charles Atlas ads. The old men who summon a teen-aged Albert Goldbarth to *daven* [pray] with them so that they can make a ten-man *minyan* and say the mourner's Kaddish aren't just aging synagogue goers, the poet here decides. "They were the Muses, you see. There were nine of them."

Of Poets, Rabbis, and Readers: The Future of Jewish American Poetry

For many poets the issues of Jewish sources, multiple identities, and even questions of poetics get bound up in the relationship between two archetypal figures, the poet and the rabbi. These figures tend to be presented rather differently, however, by women and men, a contrast that points out the central importance of gender to the work of Jewish American poets. For the men, the image of the rabbi is often invoked in opposition to the poet. "You've lost your religion, the Rabbi said. / It wasn't much to keep, said I." The poem to which these lines belong, "Debate with the Rabbi" by Howard Nemerov, is one of the paradigmatic poems to express this theme. For the women here, by contrast, the figure of the rabbi is more often a synonym for the poet: as we noted before, two of the poets, Marcia Falk and Marge Piercy, are well-known and widely loved writers of new liturgy and liturgically useful verse. While we might make take this opportunity to make sense of this opposition in a variety of ways, particularly now that the New Jewish Cultural Studies has taken up questions of gender in considerable detail, for now, we wish only to say that for most, but not all, of the men the conflict between community expectations and individual desire marks the speaker as a classically American isolato. And for most, but not all, of the women, community associations prove to be both liberating and enlightening. For others, finally, the poet is a mediating figure, resting uneasily between the two poles of isolato and communal voice. As Norman Finkelstein puts it, in the voice of his renegade rabbi-poet Acher, "They cast me from the congregation /—but they still come to hear me teach."

No doubt each reader will find yet more themes still. In hopes of encouraging this, we have added our second section, Part II, where we include ten introductory essays as a way to open yet more doors of insight. Together, these essays also tell a story about the past 150 years of Jewish American poetry; to frame them, and in the hope that they might be read as paths back to our contributing poets, we have written introductory notes to these pieces in the second half of this book.

Finally, a few words concerning the poets and poems included here. No attempt was made to be definitive or canonical about contemporary Jewish American poetry. Instead, our main goal was to get a representative selection of the various kinds of American poetry currently being written. We also wanted to represent the wide variety that is the American Jewish experience. In the end, through a combination of serendipity, good luck, and much cajoling, we collected twenty-six poems and commentary. This does not mean we only wanted twenty-six poems. It means only that serious space limitations prevented us from asking all of the poets we had planned to ask. It also means that busy schedules and other random events prevented a number of fine poets from participating. (Among those who, for various reasons, could not participate in this anthology, we particularly regret the absence of Robert Pinsky, the only Poet Laureate of the United States appointed to three succesive terms.) The twenty-six poems that follow do represent the best of what Jewish American poetry has to offer: not as a definitive canon, but as shining examples—representatives of the kinds of Jewish American poetry now being written. As to the poems themselves, we asked each poet to choose his or her own poem. Each of the twenty-six poems, in other words, was selected by the poet with the understanding that he or she would also write, for this collection, a commentary about its relationship to the poet's own sense of his or her "Jewishness."

In the spirit of Jewish tradition, then, we encourage an active interpretation of these poems and commentaries. Finding the connections, the meanings, the associations between texts and among texts has long been the sacred delight of Jewish scholarship. We hope it will delight readers of these seemingly more secular works as well.

Together, both sections of this anthology, the poems and commentary, and the essays, will introduce the world of Jewish American poetry to those still unfamiliar with it. And for those who are already familiar with its joys we hope to encourage even more exploration, even more questioning. For ultimately, our main goal is to announce the existence of a major contribution to American poetry: the various and increasingly self-conscious Jewish American poetic tradition. It is time for serious critical discussion about the theoretical and historical issues raised by this poetry, in terms of both Jewish culture and American poetry. But as jokes, old family quarrels, new political debates, Biblical riffs, *midrashim,* and other verbal sparks fly from poet to poet here, and from poem to essay, essay to poem, it is also time for us, as readers, simply to enjoy.

Works Cited

Emerson, Ralph Waldo. "Nature." Pp. 5–49. In *Ralph Waldo Emerson: Essays and Lectures.* New York: Library of America, 1983.

Ginsberg, Allen. "How Kaddish Happened." *The Poetics of the New American Poetry.* Ed. Don Allen and Warren Tallman. New York: Grove, 1973.

Gioia, Dana. *Columbia History of American Poetry.* Ed. Jay Parini and Brett C. Millier. New York: U of Columbia P, 1993.

Heller, Michael. *Conviction's Net of Branches.* Carbondale: Southern Illinois UP, 1985.

Howells, William Dean. *Criticism and Fiction.* New York: Harper, 1891.

Lazarus, Emma. "In the Jewish Synagogue at Newport." *Admetus and Other Poems.* New York: Hurd and Houghton, 1871.

————"The New Colossus." *Poems of Emma Lazarus.* Vol. 1, Boston: Houghton and Mifflin, 1889.

Longfellow, Henry Wadsworth. "The Jewish Cemetery at Newport." Pp. 33–36. In *The Poetical Works of Henry Wadsworth Longfellow.* Vol. 3. Boston: Houghton Mifflin, 1890.

Monteiro, George. "Robert Frost's Speech at Wesleyan University: An Uncollected Transcription." *Robert Frost Review* (Fall 1997): 17–24.

Neal, Larry. *Visions of a Liberated Future: Black Arts Movement Writings*. New York: Thunder's Mouth Press, 1989.

Nemerov, Howard. "Debate with the Rabbi." *The Collected Poems of Howard Nemerov*. Chicago: U of Chicago P, 1977.

Pound, Ezra, and F. S.Flint. *Poetry* 1.6 (March 1913): 198–206.

Rukeyser, Muriel. "Poem Out of Childhood." *Out of Silence: Selected Poems*. Ed Kate Daniels. Evanston: Triquarterly Books, 1995.

Shapiro, Karl. "Recapitulation." *Karl Shapiro: Selected Poems*. New York: Weiser and Weiser, 1968.

Thoreau, Henry David. "A Winter Walk." Pp. 57–75. In *The Vikiing PortableThoreau*. Ed. Carl Bode, New York: Penguin, 1982.

Zukofsky, Louis. "An Objective." Pp. 12–18. In *The Collected Critical Essays*. New York: Horizon, 1968. Expanded edition, Berkeley: U of California P, 1981. Forthcoming: Wesleyan UP/UP of New England.

I

Poems and

Commentary

Ammiel Alcalay

Ammiel Alcalay, currently living in Brooklyn, New York, is a poet, translator, and Professor of Classical and Oriental Languages at Queens College. He is the author of, among other books, a volume of poetry, *the cairo notebooks* (Singing Horse, 1993), a critical work, *After Jews and Arabs: Remaking Levantine Culture* (U of Minnesota P, 1992), and an edited collection, *Keys to the Garden: New Israeli Writing* (City Lights, 1996).

from *the cairo notebooks*

braided bracelets hair eyes mouths ships at sea breasts your

wrist embroidered pillow cases legs your head naked spine rain

water the beach quilts clothes the ghosts of our bodies a watch

skin and straw to dive and breathe whispers my arms this time

weaving long all my life my face resting the room laceless

drying my hands lying half-naked in winter this time voices

clinging to our bedclothes the air over his body my child gold

my dress go ahead this time which I loved lying my back

I don't mind almost never time badly torn stand clinging

the light the air almost fire taking off all my clothes

my stomach your face swim the window kissing delicate skin

Terrible shoulder pain. The stereo was upset, tape deck askew but in a kinky, stylized way. One record played the whole night through but it was all jerry-rigged, a knife on for weight, a weird white plastic thing on top of the disk. I only got to it in the morning to see what was happening and turn it off. Outside kids kept throwing things into the courtyard. One, hair cut close, kept reappearing inside the fence, throwing stones then waiting like he hadn't done anything. A taxi came tearing down the street headed straight for the fence which it vaulted, ending up in the backyard. My first impulse was to make sure K. was alright. I called for her and went to the bedroom where she was still asleep. Then I went to the window and started yelling to the driver before calling for an ambulance.

Several weeks of heavy dreams. The air itself permeated by silence and the violence beneath it. The camps war continues. Religious authorities have given residents permission to eat flesh. Sea piracy. Food and medicine seized. Committee meetings. Taking testimony, writing accounts. Pickets. Public discourse admits a breach grinding off to a halting start. Rocket stages admit a breach. In the dusty thicket intrepid liberty traps light. Tomorrow it will be someone even closer. Submerged in a return that had begun when. At whom was I angry. When she called to say how good it had been. When it's all alien to me. And the intention of that desire carried by a language that grows out of itself and is the magic of fully living within the mother tongue: anyone from someplace can feel it. The brutal anonymity. The ripe the ready the soft naked flesh. Memory of another time. This crowd, these vistas. Not enough noise. Excessively punctual. We are going (CLIPPETY) to the good (CLOP) people of Zamalek.

There are 28 one minute films of Cairo in Lumiere's catalog.

1895. The first film shown in Alexandria, 10 days after Paris.

Muhammad Karim acted in METROPOLIS.

Long talk with Jill (A's friend) at the picket. The first normal account I've gotten of a visit to Egypt. And a description of the *beauty* of Cairo and the fact that it's the only big city we have access to now.

3 shot and killed at a roadblock. F. in another six months. His wife and daughter visit once a week. Not to mention. More these days. Not just

Gaza. Army spokesmen assure. 4 dead the day before yesterday. 5 more yesterday. 16 wounded. Names? Helicopters tear gas hospital compound to disperse family members trying to seize corpse for burial. Blood donations not acceptable. More or less presentable leaders:

(Creon forbade Antigone to bury her brother because of the demonstration that would follow; Solon, besides "institutionalizing the distinction between good women and whores, legislated against ostentatious funerals to curb the power of the aristocracy." Not to mention the Trojan War.)

Soldiers or guerillas tracking after something. I was the last one to get by so they had to make sure I was dead. Pretended to be a corpse. Saw K. spinning away and two snails grow out of the pillow. Searched for something to write with. Red pen didn't work. Then the city: uptown but a sign said NO EXIT TO WEST VILLAGE, turned out to be THE MARITIME HOUSES. Everyone split up on the middle level in the subway. An announcement comes on that the 4 is coming in on the lower level. Stampede, a woman falls. We get down below and it's like a war movie. Doctors. Nurses. Tracks filled with disoriented people, some lying around with huge swollen lips. Chemical warfare.

The nurses that we met from Sabra and Shatilla.

Happy to be in Gaza.

Some people at the vigil had relatives up there.

The doctor was quoted as saying six people
died, and she amputated the legs of seven
others gunned down when they rushed to
meet the food trucks trying to get in.

"After all the cats, dogs, mules and other animals

in the camp were eaten, a mother and her five children

committed suicide to avoid having to turn to cannibalism."

In Geneva, all the revolutionaries stayed in 5 star hotels.

Tel Aviv. The Ayatollah floats over the Central Bus Station.
Textiles. Cassettes and tin. Posters of Saddam whirl and spin
over the river Jordan. Mine eyes have seen the glory

COMMENTARY

On one side of my work is a small stack of books that includes my translations, essays, and other critical and scholarly texts. On the other I have a very thin volume: *the cairo notebooks*. Everything in the larger pile can be found in the small one, but I don't think the reverse is true. Let me begin with some ideas from the first set of writings, in order to reach and reflect on the second, the poem at hand.

There is a deep contradiction running through Enlightenment and East European Jewry's image of itself. In this self-image, I wrote in *After Jews and Arabs: Remaking Levantine Culture* (1993), "Stress is put on the division between something conceived of as 'tradition,' a hermetically sealed area cut off from the 'worldly' concerns of other writers, and the 'perils' of attraction to that worldliness that is secretly admired and often considered or assumed to be superior to 'tradition.' This self-imposed bind isolates and diminishes the fuller possibilities framing less familiar cultural configurations."[1] At the time I was writing about what is euphemistically termed the "pre-modern." But it has become more and more apparent to me that this old contradiction still largely dictates the legitimate vocabulary for most American accounts of "Jewish" writing.

As someone involved in the cultural politics of the Middle East, I have run into a second set of self-imposed limits on American discourse. Following the

war of 1967, American writers and reviewers have been spellbound by trium-
phalist assumptions, their work permeated and circumscribed by the terms of
Zionist ideology. This might sound like the ravings of a paranoiac. But I would
assert that this state of affairs has not only severely limited the range of litera-
ture making its way into America; it has also made the writings of American
Jews not subscribing to these assumptions almost unimaginable, placing it well
beyond the pale. This, however, should not be particularly surprising since
these arbiters of taste would be more inclined to look toward official American
verse for its models rather than to what has always been most vital in the Amer-
ican tradition, what has made this century a renaissance of the word.

In a more recent article, "Exploding Identities: Notes on Ethnicity and Lit-
erary History" (1997), I wrote that "the study of Hebrew literature and the
writings of Jews in other languages stands at a crucial juncture. A combination
of chauvinism, ideological blinders, political blindness, and the lack of a true
comparative perspective has severely tested the abilities of students to emerge
intact from most of the contexts now available in which such studies can be
pursued. We can either expect more of the same or strive to open the field up to
new directions and new definitions. Entire periods are waiting to be defined
and examined."[2] Here, again, I think that much of what I wrote can be applied
to studies of writing—such as there are—by American Jews, or at least those
who've been so defined. Having said this, I think we may be poised at a mo-
ment when what I call "inaugural writing," that is, the kind of writing that
creates the conditions for the invention and emergence of its own idiosyncratic
critical vocabulary, can be reclaimed to what is most alive in the American
idiom.

Historical conditions work in all kinds of ways, depending on the degree to
which you've been touched or made conscious by them. Various forms in-
struct, inform, or translate, historically and politically, as well as emotionally.
As the Egyptian film maker Yousef Chahine has written: "Memory is confron-
tation, a confrontation with yourself. You must first confront yourself before
confronting other people, or a whole country—that's also the political context
of memory."[3] As someone barely born here (in larger historical/chronological
terms), much of my work has involved the process of both finding and losing
my "self" within the gaps I find in American discourse, gaps primarily having
to do with either the lack or the suppression of any tangible global political and
historical space or consciousness, however these end up getting defined. Part
of the difficulty of working through such a situation is that I feel as if I have
embarked upon an enormous journey only to come back to where I started
from: in my case, a distinctly American language and American idiom, only to
wonder what happened along the way. Every now and then I wish myself inno-
cent, as if I could simply have gone on writing, from the age that I seriously

began to occupy myself with writing, just letting myself work out of and through the language and the circumstances given to me without taking the actual physical and linguistic and cultural and political and experiential steps back and forth to other places that I did take. But when I read work by people who I think I should know better, I realize that I *had* to traverse those territories: Even if afterward the words I write remain identical, they would have to, at some level, be marked by knowledge picked up or shed along the way. "Coming back" for me, to an American idiom, means opening that idiom up to meanings that either have been suppressed or haven't yet been expressed in it. Both the idea of place and particular places play an enormous role in this itinerant work.

I've come to call *the cairo notebooks* a "condensed" "novel," with its most obvious antecedent, at least in my mind, in the William Carlos Williams of *Spring & All* and *Kora in Hell*. It was written almost as a series of messages in a bottle, partly because I simply didn't have time to write the longer texts and wanted to leave myself reminders and commentaries on the possible futility of pursuing longer forms. The particular genesis, in terms of process, is as follows: I was living in Jerusalem from 1978 to 1980 and then again from 1984 to 1989. From 1984 to 1989 I was immersed in active politics as well as research that ended up in both *After Jews and Arabs* and *Keys to the Garden*. This was, needless to say, a kind of massive undertaking. I was tangentially following the U.S. poetry scene through the mail. Upon returning to New York in 1989, I realized that I had a very brief moment to, as Jack Spicer would put it, tune in to that particular poetry channel of my radio. This I did by pillaging older writing that I could now begin to find my way back to, having taken such a long and circuitous journey to, literally, the old world, and juxtaposing it with work that I had done or begun doing in Jerusalem. I was not there, however, as a tourist but as a participant. Nor was I there to be nostalgic—I couldn't really imagine anything particular to be nostalgic about. I was there to inspect and incorporate shards of myself that I sensed as absences through family history and the oddity of growing up in some kind of vacuum, with a fairly tenuous hold on America but clearly, at the same time, very American in language, culture, and manner.

The book includes texts that were written over about fifteen years; in other words, there are very different strata of the self, of (my) linguistic and remembered self in it. The nature of place is both utterly specific and purposefully vague. While one might assume that everything "takes place" in the "Middle East," much of the imaginative space is set elsewhere. The materials in the book, like much else of what I have occupied myself with as a writer, translator, critic, and scholar for the past twenty years, are not easily assimilable to any expected context that American Jewish writing might refer to. In fact, changing reactions to my varied writing roles can almost be measured by the seismograph of Middle East politics, particularly as it tracks relations between Jews and Arabs and Palestinians and Israelis. But even beyond these external or more obvious markers, the book is designed to make things "safely hidden in plain sight."[4] For instance: "notebooks" is the English equivalent for *mahberot*, a medieval translation into Hebrew from the Arabic word *maqam*—*maqam* being "musical mode," but also coming to signify rhymed prose narrative, a prevalent genre in Arabic that was taken up by early medieval Hebrew writers and has come down to us, most obviously, through Chaucer. So there is an immediate entanglement: That is, *notebooks* have all the connotations engendered through Gramsci, Wittgenstein, or Rilke, along with what amounts to a history of the movement of narrative from Arabic and Hebrew into the European vernacular. The photographs on the outer and inner covers of the book were originally part of a long story board accompanied (beneath the pictures) by the opening text ("Going from the Grand Canal to Lido / and seeing St. Mark's Square for the first time, the words / 'I hear Arabia calling' kept running through my head over and over again, / like a long lost amulet I could finally feel touch me:"). That visual story begins on the inside back cover and winds its way back to the front—a not so subtle allusion to the reading direction (right to left) of Hebrew and Arabic. There is a further stage to this within the text itself in which I have sought my own direction, or horizon line, as all the texts actually end at the bottom of the page and find their starting point as if you were scrolling backward. That is, they rest at the point away from which they've been anchored.

Way beyond the particular words just noted, there is an effort to stretch what might be thought possible in an American context, something that I have very consciously striven for in my choices as a writer and translator; that is, I look for work that I would like to have seen somebody write here, but they can't, or haven't, or wouldn't be able to because the circumstances for that writing don't exist in quite such a configuration. As "translator" of my own work, I engage in this very process, displacing in order to reconfigure. Without getting too atavistic about it, you would have to be kidding yourself if you think divorcing yourself from the past, any past, is a simple matter. The question then becomes how strong the pull is and what one does to negotiate resistance or attraction to it. Without losing sight of the possibility of universal desire, claims, and responsibilities, I find it crucial to maintain a diversity of selves and roles that can act locally in many places at once.

Notes

1. Ammiel Alcalay, *After Jews and Arabs: Remaking Levantine Culture* (Minneapolis: U of Minnesota P, 1993), 23.

2. From "Exploding Identities: Notes on Ethnicity and Literary History." In *Jews and Other Differences: The New Jewish Cultural Studies*, ed. Jonathan and Daniel Boyarin (Minneapolis: U of Minnesota P, 1997), 341.

3. Interview from Ferid Boudjedir's 1987 film *Camera Arabe*.

4. Peter Gizzi, in his afterword to *The House that Jack Built: The Collected Lectures of Jack Spicer* (Hanover: Wesleyan UP/ UP of New England, 1998), 177.

Charles Bernstein

Charles Bernstein, born 1950 in New York City, is David Gray Professor of Poetry and Letters at the State University of New York at Buffalo. He is the author of twenty books of poetry, and is one of the primary poets in the avant-garde Language poetry movement. Among his most recent books are *My Way: Speeches and Poems* (U of Chicago P, 1999), an edited collection, *Close Listening: Poetry and the Performed Word* (Oxford UP, 1998), a collection of essays, *A Poetics* (Harvard UP, 1992), and the poetry collections *Dark City* (Sun and Moon, 1994) and *Republics of Reality: 1975–1995* (Sun and Moon, 1999).

Solidarity Is the Name We Give to What We Cannot Hold

I am a nude formalist poet, a sprung
syntax poet, a multitrack poet, a
wondering poet, a social expressionist
poet, a Baroque poet, a constructivist poet,
an ideolectical poet. I am a New York poet in
California, a San Francisco poet on
the Lower East Side, an Objectivist poet
in Royaumont, a surrealist poet in Jersey,
a Dada poet in Harvard Square,
a zaum poet in Brooklyn, a merz poet
in Iowa, a cubo-futurist poet in Central Park.
I am a Buffalo poet in Providence, a London
poet in Cambridge, a Kootenay School
of Writing poet in Montreal, a local poet
in Honolulu.
I am a leftist poet in my armchair
and an existential poet on the street;
an insider poet among my friends,
an outsider poet in midtown.
I am a serial poet, a paratactic poet, a
disjunctive poet, a discombobulating poet,

a montage poet, a collage poet, a hypertextual
poet, a nonlinear poet, an abstract poet,
a nonrepresentational poet, a process poet,
a polydiscourse poet, a conceptual poet.
I am a vernacular poet, a talk poet, a dialect
poet, a heteroglossic poet, a slang poet, a
demotic poet, a punning poet, a comic poet.
I am an iambic poet I am,
a dactylic poet, a tetrameter poet,
an anapestic poet.
I am a capitalist poet in Leningrad
and a socialist poet in St. Petersburg;
a bourgeois poet at Zabar's, a union poet
in Albany; an elitist poet on TV,
a political poet on the radio.
I am a fraudulent poet, an incomprehensible poet, a degenerate
poet, an incompetent poet, an indecorous poet, a crude poet
an incoherent poet, a flat-footed poet, a disruptive poet, a
fragmenting poet, a contradictory poet, a self-imploding poet,
a conspiratorial poet, an ungainly poet, an anti-dogmatic poet,
an infantile poet, a theoretical poet, an awkward poet, a sissy
poet, an egghead poet, a perverse poet, a clumsy poet,
a cacophonous poet, a vulgar poet, a warped
poet, a silly poet, a queer poet, an
erratic poet, an erroneous poet, an anarchic poet,
a cerebral poet, an unruly poet,
an emotional poet, a (no) nonsense poet. I am a language
poet wherever people try to limit the modes of
expression or nonexpression. I am an experimental poet
to those who value craft over interrogation, an
avant-garde poet to those who see the future
in the present. I am a Jewish poet hiding in the shadow
of my great-grandfather and great-grandmother.
I am a difficult poet in Kent, a visual poet in
Cleveland, a sound poet in Cincinnati.
I am a modernist poet to postmodernists and a postmodern poet
to modernists. I am a book artist in Minneapolis
and a language artist in Del Mar.
I am a lyric poet in Spokane, an analytic
poet in South Bend, a narrative poet
in Yellow Knife, a realist
poet in Berkeley.

I am an antiabsorptive poet in the morning,
an absorptive poet in the afternoon,
and a sleepy poet at night.
I am a parent poet, a white poet, a man poet, an urban poet, an angered poet, a
   sad poet,
an elegiac poet, a raucous poet, a frivolous poet, a detached poet, a roller-
   coaster poet, a
volcanic poet, a dark poet, a skeptical poet, an eccentric poet, a misguided
   poet, a reflective
poet, a dialectical poet, a polyphonic poet, a hybrid poet, a wandering poet, an
   odd poet, a
lost poet, a disobedient poet, a bald poet, a virtual poet.
& I am none of these things,
nothing but the blank wall of my aversions
writ large in disappearing ink—

COMMENTARY

But is it Jewish?
—I think, probably, maybe so
But it could also be not Jewish
—Exactly

Chana Bloch

A poet, translator, and literary scholar, Chana Bloch, born in New York City in 1940, is W. M. Keck Professor of English, and Director of the Creative Writing Program at Mills College, Oakland, California. Among her books of poetry are the recent winner of the Felix Pollak Prize, *Mrs. Dumpty* (U of Wisconsin P, 1998), *The Past Keeps Changing* (Sheep Meadow P, 1994), and *The Secrets of the Tribe* (Sheep Meadow P, 1980). She has also translated the Israeli poets, Dalia Ravicovitch, *The Window and Other Poems* (Sheep Meadow P, 1989), and with Stephen Mitchell, *The Selected Poetry of Yehuda Amichai* (U of California P, 1996). Her translations regularly appear in *The New Yorker* and other magazines. She has also written the critical study, *Spelling the Word: George Herbert and the Bible* (U of California P, 1985).

Don't Tell the Children

I

Daddy's sad. Soon he'll be
happy again. A story I'm reading them
for the first time. Little spurts of
hot paint stain the page,
green spiky leaves.
They don't know the words yet.

I don't know the words.
I'm a child who has heard things
she shouldn't. Listening all night
at the grownups' door and I can't
make sense. Won't. I'm a child
hiding from my children.

II

Bedtime stories for the children: The cheetah is the fastest land animal.
It has tawny fur marked with black spots. It is easily tamed. Giraffes are

the tallest animals on earth. They eat leaves from the tops of trees.
Snails move very slowly. They carry their shell-houses on their backs.

And for the grown-ups, an ancient tale: The war horse says *Ha! ha!*
among the trumpets. The eagle drinks blood. The ostrich leaves her eggs
in the dust. She forgets her young. The bones of Behemoth are iron and
brass. Leviathan churns the waters to a boil. His nostrils are a caldron;
his breath, flame.

III

The children sit on the rumpled blankets
and listen. They listen hard.
They're getting it all down
for future reference. Tuned to our breath
they hear even the quarter tones.
They give off
vibrations too keen for the ear,
like a struck tuning fork that goes on trembling.

COMMENTARY

A taste for language was my inheritance as the child of immigrants. My father,
who had learned English in night school, recalled one homework assignment
with relish: a letter of condolence to President Coolidge on the death of his son.
"Dear Mr. President, I share your *bereavement*," he began. The teacher asked
him to copy his letter onto the blackboard for everyone to read—the first pub-
lished work in our family. "I really went fishing for that word," he confided to
me in his heavily accented English.

   At home my parents spoke English, not Yiddish—they wanted to be "Amer-
ican," whatever that meant – though they sent me to a Yiddish *folkshul* every
day after school. Not a Hebrew school: Hebrew belonged to the men and the
boys. We lived in the South Bronx, in the shadow of the Jerome Avenue El, a
neighborhood soon to become loud with gang wars, but at that time almost too
quiet: My friends and I referred to it with disdain as the Bronx Bourgeoizoo.
My parents had settled into a life of placid routine, and who could blame them?
They'd endured their quota of violent uprootings. But the safety they plotted
for me I experienced as a constraint. I was impatient to lose my innocence.

Yiddish and Hebrew literature offered tastes, smells, pungencies of experience that I found nowhere else. In Yiddish poems by Jacob Glatstein and stories by Isaac Bashevis Singer I sought the life of Eastern Europe that my parents had escaped. The road to Palestine that they hadn't taken, the wars, the everlasting aftershocks, I discovered in Yiddish poems by Abraham Sutzkever and later in Hebrew poems by Dahlia Ravikovitch and Yehuda Amichai. I began translating these writers in much the same spirit that I went to Budapest, Prague, East Berlin, Warsaw, and Auschwitz one summer to see and hear what remained of Jewish life in Eastern Europe. Reading brought me close, to the very threshold, but the act of translation brought me inside.

For their part, the Yiddish and Hebrew writers I met shared an urgency to be heard that was different from anything I'd encountered among writers of English. For those who wrote in Yiddish, especially, translation was a necessary condition of survival. Who, after all, was reading them in Yiddish? Or who would be, in a couple of years? As Irving Howe put it, "the potential readers of Glatstein became the actual readers of Eliot." In America, Yiddish is preserved mostly in a debased form, in the jokes of stand-up comics and the handful of words that have made it into Webster's: *shlep, shmooze, schlock, schmear, shtick* (this is celebrated in some quarters as a cultural achievement). Cynthia Ozick has a painful story called "Envy; or, Yiddish in America" about Ostrover the fiction writer (a shrewd portrait of Bashevis Singer) and Edelshtein the poet (who in some respects resembles Glatstein), the first reaching a large audience through his translators, the second desperate because he has none. Behind both of them stands the destruction of Jewish life in Europe, the death of Yiddish. Ozick writes, "Of what other language can it be said that it died a sudden and definite death, in a given decade, on a given piece of soil?"

One of the first poems I translated was Jacob Glatstein's "Smoke":

> From the crematory flue
> A Jew aspires to the Holy One.
> And when the smoke of him is gone,
> His wife and children filter through.
>
> Above us, in the height of the sky,
> Saintly billows weep and wait.
> God, wherever you may be,
> There all of us are also not.

The bitter irony in that voice thrilled me; the poem gripped me and would not let go until I'd turned it into English. Never having done this thing called translation before, I wasn't at all sure I was doing it right. I sent my version to

Glatstein with a letter half apologizing for the freedoms I had taken. When he wrote back asking me to translate more of his work, I understood his invitation as an assignment. I was longing for what I called real life, the life of tragedy that lay beyond the pale of my uneventful girlhood. I went toward those Yiddish poems as eagerly as my father had come toward English, happy to be bereaved.

I was drawn to translation for another reason: I wanted to be a poet. In a workshop with Robert Lowell, I submitted some translations along with my own poems, and Lowell suggested that I could learn from my translations. I soon discovered what he meant. If I was attentive to meaning and mood, imagery, rhythm and patterns of sound, I could translate a line of verse any number of different ways; each time I chose among possibilities, I was exercising muscles that I needed in shaping my own work. When I first began translating, I would write down every conceivable variation of a line, hesitating among alternatives, anxious and unsure—the way I feel when the eye doctor asks, "Which is better, *this* or *this*?" Now, after many years of practice, I have learned to trust my choices. Translating poetry proved to be a strenuous but efficient way of teaching myself to write.

My first collection of poems, *The Secrets of the Tribe*, is my most consciously Jewish book. There are poems here about Shabbos and Yom Kippur, about the pogrom that brought my father's family to America, my father's funeral, sitting *shiva*. About the Yiddish theater on the Lower East Side of New York where immigrants got their first taste of Shakespeare—in Yiddish (according to one story, the program notes read, "Shakespeare *fartaytsht un farbesert*," translated and improved):

from Watching

You and I used to talk about
Lear and his girls
(I read it in school,

you saw it on the Yiddish stage
where the audience yelled:
*Don't believe them,
they're rotten)*—
that Jewish father and his
suburban daughters.

In *The Secrets of the Tribe* I wrote about the gradual erosion of the certainties that governed my childhood:

Furniture

Last night we talked about God
as metaphor, like
the head of the table
the leg of the chair
God of the Universe.

I haven't got a God to stand on, I said.
And flinched.
No thunder.

Shame on you,
God will punish you, my mother would say,
if you write on Shabbos.
When I wrote, I pulled down the shade.

In those days there was thunder like furniture moved in heaven.
God came down from the mountain.
My heart ticked evenly as a clock at the head of the bed.
On Friday the candles stood lit on the table,
and four chairs, one at each side,
squaring the round world.

There were crumbs on the tablecloth
and hot wax dripped from the candles
so quietly
we never heard them
go out.

And I wrote about my yearning for something to replace the lost certainties. One Yom Kippur, at an alternative service in the home of a rabbi-turned-academic, I noticed a group of converts sitting together and *davening* with more devotion than anyone else in the room, and I found myself envying them:

The Converts

On the holiest day we fast till sundown.
I watch the sun stand still
as the horizon edges toward it. Four hours to go.
The rabbi's mouth opens and closes and opens.
I think: fish

and little steaming potatoes,
parsley clinging to them like an ancient script.

Only the converts, six of them in the corner,
in their prayer shawls and feathery beards,
sing every syllable.
What word
are they savoring now?
If they go on loving that way, we'll be here all night.

Why did they follow us here, did they think
we were happier?
Did someone tell them we knew
the lost words
to open God's mouth?

The converts sway in white silk,
their necks bent forward in yearning
like swans,
and I covet
what they think we've got.

Among my earliest published work was a long cycle of poems about the narratives of Genesis, six of which I included in *The Secrets of the Tribe*. That cycle had its origin in an exhibition of Chagall's works on Biblical themes. I always had a rather skeptical attitude toward Chagall, but I found his 1931 gouaches on subjects from Genesis fresh and sprightly. In their forms and colors they carried the inflections of the shtetl, as if Chagall had painted them in Yiddish; they presented the Biblical text as it was domesticated in the lives of Eastern European Jews.

The stories of Genesis had always fascinated me, but after seeing the Chagall exhibit I began to reread them with renewed interest and to conceive them in visual terms. Intense, complex, full of violent feeling, often profoundly disturbing, these stories tell us with unsparing clarity how we are formed and deformed by family life. True, they come from a world very different from our own, yet they seem uncannily close to home when we read them with our own lives in mind. As Jews we are taught to read the past in this way. On Passover, at the Seder table, we proclaim, "In every generation let each man look upon himself as if he came forth out of Egypt"—for me, one of the high points of the evening. That act of imagining gives us the gift of the long view, a way of explaining to ourselves why we behave as we do.

The narratives in Genesis also ask to be read as communal history. They are the opening chapters in a tribal chronicle: "Let every reader look upon himself as if he came forth out of this family." Or, considering what passes between Cain and Abel, Jacob and Esau, Joseph and his brothers, and many of the other characters, we might say, in the jargon of our time, "this dysfunctional family." We understand our mysterious lives better when we recognize ourselves as the children of these complex, impetuous men and women. By taking the text personally, we make it our own, we make it "usable." That is, we bring it into the thick of our lives, where all great literature belongs.

Actually, it was a Christian poet, George Herbert, who showed me the way to some of my Jewish poems. I began to read Herbert when I was writing the Genesis cycle; later I would write a book about his work, *Spelling the Word: George Herbert and the Bible*. A devout seventeenth-century Protestant, Herbert read the Bible as if his life depended on it. He believed that his personal experience gave him a deeper insight into the meaning of the text, and at the same time that the Bible helped him to see his life more clearly. Herbert was a Christian, and his theology was remote from my concerns, but there was something familiar—almost Jewish, I would have said—in his intimate identification with the Biblical text and the uninhibited energy of his arguments with God.

Chagall's paintings and Herbert's poetry provided the impetus for my Biblical poems. Although my childhood had been outwardly quiet, my inner life was full of turbulence. In writing about the first murder, the flood and the binding of Isaac, I was coming to terms with my unacknowledged rivalry with my brother, the strain of leaving home, and the continuing pressure of my parents' judgment:

from **Brothers**

Our smile was made of teeth,
the first
human weapons.

from **The Flood**

The great hulk of houseboat beached
on top of Ararat.
Drying, the timbers crack.
It will stay there forever, shrinking
invisibly.

from **The Sacrifice**

> He will remember the blade's
> white silence,
> a lifetime
> under his father's eyes.

These subjects took on a startling clarity when I saw them through the lens of the Bible. The Biblical tales allowed me to frame what I discovered in a new way.

The narratives in Genesis continued to intrigue me in my second book, *The Past Keeps Changing*. When I wrote "Goodbye," I was teaching the story of Adam and Eve, to which I usually devote a good deal of time in the classroom. One of the commentaries, I told my students, found a difficulty in Genesis 2:17—"In the day that thou eatest thereof, thou shalt surely die"—since Adam and Eve live for a long time after eating the forbidden fruit. That commentary inspired the ending of "Goodbye," a poem about my first love:

> It's thirty years since you and I invented
> a ritual for leaving.
> Back to back in the city street,
> we walked five paces apart and were swallowed up
> by our lives.
>
> When they said, "If you eat this fruit
> you will die,"
> they didn't mean right away.

Like Herbert, I have been drawn to the energy of protest in the Hebrew Bible—the voice of Abraham, the prophets, the Psalmist and Job arguing with God. I hear that voice in "White Petticoats," a poem that takes issue with the rigidity of rabbinical law:

> If the egg had one spot of blood on it
> the rabbis said, Throw it away!
> As if they could legislate
> perfection.
> Dress the bride in white
> petticoats! Let there be
>
> no stain
> on your ceremony! As if

> we could keep our lives
> from spilling
> onto our new clothes.

In words that now seem to me uncannily prophetic, this poem speaks about embracing life in all its predictable uncertainty:

> There's a bravery
> in being naked.
> We left our clothes
> on the doorknob, the floor, the bed,
> and a live moon opened its arms
> around the dark.

In my latest book, *Mrs. Dumpty*, I return to the story of Adam and Eve, and to the subject of marriage:

from Esperanto

> I'm a married woman. You and I are a
> man-and-wife, one flesh. *Married:*
> you leave father and mother to become
>
> that word. One word
> for the hardness that needs to bury its head
> in softness, the need that grows teeth,
> the feast, the naked cleaving,
> the flooding that can't stop itself
> and the sadness, after.

Mrs. Dumpty is about "a great fall": the dissolution of my marriage of twenty-five years because of my husband's mental illness. (The "real life" I dreamt of as a girl was mine at last, though hardly in the form I'd imagined.) These poems chronicle the customary strains in a long marriage—aging, dependency, the erosion of feeling—as compounded by mania, depression, the locked ward, electroshock therapy. And the aftershocks of history as well: My husband and his parents were refugees from Hitler's Germany, and the trauma of that displacement left its mark long after the 1930s. *Mrs. Dumpty* is also the story of a woman's transformation—my own—in which "the end of safety" proves to be the beginning of freedom. As in my earlier poems about the Bible, what concerns me is the inner life: how we are formed by our losses and those of our parents, how we learn what we know through our intuitions and confusions, how we deny and delay and finally come to understand ourselves.

As I was writing the poems in *Mrs. Dumpty*, I found myself reflecting on the Book of Job, which questions fundamental Biblical teachings about reward and punishment, and about the place of human beings in the scheme of things. When Job complains bitterly about the griefs that have befallen him, his friends, who are right-thinking to the point of sadism, insist he must be guilty of a hideous sin. But God himself answers Job "out of the whirlwind," brushing aside the conventional pieties. He confronts Job with the wonders of light and darkness, rain, snow, hail, lightning, the constellations, then reads off the roster of undomesticated animals, from the real to the mythical—animals that do not serve man and are not known for their good behavior: the young lions, the raven, the wild goat, the wild ass, the ostrich, the eagle, Behemoth and Leviathan.

What kind of an answer is that to the problem of human suffering? I remember telling my students years ago that I found it far from satisfactory. God sounds like a colossal bully; what's more, he's evading the question. But lately I have come to appreciate the bracing wisdom of the Voice from the Whirlwind. In the synagogue we repeat the Biblical promise that, if we behave, God will provide the rains in their season, though most of us today don't take those words literally. The sobering truths of adult experience find a more accurate reflection in the magnificent speech at the end of Job, which proclaims that human beings are not at the center of the universe, and which emphatically denies that we are punished if we're naughty and rewarded if we're nice—something our children inevitably discover as they grow up.

But how do we talk to our children about the problems that we face? Often we try to shield them from what they already know. "Don't Tell the Children" in *Mrs. Dumpty* is about innocence and experience, the wisdom of children and the vulnerability of adults. In the first section of the poem, a mother is telling her children some bad news in easy English, in a tone of resolute cheerfulness, as if she were reading them a bedtime story. In the third section, the children instinctively know the truths of their parents' lives, even the hidden truths.

The second section, in prose, begins with a paragraph of animal lore of the kind one finds in children's books, where the world seems a safe and friendly place:

Bedtime stories for the children: The cheetah is the fastest land animal.
It has tawny fur marked with black spots. It is easily tamed. Giraffes are
the tallest animals on earth. They eat leaves from the tops of trees.
Snails move very slowly. They carry their shell-houses on their backs.

Those lines are followed by a paraphrase of the Voice from the Whirlwind, which offers a very different view of the world:

And for the grown-ups, an ancient tale: The war horse says *Ha! ha!*
among the trumpets. The eagle drinks blood. The ostrich leaves her eggs
in the dust. She forgets her young. The bones of Behemoth are iron and
brass. Leviathan churns the waters to a boil. His nostrils are a caldron;
his breath, flame.

The Book of Job found its way into this poem because its clear-eyed view of re-
ality helped me to understand the difficult situation in which we as a family
found ourselves.

I am deeply committed to the Jewish world I inhabit, a verbal culture in
which languages and texts are at the center, though I can't help questioning
many aspects of that culture. Luckily, the act of questioning is not only sanc-
tioned by Jewish tradition, it's an honored part of it. That the Hebrew Bible
carries within itself the critique of its received ideas is one of its glories.
What could be more unorthodox than the Book of Job? Yet is was included in
the canon of Scripture. A few years ago I translated the *Song of Songs*, which
celebrates the sexual awakening of two unmarried lovers; no one knows for
sure how this book survived the last cut of the canon-makers. Now I am
translating *Open Closed Open* by Yehuda Amichai, a book in which the poet
contends with Biblical and rabbinical teachings on nearly every page. I find
the quarrel with tradition one of the most distinctive features of Judaism, and
one of the most compelling. To quarrel with the tradition is to remain en-
gaged with it.

Poetry has gradually come to occupy a central place in my life, providing a
way of ordering my experience, dealing with pain or confusion, and moving to-
ward clarity. In writing *Mrs. Dumpty*, I was finding words for "bereavement,"
but the process, paradoxically, was often joyful, even exhilarating. This process
is the subject of a new poem, "Spell," which brings together passages from
Isaiah, Job, and the story of Elijah to articulate what I have learned about the
difficult but rewarding work of writing:

Spell

> What I am given is too hot to touch.
> Live coal, live
> pain from the altar. I take it
> in the tongs of language,
> of metaphor, so it won't burn.
> It does burn. I reach for it
> anyway. Slowly. The poem

is a miracle
of perversity. It knows before I do how words
give what they take away. Slake
what they sharpen. Salt what they
save. I leave a place at the table

for the Prophet Elijah who rose in fire
in a cloud of words.

Michael Castro

Michael Castro, born in 1945, teaches English at the University of Missouri, St. Louis, Missouri. He is the author of several collections of poetry as well as a critical study, *Interpreting the Indian: Twentieth-Century Poets and the Native American* (U of Oklahoma P, 1991).

The Grandparent Poems:
Self-Reflections in a Smoky Mirror

I. GRANDFATHERS

One chain-smoked cigarettes,
rolled his own
with slow deliberate movements,
never wanted matches,
lit each new smoke
with the butt of the last.

Worked as caretaker
for a club of rich French
& German businessmen
in Salonika,
by the Aegean Sea,
where he watched
the Greeks & Turks unite
to drive out the Bulgarians.
They'd shoot at
the Bulgarians,
driving them back,
street by street.
Then they'd shoot at
each other.

Like most who lived there,
this grandfather

didn't give a damn
who won, when the smoke
cleared.
But the Germans,
the Germans cared,
& so they tried out their bombers
over the city, warming up
for 'The Great War.'

The city smoked
with this grandfather.
But each work day
ended the same way for him.
He'd sweep up his own butts,
throw them away in the trash
& consign the pile to flames.

He was a disgrace
to the family,
for he worked on the Sabbath.

His grandfather
had been head rabbi
in Palestine,
& his brother
was a rabbi in Salonika,
& a money-changer
on the side—
working out of a little booth
on a busy corner.
My father,
who became a grandfather,
remembered it well.

This changeling brother
was thought highly of
by the family.
But my grandfather,
the black sheep, swept
& saved his money.
He left for America by steamship
with his wife & oldest son, Alberto,
to keep the boy from being drafted.

My father, the grandfather,
the orphaned son,
stayed behind with his sisters,
slept five in a bed
with uncles & cousins & aunts,
& sold needles & postcards & thread
to soldiers' outstretched hands
through barbed wire fences.

He was in Salonika
during the Great Fire of 1917.
He saw British troops,
a few blocks ahead of the blaze,
spraying buildings in the Jewish quarter
with gasoline.
They preferred to destroy the city
than to let the Germans have it.
People jumped into the harbor
to escape the conflagration.

All that smoke.

When my father came to America
he took up cigars,
& eventually opened a cigar store
on Chambers Street,
near the Immigration Bureau.
His grandfather, the chain-smoker,
died of Nazi gas,
age 101.

Smoke was everywhere.

On the other side,
my mother's father
was from Jannina,
from an ancient line of Greek Jews.
In America, this grandfather
worked in a cigarette factory
& lived in Harlem.
He is best remembered
for his big, beautiful brown eyes

& for the love he showered on his wife,
his three children,
& even on distant relatives
emerging from steerage
on fogbound Ellis Island.
He died young, coughing,
in the influenza epidemic of 1919,
two years after Salonika went up in smoke.

Heartsick, my grandmother followed him
six months later, dying
before her children's eyes
on a borrowed cot—

For years
my mother thought the "deathbed"
was a special bed
people brought in for the dying.

All those babushka'd aunts
& kimona-peddling uncles
wept at the funerals,
but none took in the children.

Somehow my mother, the grandmother,
survived, taking care
from age ten
of her two younger brothers,
not letting anyone break up the family,
shifting from foster home
to foster home
& back again
to the Hebrew Orphan Asylum.

She met my cigar-smoking father,
married, &
        just after his father (my grandfather) &
about the time his chain-
smoking grandfather died,
made him a son.

The son worked in the smoke shop,
handed over Turkish
blend Camels
to hacking chain-smokers
(old proverb of Salonika Jews,
"The camel doesn't see his own hump")
swept up their butts
as they disappeared down Broadway
in their own smoke,
didn't smoke cigarettes, cigars,
didn't think he knew
his own grandfathers;
but carried on,
      imagined them
as incense smoke curled
in the lamplight, wondered;
eventually
married, became a father
of a son; a grandfather
of grandsons in the hazy future;

      lit a candle, a joint,
      watched the smoke rise,
      linger around the ceiling;
      it vanished into thin air,
      except for what remained
      inside him

II. POEM FOR GRANDMA

The room was dark & full of musty furniture
plush, velvety, worn armchairs, a velour couch
draped with the lacy yellowing doilies she embroidered,
bowls filled with sucking candies on every surface,
a sense of the grave closing in, the sun banished
for some unseen offense.
Somewhere in the Bronx, circa 1950.
The radio abuzz with guys, like my father, named Joe—
DiMaggio, McCarthy, G.I. (& only last week,
I met a Cheyenne Indian who said, "My name's Joe,

but call me Angel. Too many 'Joes' in this world,
not enough 'Angels'"). She came from Ios, the island
where Homer was born, or so the story goes, as Rebecca tells it.
    She was a Romaniot,
who Grandpa had to teach Ladino.
Got out of Salonika
before the Great Fire set by the British
destroyed the Jewish quarter, before the Turkish bombings, before
World War I, before
the Holocaust, before
all her children.

From that clear Greek birthlight
to smoky steerage, Harlem, another
language (she'd teach him), another walkup
cave on another island, another
beginning to manage: brisses & weddings,
the complexities of lives
    never fully here;
    & the burial arrangements, remembering . . .
    passage . . .
of time, each moment a gravestone
knocked over, a piece of candy offered
to sweeten the conversation.
    the accented word
exhaled into the traffic's exhaust,
a stitch in the tapestry, steady
gnarling hands
barely moving in the dimness,
slipping the needle in
& out, & later, lighting
yartzite candles, dark-eyed wrinkles
turning back, & squinting, to see
the pattern.

    Dusk
in the worn plush Bronx, alone,
toothless, still squinting

(outliving the others),
in this oppressive shade. Lucky

to be an immigrant smile slowly woven
through New York's patchwork bustle.
    A fixed jaw. A crack
    in the drawn curtains of the twentieth century.
A patch of light on the drab dusty rug.
An imperious, stubborn strength beaming down
on her little grandchild
Michael

COMMENTARY

I didn't know my grandparents. All but my paternal grandmother died before I
was born, and she—an austere, aloof, larger than life figure as I remember
her—died when I was six. These "Grandparent Poems" were an attempt to
gather and explore what knowledge I had, to draw on scraps of anecdotes,
photographs, memories, impressions to honor my grandparents, and in that act
to recover something of the roots that shape, feed, and nourish me like the si-
lent working of the autonomic nervous system, roots connecting me to the his-
tory and consciousness of an older, deeper world.

It was a Sephardic world I had tasted: in the Ladino (the language of Se-
phardic Jews, a fifteenth-century Spanish, spiced with Turkish, Greek, or other
local flavors) that was bandied about when my father's relatives gathered; in
the *birechas* (a knish-like delicacy filled with spinach or cheese), the feta,
olives, and hoop breads picked up in little bodegas in the Sephardic neighbor-
hood around Mt. Eden Avenue in the Bronx where my cousins lived in the
1950s; in occasional visits to the Sephardic synagogue in that same neighbor-
hood, and memorable Passover nights at my Aunt Jean and Uncle Morris
Hassan's. But most powerfully, I had absorbed Sephardic character in count-
less more subtle ways having to do with the way my family elders carried and
expressed themselves.

Nevertheless, not having steady doses of the exotic tastes of language,
foods, and religion, not living in a Sephardic community, made being Sephar-
dic mysterious to my conscious mind. It was a fact I acknowledged with very
little comprehension. We didn't talk much about it, or express it regularly so
that I could see. My mother, a Greek Jew like my father, had been orphaned by
the influenza epidemic of 1919 and not raised among Sephardim, so she did not
speak Ladino. Later we found out she was a Romaniot, from a line of Jews who
had been in Greece since the time of the Roman Empire and who spoke Greek
rather than the language of the dominant Hispanic immigrants. So Ladino was

more exotic than familiar to me, and the inflection in our household was toward assimilation; we were pitched toward the New World, rather than the Old.

Asking questions, doing research, exploring what I found and felt in poems was a way of knowing, giving what was inside me language, and life. An act of will was required to keep the ancient connection vital. A parallel act of will, on an infinitely more profound level, was involved in my mother's childhood efforts to keep her heritage, her family of herself and two younger brothers, together after they were orphaned and in and out of foster homes and the Hebrew Orphan Asylum.

In "Grandfathers" I instinctively found images of smoke to suggest the haziness of my impressions, the tenuousness of the connection to that older world, that source of who I am. Ancestry here is perceived through a smoky haze; and, contemplating smoke, *like* smoke, dispensing smoke in the smoke shop, we all disappear into thin air—kept alive only in the breaths, the acts, the thoughts of our descendants.

Words preserve us too: written words, the nuanced qualities of conversation; and ancient words, formulae kept alive through proverbs like "The camel doesn't see its own hump," which appears in "Grandfathers" and exemplifies a rich tradition of Sephardic folk poetry I routinely heard, groaning, growing up. Yet undoubtedly these pithy sayings helped shape my poetic ear and consciousness. Many, like the following, have a memorable music and concision in their Ladino expression:

> *Asno callado, por sabio contado.*
> The silent ass is considered wise.

> *Aboltar cazal, aboltar mazal.*
> A change of scene, a change of fortune.

> *Non mi mires la color, mirami la savor.*
> Don't judge me by my color, judge me by my flavor.

> *Cominos macarones, alambicos corazones.*
> We ate macaroni, and licked our hearts.

The proverbs, many of which I heard first from my cousin, Rebecca Camhi Fromer, transmit much of Sephardic character, temperament, experience, and wisdom. They suggest the history of displacement, exile, and struggle that has been our collective lot, the sadnesses directly cited and standing behind the "Grandparent Poems."

Sephardim experienced all the ancient Jewish woes that culminated in diaspora, and then had to deal with the Inquisition and the Expulsion from our beloved Spain, which some say is the mysterious Sepharad mentioned in the Bible's Book of Obadiah. The Balkan Wars prior to World War I created another displacing trauma for many Sephardic communities, including my father's Salonika, as is related in "Grandfathers." And the Holocaust was devastating for Greek Jews, with over 90 percent of our people killed. Salonika, which had the largest per capita Jewish population of any city in the world one hundred years ago, today has but a handful of Jewish families.

This tenuousness is incorporated into our outlook. In my family this was compounded by my mother's orphanhood in America. Roots are hard to put down too firmly, for we know the ground is always capable of erupting, expelling, or swallowing us whole. We have a proverb, "He who knows nothing of the sea, knows nothing of suffering," that reflects this recurrent experience of leaving home to start over again.

After expulsion from Spain, Sephardim stuck together in insular communities in the Mediterranean region where Ladino was retained as the first language, ingraining a clannishness basic to our nature. This clannishness was expressed in the New World in tensions between Sephardic immigrants from different countries or even cities; I explore them in another poem, "La America" (indebted to Marc Angel's book of the same title), which is about the editor Moise Gadol, who struggled to unite the communities from 1910 to 1925 with *La America*, a Ladino newspaper.

Clannish even among ourselves, we certainly have never felt particularly close to our Ashkenazic cousins, nor they to us. Our Mediterranean Afro-Asian traditions are differently flavored from their European ones. Our Ladino doesn't speak to their Yiddish. Our dark complexions offend their fair eyes. We tend to resent a perceived superiority complex toward us, rooted in European attitudes toward the depressed citizens of the Ottoman Empire of the eighteenth through early twentieth centuries. Sephardim were regarded as primitives, charity cases, pitied by European Jews. In Israel, where the term Sephardic includes not only Hispanic descendants but "Oriental," non-European Jews, mostly from the Middle East, the issue of prejudice by the economically and politically dominant Ashkenazi community against us has been a significant tension in a nation where Sephardim now constitute a majority.

These attitudes and perceptions result in a certain tenuousness, an otherness in our relation to any larger picture, including what I call Big Picture Judaism. Our otherness was never directly talked about in my upbringing, but the fact is I did feel *different* from my Ashkenazic Jewish friends. When we broke down into teams for the schoolyard punchball games at PS 98 in Manhattan, for instance, I played on the team of Blacks and Hispanics against the team composed of Whites and "normal" Jews. So somehow the distinctiveness of my brand of Jewishness was absorbed.

But we were never raised to see ourselves as "victims" or black sheep Jews.

We were too proud for that. I tried to convey some of that Sephardic stubborn pride in the image of my grandmother Anna Amirez in "Poem for Grandma." Pride is not necessarily a great quality, it has its dark side (we Greeks should know about hubris); but it is ours. Deep in our Sephardic souls, if truth be told, we see ourselves as the superior ones.

We are the descendants, after all, of the Golden Age of Spain. Our poets, philosophers, physicians, mapmakers, diplomats, and merchants flowered in and shaped this period of harmony between Muslim, Christian, and Jew when Spain was the world's cultural and intellectual mecca. Mythologized over centuries of nostalgic recall, their great accomplishments imprinted themselves on us through the generations as a utopian vision and a kind of animating spark we carry with us. We want to bring people together like Hasdai Ibn Shaprut, the poet/physician/diplomat who orchestrated the Muslim-Christian-Jewish court culture of Abdul El Rachman. We think language can solve problems, resolve differences. We offer candy to sweeten the conversation. We are sociable, accommodating people, like my father pushing cigars over the counter and testing his street smarts and language dexterity with fellow immigrants who'd wander into his store seeking directions in halting English only to have him reply in versions of Spanish, French, German, Turkish—whatever it took to meet people where they lived and breathed. Sephardim believe whatever we do, we can do well; we *can* make it better.

Tenuousness, suffering, and pride. Elements of a heritage. Each embodying an attitude toward life, each a wellspring for a poet. Couple these elements with a cultural taste for language: a rich folk poetics of ballads and proverbs; a tradition of great poets—Judah Halevi, Solomon Ibn Gabirol, Shmuel Ha-Nagid, and Moshe Ibn Ezra; we developed the Kaballah, for God's sake! And for our own. This is a tradition in which manipulation of language can lead to enlightenment.

It's a heritage for a poet to take pride in, with a poetic tradition that humbles one. A great heritage for a poet, as I think about it. In fact, I'd like to think that being a poet is, in itself, a natural expression of the Sephardic heritage, spirit, and yearning.

Marcia Falk

Born in New York City, poet and translator Marcia Falk received a B.A. in philosophy from Brandeis University and a Ph.D. in English and comparative literature from Stanford. She was a Fulbright Scholar and Postdoctoral Fellow at the Hebrew University of Jerusalem, where she studied Bible and Hebrew literature. A university professor for many years, she now lectures widely. Her books include *The Book of Blessings: New Jewish Prayers for Daily Life, the Sabbath, and the New Moon Festival* (HarperCollins, 1996; paperback edition, Beacon Press, 1999), *The Song of Songs: A New Translation and Interpretation* (Harper, 1990), and an annotated volume of translations from the Yiddish, *With Teeth in the Earth: Selected Poems of Malka Heifetz Tussman* (Wayne State UP, 1992).

Winter Solstice

I

Here you are, back
in the blue-white woods—

how tall the birches,
how delicate the pines!

Standing on the frozen plot of snow,
you suddenly know these trees

will be your gravestone.
Nothing stirs—but what

are those sounds?
You balance on the crusty edge

while all around you ice
invisibly thaws,

beneath the snow
the mushrooms smolder,

58

and under your feet the unborn grass
hums in its bed.

2

Warm breeze across the winter sky,
the birch trunk shedding its skin,
ice beginning to give beneath your feet—

It's alive, alive beneath the stillness,
under the frozen surface of the pond,
in the moss-webbed rock, alive!

In the unseen hoof of the deer
whose quick track lightly pierced the snow,
and in all the unnamed footprints,

and in all the longed-for music
of the last dead leaves
and the still-twittering birds, alive!

And in the bronze of the inert star
that melts the snow
and erases the deer tracks,

and turns wet skin to parchment,
flesh to fossil, water to stone
again—

C O M M E N T A R Y

"Winter Solstice" came to me—as most of my poems do—unbidden and un-
intended, gently poking at the edge of awareness, pushing itself toward the
center of the conscious mind. I did not set out to write it (or anything in partic-
ular) that afternoon in the woods when I first scribbled some lines in my
pocket notebook. And even later, when the scribbled lines began to coalesce
into a poem, I still did not intend to write a piece of liturgy. Yet ultimately
"Winter Solstice" found its way, along with other poems I had either written

or translated from Hebrew and Yiddish, into a new prayer book—a book I never specifically set out to write but which, nonetheless, I came to write. (To say that I never meant to write a prayer book is an understatement; no one was more surprised about the fact that I had done so than I. I saw myself as a poet and a translator, at times a literary critic. I had engaged in Bible scholarship while translating the Song of Songs, but my interest in the Bible was, and remained, primarily literary.)

The Book of Blessings: New Jewish Prayers for Daily Life, the Sabbath, and the New Moon Festival had, over the course of thirteen years, evolved from the slender, poetry-sized volume it was first imagined to be, into over 550 pages of Hebrew and English blessings, prayers, poetry, essays, and commentary, organized along the themes and structure of the traditional Jewish liturgy. It had begun as a personal challenge, an attempt to give voice to various and sometimes contradictory aspects of my self—as a woman and a Jew, a feminist and a poet, an American-born native speaker of English with a passion for the Hebrew language (and a love of Yiddish, too). *The Book of Blessings* emerged out of ordinary human aches and joys, especially the yearning to feel oneself part of a greater whole. (I might bring the word "spiritual" into the conversation here if the concept of "spirituality" were not so hopelessly dualistic, invoking as it does the whole history of the mind-body split in Western civilization. As if that weren't problem enough, the marketing of "spirituality" in the current frenzy of New Age millennialism has reduced the concept to inanity.)

A Jewishly educated Jew who had grown up in a traditional Jewish home, I had become increasingly uncomfortable in my adulthood with the patriarchical theological language of Judaism; at a certain point, the very word "God" felt idolatrous to me. Coexisting with the discomfort, however, was the wish to see Jewish civilization—and, specifically, Hebrew liturgy—continue to survive. While other kinds of Jewish texts—Torah, Talmud, *midrash*, and more—can be kept alive through study, commentary, and critique, in order for prayer to survive, it has to be usable as a performance language with which we bring our awareness to the present moment. Thus prayer has to speak honestly to both the heart and the mind. This is the reason, I think, that the *siddur*—the Jewish prayer book—is the one sacred text in Judaism that has never been completed or fixed; rather, it has been adapted and shaped, added to and altered many times over the course of nearly two millennia. My belief is that the evolution of Jewish liturgy must continue if the liturgical culture is to survive.

The Book of Blessings became the vessel of my creative output for over a decade, and although not all the poems I wrote during that period ultimately found a place between its covers, "Winter Solstice" was among the ones that did. In the end, the liturgical framework I was shaping with *The Book of Blessings* became a context affecting the parameters of meaning of this and all the poems in the book. In order to begin talking about how liturgical context affects poetic meaning—what it means to have poetry as prayer—I'd like to explain the particular place of "Winter Solstice" in my prayer book.

"Winter Solstice" appears as part of a "sevenfold prayer" re-creating the traditional prayer known as the *amidah* ("standing" prayer, so named because it is recited while standing). The traditional *amidah* is the central prayer of every synagogue service; with its recitation, the individual stands in community to speak "the prayer of the heart." In my new version, the theme of each of the seven sections of the traditional *amidah* for the Sabbath is revisited, revisioned, and, finally, respoken in a collage of blessings, poems, and meditations. Included in this assemblage of genres is a multivocal selection of poetry by Jewish women (more about this later). It is here, in the chorus of women's voices, that "Winter Solstice" takes its place. Specifically, "Winter Solstice" appears in the second section of my new *amidah*, which re-creates the traditional theme of *g'vurot*, "strength," affirming God's power as *m'hayeyh meytim*, "reviver of the dead."

I should say right off that, in contemporary American Jewish culture, the concept of *t'hiyat hameytim*, "revival of the dead," tends to be seen as problematic—so problematic, in fact, that both the Reform and Reconstructionist movements have dropped all explicit references to it from the latest versions of their prayer books. The Reform movement instead praises a God who "revives all," *m'hayeyh hakol*, and the Reconstructionist prayer book speaks of God as "reviving all that lives," *m'hayeyh kol hay*. These euphemisms, however, only beg the question, for what is it that can be brought back to life *except* that which has passed from life; what can be revived that is not first dead? Although we may not share Ezekiel's messianic vision of the dry bones rising from their graves, it seems to me a mistake to expunge all mention of death from the liturgy. (Surely the question of what happens to us after we die continues to be asked today!) Because this blessing is the primary place in the synagogue service where death is dealt with (the *kaddish* prayer for mourners does not explicitly talk about the dead but rather about God's holy name), it offers an important opportunity to reflect on the theme of the relationship of death to life. In this section of my new *amidah*, which is entitled "Sustaining Life, Embracing Death," I present some contemporary responses to the ancient theme of revival and the ages-old human struggle to understand our mortal condition.

"Sustaining Life, Embracing Death" follows the same basic structure as all the sections of my *amidah*. (While I often think of this prayer as a "collage," a musical term—cantata, perhaps?—may better convey the presence of an underlying structural pattern, in which each part plays a specific role.) It opens with a meditation introducing the theme:

> To celebrate life is to acknowledge the ongoing dying, and ultimately to embrace death. For although all life travels toward its death, death is not a destination: it

too is a journey to beginnings: all death leads to life again. From peelings to mulch to new potatoes, the world is ever-renewing, ever-renewed.

Then comes the blessing itself, the essence of the section (it will be repeated at the section's end). Like all the blessings in the book, the blessing for "Sustaining Life, Embracing Death" is brief. It is unlike others in *The Book of Blessings*, however, in that it takes the form of a rhymed quatrain, in both Hebrew and English, its shape emerging from its theme, folding back on itself to connect its end with its beginning:

נְבָרֵךְ אֶת הַמַּעְיָן

עֲדֵי־עַד מִפַּכֶּה—

מַעְגַּל הַחַיִּים

הַמֵּמִית וּמְחַיֶּה.

Let us bless the well
eternally giving—
the circle of life
ever-dying, ever-living.

After the blessing comes the main corpus of the section, a selection of poems that further develop the theme. These are by a variety of Jewish women poets writing in Hebrew and in Yiddish. As far as I know, none of these poems was written specifically to be used as prayer, yet each contributes a different perspective or insight that enhances the resonance of the blessing. Taken together, they function as an integral aspect of this new liturgy; they might even be seen as a contemporary equivalent of the traditional *k'rovot,* special poems that were individually composed and added to the (traditional) *amidah* prayer on Sabbaths, holidays, and special weekdays.

The introduction of a chorus of Jewish *women's* voices here is a small step toward correcting the imbalance of a tradition that has barely recorded women's voices at all and of a liturgy in which women's words have gone virtually unheard. As men's words alone have been expected to speak for all of us for the past two millennia, let it go without saying that these poems by women are not intended to be only *for* women but rather to speak to the whole community. The ultimate point of these poetry selections is not just to introduce a diversity of women's voices but to encourage each individual to add her or his own voice to the communal chorus.

Among the poems in "Sustaining Life, Embracing Death" is a triolet by the great twentieth-century American Yiddish poet Malka Heifetz Tussman. This poem is a personal favorite of mine, in part because of its wonderful music and in part because of the sheer joy it brought me while translating it. I included it in "Sustaining Life, Embracing Death," however, because I believed

it embodied the theme of the section perfectly. Here is the English version (in
The Book of Blessings, the original Yiddish appears alongside the translation).

Leaves

Leaves don't fall. They descend.
Longing for earth, they come winging.
In their time, they'll come again,
For leaves don't fall. They descend.
On the branches, they will be again
Green and fragrant, cradle-swinging,
For leaves don't fall. They descend.
Longing for earth, they come winging.

While the inclusion of "Leaves" in "Sustaining Life, Embracing Death" was
an obvious choice, it was not until after I saw it there that I knew I would also
bring "Winter Solstice" into the section. Tussman's dying autumnal leaf, which
calls up an image of its own reincarnation in spring, put me in mind of the sea-
son *between* fall and spring, when both births and deaths are more hidden from
view. Context, of course, is everything. Following Tussman's "Leaves" in a sec-
tion of prayer on the connection of living to dying, the personal meditation of
"Winter Solstice" takes on different meaning from what it had when it first took
shape on the page. The inscrutable motion of ice beginning to melt underfoot on
a winter day now becomes the ineffable moment poised between the descend-
ing and ascending movements of Tussman's ever-living, ever-dying leaves. The
voice of one poet answers the voice of another, as the connection between sea-
sons echoes the connection between the earth's cycles and the human life cycle.
And what of the larger ritual context, which keeps these moments juxtaposed in
a *weekly* cycle, as part of a Sabbath prayer? Reenacting the cycles of the natural
world in the context of human time emphasizes the congruencies of *all* time, all
cycles—our connections to greater wholes and to *the* greater whole.

Yes, context is everything. As we know but do not always remember, the poetic
and the prophetic modes emerged out of similar origins in oral tradition—a cul-
tural background with which, to a great extent, we have lost touch today. We
often forget that the distinction between the secular and the sacred is a modern
one; we are no longer used to viewing poetry as the mode of sacred expression
it once was; we are confused by any convergence of poetry and prayer. Since
the publication of *The Book of Blessings* in 1996, I have received a great deal of
response to my conflation of these two realms. Part of this response has been a
rather peculiar concern with the amount of "blank space" in the book. Al-
though many people appreciate the book's design, finding it aesthetically

pleasing and helpful, there are those who express surprise and even dismay to find so much "unused space" in it. Such readers are unaccustomed to seeing a single prayer laid out on a page; rather, they are used to seeing as many words as possible filling the pages of Jewish prayer books.

Indeed, not just prayer books but all the sacred books in Judaism tend to look crowded, stuffed with words—beginning with the (orally composed) Hebrew Bible, which does not preserve in written form the pauses for breath that are detectable when the text is read aloud. The earliest manuscripts of the Hebrew Bible present the same dense, proselike passages regardless of the particular biblical genre, be it poem, story, or declaration of law. The later, printed texts of the Bible are even denser-looking on the page; the traditional Bible-with-commentaries (*mikra'ot g'dolot*) offers text surrounded by texts in historical layers, so that what would normally be a margin is now itself a column of words. Such ink-filled margins surround the traditional page of Talmud as well. No wonder it's a shock to open a (new) sacred text and find lines of verse surrounded by nothing but white space on all sides!

In contrast, the ordinary poetry reader doesn't blink at this arrangement—for what is a poem but language in lines, and how can you have line breaks without *space*? In a poem, white space is every bit as important as black ink: the one creates the silence that makes intelligible the other's sound. The regular reader of poetry takes for granted that speech without pause—sound without silence—is not language but merely noise. Yet, in its emphasis on speech as a sacred mode of communication, Jewish liturgical tradition has never completely recognized silence as an equal partner with sound.

As one nurtured from an early age by classical Jewish books side by side with literary/poetic texts, I have long yearned to bring the two realms closer. To me, it has always seemed obvious that a book of prayer should look like, feel like, *be as spacious as* a book of poems. How else to allow room for the prayer to breathe, time for the blessing to be taken in? Pauses between strings of spoken words are not just necessary but crucial to verbal prayer, for they provide the time—the space—in which the heart is allowed to awaken.

It was not easy to structure and design *The Book of Blessings*—there simply are no models for wholly new books of Hebrew/English prayer, and the aesthetic structure of the traditional prayer book is so buried in its accumulation of words as to be virtually invisible. Yet I always knew that once I had created the architecture for this project, the internal components would reveal themselves in naturally poetic forms. I suppose I just could not imagine genuine prayer as all that different from genuine poetry.

And so, each time I am asked, as I often am these days, to explain my use of poetry as prayer, I am surprised anew. If poetry is, in a minimal definition, authentic speech, can liturgy be anything short of that? In the end, can a verbal prayer be anything *other* than some kind—some genre—of poem?

Norman Finkelstein

Born in 1954, Norman Finkelstein is currently Professor of English at Xavier University in Cincinnati. He is the author of two important studies of American literature: *The Utopian Moment in Contemporary American Poetry* (Bucknell UP, second edition, 1993), and *The Ritual of New Creation: Jewish Tradition and Contemporary Literature* (State U of New York P, 1992). His books of poetry include *Restless Messengers* (U of Georgia P, 1991), and *Track* (Spuyten Duyvil, 1999).

Acher

It was like this in the garden:
Ben Azzai looked and died,
Ben Zoma looked and went mad;
Akiba and I went forth in peace,
but they said I cut down the young plants.

I said that one is two
and they answered if two why not a thousand:
so they cast me from the congregation
—but they still come to hear me teach.

Meir went with me to the boundary;
I rode and he walked by my side
until I reminded him that he could go no further
since he honored the Sabbath and the Law.
But he longed to hear me finish the argument,
and he waited there till I returned.

I went on to visit the fairest of my disciples,
but I will never see her again,
for she spoke for civilization
and I for its discontents.
Teku I said, and so we parted,
for the dispute cannot be resolved.

This is how it must be
for one who cannot reconcile his desires:
the soul is a spark that consumes the body:
      let no one seek to rest.
There is a Law beyond the Law and we may not know it
      except through all our wanderings.

I said do not look for the book nor its author,
      Elisha ben Abuyah, called Acher,
      the other, the stranger in your midst.

COMMENTARY

"Acher" was written on September 1, 1990. From the way it appears in my notebook, it seems to have been composed in one fell swoop, and the only significant change I made while working was a reordering of the stanzas, a move I make frequently, since the lines I "hear" first are not necessarily the beginning of the poem. Like most of the poems I was writing around that time (including the majority in my book *Restless Messengers*), the overall form is based loosely on the Romantic ode, the subject matter is remote from everyday modern life, and Jewish tradition figures significantly but rarely in a normative fashion. What distinguishes the piece from its fellows is the fact that it is a dramatic monologue, spoken directly by Elisha ben Abuyah, declared an apostate and called Acher (the Other) by his former rabbinic colleagues. In my edition of the *Pirke Aboth*, he is described as "the Faust of Talmudic literature" (79). I tend to avoid poems spoken in an assumed persona, preferring a mode in which the "I" (among other pronouns) hovers in a less determinate manner between self and other. Of course, this could also be said of the traditional dramatic monologue, and when I recall my emotional state at that time, I know all too well why I was tempted to speak from behind the clearly defined mask of such a troublemaker. But I should also point out that around that time, I was completing my *Ritual of New Creation*, a work deeply concerned with the revisionary processes that shape Jewish tradition. So although I am no Talmudist, I had a scholarly as well as a personal interest in the figure of Elisha ben Abuyah.

My first encounter with Acher was probably in Gershom Scholem's essay "The Meaning of the Torah in Jewish Mysticism," in which Scholem speaks of a lost work by Moses de Leon, author of the *Zohar*, called *Pardes* or "Paradise." The title refers to the passage in the Talmud (Hagigah 14b) that tells of "four great rabbis who engaged in esoteric studies in the second century. These four were the Rabbis Akiba, Ben Zoma, Ben Azzai, and Acher. 'One saw and died, the second saw and lost his reason, the third laid waste the young plants [that is, became an apostate and seduced the young]. Only Rabbi Akiba entered in peace and came out in peace'" (57). Scholem notes that *pardes* becomes a widely known pun, "a cipher for the four levels of interpretation," the literal, the allegorical, the Talmudic, and the mystical. "The *pardes* into which the four ancient scholars entered," Scholem writes, "thus came to denote speculations concerning the true meaning of the Torah on all four levels" (57).

This was all rather heady stuff for someone already enamored of textuality, someone who had pored over Yeats's *A Vision* when he was eighteen, and who had known of Ben Zoma since his earliest childhood, when he would hear the adults at the Seder table read of the rabbis recounting the story of the exodus at Bene Berak. "The Bible commands us, saying: 'That you may remember the day of your going out from Egypt all the days of your life.' Ben Zoma explained: *The days of your life* might mean only the days; *all the days of your life* includes the nights also. The other sages, however, explain it this way: The *days of your life* refers to this world only, but *all the days of your life* includes also the time of the Messiah." Listening to the Passover Haggadah was my first introduction to *midrash*, though it would take another thirty years before I recognized it as such. And here was Ben Zoma again, in the company of Rabbi Akiba (of whom I had heard many tales in Hebrew school) and two other sages, in a mystical paradise of pure language. And Ben Zoma went mad! Ben Azzai died! So who was this mysterious Acher?

Not long after, Acher and the Talmudic anecdote cropped up again, this time among the speculations of Harold Bloom: "The Talmudic parable of the four sages who entered Pardes is sufficient indication of why Acher outraged normative rabbis. Cutting down the young plants of Paradise signifies the destructive effect of Gnostic dualism, of Acher's belief in two principles—presumably principles of God and of a demi-urge—rather than a monostic belief in the absolute power of God. Today many readers, schooled in the insights of Scholem, may reflect with some melancholy that they are more in the mode of Acher than in that of the great Akiba" (*Poetics of Influence*, 385). This conclusion becomes even more extreme in Bloom's essay on Jewish culture and Jewish identity: "In a phantasmagoria that I believe to be already existent, many of us shape a still inchoate and perhaps heretical new Torah out of the writings of Freud, Kafka, and Scholem. I say 'perhaps' because who can say, or who ever could say, what is heretical in regard to our traditions? We call Elisha ben Abuyah *Acher*, but was he truly 'the other' for us, simply because like the Gnostics he believed in two Powers, rather than one?" (*Poetics of Influence* 368). Bloom's guarded admiration for Acher reflects his general predilection for strong writers and thinkers who stand against normative literary and cultural traditions, though he also has great respect for the psychohistorical processes through which the normative or canonical comes into being. The phantasmagoric idea of a heretical new Torah coming forth out of Freud, Kafka, and Scholem indicates that for Bloom, even in the face of the current Orthodox revival, the boldest and most imaginative Jewish thought and writing will be the result of great swerves from the normative, which will in turn preserve itself in the most uncanny ways. I tend to see the world in dialectical terms, and my Jewish heritage is closely bound up with my (post-Romantic) poetic identity. Thus the tension Bloom describes between the rebellious, transgressive imagination and the weighty historical power of cultural authority has great appeal to me, as does the weird idea that works such as *Moses and Monotheism* and *The Castle* can form the basis of Holy Scripture. The antithetical figure of Acher, somehow anticipating such modern developments, inevitably worked itself into a poem.

If such a heretical new Torah is coming into being, then surely one of its most important passages for me may be found in *Civilization and Its Discontents*, when Freud writes of the way in which the "super-ego torments the sinful ego," always "on the watch for opportunities of getting it punished by the external world" (86). In modern society, "Instinctual renunciation now no longer has a completely liberating effect; virtuous continence is no longer rewarded with the assurance of love. A threatened external unhappiness—loss of love and punishment on the part of the external authority—has been exchanged for a permanent internal unhappiness, for the tension of the sense of guilt" (89).

But is this only a modern phenomenon–and just as importantly, in what ways is it a Jewish one? It has often been observed that the conscience is a Jewish invention. Powerfully anachronistic, Bloom reads Freud backward into the Hebrew Scriptures (or reads the *Book of J* ahead into Freud), arguing that

> J's uncanny Yahweh erupts in late Freud as the Superego of *Civilization and Its Discontents*. The Freudian Superego just about is J's Yahweh, and causes our unconscious sense of guilt, a "guilt that is neither remorse nor the consciousness of wrongdoing. . . ." And precisely here, in one of the greatest ironies, Freud is J's descendent and is haunted by J's Yahweh in the figure of the Superego. The Punch and Judy Show element in Freud's scenario of the relations between Superego and hapless Ego is precisely like J's dark comedy of the relations between Yahweh and the hapless Israelites in the Wilderness. Yahweh and the Superego keep demanding that Israelites and Ego surrender all their aggressivity, and with each fresh surrender the wretched Israelites and Ego are berated still more strenuously, whacked harder for harboring unconscious aggressivity toward the creator and father. (*Book of J,* 305–306)

In my poem, the disciple who is both young lover and archaic mother (i.e., Bloom's J herself) speaks ironically for the normative power of civilization and all that it entails. No longer opposed to civilization, as Freud claims that all women must be, she is confronted by her erstwhile teacher, the gnostic ben Abuyah, with his vision of the personal *pneuma* or spark of the Outside God, who answers for the hapless Ego, the hapless Israelites. Whack, whack: The interminable nature of this Punch and Judy Show seems to have become a salient dimension of Jewish life. Or as Roth's irrepressible Portnoy cries, "Doctor Spielvogel, this is my life, my only life, and I'm living in the middle of a Jewish joke! I am the son in the Jewish joke—*only it ain't no joke!*" (*Portnoy's Complaint*, 36–37).

There is no cure for this condition, no solution to this problem; and any writer who engages in this discourse will only find temporary consolation in the utterance itself. *Tishbi yetzaretz kushyot ve'abayot*: The messiah will answer questions and problems. In the Talmud, the phrase denotes the contradiction or inconclusiveness of an argument that cannot be resolved. The answer is infinitely deferred, and with it the satisfaction that comes of intellectual or formal closure. It appears as an acronym: *teku*, a word that in modern Hebrew means a tie score. Overdetermined, anachronistic, and messianicly "pressing for the end" despite its apparent reconciliation to the definitive Jewish condition—and trope—of wandering, my poem is yet another little Jewish joke, balanced uneasily between the sublime and the parodic. The very idea of *this* text, a commentary upon what is already a commentary, only increases its uneasiness (it is an uneasiness that its author has long taken for granted). But this seems to be the nature of its fate.

Works Cited

Bloom, Harold. *The Book of J.* New York: Grove Weidenfeld, 1990.

———. *Poetics of Influence: New and Selected Criticism.* Ed. John Hollander. New Haven, Conn.: Henry R. Schwab, 1988.

Freud, Sigmund. *Civilization and Its Discontents.* Trans. James Strachey. New York: Norton, 1961.

Roth, Philip. *Portnoy's Complaint.* 1969. New York: Vintage Books, 1994.

Sayings of the Fathers or Pirke Aboth. Trans. Joseph H. Hertz. New York: Behrman House, 1945.

Scholem, Gershom. "The Meaning of the Torah in Jewish Mysticism." *On the Kabbalah and Its Symbolism.* Trans. Ralph Manheim. New York: Schocken, 1965.

Albert Goldbarth

Albert Goldbarth was born in 1948 in Chicago, Illinois. He is currently Distinguished Professor of Humanities at Wichita State University. His twenty books of poetry include *Heaven and Earth: A Cosmology* (U of Georgia P, 1991), which earned the 1991 National Book Critics Circle Award for Poetry. Other collections of poetry include *Beyond* (Godine, 1998), and *Troubled Lovers in History: A Sequence of Poems* (Ohio State UP, 1999). He is also the author of a collection of essays entitled *Dark Waves and Light Matter* (U of Georgia P, 1999) and has been the recipient of an NEA Fellowship.

Parnassus

for Herb Leibowitz

Technically I was a man.

This spindly squeaky thing with the adam's apple accent was, by virtue of being thirteen and bar mitzvahed, a technical man.

And so the phone call came: they needed a tenth for a *minyan*. Nathan Kaplan—I remembered Mr. Kaplan, didn't I?—needed to say the *yiskor* prayers for his wife, and if I weren't there in attendance, lending my lame but official singsong to these *daveners*, the God Who Demanded a Threshold of Ten would never turn His Ear of Ears to their puff of plaintive Kaplan imploration.

I didn't *want* to; but I went. I *wanted* to—what? Watch television? Play with my willie? Stare at a smear of clouds and wish a burning pinpoint of myself up through them, into the currents of outer space? The angsts and overbrimmings of being technically a man are many. In any case, yes, I went.

There isn't much more to say. They were ancient and stale of breath, and silked and fringed in the ritual synagoguewear, and I stood among them, following their lead and saying *amen* whenever someone's gnarled radish of a finger thumped the word out in my opened book. I loaned my voice, it took its place in a single wing of voice that made its technical way through the top of the ionosphere, and into a realm of shimmering off the scale of human perception.

This is why I believe in the muses, of course.

There were nine of them.

And ever since, if I've been invited to join them for a moment, to sing along as a tenth—though they may have scraped the bottom of the barrel to get my number, I go.

COMMENTARY

When ten adult males are gathered to pray, *this*—not the building; even *without* a building—is a "synagogue." "Solitary prayer," Leo Rosten says, "is laudable, but a *minyan* possesses special merit." When I was growing up, in my lower-lower-middle-class and demi-Jewish 1950s Chicago neighborhood, this idea was just as much a given as were, for others in other existences, Newton's laws of thermodynamics. Maybe in its own way it *was* thermodynamic: "The radiant Presence of God," the *Shechinah*, will dwell among the worshipers—*if* critical mass is reached, and ten are gathered.

In kabbalistic thought, the *Shechinah* is "the dwelling feminine principle" of divinity. According to the *Zohar*, a bride is married under a decorated canopy "in order thus to honor the Supernal Bride above, who comes to partake of the joy." Also, when a man returns from travel, "it is his duty to give his wife pleasure," and this "gives joy to the *Shechinah*."

I don't know what feminist criticism might wring from these ten roly-poly, grizzled, retired wholesale draperies salesmen inviting a Celestial Woman to give grace to their worship, but for me that magical ten and its magical efficacy have always been a powerful idea.

In fact, the power of ten runs richly through the lore. After all, it isn't called the "Decalogue" for nothing. Plus, the ten plagues the Egyptians suffered; the ten tests of faith God visited upon Abraham; the ten "lost tribes"; "the Ten Words by which the world was created"; the *sefirot*, "the ten aspects of God"; and more.

All that might be coincidental; but it's easy to posit our own first portable digital calculator—our ten fingers—as the inspiring template. I remember being a kid in *shul*, and struck by simply how *neat* it was, that the image of two hands clasped in prayer became the entire viably *davening* congregation *in reductio*.

Anyway, despite the importance of ten, it was resignedly understood in my childhood neighborhood that its dwindling Jewish population, further depleted by adult male Jews who were otherwise occupied during their afternoons in the work force, often enough would mean a daily congregation of less-than-*minyan* size. And this was pitifully unfortunate if a mourner was in attendance, who wanted his prayers for the dead—the *yiskor*—to be received by God with full official backing.

And so the corollary understanding was that, in a pinch like this, emergency phone calls swept the neighborhood like a dragnet, hoping to find at home some recently bar-mitzvahed shmo who, even if his mind was sticking like goo to TV baseball or a stolen issue of *Playboy*, might—well, *barely*—serve as the final sanctioning congregant. Just when you thought you were done . . . Hebrew School, over . . . *haftorah* lessons, over . . . the whole bar mitzvah, over . . . nothing but secular pleasures ahead . . . at any moment, The Dreaded Call could come, and inveigh you back into that ancient, suffocating cell. Among my set, The Dreaded Call was a horror of legendary status.

And beyond that, of course, it invokes the interesting Hundredth Monkey Theory. You know: ninety-nine monkeys on some far island can undertake a seemingly new practice, like dipping their food in the sea before eating, and it means nothing more than ninety-nine monkeys dip their food in the sea before eating—only that; but suddenly a hundredth monkey does it, and some ethereal line is breached, and monkeys *on other islands* all over, simultaneously, and with no role models, start to dip their food in the sea. There are verifying studies.

And one day, I got The Dreaded Call. I could complete the magical ten. I could raise a mourner's wishes above the ethereal line. Me, hundredth monkey.

I'd always wanted this to inform a poem. As a way of loosely studying individual desire versus communal responsibility, it especially seemed a promising notion. For years, though, nothing clicked. And I really don't much believe in simply tricking up an anecdotal moment, "Albert Makes Ten," with a handful of images and a run of enjambment, and calling it a "poem." *Whatever* poems are, they aren't journal entries broken into lines.

But an enabling architecture came unbidden, when I was asked to provide a celebratory birthday piece for the editor of *Parnassus* (the poetry criticism journal), Herb Leibowitz. *That* was it: Parnassus . . . Greek mythology . . . yes, nine muses . . . nine, inviting a tenth to accompany them for a moment. And something like thirty-five years after my bar mitzvah, there it was, down on a page.

And it felt good and right to extend the borders of High Parnassian Song into the realm of the phlegmily lubricated gutturals of immigrant prayer. For all of what appears at first to be the limiting nature of the insistence on a symbolic ten, the *minyan* was intended as a liberating gesture: It freed a people in wandering exile from the need to attach themselves to a central, physical site of worship. You can assemble a *minyan* wherever you are, like a tent.

And in its own way, it was a very populist gesture. There's a wonderful saying that goes "Nine rabbis don't make a *minyan*; ten peddlers do." Or, as it turns out, nine plus one reluctant but well-intentioned boy-man less with *shechinahs* stirring his mind, and more with *shiksas*.

Allen Grossman

Born in 1932 in Minneapolis, Allen Grossman was educated at Harvard and Brandeis universities. He is currently Professor of English at Johns Hopkins University, and is the author of collections of poetry and critical studies, including *The Philosopher's Window (A Romance) and Other Poems* (New Directions, 1995), *The Long Schoolroom: Lessons in the Bitter Logic of the Poetic Principle* (U of Michigan P, 1997), and *The Sighted Singer: Two Works on Poetry for Readers and Writers* (Johns Hopkins U P, 1991). He has also been a MacArthur Fellow, and a recipient of both a Guggenheim and a NEA fellowship.

How To Do Things With Tears

In thy springs, O Zion, are the water wheels
Of my mind! The wheels beat the shining stream.
Whack. Dying. And then death. *Whack.* Learning. Learned.
Whack. Breathing. And breath. *Whack.* Gone with the wind.

I am old. The direction of time is plain:
As the daylight, never without direction,
Rises in a direction, east to west,
And sets in a direction, west to east,

Walking backwards all night long, underground;
So, this bright water is bent on its purpose—
To find the meadow path to the shore and then
The star ("Sleepless") by which the helmsman winds

And turns. Zion of mind! This is the way:
Towards nightfall the wind shifts offshore, north by
Northwest, closing the harbor to sail
And it stiffens, raising the metal water

In the roads. The low sun darkens and freezes.
The water shines. In the raking light is
Towed the great ship home, upwind, everything
Furled. And, behind the great ship, I am carried,

A castaway, in the body alone,
Under the gates of Erebus—the meeting
Place of daylight underground and night wind
Shrieking in wires, the halliards knocking and

Ravelled banners streaming to the south-east
Like thought drawn out, wracked and torn, when the wind
Shifts and rises and the light fails in the long
School room of the setting sun. What is left

To mind but remembrances of the world?
The people of the road, in tears, sit down
At the road-side and tell stories of the world
Then they rise again in tears and go up.

The mill sits in the springs. Water wheels whack
Round: Alive, *whack*. Dying, *whack*. Dead *whack*. Nothing.
How, then, to do things with tears?—Deliver us,
Zion, from mist. Kill us in the light.

C O M M E N T A R Y

"How To Do Things With Tears" is a "how to" poem. How to think about grief
for all death but also for your own. It ends with a prayer to God for a lucid
death. *Kill us in the light*. It's the best you can do. But the light is a great thing.
The Jew studies his God, and thought about the Jew's God can help anyone to
see what's there and what is not there.

My poems, like most poems, are mostly pictures of a man thinking, and this is
one of that kind. All of everyone's conscious life is experienced as a moving pic-
ture of a man or woman thinking about the common world. Thinking is common
and assumes (takes as given) a common life for all; hence, poems are part of
the general picture of a man or woman sitting on a rock in the stream of thought
and then at the shore of ocean and then cast away and wet with the water of it.

Hard thought such as we see a man or woman thinking in poems (the stay is
wrung by it, the pennant wracked and torn) is mostly thought made possible by
a poem that has come before. In this case Psalms 39 and 87 ("All my springs
are in thee") and another which I have forgotten. Also, Cowper's "Castaway."

There is, then, a common world. Any rumor to the contrary makes no sense.
To those for whom there is no such world, there is no poetry. Also, no way of

doing anything with tears (let alone doing anything with words). Even though we are solitary, *the common world is what we know.*

What do we want from thought when we call it?

In that world, where we now are, thought like water flows from upland springs down to the sea according to the Law of Thought (the gravity of water). The consciousness of each of us struggles to make a way, her way or his way, in accord with the Law of Water: how the water tears at the wheel and then flows downward across the meadow and over the rocks until it falls into a hole and goes underground to the sea. But it is the Law of Water Falling that teaches us, "Thou shalt fall down like water and be still and be no more and be ocean with wind on it and the ship above you and down wind—beyond all calling— for you are cast away. . . ."

That is what thought is. Death is a thought in that world.

What I write about is thinking. Thinking is like the action of the mill wheel. After a while one hears the sound, the sound of the wheel striking the water— *Whack, whack.* And then after another while one hears the meaning of the sound—for example the difference between dying and death.

Everyone has heard of her own birth or his own birth and can speak of it (birth) and also to it. Poems begin that way—speaking to their "own birth," natality.

> In thy springs, O Zion, are the water wheels
> Of my mind! The wheels beat the shining stream.

Marilyn Hacker

Poet and translator Marilyn Hacker was born in 1942 in New York City, and educated at New York University. Since 1997, she has been Professor of English at Hofstra University. She is the author of numerous award-winning volumes of poetry, including *Squares and Courtyards* (Norton, 2000), and *Winter Numbers* (Norton, 1994). She has been a three-time recipient of a National Endowment for the Arts grant (1974, 1985, 1995), and has won the National Book Award in Poetry, as well as a grant from the Guggenheim Foundation.

The Boy

Is it the boy in me who's looking out
the window, while someone across the street
mends a pillow-case, clouds shift, the gutterspout
pours rain, someone else lights a cigarette?

(Because he flinched, because he didn't whirl
around, face them, because he didn't hurl
the challenge back—"*Fascists*"—not "*Faggots*"—"*Swine!*"
he briefly wonders—if he were a girl . . .)
He writes a line. He crosses out a line.

I'll never be a man, but there's a boy
crossing out words: the rain, the linen-mender,
are all the homework he will do today.
The absence and the privilege of gender

confound in him, soprano, clumsy, frail.
Not neuter—neutral human, and unmarked,
the younger brother in the fairy-tale
except, boys shouted "Jew!" across the park

at him when he was coming home from school.
The book that he just read, about the war,
the partisans, is less a terrible
and thrilling story, more a warning, more

a code, and he must puzzle out the code.
He has short hair, a red sweatshirt. They know
something about him—that he should be proud
of? That's shameful if it shows?

That got you killed in 1942.
In his story, do the partisans
have sons? Have grandparents? Is he a Jew
more than he is a boy, who'll be a man

someday? Someone who'll never be a man
looks out the window at the rain he thought
might stop. He reads the sentence he began.
He writes down something that he crosses out.

COMMENTARY

"The Boy" was written in my studio in the 3rd *arrondissement* in Paris, where
my worktable faces a window with a vis-à-vis, beyond which the lives of the
people living opposite, framed by door-sized windows, go on more or less be-
fore my eyes, as mine does before theirs. A schoolchild doing homework in one
of those flats would face me as I'd face him or her. But there is no such child; it
was I who watched the elderly widow (I think she's a widow) with the enormous
rubber plant in her front room sitting at the window hemming a pillowcase that
day, while her young neighbor-on-the-landing leaned out the window with a lit
cigarette, watching the street. I had just read a book review by a younger Ameri-
can poet friend, of two books by two other young poets, one female and one
male, in which the reviewer posited that the characteristic stance of the male
poet was (indeed) the seat at the window of his consciousness, looking out on
the world, where the woman poet was more likely to be examining the goings-on
within the room (the room of the self). Since I was quite literally writing while
looking out the window (and since I have an ongoing dialogue-in-poems with
the writer of the book review), the idea of "the boy" who fulfilled the essay's ex-
pectations was an attractive one. Gender is only one aspect of identity, though,
and the boy looking out the window over the notebook in which he was meant to
be writing an *explication de texte*—who had not thought much before about
"being a boy" the way a ten-year-old girl is often obliged to consider the impli-
cations of gender—had just (I discovered) had another of its aspects flung at
him, so that he could not, that late afternoon, take the "secular and republican"

universality of his subjectivity for granted. I could invent the rest of his history—
I know that he is not a son of the Tunisian and Eastern European Orthodox Jews
repeopling the quarter of the rue des Rosiers after the Occupation thinned its
numbers, not a *yeshiva* student who thanks God every day for not making him a
woman. But their proximity must have made him think more than once about the
Jewishness his secular parents, *soixante-huitards* pushing fifty, perhaps uncom-
fortable with their own parents' (uncomfortable) war stories, present to him as a
part of history he'll learn more about later, which has become something he
seeks out, as another child might look for sex, in novels and first-person ac-
counts not necessarily written for children. Perhaps it was that consuming curi-
osity about he's-not-quite-sure-what that prompted the taunts on the way home
from school. And I'm not sure which of us, he or I, thought first that the other
identity of "boy" "girl" "man" "woman" might be as mysteriously fluid as the
name and notion "Jew"—an insult or a proud blazon depending on the context,
something that could be flung out as one and accepted as the other. "The boy" turns
back into the middle-aged woman writer at the end, who will "never be a man,"
but he remains himself, too, someone who may one day reject the stone tablets
of gender in the same spirit as he questions what it is that makes him "a Jew."

Anthony Hecht

Anthony Hecht was born 1923 in New York City and educated at Bard College and Columbia University. He won the Pulitzer Prize in poetry in 1968 for *The Hard Hours* (Atheneum, 1967). His recent volumes of poetry and criticism include *Flight Among the Tombs: Poems* (Knopf, 1996), *The Laws of the Poetic Art* (Knopf, 1995), and *The Hidden Law* a study of the poet W. H. Auden (Knopf, 1993). He has also twice been a recipient of a Guggenheim Fellowship.

The Book of Yolek

Wir haben ein Gesetz,
Und nach dem Gesetz soll er sterben.

The dowsed coals fume and hiss after your meal
Of grilled brook trout, and you saunter off for a walk
Down the fern trail, it doesn't matter where to,
Just so you're weeks and worlds away from home,
And among midsummer hills have set up camp
In the deep bronze glories of declining day.

You remember, peacefully, an earlier day
In childhood, remember a quite specific meal:
A corn roast and bonfire in summer camp.
That summer you got lost on a Nature Walk;
More than you dared admit, you thought of home;
No one else knows where the mind wanders to.

The fifth of August, 1942.
It was morning and very hot. It was the day
They came at dawn with rifles to The Home
For Jewish Children, cutting short the meal
Of bread and soup, lining them up to walk
In close formation off to a special camp.

How often you have thought about that camp,
As though in some strange way you were driven to.
And about the children, and how they were made to walk.
Yolek who had bad lungs, who wasn't a day
Over five years old, commanded to leave his meal
And shamble between armed guards to his long home.

We're approaching August again. It will drive home
The regulation torments of that camp
Yolek was sent to, his small, unfinished meal,
The electric fences, the numeral tattoo,
The quite extraordinary heat of the day
They all were forced to take that terrible walk.

Whether on a silent, solitary walk
Or among crowds, far off or safe at home,
You will remember, helplessly, that day,
And the smell of smoke, and the loudspeakers of the camp.
Wherever you are, Yolek will be there, too.
His unuttered name will interrupt your meal.

Prepare to receive him in your home some day.
Though they killed him in the camp they sent him to.
He will walk in as you're sitting down to a meal.

COMMENTARY

Three things coalesced as ingredients for a poem of mine called "The Book of Yolek." The first of these was my experience as a member of an infantry company, in the 386th Infantry, 97th Division, which liberated the Flossenberg Concentration Camp. That camp, an annex to Buchenwald (near Weimar), boasted a Messerschmitt factory where prisoners were compelled to work making planes to defeat their own countrymen (many French and Russians were imprisoned there) as well as a large, elegant, three-story brick building used as a torture center for special prisoners. Pastor Dietrich Bonhoeffer, one of the German resisters to Hitler, was executed here, as were a number of distinguished French political prisoners. At the time we arrived, prisoners were dying at the rate of about five hundred a day from typhus. The S.S. personnel that ran the camp had fled, though one former *commandante*, Obersturmbannführer

Kunstler, "was removed from his post because of 'feasts and drunkenness.'"[1] There remained, of the original staff, one civilian, an engineer who oversaw the operation of the Messerschmitt factory, and who was eager to continue production immediately (presumably using the same enfeebled prisoners who were still living) to make planes for use against the Russians, who, he assumed, would be as much our natural enemies as his. At the time I was temporarily assigned to the counterintelligence corps, and this engineer was one of those I interrogated with the purpose of identifying (and subsequently arresting) the rest of the men who ran the camp. (The engineer himself, being a civilian, was not subject to arrest by the military.)

I was twenty-two when I encountered that camp. I had come from a family that regarded stories about concentration camps—they were, for us, little more than rumors—with a marked skepticism. My father had served in the navy in the first World War, when dimly comparable accusations of German atrocities in Belgium turned out to be a fraudulent means of galvanizing a suitable ferocity and hatred of the enemy. The manipulation and focusing of public opinion for military and morale purposes was something I held to be highly suspect. So when I saw with my own eyes men too sick to move, too emaciated to stand, I found it inexpressibly horrible. And thereafter I was prepared to believe that there was no barbarity or perversity of which mankind was not capable.

It was not something I cared to dwell upon at the time, and it was a kind of blessing for me that I had many army duties to perform each and every fatiguing day before the war was over in Europe. (After that, narrowly escaping death in the Pacific Theater, I did eight months of occupation duty in Japan.) After my discharge, I was continuously drunk for at least two weeks. And the next few years were spent devotedly in studies of English and American literature—out of love for it, of course, but as a means of distancing myself from what I felt was intolerable to think about. I suspect many newly discharged soldiers felt much the same way. Nevertheless, the time came when I felt the need to know more about what it was that I, and the rest of the world, and especially the Jews of Europe—of whom I could easily have been one, had fate so determined—had gone through. So I began to read, very hesitantly at first. One of the books I encountered early, and which deeply moved me—a poem of mine is based on an incident it describes—is *The Theory and Practice of Hell* by Eugen Kogon, who was himself a survivor of Buchenwald. There was *Night* by Elie Wiesel, another Buchenwald survivor. These things had to be read slowly, and with long intervals between them. There was Simone Weil's *Waiting for God*, *The Jews of Paris and the Final Solution* by Jacques Adler, the unspeakably eloquent photographs by Roman Vishniac published under the title *A Vanished World*, Martin Gilbert's *The Holocaust*, which I was only able to read in short segments over a long time, Peter Matheson's *The Third Reich and the Christian Churches*, and, among others, but most pertinently for present purposes, the *Anthology of Holocaust Literature* edited by Jacob Glatstein, Israel Knox, and Samuel Margoshes. This extraordinary volume, divided into sections that include "Life in the Ghettos," "Concentration and Death Camps," "Resistance," and "Non-Jews," also has one devoted to "Children," and it is from this section, and an account by Hanna Mortkowicz-Olczakowa of what she calls *Yanosz Korczak's Last Walk*, that I found my occasion. Yanosz Korczak was a famous Jewish educator in Poland who, having been ordered to lead the children of the orphanage where he taught to an assembly point from which they would be taken to death camps, refused to part from them, and went with them to their deaths. Among these children were "little Hanka with the lung trouble, Yolek who was ill. . . ." The reader of my poem will discover that, recollecting this account imperfectly, I gave the bad lungs to Yolek instead of little Hanka. But the grotesque feature that stuck in my mind was what I associated with one of the most famous photographs to survive from the Warsaw ghetto: It is of a small boy, perhaps five or six, hands raised, bewildered, while behind him, uniformed, helmeted soldiers level their rifles at him.

The third ingredient was the consequence of my reading and meditating upon the sestina form itself. It is a curiously difficult and demanding one, dating back to the troubadours, its invention commonly attributed to Arnaut Daniel, to whom Dante pays tribute. The six terminal words rearranged according to a fixed, inflexible law, recurring, of necessity, six times (once in each stanza) plus a seventh, in which two of these words recur in each of the three lines that end the poem, are technically binding, and in some ways severely limiting. In any case, the form, by its insistent repetitions, lends itself particularly well to an obsessiveness, a monomania, a kind of hypnotic fixation on some idea or feeling. Of Sir Philip Sidney's brilliant double sestina that appears in his *Arcadia*, William Empson wrote,

> The poem beats, however rich its orchestration, with a wailing and immovable monotony, forever upon the same doors in vain. *Mountaines, vallies, forrests*; *musique, evening, morning*; it is at these words only that Klaius and Strephon pause in their cries; these words circumscribe their world; these are the bones of their situation; and in tracing their lovelorn pastoral tedium through thirteen repetitions, with something of the aimless multitudinousness of the sea on a rock, we seem to extract all the meanings possible from these notions.[2]

In much the same spirit, Karl Shapiro and Robert Beum, in their useful *A Prosody Handbook*, observe: "The sestina would seem to require the poet's deepest love and conviction, involve his deepest impressions as these take on a rather obsessive quality—if the poem is to offer us more than the pleasures of contrivance."

I emerged from the war unscarred by weapons, though the worse off for having learned how to smoke in the army, and being able to obtain cigarettes almost free from the government, and continuing to smoke heavily for thirty years thereafter. I must count myself fortunate in that a good number of the men in my company were killed or very badly wounded. Still, in another way, of which I dare not make too much, I was scarred in thought and memory. If obsessiveness is what usually characterizes the sestina, it is also what characterized the "Final Solution," as well as the Jewish need to remember, to memorialize, to honor in spirit and in grief.

Notes

1. Raul Hilberg, *The Destruction of the European Jews* (New York: Holmes and Meier, 1988) 579n.
2. William Empson, *Seven Types of Ambiguity* (New York: New Directions, 1990) 36–37.

John Hollander

John Hollander, born 1929 in New York City, was educated at Columbia and Indiana universities. He is the A. Bartlett Giamatti Professor of English at Yale University. He won the Bollingen Prize in 1983. He is author of numerous critical studies and the editor of, among other works, the two-volume *American Poetry: The Nineteenth Century* (Library of America, 1993). His most recent volume of poetry is *Figurehead: And Other Poems* (Knopf, 1999). He has been a MacArthur Fellow, and received a Guggenheim Fellowship.

At the New Year

Every single instant begins another new year;
   Sunlight flashing on water, or plunging into a clearing
In quiet woods announces; the hovering gull proclaims
   Even in wide midsummer a point of turning: and fading
Late winter daylight close behind the huddled backs
   Of houses close to the edge of town flares up and shatters
As well as any screeching ram's horn can, wheel
   Unbroken, uncomprehended continuity,
Making a starting point of a moment along the way,
   Spinning the year about one day's pivot of change.
But if there is to be a high moment of turning
   When a great, autumnal page, say, takes up its curved
Flight in memory's spaces, and with a final sigh,
   As of every door in the world shutting at once, subsides
Into the bed of its fellows; if there is to be
   A time of tallying, recounting and rereading
Illuminated annals, crowded with black and white
   And here and there a capital flaring with silver and bright
Blue, then let it come at a time like this, not at winter's
   Night, when a few dead leaves crusted with frost lie shivering
On our doorsteps to be counted, or when our moments of coldness
   Rise up to chill us again. But let us say at a golden
Moment just on the edge of harvesting, "Yes. Now."
   Times of counting are times of remembering; here amidst showers

Of shiny fruits, both the sweet and the bitter-tasting results,
  The honey of promises gleams on apples that turn to mud
In our innermost of mouths, we can sit facing westward
  Toward imminent rich tents, telling and remembering.

Not like merchants with pursed hearts, counting in dearth and darkness,
  But as when from a shining eminence, someone walking starts
At the sudden view of imperturbable blue on one hand
  And wide green fields on the other. Not at the reddening sands
Behind, nor yet at the blind gleam, ahead, of something
  Golden, looking at such a distance and in such sunlight,
Like something given—so, at this time, our counting begins,
  Whirling all its syllables into the circling wind
That plays about our faces with a force between a blow's
  And a caress', like the strength of a blessing, as we go
Quietly on with what we shall be doing, and sing
  Thanks for being enabled, again, to begin this instant.

COMMENTARY

I'm reluctant to address the issue of what some people consider to be Jewish content in modern poetry—mine or another poet's—because poetry is not merely descriptive, anecdotal—and certainly not sentimental—writing in verse of some kind on what might be construed as Jewish "subjects." There has come to be a good deal of this in the past thirty years, but it has no relation to my own work and will not be discussed here. This is partially because poems, unlike pieces of expository prose of any length, don't *have* "subjects," but rather *are* representational objects themselves. A statement as to what any poem is "about" is always equivocal: Its virtue would at best be to point out something in (or on or under or . . .) the poem important enough to be singled out for consideration. In responding to the invitation to discuss a poem of mine in a Judaic context, I can only speak of where it is that my work engages questions of Judaistic knowledge as part of the fabric of experience of my world and of the language that is part of it.

My poetry is generally allusive, and I suppose that it seems more so now that readers of poetry have read less generally: Certainly the Greek mythology and the text of the King James Version of the Bible that composed part of the fabric of the literate language in English have become more arcane. But when my experience of the world and its representations began (after I'd really learned to write what I now consider really to be poetry—by my third book, perhaps) to include the Judaic tradition that had enveloped my childhood, the demands my writing made on readerly knowledge increased. Even a tiny epigram of mine—a one-line poem, in fact—"On Simon Called Peter" might need too much explaining to both the Jewish and the Gentile reader. It refers to the moment (Matthew 16:18) when Jesus's disciple Shimon bar-Yonah is renamed Peter, with an allusion to the meaning of *petrus*—"rock" (in this case, the rock upon which the church will be built), and goes

He who once hearkened darkened into stone

But the point depends upon knowing that the names Simon, Simeon derive from Hebrew *shama'*—"to hear" (as Bereshit 29 [Genesis 29:33] glosses it), even as the poetic action depends upon the movement of hearkened→darkened . . .

This kind of interplay of Judaic lore, text, interpretive traditions with those of poetic traditions of the English language and classical and romantic mythologies has increasingly marked my writing. Many of the poems, from my third book, *Visions from the Ramble*, on, have alluded to Judaic matters. I won't say anything about Jewish "subjects": Poetry is not of the stuff of novels, and the very word "about" when said of a poem can be misleading. Among the poems of mine that have needed most glossing with respect to Judaic matters have been "The Ninth of Ab" (from that third book); "Letter to Borges" (concerning my mother's probable descent from Rabbi Loew of Prague); "Tales Told of the Fathers"; "The Ziz"—a piece of mock *midrash* based on a linguistic misapprehension in English of the Tsits, a fictional huge bird of actual rabbinic writing, in which I supplied commentary from three rabbonim each with a bird-name himself; "Cohen on the Telephone"—alluding to a pre-World War I comical Yiddish-accent 10-inch 78 rpm record. And certainly the *"ki hinne cachomer,"* from twelfth-century France, one of the poetical texts inserted in the liturgy for the High Holidays with its opening trope of the potter shaping clay, and which affected me deeply in childhood, returned in complicatedly revised form in a number of poems of mine, particularly in my *Powers of Thirteen* and "The Mad Potter."

The long poem called "Spectral Emanations" deliberately sets out to invent for itself a particular fable of what American Jewish poetry might be; I might discuss it here, but it is too long, and has been glossed very well elsewhere, in Harold Bloom's *Agon* ("The White Light of Truth"); it arises from a fable retold in Hawthorne's *The Marble Faun* about how the menorah from the Temple of Jerusalem, carried to Rome by Titus, still lies at the bottom of the Tiber. Hilda, an American painter in Rome and one of Hawthorne's heroines, proposes that its recovery and relighting could generate a parable or "seven-branched allegory": "As each branch is lighted, it shall have a differently colored lustre from the other six; and when all seven are kindled, their radiance shall combine into the white light of truth." My poem is indeed in seven sections, each for a different color of the solar spectrum (the old one, including indigo, the story of whose disappearance is considered in one of the sections). The poem is full of Judaic textual and historical motifs and references throughout, but, as I have observed, it is too long and dense to deal with here.

Instead, I shall discuss a poem called "At the New Year" (1970), which is in no way an anecdotal vignette for the season. It was never intended to be an occasional poem for *Rosh Ha-Shanah*—the title came only after the poem was finished—but as the reader will observe, it ends up with a peculiar adaptation of the formulaic blessing ("*shehecheyanu, v'kiymanu vhigiyanu*") for festivals. As a child I felt something paradoxical about the ordinary school year and that of the Jewish calendar both starting around the autumnal equinox, that of the official calendar starting shortly after the winter solstice, and that of a kind of natural cycle of renewal at the vernal equinox—a new year beginning in March. (I knew nothing then of the relation between the Julian and Gregorian calendars with their different options—March and January—for the start of the year.) The poem starts out with a meditation on the arbitrariness of breaking into the circle of months at any one point and saying "this is it"; and while only a center can, with respect to a circle, be considered as point of origin (in the sense that the circle is generated from it, and defined by a constant distance from it), any point on its circumference, any instant of time, can claim to begin a new cycle.

But the poem argues, from its outset, for the privileged autumnal beginning: It might be considered a kind of secular *midrash* on why the New Year must start when it does. I think that the image early on of the page turning in some universal book resonated with overtones of the proverbial "turning over a new leaf." But also present was the *catvenu besefer hayyim tovim*—"inscribe us in the book of good life"—from the *avinu malkenu* prayer; again, in childhood, although I knew that the *sefer* was indeed a scroll, I couldn't help but visualize a codex—a bound book with pages that could turn over and flutter like wings in the wind—when throughout the High Holidays the prayer was sung. The ritual specifics—rather than merely the calendrical instance—of the Judaic New Year are initiated in the poem (and indeed were, in the writing of it) by the "screeching ram's horn." This, and the apple dipped into honey at the *kiddush* on *erev Rosh Ha-Shanah*, and the "imminent rich tents" of *Succoth*, emerged as being as prominent in my consciousness as anything else about the poem— its metrical form, for example (loosely accentual six-beat lines indented so as to suggest couplets), or its ultimate affirmation. But the whole poem remains a meditation on certain aspects of commencement, rather than some kind of non-liturgical *piyyut*.

And so the concluding of "this instant"—the "instant" of the poem's own opening line. It retranslates the formulaic "*laz'man hazeh*," usually given in

English as "this season." (I suppose that the various temporal meanings of "moment" might ordinarily cover both "instant" and "season.") The thanks are given here not for survival and preservation, as in the *berakha*, but for the endowment of the kind of consciousness that discerns the uniqueness of instants, of moments, of flashes of experience. And I suppose that by extension, then, it can be an acknowledgment of survival of another kind, that only a poet might care to make, but not only for him or herself, but for everyone.

Rodger Kamenetz

Rodger Kamenetz is the author of *The Jew in the Lotus: A Poet's Rediscovery of Jewish Identity in Buddhist India* (Aronson, 1995), and *Stalking Elijah: Adventures With Today's Jewish Mystical Masters* (Harper San Francisco, 1998); he has also written three collections of poetry, notably *The Missing Jew: New and Selected Poems* (Time Being Books, 1992). He teaches literature at Louisiana State University in Baton Rouge and lives in New Orleans. His most recent work is *Terra Infirma: A Memoir of My Mother's Life in Mine* (Schocken, 1999).

Grandfather Clause

for David Kamenetz, z"l

If only you'd done what you'd been told to do.
If only you'd not been lifted by a chance wind
blown west across the wheat tips of the Ukraine
the thunder of knouts, the Czar's knappers.
If you had stayed instead to be murdered
by the Einzatsgruppen, then old men like you
fingers palsied on the trigger, bellies shaking at the recoil
would have shot you dead at the edge of a pit
slaughtered you on the outskirts of a town
Jews could not enter after sunset.

There is a clause that refers to you
in the inner lining of a foreign language
where Jew is the dirtiest word ever.
This clause prepared in advance of your name
is the secret history of your death
decreed in a grammar strange to your Yiddish
as the language I struggle to speak is inflected
by the death that might have been.

Yet you entered America like a pilgrim or a germ—
Which was it? Or both, as America decided

with your Jewish heart and lungs and your Jewish disease
and two strong fingers and a needle.

Why should I tell that old story again?
I'm still immigrating into this moment, this day
learning that the words applied to you apply to me.
Even after all this time, I will not allow anyone
to annihilate your name and mine.
I am grandfathered in.

COMMENTARY

I was very surprised when I wrote this poem because after all the time I'd spent
since *The Jew in the Lotus* meditating and thinking about the problems of Jew-
ish anger, this came out with so much anger and ferocity. But much as we try
we can't control how our poems speak out of us. In one sense the poem is look-
ing back on my own work in poetry, especially in *The Missing Jew*, and how
that book originally arose in the 1970s as an attempt to recover my grand-
father's voice after his death. *The Missing Jew* never stopped growing as a
book—I've always conceived it as a life time project, with additions and com-
mentaries added on. The first time it came out with Dryad Press as a slim
skinny volume and I was a slim skinny guy (1979). That book was so tall and
skinny it couldn't stand up in a bookstore shelf (didn't fit). But it soon went out
of print. Then Time Being Books brought it out again in 1992, much fatter. I'd
added poems by using a midrashic method. A poem always raises questions
about itself if it's any good, and those questions are best answered by another
poem. The process goes on, open ended—very Jewish kind of writing. Some
day I hope it will be bigger and fatter—though I hope I can keep my waistline.

But the deeper question is, why? Why do I write about Jews, Judaism, ob-
sessively in my poetry? There's a wonderful poem by William Carlos Williams
about death, "he's dead . . ." and Williams just rails on and on against death and
the frustration is obvious. But maybe there's a different response and that's
what I'm trying to get at here. I think my connection to my grandfather, and to
the death he might have had had he lived out his life in Kamenetz-Podolsk in-
stead of emigrating, is part of the reason I'm a Jewish poet and not just a poet
poet. Because it's one thing to talk about the "life he might have had" and quite
another to talk about the "death he might have had." But the death he might
have had is what I'm stuck with—I owe an allegiance to it that I can't forsake.

Maxine Kumin

Maxine Kumin, born in 1925 in Philadelphia, was educated at Radcliffe College. She currently calls Warner, N.H., home. She won the Pulitzer Prize for poetry in 1973 for her volume, *Up Country: Poems of New England* (Harper, 1972). The author of twelve books of poetry, as well as several novels and children's books, her most recent works include the murder mystery *Quit Monks or Die!* (Story Line, 1999), *Connecting the Dots: Poems* (Norton, 1998), and *Women, Animals, & Vegetables: Essays & Stories* (Ontario Review P, 1996).

For Anne at Passover

I

Cold Easter week and the hard buds, forming, shake
their miter caps at me. The tower bells
sing Christly sweet, and everywhere
new scents—honey and blood—work the air.

My students, outside the college halls, regroup,
share notes, and smoke. Coats open; no hats, no gloves.
Some metabolic principle
keeps them warm enough until the bell.
Or love. Or thoughts of going home. Time now,
we mind the syllabus which juxtaposes
Socrates, inviting the poison cup,
saying, *there is no fear that it will stop
with me*, and Jesus, apportioning His week,
however accidentally, with our Greek.

A kind of water-walking, Socrates
goes barefoot and uncaring over ice,
stands tranced through two dawns, is able
to drink all comers underneath the table,
and takes no lover in his night
except philosophy, *that dear delight.*

In air heavy as damask roses we read
the prison scene together. The weather abets us
and a great poking rain commences.
We smell resurgence prickling our senses;

Son and sage hear voices. They keep no books,
but loose principles on the world to tell
their missions, miracles, and choices;
in Christ's name, Joan burns for her voices.
In Christ's name shunned, historic news,
the Jews their own stoned Jew refuse.

And Socrates, messiah true or false,
how might the Christ have come to take our sin
without you, *terribly at ease in Zion?*
You die now, for no man, and in no pain,
bathed and bedded according to the fashion,
friends who see you out your only Passion;
no nails, excepting as the soul is hung
against the flesh till death unfasten it.
One student says you sinned the sin of pride.
Another consecrates your suicide.

I say myths knit the world up when men die
for love; and if they lie, love needs the lie.
Time now. In Holy Week the tower bell
returns us to a faithful Friday rain.
Baggage and books, my students move about,
wish me a happy Easter, and go out.

II

Home by subway, I dare to see
my eye stare in my eye
and black it out;
and see my head, which best of all
I thought I knew,
elongate, squash, or disengage
itself; swim off and leave
my motiveless shoulders
lost in doubt.

Still, I get out
uptown, as decorous as the next,
feel useful in the buildings
out of habit,
peer through a window
at fat chocolate rabbits
and price Madonna lilies,
and buy an egg
with a crystal candy scene
sweetly inside—a peephole
for the eye of a child—
and look before I eat,
and put up my umbrella
in the three o'clock street.

They have unpinned Him in the rain.
Cabs spin from St. Philip's
and cars unpark
and I walk where disbelief
clacks at my soul,
an old god in my pocket
worrying the hole;
now all the saving bells begin.
I could not make Him to unmake my sin.

III

Tonight, the damask cloth laid, the loving cup
brimmed with sweet wine, I think of those my kin
who sat that Friday, inviting Elijah in
and swore he never came, nor comes again.
I think of Judas, the prophecy fetched up
to truth at our mutual season: yours to take
your pierced and honored Son out of His cave
and sing *resurgam*, drink His winey life;
    there at the rail for pity's sake
    redeem yourself, all men, as if
there were still time in this hard-budding time;

and mine to mind another book: remind
my blood relations we are marked in the blood

of an earlier lamb, and call God good,
Who thumped our Moses so to send us out
and turned aside and hardened Pharaoh's heart
    ten times, Antagonist! to put
    us on that dusty pathway through
Your hot sea. So we come to praise You.

Yearly, the youngest child, asking why
this night is different from all other nights,
is told, his soft mouth crammed with bittersweet,
the bondage years in Egypt, and in some way
learns to perpetuate them from that day.
I remember my father's mother boiled
chickens with their feet on, and we ate,
blasphemous modern children, from her plate
both meat and milk and stayed up loved and late,
no letter law applying to a child.
I have sealed her in me, her fierce love
    of kindred all she had to give,
    and my drowned Polish ancestry,
washed out of Europe, rises up in me.

We pray tonight, dip herbs, and pour out wine,
forever what we are. I hear the rain
swelling the hard buds, all our fetishes
the simple sun of promises or wishes:
a radioactive rain in Pakistan
and Haifa, Yucca Flats, the Vatican,
    on all my kind: Manhattan rich
    or Yemen poor, who break hard bread
tonight and bless their unforgotten dead.

What do we do, who eat to celebrate
with Eucharist and matzo man's old fate?
I take a funny comfort, reading how
Bakongo folk, hard on the pulsing spew
of the afterbirth, would kiss that cord
and fix it in the belly of their god
    so that its navel bud protrudes
    where we are, mewling, swathed to hold
our secret in. We die, that knob unsealed.

Now God forgive us where we live
the ways we love are relative.
Yours, Anne, the sacramental arts
which divide Him in three parts;
mine, the vengeful King of pride
despite Whose arm his Chosen died;
theirs, the unction and the fuss
who bless the lost umbilicus.

Guests of our glands, slaves to our origins,
we pray and eat tonight in greening weather.
Time swells the buds. A sharper rain begins;
we are all babes who suck at love together.

COMMENTARY

When I opened a long-shelved copy of my first book, *Halfway* (Holt, Rhinehart
& Winston, 1961), a yellowed newspaper review fluttered from it. I suspect it
was sent to me by some member of my Philadelphia family, possibly clipped
from the *Philadelphia Enquirer*, but the sender failed to include any attribu-
tion. Today, I have no idea who wrote these lines:

> Mrs. Kumin has no bohemian vices or minority scars. Her "Jewish heritage"
> mentioned in the blurb is not that of the slums nor even of the big city but is a bib-
> liographical detail coupled with her love of the turbulent New England coast. . . .
> One might wonder why the Jewish fact was brought up at all; it does not affect
> her rhetoric or end up in her subject matter only through such *New-Yorker*ish ex-
> otica as "our lop-eared Menorah. . . . the membrane scroll of Torah" in a poem of
> friendship to a Chinese. . . . Her poem to Passover, major statement in the collec-
> tion, is equally a poem to Easter and to a rite of the Bakonga, the blended style
> perfectly mirroring a blended humanity.

Not only is my Jewishness a mere biographical detail for this reviewer; it is
an exotic mannerism in the style of *The New Yorker*, to which I confess I as-
pired but in which I had at that time published only one poem, a secular paean
to springtime.

I am not much given to quarrels with reviewers. It is bad form to protest any
but the most egregious comment, and this one is raised, as it were, from the dead.

Nevertheless, it seems to me that my Jewish consciousness is present in a goodly number of my poems from that first book onward. Frequently, my awareness is set against a Christian landscape, often Catholic, sometimes Southern Baptist.

I grew up in suburban Philadelphia, in an observant Reform Jewish household next door to the convent of the Sisters of St. Joseph, a teaching order, with whom we enjoyed cordial relations. For the sake of convenience—public school was a mile away—my parents enrolled me in their kindergarten. I further attended the first two years of elementary school in that cozy setting. But after I stole a rosary in my zeal to belong to the group (cf. "Mother Rosarine": "Wrong, born wrong for the convent games / I hunched on the sidelines beggar fashion"), my parents saw the light and hastily enrolled me in public school.

Thematically, the solidarity of the convent and the benevolence of Jesus present themselves in such poems as "Sisyphus" ("One day I said I was a Jew. / I wished I had. I wanted to."); "Mother Rosarine," which retells the theft of the praying beads; "Young Nun at Breadloaf," which contrasts "Sister, Sister Elizabeth Michal / says we are doing Christ's work, we two, / She the rosy girl in a Renoir painting" with my own agnosticism, "I an old Jew"; "The Nuns of Childhood: Two Views," which narrates my adoring worship of the sisters in their habits ("I, the Jewish child next door / came through the hedge to that swaddled lap"). Interested readers can follow the thread of my self-declared Jewish heritage through a spectrum of other poems ranging from "On Being Asked to Write a Poem on the Centenary of the Civil War" to "Living Alone with Jesus" ("Can it be I am the only Jew in Danville, Kentucky / Looking for matzoh in the Safeway and the A & P?"), "In the Absence of Bliss" ("The roasting alive of rabbis / in the ardor of the Crusades . . ."); "The Poet Visits Egypt and Israel," "The Riddle of Noah," and so on.

"For Anne at Passover" is the first poem in which I addressed the issue of living as a Jew in a Christian world. My friendship with Anne Sexton served as catalyst. We were by then—1957 or '58—exchanging worksheets and ideas, arriving at the sisterhood that was to sustain us for the seventeen years of our friendship, which ended so abruptly with her suicide in 1974.

This past year, Good Friday coincided with the first night of Passover, as I believe it did the year I was working on the poem. Despite my early Catholic education, I think I was a college student before I understood that the Last Supper depicted Jesus and his disciples ranged around the Seder table. It was not a point discussed in Sunday School classes at Rodeph Shalom, nor was it addressed in Fine Arts V, when we studied the composition of the painting, any more than the enthusiastic slaughter of Jews during the Crusades was a topic for investigation in History I. Certainly I was a college freshman before I read the New Testament and encountered the aphoristic magic of the Sermon on the Mount. Moreover, I had never attended a church service (discounting my early indoctrination) until I was in my twenties.

I deplore the parochialism that still locks away recognition of the common heritage and religious practice between Jews and Christians, and among Jews, Christians and Muslims. To Anne at that time, Judaism was a curiosity, faintly tinged with disrepute. In her role of suburban housewife and mother, she was not much of a church-goer. Nominally an Episcopalian, Easter signified new dresses and hats for her daughters and herself, Easter baskets and Easter egg hunts. The Hours of the Cross on Good Friday passed unacknowledged; the Resurrection appeared to have little resonance. Only years later as she undertook a spiritual quest for relevance and meaning in her personal life, an absolutism to cling to, did the intensely moving poems about Jesus and God the Father begin to take shape.

What Sexton knew about Jews was stereotypical anti-Semitic doctrine, acquired from the culture in which she was raised. The country club to which her parents belonged did not admit Jews. Jews were a token and somehow alien presence in the schools she attended. It was remarkable luck that we were able to break through all the barriers of prejudice and received opinions on both sides (on meeting her, my mother asked me in private, "Don't you have any good *Jewish* friends?"), and forge a deep personal and professional friendship.

Thanks to the kind offices of Professor John Holmes, whom I have described elsewhere as my Christian academic daddy, I had an adjunct appointment to teach freshman English at Tufts University; Plato was part of the core curriculum. The readings were designed to encourage students to think through their philosophical and religious convictions, minimal as these were; the syllabus required me to read closely texts I had bare acquaintance with from my own educational experience and to stay one step ahead of the freshmen.

All of us young instructors were required to stick to the reading list, to hold common hour exams at midterm, to participate in composing multiple-choice questions for these exams, and to grade lengthy essay questions on the final. It was hard work and I am happy to reflect back on its rigors. *The unexamined life is not worth living*, the philosopher taught us. Without the noble example of Socrates, without the many-times-told tale of the New Testament and its central tragedy, without the Jewish notion of divine election from which derives the much-abused epithet "the Chosen People," my life would have been, if not unexamined, at least underexamined.

Sexton and I were both formalists, loving the challenge of working in meter and rhyme and finding in the rigidity of a chosen form the permission to tackle emotionally charged or difficult topics. In this case, I more or less invented a nonce form as I went along and then tried to hew to it. In Part I, I relied heavily on couplet rhymes to hold the stanzas together, balancing these against unrhymed lines that precede the rhymed ones. The poem opens with a stanza of four lines, followed by ten, then six; then it changes the pattern to four, six, ten, followed by a six-liner.

The chronology is simple. During the final class before Easter recess, students discuss their reading assignment, the scene in which Socrates calmly drinks the cup of poison hemlock. It is an execution that invites sharp contrast with the crucifixion of Jesus; the Greek philosopher is "bathed and bedded according to the fashion, / friends who see you out your only Passion. . . ."

Part II simply moves the narrator from the university to the city. It is three o'clock: "They have unpinned Him in the rain." I contrast the commercial aspect of Easter—store window chocolate rabbits, eggs—with the church bells that announce the end of the Hours of the Cross. Even so, ". . . I walk where disbelief / clacks at my soul, / an old god in my pocket / worrying the hole. . . ." Here, the lines are looser, the rhymes present but irregular.

As deeply affecting as the crucifixion is, as deeply embedded in my consciousness from my early childhood experience in the convent, I continue to disbelieve in anything supernatural. As Santayana said, "Poetry is religion which is no longer believed." The god of any creed is for me little more than a metaphor; the resurrection of Jesus is perhaps the most elaborate and compelling metaphor of all.

Part III takes up the story of Passover. Judaism is to a pleasing and considerable extent a kitchen religion, perhaps reflecting its enclosure over centuries in the home or community. Every holiday seems to have its special foods. The Seder meal is long and full of ritual, with symbolic structures: the lamb shank, the roasted eggs, the bitter herb. The readings from the Haggadah are intended to recreate the exodus from Egypt for every child present. In a sense, the Seder service provides an indoctrination not dissimilar from, say, the Baltimore catechism, for every culture initiates its children into its own history. The roots of Jewish holidays are centuries deep and the Seder service carries a lot of emotional baggage. One need not be a true believer to be moved by the spirit of Passover.

Implicit in the story of the plagues that led to the Jews' exodus from Egypt is the portrait of an Old Testament God, as mercurial and passionate as any human. This is not the latter-day refined God of love, or the detached, indifferent *deus absconditus* of contemporary thought. This vengeful God first sends a plague, terrifies the Egyptian ruler into submission, then "turn[s] aside and harden[s] Pharaoh's heart / ten times, Antagonist!" He is a Pat Robertson sort of God, delivering divine retribution with a primitive relish.

But even as the children are told the old story, even as "[w]e pray tonight, dip herbs, and pour out wine, / forever what we are" I find myself linking what I call "our fetishes": the sacrament of the Eucharist, the symbolology of matzoh, the unleavened bread, the worshipful care taken with the placenta among the Bakongans.

The stanzaic patterns in Part III rely heavily on rhyme and meter. Iambic pentameter prevails except in the indented lines, which are deliberately set apart; the rhymes are closely placed. The intent is to move the poem's expository passages forward without ever sacrificing the natural word order to achieve rhyme. Many of the lines are quite heavily end-stopped, which emphasizes the rhyming pattern. I look at this and wonder how I did it.

Forty years removed from the composition of this poem, I have to say that I cringe at the first line of the concluding quatrain. Today, it seems facile, smart alecky. But the motivation for all of these rites still rings true to me. "We are all babes who suck at love together."

Philip Levine

Philip Levine was born in 1928 in Detroit, Michigan. He received his education at Wayne State University, the University of Iowa, and Stanford University. He ultimately settled in Fresno, California, and taught at both Fresno State University and Tufts University until his retirement. The many awards his books of poems have received include the Pulitzer Prize, the National Book Award (twice), and the National Book Critics Circle Prize for Poetry. His most recent volume of poetry is *The Mercy: Poems* (Knopf, 1999).

The Old Testament

My twin brother swears that at age thirteen
I'd take on anyone who called me kike
no matter how old or how big he was.
I only wish I'd been that tiny kid
who fought back through tears, swearing
he would not go quietly. I go quietly
packing bark chips and loam into the rose beds,
while in his memory I remain the constant child
daring him to wrest Detroit from lean gentiles
in LaSalle convertibles and golf clothes
who step slowly into the world we have tainted,
and have their revenge. I remember none of this.
He insists, he names the drug store where I poured
a milkshake over the head of an Episcopalian
with quick fists as tight as croquet balls.
He remembers his license plate, his thin lips,
the exact angle at which this seventeen year old dropped
his shoulder to throw the last punch. He's making
it up. Wasn't I always terrified?
"Of course," he tells me, "that's the miracle,
you were even more scared than me, so scared
you went insane, you became a whirlwind,
an avenging angel."
                                I remember planting

my first Victory Garden behind the house, hauling
dark loam in a borrowed wagon, and putting in
carrots, corn that never grew, radishes that did.
I remember saving for weeks to buy a tea rose,
a little stick packed in dirt and burlap,
my mother's favorite. I remember the white bud
of my first peony that one morning burst
beside the mock orange that cost me 69¢.
(Fifty years later the orange is still there,
the only thing left beside a cage for watch dogs,
empty now, in what had become a tiny yard.)
I remember putting myself to sleep dreaming
of the tomatoes coming into fullness, the pansies
laughing in the spring winds, the magical wisteria
climbing along the garage, and dreaming of Hitler,
of firing a single shot from a foot away, one
that would tear his face into a caricature of mine,
tear stained, bloodied, begging for a moment's peace.

COMMENTARY

I would like to consider what it is to be a Jewish poet in America, not any Jew-
ish poet or all Jewish poets, but simply one, this one. And I would like to do so
while meditating on aspects of one of my poems, "The Old Testament." It's a
question I've been asked for years without answering, and perhaps the time has
come to answer.

Let me first submit to the temptation to say the truth. I have no idea what it
means to be a Jewish poet in America. I'm also an identical twin, and when I
was young people would ask me what it was like being a twin. I had no way of
answering because I didn't know what it was like not being a twin. If a robin
could talk and you asked what it was like being a robin, the answer might be,
"Different from being a nightingale or a pelican, none of the gorgeous singing,
none of the daily hunt for sea food." Or it might be, "You know, building the
nest, searching for grubs, sitting on the eggs until they hatch, the whole robin
thing." By the same token I could answer the Jewish-poet-in-America question
by saying different from being a coal miner or a film star. In the morning I
don't lay *tfilun* as I did for some months as a boy. Instead I rise from bed,
have some coffee, and go into a room by myself and sit and write and most
often throw away what I write. I imagine Charles Wright, who is certainly as

productive as I, would probably say something quite similar, skipping the part about once laying *tfilun*. I read Charles as essentially a religious poet, one concerned with the search for the relationship between the temporal and the eternal, one who finds in ordinary daily life hints at that relationship, one whose poems struggle, often successfully, to encapsulate those hints, which we might call moments of *satori*. I believe that often I'm trying to do something similar. We go about it in different ways. I'm most often a narrative poet, whereas Charles relies more on his capacity to make his language sing and on his seemingly inexhaustible fund of images. I don't know that my penchant for narrative derives from being a Jew or that his singular gift for phrasing is the gift of his Christian heritage. What I am struck by is that we are both deeply influenced by that great Christian mystic, William Blake, and such bold statements as "Time is the mercy of eternity" and "Eternity is in love with the productions of time."

As you can see, I'm trying to define myself by comparing myself to what I am not. I notice that in my poem "The Old Testament," the speaker—whom I intended the reader to take for me—is himself defined by others, larger boys who label him "kike." He does not behave as we are told Christians are instructed to behave—and obviously in my boyhood did not behave—he does not turn the other cheek either metaphorically or literally. He fights—or so is told by his brother—with an abandon and a ferocity he did not know he possessed.

The poem grew out of a meeting in my early fifties with my twin brother, who described me to his new wife as the brother does in the poem. I had no idea what he was talking about, and yet he was so specific regarding the details of these events I had to believe he knew what he was talking about, and I also knew without the least doubt that his memory for our teen years was far sharper than mine. I later meditated upon his description and joined it with other "facts" of my life as I recalled them, my passion for gardening, my hatred of Hitler, my desire for peace—that is, my profound need to be left alone, to simply do what I wanted to do without interference.

What does this have to do with being Jewish? Jewish kids are by no means the only ones persecuted by more powerful kids for nothing they've done but for just being who they are or for simply being somewhere. My Detroit, that is, the Detroit of my growing up, was a viciously anti-Semitic city possessing such outstanding Jew-haters as Father Coughlin, who spouted his Nazi filth every Sunday from the Church of the Little Flower in Royal Oak, a few miles from where I lived, and Henry Ford, whose Dearborn newspaper published the so-called Protocols of the Elders of Zion. It's little wonder I was in the eyes of many—schoolmates and others—first and foremost a Jew, and for some, nothing else. I thought of myself as a boy, one in love with planting and growing, which I never considered Jewish or non-Jewish, the passion having been passed to me by my mentor, Sophie Psaris, my neighbor to the north who was born and raised in Salonika and possessed what appeared to be a boundless love for all things that lived. It's a shame that at that age I was not familiar with Freud. He would have helped. As Alfred Kazin notes in *God and the American Writer*, "Freud as a Jew was enthralled by the survival of his people and, whether he admitted it or not, attributed the survival not to persistent loyalty to God but to anti-Semitism, which kept one fighting back. 'Being a Jew I knew I would always be in the opposition.'"

My sense of who I was at that age, fourteen, is not the same as my brother's, though on some matters we would agree. Although my mother was not a practicing Jew—nor had my father, who died when I was five, been—she insisted that we have a joint bar mitzvah; this because my father would have wanted it, she claimed. We submitted and were then given the option to keep the faith or not; we were men now and could choose for ourselves. I'd been going to a small orthodox *shul* on the east side of Detroit since I was six or seven in the company of my grandfather, Zaydee, as I called him, a man I deeply loved. There were many things at the *shul* that I liked: the perfumes of the small, crowded room—a mixture of tobacco, wine, old wool, and sweat. "The visuals": the glorious *talisem*, the prayer shawls, white fringed with bands of dark blue or black, the Torah itself, brought so reverently forth from the Ark. I liked the sense of men worshiping together, the sense of community, which also included a sense of privacy as each man seemed to *doven* at his own sweet will. I would think my brother appreciated the same things, and like me soon grew bored because of the simple failure to comprehend the meaning of what we were witnessing. Zaydee was not a believer and explained nothing. He was there to meet with business cronies; once he located them their *dovening* would come to an end to be replaced by *handling* in Yiddish. I wanted to become like these men, not because I shared their faith but because I wanted to grow into manhood, and this was how manhood looked to me. However, when my chance came I opted out after some weeks of laying *tfilun* and Saturday *shul* attendance. Here my twin and I were in complete accord: This all-powerful God whose name was unspeakable was allowing the slaughter of our people, his chosen people, in Europe and the raging anti-Semitism at home. To put it simply, we did not believe He was who we had been told He was, and if we were His chosen people we were chosen for disaster. Even my fasting on Yom Kippur failed to give me a sense of closeness to our departed father, whom both of us still adored. To make matters worse, his sudden departure was explained by my aunt as God's will. "He always takes," she said, "the best to Himself." He had the universe and all time, and yet He deprived us of the man we most needed. If in fact He was all powerful, He was also incredibly selfish in our eyes.

In the poem "The Old Testament," the boy turns away from the social world so fraught with hatred and violence to a rapport with the natural world and its beauty. His gardening begins as part of the war effort, the fight against Nazism, and the raising of vegetables, but he soon turns toward the luxury and beauty of flower gardening. What the adult poet recalls is the glory of roses, peonies, pansies, but even his dream of Edenic perfection is interrupted by his need for revenge against the one he identifies as the ultimate source of his pain, Hitler, who he hopes to make suffer as he has suffered. "Vengeance is mine, saith the Lord," but it is not in the Lord's name he dreams of vengeance. He knows without the least doubt he has been wronged, and his dream is to right the litany of personal wrongs and finally achieve justice. Is this a Jewish dream or simply a universal dream, to right the wrongs against one's self and one's people and thereby achieve justice? I can't imagine a people who would feel differently about persecution.

Of course today I am fifty-six years older than the boy in the poem and have spent some years studying the *Old Testament*, as it was called in my youth. I was dazzled by many of the books. I loved the fury of Amos, the wisdom and the language of Ecclesiastes, the beauty of the Psalms, and the astonishing characters who marched through the two books of Samuel. I read them over and over and grew to love my people, their devotion, their courage, their endurance, but their God felt no closer to me than He did at fourteen or than He does today. Why did I call my poem "The Old Testament"? Because the poem is a statement of belief, this is what I apprehend regarding the covenant between man and God: We will live in an unjust world in which we may dream of peace and never achieve it. And we will, like the God of the Old Testament, exact revenge whenever we can. (Curiously enough, in my years of reading and living I have learned of others who are so astonishingly moral they can truly forgive even when forgiveness is not asked for, men and women who seem more god-like than the god of the Book.)

Notice, there are two miracles in the poem. One in the first stanza when the boy, though terrified, turns into an avenging angel and acts not out of his fears but out of something deeper, his sense of indignation. The little *shlepper* turns into a warrior, a young David, if you will, outweighed, outmanned but defiant. It's a miracle in his brother's eyes, the victim transformed into an avenger, an unkillable force even though beaten, for it's the tall, lean Episcopalian who throws the final punch. The speaker refuses to accept defeat and thus he triumphs. Even the knowing brother cannot explain it. And then there are the miraculous moments when the plants come from seeds or bulbs or bare roots into their fullness, "the pansies/ laughing in the spring winds, the magical wisteria/ climbing along the garage . . ." A second set of transformations as inexplicable to the brothers as the first and as much a part of the covenant with creation as the roaring wars of human society.

For me the Bible became a book, a book of wisdom, lamentation, prophecy, erotic poetry, sagas full of heroism and memorable characters, a great book and one I know has influenced both my life and my writing. I don't know that it's had a greater influence on me than Whitman's "Song of Myself" or the works of William Carlos Williams. I don't know that it's been more useful to me than Whitman's astonishing claim, "There is that lot of me and all so luscious," which has helped me to define myself to myself. I know I have had trouble with the Bible's claim that a special relationship exists between the Jews and God. Growing up during the rise of Nazism I became very skeptical about such racial claims. Regarding racism—one of the greatest evils I've witnessed during my life—in my own experience Jews have been no better than many other people, and when I saw in Israel the hideous practices against the Arabs I was both shocked and shamed. Not surprisingly, the most outwardly pious appeared to be the worst; was their excuse—if in fact they felt they needed one—the special covenant they had with God? (Did not the Lord God speak to Moses, "Ye have seen what I did unto the Egyptians and *how* I bore you on eagles' wings, and brought you unto myself. Now therefore, if you will obey my voice indeed, and keep my covenant, then ye shall be a peculiar treasure unto me above all people; for all the earth *is* mine: And ye shall be unto me a kingdom of priests, and an holy nation." Exodus 19:4–6) How unfortunate their Palestinian brothers were not chosen for God's work. Of course, if we study the Koran we find God is more generous to them; what I saw in Israel had more to do with power, race, and class than it did with religious belief, although religious belief had become more useful in maintaining the exploitation of one people by another.

As a younger poet I did not think of myself as religious. Indeed, I did not think of most of those who in my experience professed religious faith as religious. They seemed obsessed with ritualistic observances that to my eyes had nothing to do with love for God and all the creations he'd placed on earth. Now and then I would meet someone—like Sophie Psaris—who in his or her ordinary actions embodied a reverence for life as it is, and I would think, She is special. At age sixteen I met an older black man in a grease shop I worked in who would not permit the world to demean him. He was gracious and charitable to everyone who treated him with respect, and toward me he showed a beautiful masculine tenderness I had received previously only from my father. He was far stronger than I, and when he saw that the work of loading or unloading a truck was becoming too much for me, he would ask me to rest and he would do both our jobs. If I had no cigarettes or money for lunch he would share whatever he had with me. A few years later I read Kierkegaard and realized I had encountered one of his Knights of Faith. Still later I read the French Catholic poet Charles Peguy's astonishing essay, "Notre Jeunesse," in which I encountered the following description of his dying Jewish friend, Bernard-Lazare:

> I still see him in his bed. That atheist, that professional atheist, that official atheist, in whom resounded, with unbelievable power, with unbelievable gentleness, the eternal word; with eternal power, with eternal gentleness; whose equal I have

never found anywhere. . . . I still see him in his bed, that atheist dripping with the word of God. Even in death the whole weight of his people bore down on his shoulders. He could not be told he was not responsible for them. I have never seen a man burdened in such a way, so burdened with a task, with an eternal responsibility. As we are, as we feel responsible for our children, for our own children in our own family, just as much, exactly as much, exactly thus did he feel for his people.

I realized that without ever again entering a *shul* I might, if I improved my soul, become a religious Jew.

Let me now speak merely of being a poet in America. If any of the compositions I've written in the last fifty years turn out to be poems then I am not only a writer, I am a poet. It's a life I chose between the ages of eighteen and thirty, a life I chose day by day by doing what I believed would enliven my writing. Some choices I see now were misguided, perhaps stupid. By the age of thirty I knew I would spend the better part of my life trying to write poetry, and I knew also that America would not love me for it, and I was right on both counts. In spite of what many would consider an arcane passion, I do not feel like an outsider. Since my early twenties I have found others with a similar passion, and this has helped sustain my determination to persist, and I do so without any final assurance I will succeed. I do so because I must, because it is the only route that I've so far found that could possibly lead to happiness, and I believe in the value of happiness, that happy people beget more happy people. A friend of mine who is also a poet once stated positively that the only reason to write poetry was to relieve manic depression. Not being a manic depressive I said that was nonsense. Why then did I write? I suddenly blurted out what I never considered before but what I knew to be the truth: I do it for the glory, by which I meant not the fame but the glory of the endeavor.

Although I am not a practicing Jew and at this moment hope never to be one, I am Jewish. Being Jewish has been a basic condition of my life. I knew that's what I was before I was five, and in the streets, the classrooms, the employment offices, the drug stores, the factories, and later the bars and cafés of Detroit I was constantly reminded that I was Jewish, not that I was liable to forget. For over thirty years I've had a belief in a being I can only call God. He is present in all living things, and He comes to each of us to the degree we invite Him to enter, to make room for Him in the way we go about our lives. I once believed His presence was especially large in the hearts of the Spanish anarchists who staked their lives on the gamble that men and women could live as equals in a free society and who were willing to die for that belief and for each other. I saw these men and women as the special children of my God because what my God demanded first and foremost was justice. This I learned from the history of my people. Even the most mighty could be punished for their transgression as King Saul and David were punished: in that in God's eyes we were all equal. This was my Detroit Jewish heritage. If I betrayed my loyalty to the people I worked with regardless of their race or position I would be despised in God's eyes: I learned this from my teachers and from the actions of those who seemed most truly religious to me. And I read it in our holy book as well. Did not Amos say that those who lie "upon beds of ivory, and stretch themselves upon their couches, and eat the lambs out of the flock, and the calves out of the midst of the stall," if "they are not grieved with the affliction of Joseph" then they shall "go captive with the first that go captive" (Amos 6:4–7). Christian though their heritage was, the Spanish anarchists despised the church of Spain for siding almost totally with the powerful against the needy; their fervor was religious. For me they were true Jewish heroes whether they knew it or not. Those were heady days of hope. Today I am less sanguine. Recently in South Dakota while teaching on a Sioux reservation I was asked if I would ever write about the place. I answered that I would. Exactly what would I write about. The landscape, I said. This is where my God lives and He hasn't spoken to me in years. And having said it I knew it was true.

Jacqueline Osherow

Born in 1956 in Philadelphia, Jacqueline Osherow teaches English and creative writing at the University of Utah in Salt Lake City. She is the author of four collections of poems, *Dead Men's Praise* (Grove Atlantic, 1999), *With a Moon in Transist* (Grove Atlantic, 1996), *Conversations with Survivors* (U of Georgia P, 1994), and *Looking for Angels in New York* (U of Georgia P, 1988).

Scattered Psalms: XI (Dead Men's Praise)

Yakov Glatstein already
used this verse in a poem,
translated, in that book
(*Radiant Jews,* 1946),
Dead Men Don't Praise God

and you can see how, then,
it must have seemed that, for years,
this verse had festered in its psalm
waiting to reveal its acrid heart.

I don't blame him if he thought
all praise had ended

but I wonder if it's heartless
after only fifty years
to think—again—the praise has just begun:

The dead don't praise God,
or the ones who go down to silence,
but we'll praise God
from now on forever
hallelujah—

I'm not suggesting that we think about it:
just sing it, during Hallel,
at synagogue, the next new moon,

and get in on a little
of its stubborn bravado,
its delirious proof
of itself—*hallelujah*—

which, in my opinion,
explains the annoying epithet *chosen*
that has caused us so much trouble over the years

(though there are a host
of twentieth-century explanations:
chosen for suffering, for near-annihilation,

or—on the other hand—for the idea
of public ownership of means
of production, relativity,
A la Recherche du Temps Perdu).

I say: chosen for this
tenacious language,
to be the *we*
who get to say this word
and live forever,

and it makes me pity Handel,
gospel singers, televangelists—
belting out their hearts for a borrowed word—

when I have the whole thing,
one hundred and fifty psalms,
every single syllable a *hallelujah*

and not—you have to understand—
an English hallelujah
with its vague exultation and onomatopoeia

but a word composed of holy signs
that could actually spell God's name
if they weren't ordering the universe
to praise Him.

There's a story my friend Isaac tells
before he reads *Akdamut* on Shavuot:

how the poet Rabbi Meir ben Yitzhak
first wrote *Akdamut* in Hebrew
and the angels stole it away, page by page,

so he had to begin all over again,
this time in Aramaic,
to keep his genius secret from the angels.

I want to know how David
got away with it.

Were the angels just so riveted
by what they heard
that they left him to go on and on and on?

(With Glatstein, there wasn't any problem;
they were probably in stitches:

this poor *shlemazel* writing
in an instantaneously dead language—
irony's the soul of Yiddish—
dead men don't praise. . . .)

As for me, though it's my new goal
to have a page or two stolen by an angel

(it would have to be—let's be realistic—
a fairly boorish angel, not much of a reader,
the eyes on his wings pressed shut,

so addicted to watching television—
mostly telenovelas—he knows
the English language by osmosis).

I don't figure this page is in imminent danger.

Maybe, reading over his shoulder,
the angels rejected David's poem
(didn't they have enough of praising God?)

or maybe—that's it!—it was they who fed him lines
(*Do you think this kid will really take over? hallelujah!*)

or maybe it's nonsense about the *Akdamut* . . .
there was no Hebrew version,
are no angels . . .

and my *hallelujah*,
my precious, rising *hallelujah*
doesn't have the stamina
I need it for,

has, in fact, been burned away
before it could adorn a single tongue
for countless generations of David's offspring

and I'm not talking about the ones who turned to ash—
they're around somewhere, singing *hallelujah*—

I'm talking about the other ones, numberless as stars,
who never got to sing a word at all:

permutations of permutations
of permutations of permutations
of pairs of double helixes,

singular and brief as snow,
among the double helixes that burned,

every one an unrepeatable
and complex promise,

and, among them,
certainly, at least
a few who might
have liked, even for
an instant, to live forever.

COMMENTARY

I recently fell in love with an old Jewish joke, quoted by James Atlas in a magazine article. "What's the difference between a garment worker and a poet?" The answer: "a generation." My family is slow; it took us two generations. But the joke nonetheless comes to mind when I try to think about what distinguishes American poetry; above all, it is a poetry unabashedly close to its, as it were, garment-worker heritage, a poetry very well aware of its nonpoetic and non-American immediate past. If our poetic tradition is a short one it is also an energetic, daring, and all-inclusive one. And what poet wouldn't want to be a part of that?

At the same time—and probably not coincidentally—poetry is pretty much beside the point in America. Not only doesn't America have time for poetry, it doesn't have any interest in it, nor does it place any value on it. Being immaterial and impractical, poetry is, by definition, antithetical to the American main chance. Here, poetry is more potent as a metaphor than as itself. A perfect pass in basketball or football might be described by an appreciative sportscaster as "pure poetry," but I doubt that he would have a particular line or stanza in mind. If poetry is quoted here, it's for utilitarian purposes. I was ecstatic a few days ago to hear Ted Kennedy on the radio describing a so-called educational reform bill as placing a sign on the door of every public school that read, "Abandon all hope, ye who enter here." The commentator said, "flowery language aside," and went on to discuss the issues and I wondered if she knew that the line came from *The Inferno*, and, in any case, whether it mattered. It was a most effective line for a speech in the senate.

Perhaps poetry does have a place in American public life, after all? Perhaps what we need to learn is how to write like Dante. . . .

On the other hand, Emily Dickinson was no slouch, and no one ever paid any attention to her. She is not only the greatest poet the United States has ever produced, she's also our most vivid cautionary tale. Her life tells us that, yes, you can write great poetry in America, but if you want it published you will pretty much have to write the poems out yourself, neatly fold their pages, and bind them together with string with your own hands.

Perhaps I am perverse, or just brainwashed by Dickinson's example, but I actually think this marginality of ours could also be understood to be a strength of American poetry. There is nothing to be gotten out of writing poetry in America but the poetry itself, and this ought to make us—like Emily herself— a fairly monomaniacal bunch—interested only in the extraordinary possibilities of where the next blank page (blank screen?) might be made to go. Here, too, our garment-worker connections might stand us in good stead. After all, no one paid any attention to them, either.

I've decided to try to remind myself as often as possible how lucky I am to be at my computer every day rather than at some relentless machine in a sweat shop.

"Do I consider myself an American poet?" It doesn't much matter, since I am one. On the other hand, I'm not sure my allegiance is particularly to the American tradition. My suspicion is that poetry has more in common with other poetry—regardless of chronology or geography—than it has with anything else, and I try to put myself in contact with as much of the world's poetry—past and present—as possible. I read as much as I can in its original language, but find a peculiar pleasure in reading poems in translation—you get to imagine them, to think of how marvelous the poems might be if you only had access to them. The translation simply gives you something to take off from. The poems I read in languages other than my own provide a different sense of new poetic possibility; I find myself wondering how I can bring that linguistic approach into something of my own.

Of course I read non-American English-language poems; again, you often get interesting insights into how the English language might be used. Nonetheless, I sometimes think I miss more than I acknowledge, as I know my English friends missed more than they acknowledged about many great American poets I would show them. But there is the pleasure here of reading something that is at once yours and not yours—it is your language, but not at all the way you'd use it. For me, one astonishing find was the Indian poet Nissim Ezekiel—not only the poems, but that he should exist at all. A poet writing about the psalms in Bombay from a Jewish perspective? I was out of my mind with excitement. And I suppose I should then go on to say that, for me, this is the tradition with which I align myself, both consciously and unconsciously, despite my idealistic talk a paragraph ago about the universality of poetry. It was surely hearing the Psalms in synagogue as a child that gave me my first sense of what poetry is, and my desire to write it must have something to do with the extremely appealing notion—even to a six- or seven-year-old—that there is such a thing as a holy language. Surely, if I write out of a specific poetic tradition, it is the Jewish poetic tradition, American poet though I am.

This leads me to the question of American poetry not written in English. Lately—like so many middle-aged American Jews—I've become obsessed with the Yiddish language. This has something to do with the passing away of my four garment-worker grandparents, all of whom had Yiddish for their native tongue, and the realization that this language, which I feel so comfortable around, though I don't exactly understand it, is, if not dead already, quickly dying. As a result, I've begun to try to read Yiddish poetry and have found some extraordinary quintessentially American poets (one generation away from garment workers indeed; there's Mani Leib, who describes himself as "Not, thank God, a shoemaker who writes poems, but a poet who makes shoes")—wonderfully moving and funny poets, poets who talk about Manhattan and Arizona in their poems, but do so in the Yiddish language. I especially love Jacob Glatstein, but I'm also extremely interested in Moyshe-Leyb Halpern, the aforementioned Mani Leyb, Kadya Molodovsky, Malka Heifetz Tussman, Celia Dropkin, Gabriel Preil, Abraham Reisen, Aaron Zeitlin . . . And I'm sure it's only my ignorance and the paucity of translation that make me fail to mention many others. As I say, our America is in their poems, and we do ourselves and our own poetry a tremendous disservice if we do not learn to incorporate these great American poets into what we understand to be American literature. I can't tell you how often I have found in their work the voice I myself have longed for—born of tradition, but irreverent, deadly serious, but funny, self-mocking, but full of mastery.

Alicia Suskin Ostriker

Born in 1937 in Brooklyn, New York, Alicia Suskin Ostriker is Professor of English at Rutgers University. A recipient of a National Endowment for the Arts fellowship and a Guggenheim Foundation fellowship, she is both a poet, and a scholar. Among her recent volumes are *The Little Space: Poems Selected and New 1968–1998* (U of Pittsburgh P 1998), *The Crack in Everything* (U of Pittsburgh P, 1996) (poems), the mixed-genre book *The Nakedness of the Fathers: Biblical Visions and Revisions* (Rutgers UP, 1994), and the influential critical study *Stealing the Language: The Emergence of Women's Poetry in America* (Beacon, 1987).

The Eighth and Thirteenth

The Eighth of Shostakovich,
Music about the worst
Horror history offers,
They played on public radio
Again last night. In solitude
I sipped my wine, I drank
That somber symphony
To the vile lees. The composer
Draws out the minor thirds, the brass
Tumbles overhead like virgin logs
Felled from their forest, washing downriver,
And the rivermen at song. Like ravens
Who know when meat is in the offing,
Oboes form a ring. An avalanche
Of iron violins. At Leningrad
During the years of siege
Between bombardment, hunger,
And three sub-freezing winters,
Three million dead were born
Out of Christ's bloody side. Like icy
Fetuses. For months
One could not bury them, the earth
And they alike were adamant.

You stacked the dead like sticks until May's mud,
When, of course, there was pestilence.
But the music continues. It has no other choice.
Stalin hated the music and forbade it.
Not patriotic, not Russian, not Soviet.
But the music continues. It has no other choice.
Peer in as far as you like, it stays
Exactly as bleak as now. The composer
Opens his notebook. *Tyrants like to present themselves as patrons of the arts.*
That's a well-known fact. But tyrants understand nothing about art. Why? Be-
cause tyranny is a perversion and a tyrant is a pervert. He is attracted by the
chance to crush people, to mock them, stepping over corpses . . . And so, hav-
ing satisfied his perverted desires, the man becomes a leader, and now the per-
versions continue because power has to be defended against madmen like
yourself. For even if there are no such enemies, you have to invent them, be-
cause otherwise you can't flex your muscles completely, you can't oppress the
people completely, making the blood spurt. And without that, what pleasure is
there in power? Very little. The composer
Looks out the door of his dacha, it's April,
He watches farm children at play,
He forgets nothing. For the thirteenth—
I slip its cassette into my car
Radio—they made Kiev's Jews undress
After a march to the suburb,
Shot the hesitant quickly,
Battered some of the lame,
And screamed at everyone.
Valises were taken, would
Not be needed, packed
So abruptly, tied with such
Frayed rope. Soldiers next
Killed a few more. The living ones,
Penises of the men like string,
Breasts of the women bobbling
As at athletics, were told to run
Through a copse, to where
Wet with saliva
The ravine opened her mouth.
Marksmen shot the remainder
Then, there, by the tens of thousands,
Cleverly, so that bodies toppled
In without lugging. An officer

Strode upon the dead,
Shot what stirred.
How would it feel, such uneasy
Footing, even wearing boots
That caressed one's calves, leather
And lambswool, the soles thick rubber,
Such the music's patient inquiry.
What then is the essence of reality?
Of the good? The mind's fuse sputters,
The heart aborts, it smells like wet ashes,
The hands lift to cover their eyes,
Only the music continues. We'll try,
For the first movement,
A full chorus.
The immediate reverse of Beethoven.
An axe between the shoulder blades
Of Herr Wagner. *People knew about Babi Yar*
before Yevtoshenko's poem, but they were silent. And when they read the poem,
the silence was broken, Art destroys silence. I know that many will not agree
with me and will point out other, more noble aims of art. They'll talk about
beauty, grace and other high qualities. But you won't catch me with that bait.
I'm like Sobakevich in Dead Souls*: you can sugar-coat a toad, and I still won't*
put it in my mouth.

Most of my symphonies are tombstones, said Shostakovich.

All poets are Jews, said Tsvetaeva.

The words *never again*
Clashing against the words
Again and again
—That music.

COMMENTARY

So what is Jewish about this poem? To answer a question with a question: What
is Jewish about any poem? Or any piece of literature or work of art, for that mat-
ter? The question keeps coming up, like all those questions about gender, and
class and ethnicity, in these days—in today's daze—of identity politics, which

has become such a big thing precisely because our identities are all so fractured
and hyphenated. "Who is it that can tell me who I am?" asks a King Lear
whose identity has been stretched like a wad of Silly Putty, almost to the rap-
ture of complete rupture, thanks to his own insistence on the self's solid domi-
nance as Father and King. Avoid hardening of the categories, a friend told me
long ago, and I find this an excellent motto. Yet we all need categories.

A few years ago, asked to give a talk at a conference on "Poetry of the Fif-
ties," I decided that I needed to figure out what was Jewish about Allen
Ginsberg's "Howl." Not "Kaddish," where at least a first-order answer is obvi-
ous, but "Howl," whose only explicit Jewish references are "Moloch,"
Ginsberg's version of the pagan god to whom Israelite children were at times
sacrificed as burnt offerings, to the horror of the prophets, and "Carl Solo-
mon," a Jewish name. No chicken soup or chopped liver, no Jewish holidays,
no Sabbath, no bubbe and zayde, no Biblical characters in modern dress, no
holocaust. Yet you feel the Jewishness of "Howl" in your bones. I began by
finding parallels with the Book of Lamentations, written after the sack of Je-
rusalem in 586 B.C.E. These are numerous. They range from the parallel titles
evoking a cry of suffering (the Hebrew title of Lamentations is the book's first
word, *Eicha*, meaning "how," as in "How doth the city sit solitary, that was full
of people! How is she become a widow!" Lamentations 1:1) to imagery of mu-
tilated and humiliated bodies and even of cannibalism, to similar visions of
god as the enemy whom one must nonetheless worship. The sublimity of
"Howl" derives from the tradition of Prophetic literature, and most particu-
larly from Lamentations. On the other hand, there is so much that is anti-
sublime, tragicomic, and in fact ridiculous about "Howl." That, I decided, was
its Yiddish side. All those self-lacerating jokes, that low language, the buf-
foonery of it. And the ultimate tenderness, and the vision of social justice loi-
tering behind the outrageousness of Ginsberg's hipsters. Is it possible, not-
withstanding Ginsberg's overt rejections of Judaism, to understand "the best
minds of my generation" as an oblique version of a chosen people? Should we
see both Jews and Ginsberg's cohort of misfits as people condemned to ostra-
cism and victimization because of their stubborn rejection of the dominant
culture—Christianity on the one hand, bourgeois capitalism on the other—
and their quest for another kind of holiness? Are the "angelheaded hipsters
burning for the ancient heavenly connection," in all their "poverty and tatters
and hollow-eyed" weirdness, perhaps only a morphed version of frenzied da-
venners in some crumbling Hasidic *shul*? My point here is that certain kinds
of surface content in a poem may announce themselves as Jewish—but what
fascinates me is the question of how Jewishness gets encoded or encrypted, as
it were, in a poem's DNA.

So "The Eighth and Thirteenth" may announce itself as a "holocaust"
poem, and therefore as ipso facto Jewish. Does that mean we are to understand

Shostakovich, whose Thirteenth Symphony is the Babi Yar Symphony—and Yevtoshenko, on whose poem the symphony is based—as Jews? No, they are Russians. So what is going on here?

I began writing "The Eighth and Thirteenth" in May 1991, a half year after a mastectomy, while spending a week of solitude in a cabin my family built in the Massachusetts backwoods, up a dirt road, far from the turnpike exit. We have plumbing and a pond, but no electricity, no phone. The agenda was reading, meditating, writing, relaxing. It was a time of healing and pleasure. Some of my writing dealt with the surgery, some with swimming, flowers, mushrooms, history, art, friendship. Some of it was random scribbles. One evening as I finished my pasta and sipped my wine by the yellow light of the oil lantern, the local public radio station (Five College Radio, out of Amherst) played Shostakovich's Eighth Symphony. The effect on me was as if a hand had gripped my heart, was attempting to wrench it from my body. The grief was almost intolerable. I seized a pen and notebook and wrote while listening, and afterward.

Shostakovich's Eighth Symphony memorializes the siege of Leningrad during World War II. Premiered in Moscow in November 1943, it received a thirty-minute ovation; Stalin subsequently banned it. Patriotic art, socialist realism, was supposed to be heroic and uplifting. In truth, as propaganda designed to encourage workers and soldiers, the Eighth Symphony fails miserably. The Thirteenth Symphony, composed in 1962 after Stalin's death, was inspired by Yevgeny Yevtoshenko's famous poem "Babi Yar," which responded to the discovery of the ravine in which over one hundred thousand massacred Jews of Kiev lay. I bought both symphonies when I returned home from Massachusetts, and borrowed from the library Shostakovich's *Testimony*, an autobiography that reads as if written with an axe, not a pen, describing what it was like to survive the Stalin years in Soviet Russia as an artist, while one's colleagues were swallowed by the *gulag*. Shostakovich's raw, splendid, masculine and mordant prose is of a piece with his music. You would recognize it anywhere. The italicized sections of "The Eighth and Thirteenth" are from his text. I included them for their truth, as an homage to the composer, and for the toughness of their verbal music. Shostakovich's disgust with Wagner, and his furious indignation over the playing of Wagner in Moscow during the period of the Hitler-Stalin pact, also come from *Testimony*.

The poem went through a few expansions and contractions. For a while there was a section on Plato's cave, as a sewage tunnel of history. There was a passage on Dr. Mengele's notorious medical experiments in Auschwitz. A long meditation on the Russian qualities of the Eighth Symphony was cut down to two lines. An epigraph consisting of two lines by Margaret Atwood, "The facts of this world seen clearly/are seen through tears," lasted through several revisions. The quotation from Marina Tsvetaeva came in late in the game. I was, of course, not thinking "this is a Jewish poem" while I was composing it. I was thinking primarily about how difficult it is to respond to music in a poem, how difficult to construct a poetic music somehow equivalent to what one hears and feels. I have written many poems responding to visual art; music is harder. I wanted a fusion of beauty and pain here. I wanted cruelty, inexorability, roughness of construction. Above all, I wanted my poem to embody, without my saying so, my reverence for the genius of Shostakovich as not merely musical but moral. It is a cause of awe to me that this Russian could compose music honoring the suffering of his fellow Russians, then go ahead and compose music honoring the suffering of despised Jews. I am not sure if it is widely recognized how extraordinary a human accomplishment such empathic leaps of the imagination are. In his "Defense of Poetry," Percy Bysshe Shelley argues that "The great secret of morals is love; or a going out of our own nature. . . . A man, to be greatly good, must imagine intensely and comprehensively; he must put himself in the place of another and of many others; the pains and pleasures of his species must become his own." The ethics of poetry, Shelley claims, consists in its way of compelling readers to identify with others, and with many others. Surely this is a task only the imagination can perform, and to which it is uniquely suited.

To the Jew, the task of identifying with what is not-self is a commandment. Its first appearance is Exodus 23:9, "Thou shalt not oppress a stranger, for you know the heart of the stranger, seeing you were strangers in Egypt." An astonishing notion, if you stop to think about it. "Stranger" means, of course, resident alien, and is it not human nature to oppress resident aliens? There is a story back in Genesis 16 that might prepare us for this curious moment. Hagar, whose name puns on *ha-ger*, stranger, is the slave of Sarah, wife of the patriarch Abraham. Sarah, being barren, gives Hagar to her husband, "that I may obtain children by her." Hagar becomes pregnant, but the surrogacy arrangement sours from the start; Sarah is "despised in her eyes," and when the mistress retaliates by harsh treatment, Hagar flees to the desert. There she encounters an angel who tells her to return to her mistress, assuring her that the Lord "will multiply your seed exceedingly," that the son who is to be born must be called "Ishmael; because the Lord has heard your affliction. . . . And she called the Lord that spoke to her, God-sees-me." For a time domestic peace prevails, but after Sarah finally gives birth to her own son, Isaac, she insists that Abraham cast out Hagar and Ishmael, "for the son of this slavewoman shall not be heir with my son, Isaac." Abraham reluctantly obeys his wife, as God tells him that the covenant will be with Isaac but that Ishmael too will be made a nation, because he is Abraham's seed:

> And Abraham rose up early in the morning, and took bread and a bottle of water, and gave it to Hagar, putting it on her shoulder, and the child, and sent her away; and she departed and wandered in the wilderness of Beersheba. And the water in the bottle was spent, and she cast the child under one of the shrubs. And she went

and sat at a distance, a bowshot away, for she said, Let me not see the death of the child. And she sat over against him, and lifted up her voice, and wept. And God heard the cry of the boy, and an angel of God called to Hagar from heaven, and said to her, What troubles you, Hagar? Fear not, for God has heard the cry of the boy where he is. Arise, lift up the boy and hold him by the hand, for I will make him a great nation. Then God opened her eyes and she saw a well of water; and she went, and filled the bottle with water, and gave the boy to drink. And God was with the boy, and he grew, and lived in the wilderness, and became a bowman. (Genesis 21:10–20)

The poignance of this scene, with its empathy for the outcast, depends on its being an abrupt and anomalous digression from the dominant narrative of Genesis, with its single-minded attention to the main line of begats constituting the covenant between God and Israel. Tribalism is an *axis mundi* of Jewishness, established in Genesis and reinforced throughout Biblical narrative and throughout Jewish history. We are the chosen ones, we are to hold ourselves separate from the *goyim*, the Lord our God is a jealous God. Yet an equal and opposite ethic is also enjoined on us, not once but many times. The decalogue declares that sabbath rest applies to strangers as well as Israelites. A dozen texts in Exodus, Leviticus, Numbers, and Deuteronomy command equality under law for natives and strangers, forbid natives to vex or oppress the strangers among them, and even demand that the Israelite "love" the stranger. An absurd demand, certainly. Yet it was a truism in the family of my childhood that our experience of being alien and oppressed teaches us kindness and compassion. I have actually always believed this, fool that I am. I have cherished the Talmudic description of Jewish men as "compassionate sons of compassionate fathers," for my own father and grandfathers were gentle and kind men, personally, and socialists politically. I have treasured Hillel's famous formulation of the self-other relationship: "If I am not for myself who is for me? If I am for myself alone, what am I? And if not now, when?" It has been a source of the deepest ethnic pride for me that American Jews turn out for every movement of social justice—and of racking shame that Israeli policy has oppressed and continues to oppress the stranger, the Palestinian, in its midst. My soul vibrates to the conclusion of Grace Paley's "Midrash on Happiness:"

By work to do she included the important work of raising children righteously up. By righteously she meant that along with being useful and speaking the truth to the community, they must do no harm. By harm she meant not only personal injury to the friend the lover the coworker the parent (the city the nation) but also the stranger; she meant particularly the stranger in all his or her difference, who, because we were strangers in Egypt, deserves special goodness for life or at least until the end of strangeness.

Although the ultimate sources and meanings of a poem may remain mysterious to the poet, my speculation is that "The Eighth and Thirteenth" could be considered a Jewish poem not simply because it deals with the holocaust but because compassionate boundary-crossing is for me a core Jewish activity, and I love it wherever I see it in others. My grandparents were Lithuanian Jews who came to America in the 1880s in flight from the pogroms that were sweeping Russia and Eastern Europe in that decade. Jew-hatred remains alive and well in post-Stalin (and post-Gorbachev) Russia. That a great Russian artist could feel as Shostakovich felt for the Jews moves me to the soles of my feet; I want to feel that this compassion is inseparable from his genius, his canniness, his angry survival. I want, too, to put the suffering of the Jews alongside the suffering of the Russians. I want a recognition that the holocaust both is and is not like other disasters of war, other genocides. And I want to support the idea that art continues, relentlessly, to struggle between poles of "never again," that hopefully resolute post-holocaust slogan, and the more likely reality that the intolerable disasters of war will occur "again and again" in the future as in the past. Like the twin principles of Jewish history—our tribalism says we are uniquely "chosen," while our universalism claims God is one God and human beings one family—passionate hope and passionate despair wrestle together here.

What Marina Tsvetaeva actually said was not "all poets are Jews," but something more succinct and brutal, "Poets are Yids." I see at least two possible meanings for this aphorism. One is that poets are the insulted and injured of any society; poets are the ones you can spit on. Another could be that poets, wherever they live, live in exile. Always in Egypt, always strangers. Always, therefore, with the insight into others, the compassion born of exile? Perhaps so, perhaps no. Tsvetaeva, a pure Russian, spent most of her adult life in exile. In 1941 she hung herself.

Postscript. A decade ago, inspired by Enid Dame's *Lilith and Her Demons*, in which Lilith is a mouthy and sexy survivor, I wrote a set of "Lilith Poems" in which Lilith is a black woman speaking to Eve, a white woman. In the trajectory of the sequence, Lilith at first despises Eve (she is Eve's cleaning woman), later tries to teach her courage, and still later invokes the goddess by a series of names from the African Yemanja to the kabbalistic Shekhinah.

I have been attacked for writing in a black woman's voice, and have no defense except to say that the poems came to me in this form, that they are among other things an homage to the boldness of contemporary black women's poetry, and that the poetic imagination must be permitted to glide between self and not-self. As Whitman says: "For every atom belonging to me as good belongs to you." In a more recent book, *The Nakedness of the Fathers*, I permit myself to be inhabited by a variety of male biblical figures, and also by a Hagar who speaks with unquenched rage of Sarah's exploitation and betrayal of her. As Sarah and Isaac are ancestors of the Jews, so Hagar and Ishmael are, according to legend, ancestors of the Arabs. Genesis 21 marks the moment of a split whose tragic consequences continue to this moment. My Hagar is proud of a son who can shoot an AK-47 and whispers to him to fight to his dying breath. Reading this poem before Jewish audiences, I have scandalized and angered some. I cannot help this. I cannot help being Hagar as well as Sarah, a black woman as well as a white one.

This summer I taught a contemporary *midrash* class in which one of my male students wrote a magnificent piece centered on Miriam as a radical prophet of liberation. Like Lilith, Miriam has lately become a feminist heroine, and my student will doubtless be castigated by some feminists for trespassing on their territory. But he could not help it. He went where imagination led. Moreover, he wrote in the voice of a gay man, though he is himself heterosexual; the premise was that he and Miriam had been palace dancers in childhood, and the persona enabled the piece to leaven prophecy with campy wit. Perhaps this strategy too will be considered offensive. I thought it was very Jewish of him. Art, as Shostakovich wrote, destroys silence. Jewish art, in at least one of its impulses, may not destroy the gulf between ourselves and the stranger, the other. But it tries.

Bob Perelman

Born in 1947 in Youngstown, Ohio, Bob Perelman is a Professor of English at the University of Pennsylvania. One of the primary figures involved in the avant-garde Language Poetry movement, his recent poetry collections include *Ten to One* (Wesleyan UP, 1999), *The Future of Memory* (Segue Foundation, 1998), and *Virtual Reality* (Roof Press, 1993). He is also the author of such important studies of American experimental poetry as *The Marginalization of Poetry: Language Writing and Literary History* (Princeton UP, 1996), and *The Trouble With Genius: Reading Pound, Joyce, Stein, and Zukofsky* (U of California P, 1996).

Chaim Soutine

I

Unclose your eyes, you look ridiculous,
untip your head, shut your lips.

Listen. I'll tell you a secret.
I learned this when I left the *shtetl*

—that means home town,
everyone's from the *shtetl*. That bottle

you're clutching. In the *shtetl* it's called
the bottle of last things.

Everyone gets one. It's supposed to be
invisible, it's bad luck to mention it, they say.

But take it down from your mouth.
You didn't know you were holding it!

They say that's good luck,
and the tighter you close your eyes the better.

The world in there, all yours:
visions, powers, messiahs.

But now that you know—hoist it back up,
run your tongue around the rim,
feel the glass, if it's beveled smooth,
curl your tongue into the neck,
do whatever. It's yours.

But the big secret is . . .
It's empty! Glug glug!

You've swallowed it all! Tasted good?
Who knows! All gone!

Bottoms up must have been
your very first word!

And guess what that means?
Bad luck!

Finis! Curtains! Triumphal openings, Picasso elbowing over to chat—
nothing, forget it!

I've found out the hard way.
But at least I'm not in that ridiculous posture anymore,
squeezing the neck, eyes screwed shut, piously sucking.

Here's my advice: throw it away.
smash it on the curb,
go heave it through some stained glass.
Just get rid of it! Now:

head level, mouth shut, eyes open,
forward march . . . we're big doomed heroes!

2

God can give you the world
(glug glug!), sacred word, covered ark and all,

I can paint you
pictures of whatever—curtains blowing open,
nice tablecloths, high class space,
sides of meat, streaming red, glistening, clotted yellow.

Push the paint, whip it around.
It likes it. A strip-tease

without the tease and without stopping at the skin.
The girl thinks I want to see her body—

surprise! Keep your clothes on, sweetie,

you're here to wave away flies.
They're actually pretty, patchy fur swarming

over the side of beef if you
let them settle, but it's

much prettier bare.
Keep waving.

Your arms are killing you? So what.
After four days hanging there it doesn't
smell so great?

Hey, my blood didn't taste so great
when the god-fearing neighbors beat me up

in the name of the almighty.
Thou shalt make no graven images

and thou shalt smash the kid
who tries to paint the rabbi

and here's one for free
in case anybody forgets what No means.

3

Let's build a frame of common
sense, stating the case with deeply

received ideas and fields of trophies
to hold the still-warm ashes, yes?

What's happening? Soutine, non-verbal painter
of crooked landscapes, people, meat, is speaking,

supposedly, but it can't be, time
is a problem, and place,

one's place in the senses, facts of habit, recognition,
situations where art is produced, carefully broken windows

placed at careful distances
from customers who are always right.

The dramatic monolog is far down on the list
of living forms, supine, disgusting really.

What is an anecdotal Soutine to me,
and what am I to these

acidic bursts of no one's speech

and they to the decomposing composition?
The desire for heroic writing splits

into appetite (glug glug!) and horror
at the achieved sentence (keep waving!),

while the eye (your mind or
mine?) sticks the words like pigs,

with syntax underneath to catch the
flows of meaning. The taste

of lost things is a tyrannical pleasure
and is always in infinite supply.

    4

For the sake of art,
modernist coffee, Paris,

it would be nice
to hold some things separate,

let the anxious animal graze outside forever
on museum grass

while, inside, history's waterfall flows upward,
sharp white walls

keeping the vision of taste safe
from the mouth that wants grapes

perpetually bursting into the old original wine:
Make It New.

The Louvre
is the *shtetl* of *shtetls*.

Unless our home
is language, raising us

inside its womb. Reading its shifting glitter
I almost forget I ever learned

to write in half-lit
rooms and blocks and days.
There are lives outside

the correction chambers of this page.
Couldn't it be stronger? Time

to stop and name. Print
on paper for the neighbors.

C O M M E N T A R Y

I can't claim any significant amount of research behind this poem. I was invited
to contribute to a volume of poems celebrating the University of Iowa Art Mu-
seum; and was taken by the one Soutine reproduction in the catalog ("Femme

au chien": a seated dark-haired woman emerging out of a thin sea of red and yellow). Some rudimentary research led me to the story of Soutine asking to paint the rabbi's portrait and getting beaten up by his neighbors in the *shtetl* and the story of him in Paris employing a model to waive flies away from the side of beef. I was attracted to these stories; and I loved the courage of his paintings.

If I identify with any group, it's with secular Jews. Not the energy of self-hatred, rather the shared warmth of aggressive humor, art, and rootless cosmopolitanism, that last phrase typical in taking the horrible *volkish* phrase of Stalin and making a hamentashen out of gratuitous hatred and stupidity at least as deep as the Red Sea. Who really wants to live in rooted ruralism, blaming all the trouble of circulation and stasis on the outside insiders? But resentments are tasty.

I was not beaten up as a child, either by Jews or for being Jewish. But I do recognize the edgy feeling of being outside the large group and outside the outside group, too. How Jewish was Soutine? Much more than me, I imagine. If I identify myself as Jewish, it's a cultural, not a religious identification. Or I'm an atheist Jew, perhaps, believing in history, the occasionally humorous pathos of being situated in a time and place, in a changing chain, one that breaks, too. You say eternal, I say ahistorical; in either case they're the "lost things" of the poem. Consequently, as an artist, one is left with all the color in the world, or in my case, the words, which one then shapes in order to provide noninfantile sustenance to the neighbors.

But the infantile, elemental is a permanent as metabolism; the mouth is simultaneously intellectual and infant. I am saying that art is social, material: it's on paper, or canvas, something one learns to do; and that it is involved with infantile drives, permanently unsatisfiable desires.

Somewhere amid Zukofsky, Reznikoff, and Ginsberg; outside all of them.

In some extended logic, the poem envisions the ultimate audience as universal and as *shtetl* Jews. In fact, *shtetl* Jews are universal ("everybody's from the shtetl") and the target of universalizers who can't stand the thought of otherness. In section 3, "common sense" and "still-warm ashes" go together. I don't want to claim this as that much of a "poem after Auschwitz"—but it is a category we need to keep as firmly in mind as possible as we read and write.

Marge Piercy

Born in 1936 in Detroit, Michigan, Marge Piercy has published fifteen collections of poetry; her latest is *The Art of Blessing the Day: Poems with a Jewish Theme* (Knopf, 1999). A well-known novelist as well as a poet, she has written fourteen novels, and her books have been translated into sixteen languages.

Snowflakes, my mother called them

Snowflakes, my mother called them.
My grandmother made papercuts
until she was too blind to see
the intricate birds, trees, Mogen
Davids, moons, flowers
that appeared like magic
when the folded paper
was opened.

My mother made simpler ones,
abstract. She never saved them.
Not hers, not mine.
It was a winter game.
Usually we had only newsprint
to play with. Sometimes
we used old wrapping paper,
white sheets from the bakery.

Often Grandma tacked hers
to the walls or on the window
that looked on the street,
the east window where the sun
rose hidden behind tenements
where she faced to pray.
I remember one with deer,
delicate hooves, fine antlers

for Pesach. Her animals were
always in pairs, the rabbits,
the cats, always cats in pairs,
little mice, but never horses,
for horses meant pogrom,
the twice widowed woman's
sense of how things should be,
even trees by twos for company.

I had forgotten. I had lost it all
until a woman sent me a papercut
to thank me for a poem, and then
in my hand I felt a piece of past
materialize, a snowflake long melted,
evaporated, cohering and once
again tower-necked fragile deer
stood, made of skill and absence.

COMMENTARY

This poem began with a request from Ross Bradshaw of Five Leaves Press in England to make a compilation of my Jewish-themed poems for him to publish. Knopf decided they wanted to bring it out here in time for Pesach of 1999 [5759].

I did not like the cover design Ross first produced, and suggested to him and to my editor Ann Close at Knopf that we use a papercut. I am not exactly sure why, but it seemed to me appropriate and I had in mind a papercut with birds and animals in it. Recently a woman who was using a poem of mine in her Haggadah—I had been working on a Haggadah for at least twelve years, and I have written poems for all the items on the Seder plate as well as a *maggid* poem—wrote thanking me for the use and sent me a papercut, abstract but pretty.

Neither Ross nor anyone at Knopf knew what I was talking about, and I was suddenly unsure myself. Did such things really exist? Were they really a traditional Jewish women's art form? Why was I so sure I had seen them? Where? I put a query out on the Women's Studies listserv and wrote via e-mail to some women rabbis of my acquaintance and consulted the head of Jewish Studies at a university where I was giving a poetry reading under her auspices. Sarah Horowitz was able to help me understand that what I was seeking actually existed.

It had been primarily a women's art form practiced in Eastern Europe, particularly in Lithuania (where my Grandmother Hannah came from) and in Poland, although some men made them and still do so. The name that first came to me was *papirn shnit*. I was to learn that they have many names.

By chance as I was returning from that reading, someone I had not seen in twelve years, Rabbi Sue Elwell, was sitting across the aisle from me on the plane to Boston and asked me if I remembered her. I had met her when I was the Ellison Poetry Fellow at the University of Cincinnati and finishing the penultimate draft of *Gone to Soldiers*. Sue was then in her last year at the rabbinical college. It turned out that she knew quite a bit about papercuts, including some of their uses and including also some contemporary practitioners. I was underway. I knew now I was not deluded and that somehow I had acquired a strong feeling for papercuts and sometime in my life I had seen a number of them.

It was one of the e-mail messages in response to my query that suddenly brought two wires together in my brain. The message said that papercuts were often put on the Eastern window as *mizrachi*—object put up to indicate in which direction to pray—and another message said they were often used as decoration at Pesach and Shavuot. Sarah Horowitz called them *rayzellach* [little roses] and suggested that women made paper flowers as decoration because they could not afford real flowers, and the papercuts were cheap and portable. Another woman called them *shavuselah*—little Shavuots. Suddenly I saw a papercut on a window with the sun coming dimly through it. Cleveland. I was a child.

I received then a piece of my childhood long forgotten. My almost blind grandmother had made exquisite papercuts, bending forward (she was nearsighted and had cataracts in both eyes, as I was to have) almost nose to the paper and with a little scissors or sometimes with a small sharp knife resembling a scalpel, cutting, cutting quickly, now very slowly, snipping away so that magically trees, flowers, birds, deer, cats, cows all appeared. Further, my mother had made papercuts, although slapdash ones that she called snowflakes. And I too in my childhood had made papercuts. Grandmother had liked my papercuts and told me I had more talent than my mother at that—but then she was always saying things like that, since she had a stormy relationship with my mother and a very loving one with me. I associated papercuts with being happy, with feeling safe, with feeling cherished—all experiences none too common in my childhood and intensely appreciated.

Thus I recovered a piece of memory buried and inaccessible to me, and from it I fashioned the poem. I decided it had to be the first poem in the book, but it was too late to include it in the British collection, which had a much earlier publication date in November. Ross wanted to bring it out in time for the Poetry International London Festival, where I was to read. However, "Snowflakes, my mother called them" is firmly and proudly in the American edition of *The Art of Blessing the Day*, which is somewhat longer than the British version.

The form of the poem is straightforward narration. It is in eight-line stanzas. I often like working in stanzas, since it doesn't give the same distortion as rime in English or a fixed line length, but offers some shape and tension to the poem. I played with a six-line stanza, but went with the longer stanza, since it seemed more organic to the movement of the memories in the poem. As the last line indicates, I find the making of art through absence—the removal of paper and shaping of the void created—very intriguing. I am always telling students in workshops that poems are made out of sounds and silence, and that the silence is just as important as the sound. In papercuts, I saw something similar.

After I finished the third draft of the poem, I made the first papercut I had tried since I was perhaps ten years old. I would like to say how beautiful it was, but truthfully, it was awkward and clunky. I crumpled it up and threw it away. I shall have to be satisfied with poems instead of papercuts. However, I wish I had a beautiful papercut in place of the *shiviti* covered with fine writing that marks the eastern wall of my own house, but all of my grandmother's papercuts vanished years and years ago.

She died when I was fifteen and very rebellious against Orthodoxy. I sulked at her funeral and wrote poems about hypocrisy. My grandmother lived with us part of every year (the rest of the time with my favorite aunt, Ruth) and we slept together in the same double bed. She was a fine storyteller and gave me my religious education. She formed a lot of my ideas about being Jewish and gave a strong sense of a women's tradition, women's prayers, women's stories. All I have of hers is a cameo that my grandfather bought for her in Naples when they were fleeing Russia and seeking passage to America. They were newly wed and on the run, and he still loved her strongly. Eleven children later, he was not so devoted or loyal, but that's another story or another poem.

I am aware of the papercuts that were used to ward off Lilith in childbirthing rooms, but I do not think I have ever seen them. Hannah, my grandmother, told me stories of Lilith—Lilith the terrible, but also the free, a hint of ambiguity in the treatment of her. I am curious what these papercuts looked like, but have never seen them pictured. I suspect they are not as warm and pretty as the papercuts I so admired as a child and find delightful now. They were not what I had in mind, any more than formal, even more intricate papercuts used in synagogues. I was interested in the domestic variety used as cheap decoration.

Hilda Raz

Hilda Raz teaches at the University of Nebraska, where she is editor of the prestigious literary magazine *Prairie Schooner.* Her books of poetry include *Divine Honors* (Wesleyan UP, 1997) and *What is Good* (Thorntree, 1989). Her edited collections include *Living on the Margins: Women Writers on Breast Cancer* (Persea, 1999) and *The Prairie Schooner Anthology of Contemporary Jewish American Writing* (U of Nebraska P, 1998).

Mu

". . . the old root giving rise to mystery was *mu,* with cognates MYSTICAL and MUTE. MYSTERY came from the Greek *muein* with the meaning of closing the lips, closing the eyes."
                                                                    – Lewis Thomas

Misery a block in the head
a block I hum mmmm through, the way mother
mmmm helps me move to. Umber attaches to shadows
in hedge-ribbons. Feet mmmmmmmm, hit-sounds like murder
stitched to lips, the miles, hummm, eyes shut shuttered, cement walk
studded with dark I'm afraid mmmmmo
and now I am come alone at midnight onto the pineneedles of the park.

I am come to say goodbye in the dark but my mouth won't open.
What opens is my eye to the open edge of the metal tunnel under
the curve of the spiral slide I'm afraid to rise to. I'm standing at the base
to cry out at midnight Whose children will come down? Who
bashes into my arms so we open our mou ths to this cadence no no
no no mmm mommy up again to ride the big slide they and I falling
into the dark air. Open is the mouth of the metal tunnel.
Tomorrow, mmmmu, the knife.

COMMENTARY

The poem "Mu" from *Divine Honors* (Wesleyan Poetry Series, University Press of New England) was written the night before surgery for cancer. The poem documents the terrifying hours before the hospital. In the middle of the night I walked to the park where my children played when they were small. To leave home in the dark I experienced as a violation of both the safety and limitations of enclosure. The choice was made gladly since I was in extremis, afraid both of amputation and of the cultural meanings of body as I understood them. I walked for a long time in the middle of the night until I came to a known place. I walked to avoid silence, stasis, and the giving over of mind to speculation. I chose to abandon my house in order to return to a playground in the company of my ghost children, now grown. The maternal breast was in control. As a parent but also in the guise of a child (regressed) I went in search of my dead mother to find comfort, meaning, and order. My body, which would be cruelly hurt in the morning, worked to find in the outside world signs that in the Kabbalah signal sense. My text was the world outside my house, the site of family scripts, a place outside body that to me closely resembled body. The rational mind was on hold, but the Jewish poet was awake and finding language in sensory data. I was aware of the presence of vowels in English, their absence in Hebrew, conscious of formal textual traditions—the honoring of words inside words, clues from etymologies, and repeats, refrain, variation, numbers in patterns. I understood the flexibility of English verb tenses, which reflect subjective temporal shifts. Terrified and clamorous, eager to be moving, I walked fast to listen hard, to honor music—messages without specific meaning—and to attend to hearing, the body's final sensory connection to earth. My papa, long dead, was davening in the front bedroom of our house in Rochester, New York. I heard again the Hebrew chants that had been only repetitions to me, whispered sound without specific meaning that my grandfather uttered in his leather straps, his phylacteries, as he bowed and swayed, davened. The sounds of my feet on the pavement announced an interchange between my body and the body of the earth.

At last I came to the park. There I made a conscious exchange of new terror for old. Always I had been afraid of the high slide, of any physical experience that signaled surrender of control. (Anesthesia was one embodiment of this fear.) Any safe Jewish child familiar with the Holocaust as I was—my brother, an American soldier in World War II, left for boot camp during my fourth birthday, he was an infantry photographer at the European front—might so respond. As a child I had refused to participate in playground activities. The high slide especially frightened me. As a young mother I was afraid of my children's fascination with the slide. I had watched each one on turn climb the open and winding stairs, sit down and let go to accelerate through the steel turns and bash into my arms. I was afraid also of the winding culvert in the grass open at each end the diameter of an adult human body the children wiggled through, their voices muffled. Now I climbed the stairs to the slide, sat trembling on the steel platform, sat to let go, hurtled down, got up and crawled to and through the dank leaves in the concrete culvert. Again and again. Alone in the cold dark I played.

Returning home near dawn I brewed tea and sat down with my notebook to write. The making of the text was deliberate, an act of creation in the face of mayhem. I took from the cupboard the sticky jar of honey and remembered what my mother had told me, how we Jews put a little honey on the page so the child's first kiss of the book will be sweet. Certainly my grandmother Hilda, dead before I was born to commemorate her name, was safe in England as her Russian ghetto burned to the ground early in this century. To honor the tradition that valorizes study and text, even or especially in extremis, and to honor a tradition that makes a place for prayer in extreme as well as safe circumstances, prayer never blanched of meaning though it be meaningless, I wrote. I told myself a favorite story about a tribunal of learned elders assembled, fed, and protected in the meanest barracks of the worst camp in Poland during the Holocaust, how it was charged to debate and discover the truth of the proposition, "Our suffering proves there is no G-d, therefore no covenant," how the tribunal assembled to announce their conclusion, "There is no G-d. Now let us praise Him." I drank the fragrant tea. I wrote and exchanged terror for effort and made a symbolic exchange of text for my flesh. To honor our Jewish kin and to comfort myself with the spirit of Rabbi Nachman of Bratslaw, of whom it is said that he said "Whoever can write a book and does not, it is as if he has lost a child," this poem grew and the book around it.

I am not a learned Jew nor an observant one. But like all writers I honor, serve, and work to understand and revise traditions of ritual and learning. All poets are fascinated by etymologies and form. Leaping over the scorn felt by the immigrant generation in my family, I connect to traditions of the Kaballah, count and search for meaning in the accidental. We repeat, make refrains, catalogues, lists. We record the random sounds of feet hitting pavement. We honor the vowel. Where we are, as we can, we listen and say. The necessary and perhaps only apparent passivity of a circumscribed life in the ghettos translates in us to respect and trust in the saving actions of the mind. And whatever the rabbis might have to say about the appropriate rituals for mastectomy, for me the exchange of flesh for text was an honorable one.

Jerome Rothenberg

Born in New York City in 1931, Jerome Rothenberg has written, edited, and translated
more than twenty-five books; he is a major figure in the ethnopoetics movement.
Among his recent collections are *Seedings and other Poems* (New Directions, 1996) and
Gematria (Sun and Moon, 1993), *The Lorca Variations I–XXXIII* (New Directions, 1993.
Among his many anthologies are, with Harris Lenowitz, *Exiled in the Word: Poems and
Other Visions of the Jews from Tribal Times to the Present* (Copper Canyon P, 1989), and the
two-volume anthology *Poems for the Millenium: The University of California Press Anthology
of Modern and Postmodern Poetry* (U of California P, 1996 and 1998), which he edited
with Pierre Joris.

Nokh Aushvits (After Auschwitz)

the poem is ugly & they make it uglier
wherein the power resides
that duncan did—or didn't—understand
when listening that evening to the other poet read
he said   "that was pure ugliness"   & oh it was
it was   & it made my heart skip a beat
because the poem wouldn't allow it   no
not a moment's grace nor beauty to obstruct
whatever the age demanded   or the poem
shit poured on wall & floor
sex shredded   genitals torn loose by dog claws
& the ugliness that you were to suffer
later   that they had suffered
not as dante dreamed it but in the funnel
they ran through & that the others called
the road to heaven   little hills & holes now
& beneath   upon   among them
broken mirrors kettles pans enameled teapots
the braided candlesticks of sabbath
prayershawl scraps & scraps of bodies   bones
his child's   he said   leaping
into the mud the pool of bones

& slime   the frail limbs separating
each time he pulls at one   the mystery of body
not a mystery   bodies naked   then bodies
boned & rotten   how he must fight
his rage for beauty must make a poem
so ugly it can drive out the other voices
like artaud's squawk the poem addressed
to ugliness   must resist
even the artistry of death   a stage set
at treblinka   ticket windows   a large clock
the signs that read: change for bialystok
but the man cries who has seen
the piles of clothing   jews
it is not good it is your own sad meat
that hangs here   poor & bagged   like animals
the blood coagulated into a jell
an armpit through which a ventricle has burst
& left him dangling screaming
a raw prong stuck through his tongue
another through his scrotal sac   he sees
a mouth   a hole   a red hole
the scarlet remnants of the children's flesh
their eyes like frozen baby scallops
so succulent that the blond ukrainian guard
sulking beneath his parasol leaps up
& sucks them inward past his iron teeth
& down his gullet, shitting
globules of fat & shit
that trickle down the pit in which the victim—
the girl without a tongue–stares up
& reads her final heartbreak

C O M M E N T A R Y

I would like to take the occasion that this gathering presents, to address a theme
or presence to which until several years ago my work only barely alluded, but
which has been an ongoing subtext in most of my poetry & in that of much of
my generation.[1] In a period of barely half a dozen years (from 1939 to 1945),
there were over 40 million state-directed murders of human beings & at least

that many sufferings, maimings & tortures: a disaster so large as to be almost incomprehensible & itself only a part of the disasters & conflagrations of this century & millennium from which we're now emerging. Auschwitz & Hiroshima came to be the two events by which we spoke of it—signs of an enormity that turned myth into history, metaphor into fact. The horror of those events encompassed hundreds & thousands of like disasters, joined (as we began to realize) to other, not unrelated violence against the environment/the earth & the other-than-human world. By the mid twentieth century, in Charles Olson's words, "man" had been "reduced to so much fat for soap, superphosphate for soil, fillings & shoes for sale," an enormity that had robbed language (one of our "proudest acts" he said) of the power to meaningfully respond, had thus created a crisis of expression (no, of meaning, of reality), for which a poetics must be devised if we were to rise, again, beyond the level of a scream or of a silence more terrible than any scream.

The ground against which Olson, writing in the late 1940s, set his own poetry of "resistance" was the too familiar ground of Auschwitz & the death camps of World War II. Even now, when that ground has been sanitized & turned into a museum (a museum more than a shrine), the presence as exhibits of hair, shoes, fillings, glasses, prayershawls, toys, can still bring an immediate, uncontrollable sense of the reduction, the degradation that the modern world allows. I do not intend to single out the Jews as victims, as if the lesson is only there for us—or the suffering. Nor do I want to see us only as victims, the innocent sufferers, though Auschwitz & the Holocaust are at their most horrible the accounts of an innocent suffering. To be only the victims, as the founders of Zionism knew, was to be only partly human—a perception that has led on its negative side to the tragedy of Palestine & to a new state of oppression borne by Jews as now a nation among nations. It is for reasons like this— reasons still unresolved for me—that in writing *Poland/1931* & *A Big Jewish Book*, I did for the most part let the Holocaust speak without being spoken.

The word "holocaust" was itself a block. I'll say more of that in the poems that I'll read this evening, but I'll also say a little about it now. I grew up during the war but not in it, & the reports of the deaths & suffering—all the deaths & suffering—came back to us only by degrees. I was a child of the generation that rejoiced in the deaths of our enemies, & there is a burden in that from which I have long wanted to be free. There was a grandmother who wept for her dead, but I only cried for her weeping. At no point did she speak the word holocaust or even the word *shoah*, but the childword for me (from which I still feel a tightness in the throat & chest) was *khurbn* (*khirbn* in the dialect of where they came from). Holocaust is a Christian word that bears the image of a sacrifice by fire. A totality of fire: that is, in human terms, a genocide. The fire I believe is true; the sacrifice a euphemism for the terror. Or if one thinks of sacrifice, the question next comes up: a sacrifice to what? to whom? And the answers come rushing back, sounding themselves like questions: to God? to Adolf Hitler? to make atonement for inherent sin? or Jewish sin? to set the circumstances for a Jewish state? And it seemed to me then & now that the word itself was false, that the questions that it raised were false, that the answers that it seemed to force only increased the sense of pain & madness. *Khurbn/khirbn* was the word I knew for it: disaster pure & simple, with no false ennoblement. Nothing left to say beyond the word. No sacrifice to ponder. (And no meaning.)

Besides which, I didn't hear the word holocaust used in that sense until a decade or more after the event. By then much had been written about the suffering, some of it (the first witnessings in particular) in a language & a literature that we came to prize. But there was also a feeling that turned many of us from a participation in that writing: a revulsion at taking on the voice of those who suffered, of displaying our own feelings in such a way as to overshadow the terror of those times & places. It became necessary to talk outside it if we were to talk at all. But the impression of it was burned into our minds & hearts, so that it colored (much as Olson put it) everything we did as poets or as artists. "After Auschwitz," wrote Adorno, "writing poetry is barbaric"; but that poetry he singled out as *lyrik*. Another kind of poetry came to be our central way of speaking: our most human act. It was a poetry that Adorno also recognized, when writing of it some years later: "Perennial suffering has as much right to expression as a tortured man has to scream; hence it may have been wrong to say that after Auschwitz you could no longer write poems."

I want to speak about that other kind of poetry & to get at it through two turnings in my own work as they relate to holocaust or *khurbn*. "What have I in common with Jews?" Kafka had asked, &, as a mark of his own alienation: "I hardly have anything in common with myself." As a Jew, after Auschwitz, there were two ways to go: to move into a new Jewish nationalism as a response to the threat against this order of being in particular, or to take the legacy of Auschwitz as a call to vigilance against all forms of chauvinism & racism (even those held by Jews). (I do not count the third way here, of total separation.) Most of those I know went the second way, there to meet with others so moved by those times & by the times that would follow. What was Jewish lurked beneath the surface—or lived inside the words. A witnessing by silence.

In 1968 America was deep into Viet Nam, & I was finishing a first assemblage of tribal poetries from around the world, *Technicians of the Sacred*. The war drove me to a further, deeper alienation from America, & *Technicians* led me to explore ancestral sources of my own—"in a world" (I wrote) "of Jewish mystics, thieves, & madmen." The book that followed, *Poland/1931*, was unmistakably Jewish; but ironic also, since it accepted (on the surface) a degree of chauvinism & sentimentality I would otherwise deny. Played out as a comic encounter, it gave me a sense too of having come into a mythic, fantastic world

in which, surprised, I somehow felt myself at home. David Meltzer called it my
"jewish surrealist vaudeville," a phrase that I liked & often repeated. Beyond
the irony & myth, there was I felt a sense of history as well, but a history that
fell just short of the Holocaust, of that which was still not to be spoken. (It
didn't have to be, of course, since everyone knew it was there without the nam-
ing.) The opening poem of *Poland/1931* reads like this: [Reads]

Poland/1931: The Wedding

my mind is stuffed with tablecloths
& with rings but my mind
is dreaming of poland stuffed with poland
brought in the imagination
to a black wedding
a naked bridegroom hovering above
his naked bride mad poland
how terrible thy jews at weddings
thy synagogues with camphor smells & almonds
thy thermoses thy electric fogs
thy braided armpits
thy underwear alive with roots o poland
poland poland poland poland poland
how thy bells wrapped in their flowers toll
how they do offer up their tongues to kiss the moon
old moon old mother stuck in thy sky thyself
an old bell with no tongue a lost udder
o poland thy beer is ever made of rotting bread
thy silks are linens merely thy tradesmen
dance at weddings where fanatic grooms
still dream of bridesmaids still are screaming
past their red mustaches poland
we have lain awake in thy soft arms forever
thy feathers have been balm to us
thy pillows capture us like sickly wombs & guard us
let us sail through thy fierce weddings poland
let us tread thy markets where thy sausages grow ripe & full
let us bite thy peppercorns let thy oxen's dung be sugar to thy dying jews
o poland o sweet resourceful restless poland
o poland of the saints unbuttoned poland repeating endlessly the triple names of mary
poland poland poland poland poland
have we not tired of thee poland no for thy cheeses

shall never tire us nor the honey of thy goats
thy grooms shall work ferociously upon their looming brides
shall bring forth executioners
shall stand like kings inside thy doorways
shall throw their arms around thy lintels poland
& begin to crow

I wrote that in 1967/1968, & the other poems in that book between then &
1973. I had never been to Poland but had set the parameters of the work by Po-
land as my ancestral place-of-origin & by 1931 as the year of my birth—not in
Poland but in Brooklyn. As at the end of that first poem (with its executioners
procreated by the Polish Jewish bride & groom), you can sense the Holocaust
if you choose, or you can find it more visibly, more at surface, in another poem,
"The Student's Testimony," in which I speak of a war & of a man hidden in a
cellar while above him the stars draw letters across a ruined sky. [Reads]

from **The Student's Testimony**

Coda

once in a lifetime man
may meet a hostile spirit once
he may be imprisoned for his
dreams & pay for them
lightning is like oil the mirror
once it starts keeps
runnning
such was their wisdom though we had
no use for it
only later seeing it
reborn
in joplin on a billboard
his own shadow
was more than he could bear the war
came & he ran from it
back in the cellar drinking
too much he grew thin
the great encounter ended it
in flames the candelabrum rose did it become
a heart
that broke into sparks & letters
a shower of ruined cities from which

> my demon
> vanished fled from the light when I was born

(Auschwitz. Hiroshima.) It was as much as I wanted to say—as I thought I should say—until several years ago (1987, 1988), when I traveled by car from Germany to Poland. Crossing the line I felt myself moving into a world still in ruins—an empty world—a world of ghosts. At the border, waiting, we sat in our car beside a line of trucks filled with cattle on their way to slaughter. Bellowing. The sounds were heavy—lost & painful. The air stunk of excrement, became itself an animal. I walked into a latrine to relieve myself, to piss, & was overwhelmed by the accumulated human smells. And I remembered the books of witness I had read before, the visions of a death by excrement so often written there. I felt myself (this man, this animal) in a condition of unrest as never before—& in a condition of poetry.

Robert Creeley—the American poet who, more than anyone else in my generation, has saved (that is, transformed) the "lyric voice" for us—writes in a more recent poem:

Ever Since Hitler

> Ever since Hitler
> or well before that
> fact of human appetite
> addressed with brutal
> indifference others
> killed or tortured or ate
> the same bodies they
> themselves had we ourselves
> had plunged into density
> of selves all seeming stinking
> one no possible way
> out of it smiled or cried
> or tore at it & died
> apparently dead at last
> just no other way out

I cite this here because of Creeley's recognition that there does in fact exist a kind of poetry to which the term "holocaust [poetry]" might still be most meaningfully applied. As such it is not necessarily a poetry about the Holocaust, but a poetry that characterizes what it means to be human, to be a maker of poems (even lyric poems!) after Auschwitz. Poetry after Auschwitz is poetry that has somehow been touched, transformed, by Auschwitz & the other terrors of our time. It is altered, transformed, down to its roots (its language), & the extent of its transformation is the measure of its test as poetry. This is not an easy test to make or take, but it is for me, with all the allowances I am willing to make for myself & for my fellow poets, the measure by which our work has been, must be judged from thereon out. It underlies our discontent with regularity & clarity as a reflection of nature or of God. Reality—& let me say this as strongly as I can—is what the twisted, rotting, disbelieving dead at Auschwitz, Hiroshima, & the other hellholes of this world reveal to us. We may hide from it—& do—too often in that other mode that we confuse with poetry—I mean, "the way of Beauty," "Reason's Way."

The poetry after Auschwitz is a poetry in extremis—a poetry at the extremities of language . . . the extremities therefore of thought & feeling. It was Creeley who spoke, elsewhere, of a poem "addressed to emptiness" (the anomie & anonymity of the modern & postmodern conditions), but I would speak as well of a poem addressed to ugliness—a counter not only to anomie's numbness (its loss of law or meaning) but to that other temptation—the temptation of the beautiful—that we also feel. Given more time I would trace it with you to a range of poetries—of transformations across the arts—from both before & after Auschwitz. Its reality—coming most methodically to life at Auschwitz—is neither new nor over. It waits in Bosnia, in Chechnya, in Kurdistan and in Rwanda; it looms out (as I write this morning) in the twisted ruins, the splintered bones in Oklahoma City. It is mankind in extremis & it has its counterpart in nature in extremis: the terror of an angry & devouring god—the total god envisioned in the total state—made real by the imagination.

It is this that comes to me when writing, living, in a state of poetry—when I am most clearly in it. And I think of the bodies of the living dead, buried in excrement: the account of an ugliness, repeated many times over, that overwhelms us in the pages of the witnesses. "Hell upon hell of excrement," writes Antonin Artaud (of other places, other hells), locked in the mental hospital at Rodez, while the Holocaust was going on—& in the pit of his own body. But the century—of wars & holocausts—has worked its way into his language & the vision that his language gives us. "With my own eyes," he writes, "I have seen falling from a great many coffins I know not what black matter, I know not what immortal urine from these forms mute of life which, morsel by morsel, drop by drop, destroyed themselves. The name of this matter is caca, and caca is the raw material of the soul, whose puddles I have seen in so many coffins spread before my eyes. . . . The breath of the bones has a center and this center is the abyss of Kah-Kah, Kah the corporeal breath of shit, which is the opium of eternal survival. . . . The odor of the eternal ass of death is the oppressed energy of a soul whom the world refused to let live."

This, then, is also poetry's real voice—its most real voice perhaps, given the revelations of the Khurbn & of the century through which we have just been living. It is not an easy thing to say, since I too have been smitten by Beauty— often enough—& have felt that as an antidote to the murder & madness of the other dispensation. But that was to forget that the perpetrators themselves so often held to a cult of mindless beauty, while commiting the ugliest (because most systematically conceived) of crimes & degradations—as the final issue, so to speak, of a false & lying art.

In the light of that, I remember sitting with Robert Duncan some years ago, while another friend at a symposium I had brought together read a poem filled with fantastical Artaudian images of the grotesque & warped—so much so that it caused Duncan to withhold applause & to whisper (too loudly I thought) that the poem was nothing but pure ugliness . . . or words to that effect. The comment stuck with me, bothered me a great deal in fact, & came rushing back at me, when I felt myself dibbik-stricken on my first journey to Poland & the death camps at Auschwitz & elsewhere. I'll end my part of this panel, then, with one of the poems from *Khurbn*—a poem with the Yiddish title "Nokh Aushvits" and the English title "After Auschwitz"—which says, I think, what I've otherwise been trying to say here. It follows another poem in which I've modified Adorno's comment that there can be no poetry after Auschwitz into my own declaration: After Auschwitz there is only poetry.

[Reads After Auschwitz.]

Note

1. Much of this commentary was originally a talk, "Poetry & Extremity," for *Articulations of History: Issues in Holocaust Representation*. Photographic Resource Center, Boston. May 3, 1995.

Howard Schwartz

Howard Schwartz, poet, critic, and folklorist, was born 1945 in St. Louis, Missouri. He was educated at Washington University, St. Louis, and is Professor of English at the University of Missouri, St. Louis. His books of Jewish tales include *Next Year in Jerusalem: 3000 Years of Jewish Stories* (Viking, 1996), *Lilith's Cave: Jewish Tales of the Supernatural* (Harper, 1987), and *The Diamond Tree: Jewish Tales from Around the World* (Harper-Collins, 1998); he is also the editor with Anthony Rudolf of the ground-breaking international anthology *Voices Within the Ark: The Modern Jewish Poets* (Avon, 1980). His most recent collection of poetry is *Sleepwalking Beneath the Stars* (BkMk Press, 1992).

Signs of the Lost Tribe

One day
I found the first sign:
Old boxes stacked in the attic
In a room I had never entered.
After that
I found the signs everywhere:
In every drawer I opened
On every doorpost
I passed
When I lay down
And when I rose up.

Somehow
One of the ten lost tribes
Had wandered
Out of the desert
And all of them were living
In my house.

Since then
I have become accustomed
To their ways.
Of course

I never acknowledge
Their presence.
Who knows
What they would do
If their secret were known?

They have traveled
In exile
Ever since they were born,
Following the path of the exodus
Wherever it leads them.
Somehow
They still fulfill
The rituals
Carved out
Of so many years of wandering
Blessing the moon
At night
Counting the stars
Casting their sins into the water.

During the day
They search everywhere
For the land that has been lost
At night
They hide
From the unsuspecting
In closets filled with invisible families
In drawers crowded with sorrows
On shelves full of their sad
Songs.

They even inhabit
My dreams
There
Above all
They are at home.

C O M M E N T A R Y

My favorite writers are the obsessive kind, who keep returning to the same themes and imagery, like William Blake or Franz Kafka or Henri Michaux. They created a personal mythology, which nevertheless rings true. It might be said that they kept trying to write the same poem or story over and over, but it always turned out to be a little different. Observing the pattern of these variations is one of the fascinations of reading these authors. They force us into becoming intimate with their myths, and in the process we make them our own.

I have a similar view of Jewish tradition. The myths and legends of Jewish lore made their way into the Bible, and from there echoes and variants of these same themes are obsessively recounted in the rabbinic fantasies of the Talmud and *midrash*, the Kabbalah, medieval Jewish folklore, Hasidic lore, and even in the oral tales gathered by modern ethnologists that are found in the YIVO Archives in New York and the Israel Folktale Archives in Haifa. Thus each generation has reimagined the Bible and recast its stories and themes in its own way.

One of the most popular Jewish myths concerns the Ten Lost Tribes. This legend grows out of a historical catastrophe—the conquest of the northern Kingdom of Israel in 722 B.C.E., where ten of the twelve Jewish tribes made their home. From a historical perspective, it seems likely that the ten tribes were scattered and forced to abandon their religion. They almost certainly assimilated. But in Jewish folklore they are still out there, somewhere. There are hundreds of accounts of where the lost tribes can be found—in every country imaginable—but the most popular legend holds that they make their home on the other side of the river Sambatyon. This mythical river is said to run six days of the week, throwing up rocks as high as a house, so than no one can cross it, while on the Sabbath it magically comes to a rest. But of course the pious ones of the ten lost tribes are unable to cross then, since it would be a desecration of the Sabbath.

The myth of the lost tribes was one of those that haunted me the most. I wrote about it for the first time in 1969. That summer I drove with a friend from St. Louis to Berkeley, California. Along the way we stopped in Boulder, Colorado. We left in great spirits, but by the time we got to Boulder, we were already starting to feel exhausted. I felt like a wanderer in a strange land, and I thought of the ten lost tribes. I imagined that the tenth lost tribe was the most lost of all, and I wrote the following tale:

How the Tenth Tribe Lost Its Words

For years after the separation from their brothers the tenth lost tribe paused at dusk, raised up their tents, and assembled for the holy services. But in the thirty-ninth year they could not agree on where to seek the promised land, and one day when they had assembled for prayer no words sang out, for somehow they had lost the word *open*, and from that day on the scroll remained tightly closed.

Divining the fate this sign foretold, the prophets so frightened the people that no man dared lie with his wife. Instead all stretched out alone and discovered the silence of their empty hands, and by morning they had lost the word *hold*.

Soon afterwards their wanderings were cut short. Day after day they stayed in their tents and refused to continue their journey. At last they agreed among themselves that this place was their home, and that day they lost the word *search*.

Before long not only the people, but the animals, the birds, and even the winds had become silent. And within a year no one could speak their ancient tongue; its words were scattered through the desert like clouds of dust.

A year or so later I came back to the idea of a lost tribe and imagined it hidden in a library. This one also took the form of a parable, "The Barbarians":

During the night they hide themselves in the library. No one, they have learned from long experience, suspects their presence there. In vain, hour after hour, their hands repeat what was imprinted at the time of their first notable appearance on the planet. Since then their numbers have steadily decreased, and for thousands of years they have only managed to slow their extinction. Still, they know nothing of this success, for their primal law never permits them an instant of contentment. Nor are they aware of the other libraries filled nightly with the gesturings of their brothers, for all outside communication broke down centuries ago, and each group believes themselves the last to survive. And invariably the night itself is spent too soon, for at the first evidence of dawn, always unexpected, they rush out to hide from the unsuspecting, and search for the forests that no longer exist.

After writing this piece, I did not return to the subject of a lost tribe for more than twenty years. Then, sometime in the late 1980s or early 1990s I wrote the poem "Signs of the Lost Tribe," the third incarnation of this theme.

I cannot be certain about the date of the poem because after writing it I somehow forgot about it. It stayed in a pile of drafts for several years until one day I came across it, and at first I couldn't even remember writing it. Now I came back to it and took it through a substantial number of drafts until I felt it was finished. In the process I combined it with another poem I had recently written, called "The Lost Tribe:"

> They have traveled
> In exile
> Ever since they were born.

> All kinds of spirits
> Travel with them
> Wandering spirits
> Still following the path of the Exodus
> Wherever it leads them.
>
> They too cannot bear to abandon
> A quest that has lasted
> So long.

These lines were condensed into the fourth stanza of "Signs of the Lost Tribe." I regretted losing "all kinds of spirits travel with them" and the last stanza, but I didn't find a place for them in the combined poem.

Looking back at the genesis of "Signs of the Lost Tribe," I can see a direct connection to the parable I wrote in Boulder and to the timid barbarians hiding in the library. But there are two major changes in the theme. First, in "Signs of the Lost Tribe" the tribes are not hiding in the forest or in a library, but in my own home. They have infiltrated my life. Indeed, I read the poem as meaning that they live inside me, which is why they are most at home in my dreams. This last notion echoes the Jungian concept of the collective unconscious, in which past generations continue to bestow their blessings and curses on us from within our psyches.

Second, the Jewish element was much more prominent than in the previous works. The lines "On every doorpost / I passed / When I lay down / And when I rose up" intentionally echo the words of the *Shema*, the central prayer in Judaism: *You shall teach them to your children. Speak of them when you walk along the way, when you lie down and when you rise up. Bind them as a sign upon your arm, and let them be as frontlets before your eyes. Place them upon the doorposts of your house and upon your gates* (Deuteronomy 6:7–8).

So too does "Blessing the moon / At night" refer to the prayer of the blessing of the moon that is said at the time of the new moon on Rosh Hodesh, while "Casting their sins into the water" refers to the custom of *Tashlik*, at Rosh Hashanah, when bread crumbs are scattered at a body of water as a way of casting off the sins of the past year. However, "Counting the stars" does not refer to an actual Jewish ritual. It's an example of poetic license.

In my life I am not much of an observant Jew. But for years I've been aware of a voice (or voices) within me that still hungers for ritual. One way of reading this poem is to see the tribe suffering over the lack of ritual, which has been its hallmark for so long. In a somewhat surreal way, the poem also recalls Jewish history, blending the Exodus from Egypt with the wanderings of the Jews and especially of the lost tribes. I closely identified with this myth of wandering eternally in exile.

In time I found that I liked this version of the myth of the ten lost tribes best because it was both personal and collective. I felt more connected to it than to the preceding versions, because it had captured a personal myth of my own. It was my own tribe, living in my life, but it was also a fertile Jewish myth, with a long life of its own.

Alan Shapiro

Alan Shapiro was born in 1952 in Boston, Massachusetts. He was educated at Brandeis University and is currently Professor of English and Creative Writing at the University of North Carolina, Chapel Hill. He is the author of *The Dead Alive and Busy* (U of Chicago P, 2000), *In Praise of the Impure: Poetry and the Ethical Imagination* (Triquarterly Books, 1993), and several collections of poetry, including *Covenant* (U of Chicago P, 1991), *Mixed Company* (U of Chicago P, 1996). He is also the author of a collection of essays entitled *The Last Happy Occasion* (U of Chicago P, 1996), and the memoir *Vigil* (U of Chicago P, 1996). He has also been a recipient of a Guggenheim.

The Bath

When he called me to help him from the tub that he had somehow,
despite his blindness, palsied hands, bad back and shoulder,

gotten himself into without falling, so in the water's heat,
his body nearly forgotten, he could rest and doze,

but now lay shivering in, naked before me, helpless,
the penis slack and floating beneath the belly fat,

the spindleshanks, loose swags of flesh along the arms,
we needed customary speech but knew no custom.

This was a desolate place. Forget Ham and his father's, "Cursed
be Canaan, a slave of slaves shall he be to his brothers."

There was no curse or blessing here. If there were guides,
or avatars among us, speaking the words for us

to speak, of broken covenants, of dereliction,
and redress, we heard them only as the faint,

miasmal whispering of our embarrassment.
Forget Aeneas and Anchises. There was no place

for us to go to after I turned my back, and knelt,
and with his arm around my neck, lifted him slowly

piggyback from the water, his head against mine,
our faces there in the mirror facing us, side by side,

with nothing to say except he's okay, I can leave now,
god damn it he can dry himself, and so I let him.

COMMENTARY

The identity of the Jewish-American poet (like the identity of any American
poet of any racial or ethnic stripe) inheres in the hyphen between the modifiers.
My identity is quintessentially American because of its impurity, its mongrel
status, its jerry-built construction, pieced together as it is from a wide variety of
histories, which are in turn informed by even wider and more heterogeneous
histories. My identity is what it is because I read the Torah as a kid; because
Yiddish idioms and intonations permeated the American English that my par-
ents and grandparents spoke; because my grandfather on my father's side had
been conscripted into the Czar's army and ran away to the New World where he
became a big-shot meat dealer—Philip Shapiro, M.D., is how he'd introduce
himself; because I grew up hearing stories like this on both sides of my family,
stories of immigration, success and failure in the New World, stories that reit-
erated the Biblical stories of exodus and desert wandering. My identity is what
is because of Adolf Hitler whose evil I grew up hearing about at every dinner
conversation; because so many of my neighbors were Holocaust survivors who
warned me if I didn't learn Hebrew and get bar mitzvahed and live a good Jew-
ish life I'd be finishing the work that Hitler started; my identity is what it is be-
cause, despite these admonitions, I hated Hebrew school, hated being stuck in
a classroom learning a language no one I knew spoke while all my gentile
friends were out in the playground playing basketball, and so in protest I re-
fused to learn a word of it, and, much to my parents' embarrassment, stayed
back three years in a row and nearly failed to get bar mitzvahed ("no better than
a Nazi," my Hebrew teachers used to say of me). My identity is what it is be-
cause during the Cuban missile crisis I was certain I and everyone on the planet
was going to die in a nuclear holocaust; it's what it is because of Vietnam, be-
cause of the Six Day War, because of Woodstock, and because while my par-
ents and their friends were singing "If I were a rich man, a baba biba biba baba
biba biba biba bum," I and my friends were singing "Who put the bob in the

bob shebob shebop, who put the bam in the bamalama ding dong." My identity is also what it is because I write English and was schooled in the Classical and Christian literary traditions of English literature, traditions that are themselves edgy amalgams of different languages, different conquered and conquering cultures, city-states, empires—because the language I speak and write in is itself the effect of dispossession and displacement, murder, rape, and interbreeding.

The experience presented in "The Bath" is influenced by classical and Jewish lore. This is a poem about the difficulty of expressing filial piety in a society bereft of mediating ritual. Hovering over the poem is the Jewish tradition of filial respect, emblematized by the Biblical story of Ham and Noah. Noah curses Ham because Ham gazed upon his naked father as he slept. The curse itself affirms the moral order that the son had momentarily upset. In an orthodox household, or traditional society, where custom and ritual shape every aspect of daily life, a son would know exactly how to care for an ailing parent; and if he screwed up in some way or another, he'd know what prayers to say, or what penances to do, to make amends. On the other hand, in the classical literary tradition the great exemplar of which is the *Aeneid*, filial piety is synonymous with imperial ambition and a trans-personal sense of destiny. Aeneas carries his infirm father on his back out of the burning ruins of Troy, preserving the past as he embarks on a journey to establish the future of Rome.

Both these stories are a kind of afterimage of a world no longer available to me or my father. They help define by contrast the "nakedness" of contemporary life, the paucity of mediating ritual. Our freedom from the past leaves us naked before each other, and, in some ways as a condition of that nakedness, utterly at a loss for what to do, or what to say. He has nothing to teach me, I have nothing to learn, beyond the moment of our embarrassment.

For good or ill, in its mix of the contemporary and the traditional, the Biblical and the classical, high language and American slang, in its estrangements and devotions, its sense of the past as both essential to an understanding of the present and inadequate as a guide for what to do or how to act, "The Bath" is a deeply American poem, and maybe also a deeply Jewish one. Perhaps one reason why the Jew has been a favorite whipping boy of the Western world is because in his homelessness the Jew has always been the most uncomfortable reminder of history itself, of change, of difference, to the pedigree-loving cultures he has moved among. The Jew was the first American long before America existed.

Hal Sirowitz

Hal Sirowitz, a well-known performance poet, is the author of several volumes of poetry, including *Mother Said: Poems* (Crown, 1996), and *My Therapist Said: Poems* (Crown, 1998). A native of Flushing, Queens, he teaches special-education students at a local grade school; he has also received a NEA Fellowship and appeared on MTV's "Spoken Word Unplugged."

Sons

We're Jewish, Father said.
So we don't believe in Christ.
If God wanted us to worship Jesus
He would have arranged for us to be born
into an Italian family. I have nothing
against Him. He was probably a very nice man.
You have to give Him credit for trying.
A lot of people still believe He's the Son of God.
I don't know what He had against His real father.
But if you ever did that to me,
said you were someone else's son, I'd be insulted.

COMMENTARY

I read "Sons" at a café in Atlanta, Georgia. After the reading a woman with a large crucifix around her neck told me that just last week she found out for the first time that Jews didn't Believe in Christ. She wanted to know if it was true. I told her it was. She asked me how it made me feel. I said it made me feel like an outsider, but I was used to it.

The poem is about having to exist outside the dominant religion. Being Jewish made me feel like an outsider. Chanukah wasn't as much as Christmas. I got a small present seven days in a row. My Christian friends were getting gigantic toys, like bicycles. Finally my mother said that since she didn't want me to feel left out of Christmas, because she knew I was bombarded by it each day—songs on the radio, trees in the stores—she decided to give me a big present on Christmas.

When I was in college I studied world religions, and was very impressed with the sayings of Christ. I loved looking at paintings of His birth and crucifixion. But I could never take that step into belief. My rabbi told my religious study class when I was fifteen that the difference between Jews and Christians was that they thought Jesus was divine, but we thought He was just a great man. I was a secret admirer, but believing in Him would be eradicating my past. Jehovah's Witnesses and Mormons ring my doorbell all the time. When I tell them I'm not interested in converting because I'm Jewish they get even more excited, and act like my conversion would be a bigger prize. But I can't go against my roots and beliefs.

"Sons" is my Jewish manifesto. The rock group The Kinks have a line in one of their songs: "I'm not like everybody else." Ray Davies keeps repeating that line until it's a proud chant. My poem "Sons" is like that. I'm saying I'm Jewish, therefore I'm different. But instead of feeling bad since I'm not like most other people, I want to embrace it.

Gerald Stern

Gerald Stern was born in 1925 in Pittsburgh, and educated at the University of Pittsburgh and Columbia University. For many years a Professor of English in the Creative Writing Program at the University of Iowa, he now divides his time between rural New Jersey and New York City. He is the author of ten collections of poetry including *Last Blue* (Norton, 2000). His recent *This Time: New and Selected Poems* (Norton, 1998) won the National Book Award. He has also been the recipient of a Guggenheim and a NEA grant.

Paris

As I recall the meal I ate was liver
with mashed potatoes, and out of simple courtesy
I kept what I could in my briefcase or half hidden
under the table; I think an Underwood brought me
two months free living and the Polish architect
I sold it to whose teeth the Germans had smashed
at Auschwitz it gave him seven months at least,
depending on other forces. The whole thing
lasted maybe a year for by my reckoning
when I was ready to leave the stores were already
full of new things and they were cleaning the bridges
and polishing the squares. My own time
was somewhere between the Ordeal and the Recovery,
but there was food enough. The one thing
I remember about him we had the same
name in Hebrew though I don't know what he was called
in Polish—I hope not Gerald—we always walked
after lunch and stopped for coffee. By my
reckoning he was in his forties. I went
to Italy on that money, it was my first
grant, a little hopeless by later standards,
but that only made it easier to practice
deprivation—in one or two years—ketchup
with beans, seven pounds of lamb for a dollar,

bread eight cents a loaf. It was
more loyal that way, I was so stubborn I did it
ten years too long, maybe twenty, it was
my only belief, what I went there for.

COMMENTARY

I may have written "Paris" in ironic opposition to the dozens of other "Paris" poems, written over the course of the last eighty or so years, that celebrate the wonder of being there and the special grace of having been chosen as a witness. My "Paris" has as its subject buying and selling, "handling," as we say, and the need to live by one's wits, on air, as it were, as a condition for "receiving the blessing" and "being in the presence." It may be, though, that however I protest, I have only come through the back gate, and Paris was for me also the place of grace and enlightenment, only I insisted on its being on my own terms, as I always do. The Jewishness of the poem is a little more complicated. The events take place in a now famous Jewish restaurant on the rue de Rosier, in the old Jewish quarter; the person I negotiate with—in the poem—is a Polish Jew who was imprisoned at Auschwitz; and the "business" we do is certainly "Jewish" business, though a Jew-monger and a Jew might see it in different lights. But the poem is Jewish in a deeper sense: in the passionate and even obstinate devotion to an idea in which one's whole life is committed, or sacrificed, or put at risk, much in the manner of Talmudic devotion. And in the idea of separation and even a kind of secrecy in order to be in a condition to pursue that idea. So that "Paris," however it contains the typical historic attitude to that city, whether it be the nineties of the last century or the twenties and fifties of our own, also stands for something else, a different kind of devotion, involving belief, not just sensation.

When I arrived in Paris, in September 1949, Europe was still struggling to recover from the wartime destruction, dislocation, and confusion. There were not enough goods being manufactured, the demand was sudden and extensive, and American dollars, and American products, were highly valued. I was on the World War II GI Bill of Rights and received seventy-five dollars a month as a student at the Sorbonne, but like the others I was able to live on a dollar or so a day and save the rest. In addition, we were able to get maybe an additional 10 percent on greenbacks by trading in the market at the Left Bank cafés, a universal—even public—practice that was ignored or even encouraged by the French authorities. I trailed an Englishman one day on the metro to my restaurant—it was Goldenberg's—and stood outside while he traded my dollars back into francs—it turned out to be an additional 30 percent, I discovered later, and after he left I went inside myself. He was Jewish and from the East End. I remember we both wore belted raincoats out of some bad Bogey film. I suspect my collar was turned up, for style or against the bad autumn weather. Inside Goldenberg's I ate, talked a little with my neighbors, in Yiddish and French, earned their trust after one or two visits, and found myself, after a while, to be a kind of minor operator in the unofficial market. Goldenberg's then was an older style sit-down restaurant, with worn "white" tablecloths, and not the delicatessen it later became, nor was it famous enough yet to be selected as a bombing target by patriotic Palestinians, as it later was. Business is business I guess, though when I think of it, almost a half century later, I feel more than a little guilty making a profit from other young students, and artists, but I at least wasn't in serious soup like my friend McClean who dealt in passports, gasoline coupons, and false identities, and was on several "wanted" lists, he of the wispy beard, a good Scotchman from Pittsburgh. In addition to money, I sold typewriters, cameras, and such. Someone who came over on the Isle de France with a cumbersome new Royal or Underwood which she paid maybe forty-five dollars for was happy to get rid of it for twenty or twenty-five after a heavenly year where the terrific novel gave way to other sweet things and only a few pages were typed out. I got a hundred, they probably got two. I always have only one foot in the muck, I keep a humorous attitude and I am easily bored, so I got out of the business quickly, when I made enough to live in Italy for a while. Selling a few *machines à écrires* for the privilege of seeing Giotto in Padua and Simone Martini in Sienna wasn't such a bad deal.

Clearly I have in mind, whether it operates consciously or unconsciously, not only the role of the Jew in commerce but his underlying role of being forced, in an unsympathetic and even contemptuous world, into unpleasant, degrading, and uncreative activities. My Polish architect might have been a true master builder, or even a good draftsman, but his body and soul were ruined by the Germans, and of course the good French, though they let him survive, gave him no opportunity to practice his profession, assuming he could ever be in a state to do so. The Christian world both enabled and forced Jews to practice a certain economic role—a familiar story—and then victimized and persecuted them for doing so—another. Nor was their greedy solemn sanctimonious behavior confined to the Middle Ages. I have neat stories from my own life. The question here is what that all has to do with my trading on the rue de Rosiers, and what the poem is doing. I was not forced into commerce by Christian authorities; I had more than enough money to live on in decent poverty, and I could change my condition at any time by going home and getting a job or going back for serious graduate work. It was a time of great opportunity and I had more than one foot up. I was doing what I did for adventure, because the opportunity was there, as a lark, out of a little greed and out of contempt for authority. I think also out of a sense of revenge, though I don't know revenge on what, and out of the Rimbaudian view of the poet as above bourgeois practice and operating according to his own pure and separate code. Ironically, I hated commerce and abhorred selling and profit-taking, partly out of ridiculous artistic posturing, partly out of socialist idealism, and probably partly out of some small Jewish self-hatred or embarrassment. I opted more for nobility; which I called justice. I was sometimes a prophet, sometimes a harp-toting bard.

The poem, as it moves through its narrative to its conclusion, treats the artist-priest in contradictory and inconsistent ways. Sometimes it's matter-of-fact, as in lines 1–8; sometimes it's ironical and self-conscious, as in lines 19–25; sometimes almost on the artist-priest's own terms, as in lines 25–28. Everything depends on the language and the context of the language, as everything depends on the tone and gesture behind that language. "Practicing deprivation"—or anticipating doing it—by subsisting on ketchup and beans is a slightly funny ritual activity, by virtue of the language I use and its ordering, even if I did do that, which I did, for over six months once. And it's absurd to think of eating cheap food, or even starving a little, as the one condition of belief. Except I am clearly talking about another line of sacrifice even as I talk about food.

As far as the devotion and commitment, what I claim as the Jewish quality only in a deeper sense, that is the critical point of the poem. Jews may be responsible for the devotion to one God, but the passionate devotion to a single—or singular—idea has to be as old as the race, and the sacrificing of one's life for art and the elevation of art over all things—even the opposition of the artist to those things—was common to the point of banality from the time of the Romantic movement on and existed in various ways during and after the Renaissance and even among the ancients. My poem doesn't beat its artistic chest until the last line, or the last few lines. I was saved from that posturing just as I was saved from posturing about Paris by focusing on some other thing. I think my own commitment, in the poem, though it is grounded in artistic values, always has the other values in mind and never escapes the idea of responsibility, and even duty, to those values. I think its very attitude to the (precious) Paris poem is a case in point, for "holy" Paris is exactly the equal of "holy" artist. Nor is it accident that the restaurant I write about was the one chosen as a hated Jewish symbol, nor is it an accident that the person I traded with, and became friends with, was at Auschwitz. Nor that food dominates the poem so much. Nor that my "deprivation," which was voluntary and rather light and easy, was so connected to his, which was forced, and hideous.

I am asked over and over what it is in my poems that is "Jewish." I answer, maybe a little differently each time, the rhythms of the language, the subject matter, the humor; the brazenness, the breaking of bounds, the confrontiveness, the close interaction with others; the sense of outrage and anger; the bitterness;

the love of the past, the sense of loss, the sense of justice; the addiction to things, the naming; the lack of embarrassment at emotion; the ritual, the mourning. And I have to say, like a clock, that non-Jewish writers share these things and many Jewish writers do not.

"Paris" is a kind of meditation on my own life at a certain critical point. I had been, over a period of two or three years, declaring myself a poet, and the trip to Europe, although I still protected myself by calling myself "student," was for me definitive. The fact is, I went to Paris because it was cheap to live there—a few months earlier I was on my way to Mexico and the car broke down, an old Nash. So the concept of cheap living, and living by my wits, was already in my mind. Before I declared for poetry I was on my way to a career in labor relations, law, or social work, absolutely normal behavior for a Jewish boy in the late 1940s in Pittsburgh, and the move into poetry represented, as far as my corollary thinking, a swerving and even a betrayal of sorts as I abandoned Eugene Debs for T. S. Eliot, one belief for another. Though I came back, in my own way.

I suppose my "dieting," though it had to do with economy, inevitably brings up the issue of sacrifice, and I can't use that word without the religious association. That is, I pay attention not so much to what I didn't eat—in my deprivation—whatever kind of chop or steak or pasta it might have been I did without, but to what I did eat, the beans, the fat, the bread, what God might be pleased with. My sacrifice would unite me with Him who is the God of poetry and Him who is the God of Mercy. Or Her. Or it would unite me with other like souls, past and present, or it would put me in the right state. I'm being a little playful, but not altogether. I was enabled through denial, stubborness, devotion, to touch a hem or two. I even surprised myself. Though the sacrifice was greater than I expected.

C. K. Williams

C. K. Williams was born 1936 in Newark, New Jersey, and educated at Bucknell University and the University of Pennsylvania. He is currently teaching at Princeton University. The author of ten books of poems, his most recent collection, *Repair* (Farrar, Straus, & Giroux, 1999), won the Pulitzer prize. His *Selected Poems* (Farrar, Straus, & Giroux) appeared in 1994. He is also the author of *The Vigil: Poems* (Farrar, Straus & Giroux, 1997). He won the National Book Critics Circle Award for *Flesh and Blood* (Farrar, Straus, & Giroux, 1997).

The Vessel

I'm trying to pray; one of the voices of my mind says, "God, please
    help me do this,"
but another voice intervenes: "How conceive God's interest would be
    to help you believe?"

Is this prayer? Might this exercise be a sign, however impure, that
    such an act's under way,
that I'd allowed myself, or that God had allowed me, to surrender to
    this need in myself?

What makes me think, though, that the region of my soul in which all
    this activity's occurring
is a site which God might consider an engaging or even an acceptable
    spiritual location?

I thought I'd kept the lack of a sacred place in myself from myself,
    therefore from God.
Is *this* prayer, recognizing that my isolation from myself is a secret I no
    longer can keep?

Might prayer be an awareness that even our most belittling secrets are
    absurd before God?
Might God's mercy be letting us think we haven't betrayed those
    secrets to Him until now?

If I believe that there exists a thing I can call God's mercy, might I be
    praying at last?
If I were, what would it mean: that my sad loneliness for God might
    be nearing its end?

I imagine that were I in a real relation with God instead of just being
    lonely for Him,
the way I'd apprehend Him would have nothing to do with secrets I'd
    kept, from Him or myself.

I'd empty like a cup: that would be prayer, to empty, then fill with a
    substance other than myself.
Empty myself of what, though? And what would God deign fill me
    with except my own prayer?

Is this prayer now, believing that my offering to God would be what
    He'd offered me?
I'm trying to pray, but I know that whatever I'm doing I'm not: why
    aren't I, when will I?

COMMENTARY

I can't remember whether I ever really longed for god, or longed to long.
Maybe that's because my first needs for god were so much determined by vari-
ous theodicies. It offended me even when I was very young that god could
seem to be so obstinately dedicated not only to permitting evil on the human
earth, but apparently to maximizing it as much as possible. Later, when my
daughter was born, the Vietnam war was going full force, full, insane, irra-
tional, absolutely unnecessary force; napalm and cluster bombs, rhetoric and
lies, Nixon and Kissinger. No earthly predicate could seem to account for the
fact that somewhere in the universe creatures as lovely and vulnerable and es-
sential as my child were being torn to bits and thrown away like Kleenex.
Whose fault would it be but a god's? If a god dared to offer glimpses of his
being, dared to assert in any way his omnipotence, how could he then define
himself as capable of allowing within himself that much vileness, that much
complete evil; within himself, for isn't he supposed to encompass everything,
to be everything?

    So all the readings I'd done in Buber's lovely metaphysics of generosity, in
Scholem's evocation of meaning-crazed kabbalists; all the brooding I'd done

on the Shoah, which wasn't my evil, but the dream of evil that history had dreamed for me; and all the hints and glitters the world had shown me of the exultant-transcendent, turned against that being who claimed to be at the source of being, and it was then perhaps I came closest within myself to feeling I was in any relation at all with something beyond.

But all this of course is the kindergarten of religion. That's what a rabbi from Hillel said in order to humiliate me in front of my "brothers" the year I was in a fraternity at college. He was giving a talk to us, presumably to teach us something, and I asked him a question about afterlife, or original sin, or some such thing I'd picked up from my first immersions in Dante and Milton, and he said, "You're in the kindergarten of religion," and all the brothers, who found my ambitions to culture and intellect hilarious anyway, roared with delight. Snidely, the rabbi said it, with evident pleasure in my discomfort, which didn't surprise me since all the rabbis I'd ever met up until then were insensitive, indifferent, sometimes frankly cruel people. The pale, soft, unsmiling, crushingly tedious rabbi who drove me through my bar mitzvah studies was cruel in his indifference to anything alive in what presumably might have been called my soul. His brother-in-law, who taught one year of Hebrew school, was virile and husky, but his greatest pleasure was to lift us out of our seats by our ears if we whispered or yawned, and to drag us howling across the bleak synagogue vestibule that served as a classroom.

My father, though, conceived the idea that I should have the bar mitzvah of an overachiever, though I hardly fit the description, so I sat every day for a year with the dough-faced rabbi, who smelled fifty years older than he was, so I could mount the podium and parrot almost the entire Friday night and Saturday morning Sabbath service. I wore a blue suit, received presents, most memorably certificates saying trees had been planted for me in Israel, a place it took me another forty or so years to bring myself to visit, and where I couldn't find my trees but did meet enough remarkable people and make enough good friends to bind me even more inexorably than I already was to that maddeningly ordinary little country, a country as ready to befoul its meaning and its morals as any other. And I saw there, too, whole neighborhoods of men in black who looked like my bar mitzvah rabbi, and who thought of others unlike themselves with as much human kindness and tolerance and love as the bully from Hillel. Their most impressive achievement as far as I could tell was to look picturesque as they battered their heads against a wall and moaned with a despair they merited and an ecstasy they didn't.

But then comes this other thing, this prayer-thing, which seems in some absurd way to have nothing to do with anything else, but still brought with it moments, though I think perhaps they're all over now, when I would long towards the god I knew had to hover out beyond questions of theodicy, beyond issues of theology: I called on him to resolve that bleak, obsessive question the yes-no mind of the mortal has to ask because we can never have a yes without a perhaps or a no; the question of why existence at all, and if so, why then the twice why of the nonexistence of being dead?

And yet, so much loveliness the world has revealed to me during my life with it; wouldn't it be ungrateful to ask for still more? The attention flags, though, the light dulls for moments or hours or years; the theodicies of consciousness, too, can take you: of how inattentive (might one say sinful?) self can be in beholding what is to be beheld. And still, the temptation again to prayer: Is it that one feels a need, or more than a need, to hallow existence, sanctify it, find what in it hasn't been sufficiently praised? So, yes, one does imagine being emptied and filled, even for a single instant, not with rapture—mortal being implies sufficient rapture—but with the emotion of response the very notion of divinity despite all ever promises and, for me, alas, ever withholds.

Eleanor Wilner

Eleanor Wilner, born in 1937 in Cleveland, Ohio, was educated at Goucher College and Johns Hopkins University. She currently resides in Philadelphia, Pennsylvania. A MacArthur Fellow, her most recent volume of poetry is *Reversing the Spell: New and Selected Poems* (Copper Canyon P, 1998). She has also written *Gathering the Winds: Visionary Imagination and Radical Transformation of Self and Society* (Johns Hopkins UP, 1975).

Miriam's Song

Death to the first-born sons, always—
the first fruits to the gods of men.
She had not meant it so, standing in the reeds
back then, the current tugging at her skirt
like hands, she had only meant to save
her little brother, Moses,
red-faced with rage when he was given
to the river. The long curve of the Nile
would keep their line, the promised land
around the bend. Years later
when the gray angel, like the smoke trail
of a dying comet, passed by the houses
with blood smeared over doorways,
Miriam, her head hot in her hands, wept
as the city swelled with the wail of Egypt's women.
Then she straightened up, slowly plaited
her hair and wound it tight around her head,
drew her long white cloak with its deep blue threads
around her, went out to watch the river
where Osiris, in his golden funeral barge,
floated by forever . . .

as if in offering, she placed a basket on the river,
this time an empty one, without the precious cargo
of tomorrow. She watched it drift a little
from the shore. She threw one small stone in it,

then another, and another, till its weight
was too much for the water and it slowly turned
and sank. She watched the Nile gape and shudder,
then heal its own green skin. She went
to join the others, to leave one ruler
for another, one Egypt for the next.
Some nights you still can see her, by some river
where the willows hang, listening to the heavy tread
of armies, those sons once hidden dark
in baskets, and in her mind she sees her sister,
the black-eyed Pharaoh's daughter, lift the baby
like a gift from the brown flood waters
and take him home to save him, such a pretty
boy and so disarming, as his dimpled hands
reach up, his mouth already open
for the breast.

COMMENTARY

> And the Lord said unto Moses, Go in unto Pharaoh:
> for I have hardened his heart, and the heart of his servants,
> that I might shew these my signs before him:
>   —*Exodus* 10: 1

Welcome back to the story—God who ascribes to His own agency the harden-
ing of Pharaoh's heart, and worse—that He has made Pharaoh implacable to
justify a display of His own divine power, a weapon's test of plagues to cause
untold suffering, and I mean "untold" quite literally, since those who suffer
God's display of omnipotency get no lines—though, when the final plague, the
death of the firstborn, comes down on Egypt: "There was a great cry in Egypt,
for there was not a house where there was not one dead."

   She must have heard it then, as I hear it now—the great cry in the night for
the slaughter of innocents. Egyptian, Hebrew: It is all the same. So awakens
Miriam, a transpersonal figure in the ancient guise, but returning now with the
blood of the twentieth century coursing in her veins and with the eyes of our
contemporary—a figure revived from the legendary past by the urgency of our
own moment, and the need to envision that past anew.

   In my mind's eye, I see her by time's river, a figure who wishes to save
the seed of a people and who lives on to become, this time, not a celebrant of

victory but a figure of mourning. As she hears the wailing of her sisters, she knows the irony of the distance between intention and consequence, how the exodus of one people is stained with the innocent blood of another.

She comes to understand the world as a place of exile, where one army, and one designated enemy, replaces the next. But inside this awareness is another possible future: one where divine sanction for slaughtering innocents has been threatened by the realism of the sympathetic imagination, by sisterly feeling; where lives are of ultimate value and are made equivalent; where the tribal gives way to the ethical.

The moment when Miriam draws "her long white cloak with its deep blue threads around her," she is redefining herself and a tradition at whose headwaters she stands, using the old prayer shawl for a new conviction, and one which strikes at the heart of the old fiction of nation, with its story-God who provokes tyrants in order to prove His power, and His special protection of a people, by wholesale murder.

And here is a mass murder that mirrors exactly the nation that set the story in motion: the original order by the Pharaoh to murder the firstborn (sons) of the Hebrews, an edict that brought Miriam and her mother to place Moses afloat in a basket on the Nile in the first place. How many more times will the hands at the Seder table raise and call down, accompanied by drops of wine, like blood, terrible plagues on a whole people, and on their helpless young? How long will this be enacted? In the name of one people's freedom, how can we bear to celebrate the suffering of others? Are we indeed so free? And if the hard hearts of tyrants and the desire for revenge are in our human nature, isn't it time to outgrow the ascription of those base emotions to a Moral Being beyond us? If God is to save us from our enemies, who will save us from ourselves? And who, anyway, are "we"?

What would Miriam do after she had "wept / as the city swelled with the wail of Egypt's women," when she understood that what had been done *to* her tribe had now been done *by* them (under the aegis of God's agency) to another? The question has a long trail of tears, as well as fresh historical urgency. I did not know what she would do; I simply watched her as she went to the river, as she invented and enacted a new and somewhat riddling ritual. Its enactment is based on a knowledge given her by all the intervening centuries between then and now, both original instance and emblem of what repeats.

And like all rituals, this one rises from a sense of the sacred and, though it invites interpretations, the meaning is embodied in the action; we may investigate its sense, but only the action is fully adequate to its meanings. With what we might call cognitive economy, a ritual is always a single action with multiple meanings.

Shortly before I wrote this, I was visiting a young friend with two small children. I honestly forget which of the many bloodbaths of recent times it was, but—to the media blare of virtuous self-justification—the United States had just obliterated the lives of a number of humans, most of them innocent of anything except living in the wrong country at the wrong time. Sick with outrage, we were talking about these endless wars, the terror bombing of cities, the waste, too, of soldiers' young lives, and she suddenly burst out: "We should stop having their children until they stop this killing." I mentioned Lysistrata. "Yes," she said, "the idea is ancient, but it hasn't been tried yet." In part, her words echo in Miriam's action.

Another friend after reading this poem had mentioned that this was the trope—this placing of stones, one by one, in a floating object until it sank—that was being used by the ecology movement as a warning about where our heedless interventions in natural ecosystems are leading. I hadn't known that, but it seemed a rhyme with another reading of Miriam's ritual: a historical statement, if you will, of instance after instance of ironic consequence of actions motivated by idealism and desperation, with their admixture of bloodlust and vengeful desire for power, instance after instance of liberator turned tyrant—until the hope and the innocence once contained in that basket sink into the waters. And the loss, the deliberate giving up, of historical innocence may be the best and only protection for the innocent of the world who deserve protection. For who is it, who has clean hands?

This figure by the river recovers and reproves the two Biblical sources behind it; one is obviously the story from Exodus, the other is from Psalms. That second source breaks into visibility in the lines "some nights you still can see her, by some river / where the willows hang, listening to the heavy tread of armies. . . ." In those willows hung the harps in Psalm 137 that begins so plangently: *"By the rivers of Babylon, there we sat down, yea, we wept, when we remembered Zion."* But how does it end, this lovely song of exile that asks: *"How shall we sing the Lord's song in a strange land?"* It ends, it is necessary to remember, with these two bloodthirsty verses:

8 *O daughter of Babylon, who art to be destroyed, happy shall he be, that rewardeth thee as thou hast served us.*
9 *Happy shall he be, that taketh and dasheth thy little ones against the stones.*

Happy he may be, but she, sister of lamentation, sister of the Women in Black, is horrified at this delight in the dashing of infants against the stones. For Miriam is sister to "the black-eyed Pharaoh's daughter," as she is to the daughter of Babylon—for we women are all "daughters of Babylon," our gender used as trope for the target zone, as well as women exiled from sanity in a world not of promised lands but of warring nations with armies, led by Pharaohs of one stripe or another, bastions of inequity and humanly engineered afflictions. So it may be these very stones of Psalm 137:9 that Miriam invokes as she throws them, one by one, into the basket of God's chosen, so that the stones sink that self-conception rather than be used in the terrible way in which the Psalm rejoices.

These stones speak, in the effect of their weight, with the touchstone of the real. Here is gravity, real bodies. Here is a measure of the ethical that shows no partiality and will not fail us. A return to the real, a recovery from the delusion of a divine sanction that makes one human life mean more or less than another, that makes body count synonymous with victory. How shall we bear a terrible history unless we change it, unless we refuse to see the headstones of the dead as the place to break yet another generation of children? And how separate our children from theirs?

Speaking of what he feels about the politics of memory and the uses of atrocity in the education of young Israelis, Professor Yehuda Elkana of Tel Aviv University, a survivor of Auschwitz, spoke for many of us less qualified when he said:

> What are children to do with such memories? The somber injunction, Remember! may easily be interpreted as a call for blind hatred. It is possible that the world at large must remember. . . . But for ourselves I see no greater educational task than to stand up for life, to build our future in this land without wallowing day in and day out in ghastly symbols, harrowing ceremonies, and somber lessons of the Holocaust. . . . The deepest political and social factor that motivates much of Israeli society in its relation with the Palestinians is a profound existential "Angst" fed by a particular interpretation of the lessons of the Holocaust and a readiness to believe that the whole world is against us, that we are the eternal victim.
>
> In this ancient belief, shared by many today, I see the tragic and paradoxical victory of Hitler. Two nations, metaphorically speaking, emerged from the ashes of Auschwitz: a minority who assert "this must never happen again" and a frightened and haunted majority who assert "this must never happen to us." If these are the only possible lessons, I for one have always held with the former. I have seen the latter as catastrophic. History and collective memory are an inseparable part of any culture; but the past is not and must not be allowed to become the dominant element determining the future and destiny of a people.

The Miriam of the poem acts from that same awareness. She is not bound by the long ago moment in which she first appeared in written form, because she lives in the mythic space of collective memory. And living memory is not what is engraved on stone, or printed on a page, but what we carry within, and, insofar as we are alive, it changes with us. So, the living Miriam, woman and emblem, rises out of history and collective memory, and, stepping out of the past with our knowledge of its future, comes both to mourn, and to prevent its repetition.

The gesture of the baby reaching up, open-mouthed, for the nurture of the world he will devastate, for so the story ordains, is disarming in both senses of the word. The meeting of those two meanings is irony, and irony of the tragic sort. For tragedy, we surely know by now, is victory's twin—and even if this story had played only once, *dyanu.*

II

┿┿

Reflections

The essays that follow offer ten reflections on Jewish American Poetry: its importance; its internal history; its place in American poetry, American Judaism, and Jewish literature in general. Written by poets, reviewers, scholars, and editors, these pieces often focus, at least in part, on poets featured earlier in this volume, including Gerald Stern, Maxine Kumin, Alicia Ostriker, Jaqueline Osherow, and Michael Castro. The essays also introduce readers to dozens of other poets, past and present, whose work has shaped—or has now begun to shape—the landscape of Jewish American poetry.

In Jewish tradition the educational practice of *chevrusa,* or pair-study, encourages students to work through a holy text two by two, reading a passage and stopping to tease out its implications. We hope that each of these essays will serve as this sort of partner, raising questions and guiding each reader to reflections of his or her own.

Reflections: Editors' Introduction

We begin with "Learning, Learning, Learning: Jewish Poetry in America," by David Bleich. In this essay, Bleich reads Jewish American poetry in the context of other Jewish American cultural artifacts: notably the movies (*The Jazz Singer,* from 1927) and the well-known fiction of Philip Roth, Norman Mailer, Saul Bellow, and other male writers who came of age in the 1950s. While these more famous works dwell on assimilation and its discontents, Bleich argues, the work of Jewish American poets offers a "stance toward Jewish culture" that is "deeper, calmer, more realistic, and more generous." Attending to poems of religious ritual, the "Yiddish bridge" from the Old World to the New, and above all to the healthy and vibrant challenges to tradition offered by Jewish women poets, Bleich introduces crucial themes that apply not only to the contemporary period but to Jewish American poetry in general. These themes return, at times with bittersweet variations, in the essays that follow.

Learning, Learning, Learning: Jewish Poetry in America

DAVID BLEICH

David Bleich, Professor of English and Education at the University of Rochester, is the author of numerous important scholarly books and is one of the principal theorists of the Reader-Response school of literary theory. His most recent book is *Know and Tell: A Writing Pedagogy of Disclosure, Genre, and Membership* (Portsmouth, N.H.: Boynton/ Cook, 1998).

In *The Vanishing American Jew*, Alan Dershowitz[1] describes how the successes of individual American Jews have led to the threat of dissolution of Jews as a people in America. Because of the increasing percentage of intermarriages, fewer Jews are born, leading to an uncertain future of Jewish culture. It is tempting to agree that *assimilation* is at work: Jews, the minority group, are marrying non-Jews, the majority, leading to the end of Jewish distinctiveness as a cultural group. Assimilation, rather than combination, is the appropriate term because the majority culture seems likely to overwhelm and replace the minority: More and more Jews, for example, get into the habit of saying "Merry Christmas." Even those who say "Happy Chanukah" do so in emulation of the majority. The Jewish nonreligious festival is mistakenly balanced against the Christian religious festival and the actual Jewish tradition of Chanukah is assimilated to Christmas by using the latter's conventions of social interaction, such as cards, gifts, and greetings. Dershowitz says the results of assimilation may be both good and bad: good because it represents the free choice of Jews in the process of flourishing, bad because prosperity is achieved at the expense of a distinctive collective identity, and possibly at the expense of survival.

Dershowitz thinks that "learning, learning, learning" is the only viable way to counteract the rapid dilution of Jewish culture. This is the principal contribution of his book: to provide a rationale for learning, practicing, and "opening up" Jewish culture, making it more self-consciously flexible and accommodating of many forms of Jewish practice and belief. His stance with regard to the survival of the Jewish People in the next century is that all Jews, not only rabbis, but especially those in learned professions, should participate in the processes of Jewish education, in order to win the "minds and hearts of our Jewish youth; . . . a little healthy competition from non-rabbinical Jewish scholars will improve Jewish education" (18). Practically, this is not exactly competition, but a self-conscious combination of perspectives: Jews are urged to study simultaneously the substance of rabbinic teachings, texts, and Jewish history as a coordinate subject with the history and culture of their native society, in this case, America, or Western civilization. This style of learning can benefit all people: Students of American poetry, for example, should also study the poetry of Jewish poets, Irish poets, English poets in America to render the poetry written in American society part of a living tradition.

In poetry, more than in fiction or drama, American Jews have striven for the combination of cultural consciousness described and prescribed by Dershowitz. Poetry written by American Jews has been and can continue to be more than a feature of "assimilation"; it is part of a redefinition of Jewish culture in a friendly society. It is not obvious that this is the case, and it is not clear why it came about as it did. But in this essay, I offer a few observations, reflections, and speculations about the character of the poetry written by American Jews. These thoughts follow from the premises of the rest of this volume, namely, that until recently the general public has noticed mainly the fiction of American Jewish men as the main contribution of Jews to American literature in this century. Allen Guttmann in 1971, for example, holds up Philip Roth, Norman Mailer, and Saul Bellow as the premier Jewish writers: those who, in the opinion of some, belong with Hemingway and Faulkner. The picture, however, is considerably more complicated, in scope and in substance. In scope, both men and women contributed considerably to fiction and to poetry, yet women's fiction and poetry by both men and women took a back seat to the fiction of writers like those just listed, as well as a few others. I will not discuss why the considerable production of fiction by Jewish women did not make it into the classrooms, but given the adverse climate toward public women in this country, it is not surprising. In poetry, however, to the extent that Jewish poets became recognized, women did so in roughly equal proportion to men. It is this phenomenon that is more of interest in this essay: I want to distinguish the stance of poets (both men and women) toward Jewish culture from the stance of male Jewish novelists. The corpus of work by American Jewish poets adds up to a site for studying assimilation, but is not an example of it. In fact, I think the efforts of poets, taken collectively, reflect relatively well the ideals described by Dershowitz as likely to help Jews survive as a people in the next century in America.

Until recently, studies of assimilation have presupposed that it refers to the overcoming, by men, of exclusions. This, for example, is what Susanne Klingenstein's book[2] describes: how Jewish men made it into the academy in the 1940s. Gradually, they did, as they did in other fields from which they were previously excluded. The success of the Hollywood studio heads who became a class of millionaires paved the way for other Jews (mostly men) to enter the world of finance. But in the academy and in finance, it is more true than not that Jewish men emulated other men in the elite class, the result being that their Jewish culture only played marginal roles in the work they did. At least, whatever roles Jewish cultural consciousness played for these successful men, it was not in view to most people. Only recently, for example, in Neal Gabler's 1988 study of the Hollywood studio heads,[3] can we begin to discern how Jewish styles and values played roles in the kind of films turned out by Hollywood. Those studying assimilation still have not paid attention to its having proceeded without affecting the underlying androcentric axioms of American society.

The male Jewish novelists who "made it" wrote about mainly male problems and from an exclusively male point of view. Women also wrote novels trying to present life from their point of view, but they were simply not recognized to an extent approaching the level of the male novelists. A good example is *Portnoy's Complaint,* Philip Roth's 1969 sensational novel, whose *caricature* of Jewish men may well have been the basis of its wide recognition. The male complaints, fulminations, hand-wringing, philosophical angst, fear of persecution occupied the pages of the popular novelists such as Roth, Mailer, Bellow, and Malamud. Even Henry Roth's earlier *Call It Sleep* cannot escape this narcissistic orientation. Although the term *complaint* is given by Roth as a parody, the depth of complaint by these male writers is unmistakable and disturbing; I do not myself wish to be identified with these versions of Jewish men.

In contrast to the situation of American Jewish poetry genres, there is some reason to suppose that the genre of the novel has had a constricting effect on the ability to present a characteristically Jewish experience in the transition from a religious to a secular culture. Hannah Arendt's *Rahel Varnhagen*[4] and Anzia Yezierska's *Bread Givers*[5] give accounts of remarkably similar struggles of women in assimilationist situations—the former aiming for assimilation, the latter aiming to keep a distinctive though secular culture. Although these problems, like those presented by the male novelists, are not to be taken lightly, they are still in the category of "complaint about the struggle," with few elements of direct, authentic celebration of Jewish history, values, experience, language, and consciousness. This affirmative element, long a part of Jewish culture, is missing from the prose literature of assimilation.

The history of modern American Jewish poetry does not have this tense, urgent, near desperate quality. Nor, however, is it "emotion recollected in tranquility." It is something different and distinct, namely, an inquiry into history and society, done privately and modestly, with humor and dignity, without frivolousness or solemnity, within a tradition of American poetry that is already marginalized.[6] It is reflective, indirectly, of many educated Jews' wishes to profess secular "mainstream" culture; but it is also welcoming to interests of Jewish history, Jewish idealism, and perhaps most importantly to ordinary readers like myself, recollections and recordings of deep, consequential collective feelings that many of us can rehearse as we read through the poetry. With its relatively democratic distribution of contributors, many sides of Jewish-American experience become available to many readers. The poems I read are learning and teaching, indeed, researching the Jewish past, rearticulating it in ways that are, perhaps, freer that those available to prose-writing academics still trying to be good enough to gain entrance and respect in the non-Jewish academy.[7] The poems combine the memory of the past with the phenomenology of the present. They offer us voices that are deeper, calmer, more realistic, and more generous than those we have already accorded recognition in prose fiction. And at least as importantly, they contribute to the project of recasting a Jewish culture in a society that has been, for the most part, accommodating to Jews as to other "others." American Jewish poetry contributes to our need to find conventions, language, ideals, memories that retain a Jewish consciousness and identity that encourage life within a different society while remaining within our historic culture.

In my discussion I will suggest, through instances of poetry (some of which is included in this volume, some not), several modes in which poetry by American Jews touches on issues in an especially rich way—one that practices and encourages us to pursue the ideals of learning characteristic of Jewish life for many centuries before us. These ideals are not "ideal" in its traditional meaning; rather, they are markers of characteristic Jewish uses of language as collective gestures of solidarity, as enhancements of existing social relationships, as moments of play and comedy that remind us of the historic vitality of Jewish social mores. It is a life of peacefulness, free of the urgings of imperialism, slave-holding, and domination of others. It is noteworthy that even though Jewish life has been marked, like other cultures, by an endemic androcentrism, the practice of poetry has itself begun to pull Jewish life away from this form of domination as well, a claim that, by and large, cannot be made by the practices of prose fiction writers.

Who would imagine that one of the ideals of American society was articulated in a poem written by a native-born Jewish woman, Emma Lazarus, and that it would express an ideal that today is in doubt: the generosity of a free, rich country toward the "tired and poor" of the rest of the world? Who also would imagine that this charitable gesture is a contribution of Jewish poetry to American society? This poem marks a beginning of the modern Jewish spirit and provides a model for the solution to the problems of assimilation: the reenactment of the generous act by those who are here to those seeking a just society.

The latter ideal precedes the struggle of assimilation. The needs of assimilation got in the way of the search for, and the effort to create, a more just society. The solution of Jewish American poetry is to assert the historic loyalties to family, history, society, and language, found in a culture that has specialized in survival over millenia. An example of how this solution plays out may be seen in several treatments of a piece of liturgy still used by even less observant Jews: the Kaddish.

The Kaddish is the prayer of survivors for their beloved dead. Perhaps unknown to those who have not translated it, it does not mention the dead, dying, the next world, or anything to do with death. It is a wish that God's name continue to be sanctified through time. It is one of the moments when Jews remembering those who lived take a moment, even in ignorance, to juxtapose their own loss with a wish for the endurance of the collective. David Ignatow's "Kaddish"[8] finds the speaker sitting by his mother's death bed, she in an oxygen tent, he contemplating the eternal separation that is about to take place:

> Your face beneath the oxygen tent was alive
> But your eyes closed, your breathing hoarse.
> Your sleep was with death. I was alone
> with you as when I was young
> but now only alone, not with you,
> to become alone forever, as I was learning
> watching you become alone.
>
> Earth now is your mother, as you were mine, my earth,
> my sustenance and my strength,
> and now without you I turn to your mother
> and seek from her that I may meet you again
> in rock and stone. Whisper to the stone,
> I love you. Whisper to the rock, I found you.
> Whisper to the earth, Mother I have found her,
> and I am safe and always have been.
>
> (Rubin, 109)

The sentiment of this speaker may perhaps be contrasted with the absence of this sentiment in Jakie Rabinowitz in the 1927 film *The Jazz Singer.* At the end of the film, Mrs. Rabinowitz declares that Jakie belongs to the American audience and, actually, parts with him in spite of her deep attachment to him; she delivers him to America. Ignatow, however, in an equally "professional" context (poetry writing as professional as popular singing), *says Kaddish.* He parts with her in love, and even as he secularizes her passing by finding their common mother, Earth, the secularization takes place with reference to the historic

prayer that asks that God's name continue to be sanctified. Bringing his mother
back to earth with his love, the speaker sanctifies their common mother and re-
lates the material feelings of child to mother, loving safety, to the palpability of
the earth, the rock of the grave and to the gravestone. The context of the sanc-
tification of God's name oversees this process, and the poet has brought the two
strains of the religious and secular together in the act of mourning the beloved
parent, a feeling we all have had or will have, a feeling common to all people.

In her poem by the same name, "Kaddish," which presents an English com-
mentary on a transliteration of the mourner's Kaddish, Melanie Kaye/Kantrowitz
places her father's death in a more clearly social context of American society:

> Tuesday my father died   Wednesday
> The rabbi   who never met my father   met with us
> My mother   my father's sisters   the daughters
> 5 minutes before the funeral was to begin
> to prepare the eulogy   He asked
> if my father had belonged to any organizations if
> people from   his place of business had come
> and he said   since there were no sons
> he   would say kaddish   for my father
>
> and I did not tell the rabbi   my father was broken
> before he died
>
> . . . .
> I did not mention he beat us the children
> But not his wife   I did not reveal his high point in life
> a trip   with his buddies   to the Chicago World's Fair
> In a '32 Ford   I did not say he changed his name   he was
> Kantrowitz   he become Kaye   I did not say he built
> A business   retail   and taught me
> *never cross a picket line*
> > > Y'he sh'meh rabbo m'vorach l'olam
> > > Ulolmy olmayo
> I did not tell the rabbi   my father listened carefully
> To all things Jewish
>
> nor did I tell him
> *Save your prayers*
>
> I said, *I will speak at this funeral*
> And I did   to mourn him properly

> > > > > > > > (Beck, 108–109)

The woman mourning her father is different from the man his mother; also, much more painful. The speaker finds herself immediately excluded from her father's funeral by the rabbi, automatically following the male tradition of privileging men in religious service. The speaker, angry at the men, angry at the superficiality, yet decisively respectful of this moment of contact with Jewish consciousness, takes the initiative from the official Jew (the Jewish Official?) and "shouts" the truth to us about Mr. Kantrowitz, the maddening combination of self-indulgence and social, cultural consciousness. This moment also takes place within earshot of the Hebrew prayer/poem that exalts God, and, in this case, makes sure to cite the prayer itself: "May God's name be blessed for ever and ever." Here too, the living text of the Hebrew (Aramaic, actually) language oversees the reality of the passing of the beloved parent, this time judged more harshly by the surviving child. This offspring seizes the moment to change the elements of injustice caused by her father and other Jewish men; she creates a new moment, now, that is perhaps more just than the living relationship with her father. It is a moment at which historic Jewish feeling is realistically planted in American society, a moment analogous to Charles Reznikoff's in his second "Kaddish" poem. But is also a moment at which this society is an accepted *context* for the continued growth and development of the Jewish people.

The lyric singers organize their memory around the traditional Hebrew text and place at its disposal the passions of the present losses. Before our eyes, the speakers are learning how to adapt often-repeated words to add the secular moments to the history of the Jewish people. In Kaye/Kantrowitz's case, the contact zone of rabbinic androcentrism (their privileging of men to oversee religious rites and Jewish law) is transferred and transformed to a new Jew who takes over the work of presiding at a communal observance of death. The boredom of the pro forma eulogy, characteristic of such moments in American society, is reinvigorated by, on the one hand, the revocation of androcentrism, and, on the other, by the insistence that on such occasions, for God's sake, the truth must be told. And that is just what this poet does.

Why do Mani Leib and Jacqueline Osherow[9] after him say that a "poet among Jews" is "unneeded"? We have seen, in history, how fully the poet does live among Jews, how deeply integrated such a figure is, dating back to the songs, praising God, sung by the adulterous King David or to the songs of love sung by his lustful son, Solomon. The poets, the prophets, the sayers, the readers of history: These figures speak within, and sometimes for, the Jewish people. In her lyric, "The Yiddish Muses," Osherow searches for the sources of inspiration in the secular utopia of America. As noted earlier in this essay, the poet in America is an outsider, a marginalized figure, unaccepted because unmasculine: This second-class poet is unneeded among Jews.

The speaker in "The Yiddish Muses" is alienated from the culture of Yiddish: "Yiddish is no language for poetry, so homely / On the page, vowels instead of silences" (the biblical Hebrew has only understood vowels). Poetry has entered the vernacular, and it is no longer a purely ancient art whose works are reread today in sacral settings. Searching for the vernacular Jewish muse (the Yiddish muses), the poet is the dreamer and not the prophet, not the king, not the "official" speaker. Like Kaye/Kantrowitz, Osherow records the diffusion of the official voices into the popular voices carried through Europe by the Yiddish language. Her search overtakes her passions: "Can you blame me / If I ride and ride, unneeded as I am / And dangerous, a dreamer among Jews?" The speaker remembers her forebear dreamer, Joseph, whose embarrassing fantasies of the sun, moon, and stars bowing to him would indeed be dangerous if they were not dreams, poems, songs, idle thoughts to be interpreted rather than realized. The speaker finds the Yiddish muses in the synagogue, chuckling as they "praise the Name." The muses respect the "routine miracle" of Jerusalem's transcendence of ordinary life, even the religiously ordained commonplace of the "women's section." The history of the Jewish people, responsibility for which is now transferred to the everyday dreamer, has become, through the Yiddish muses, a secular inspiration. A poet is "unneeded" among Jews because the dreamer, the traveling singer, *a member of the common people*, has returned, and is as he/she once was, an ordinary person.

Historically among Jews, the poet is not an extraordinary figure. In a sense the lyric singer is always an ordinary person, not a king or a prophet. This poet, at home in New Jersey and in Brooklyn, "Looking for Angels in New York," insists on the immanence of God and of figures believed to be transcendental in the popular culture of America. Osherow's vision, aiming to integrate the vernacular Yiddish with the classic Hebrew, the king and the dreamer, does so in the context of contemporary American society, whose "extraordinary" possession is her discovery of "angels in New York."

> If Jacob has rested in New York, he
> Would have seen angels on elevators,
> And Saint Mark, though an insurance salesman,
> Would certainly have witnessed miracles.
>
> (Osherow, 39)

Some of the longing for home, which was expressed by the generations before Osherow as a longing for the *shtetl* (for example, in the Yiddish song "Mein Shtetele Belz"), has been transferred to a longing for New York City, which had become the new capital of Jewish life before the establishment of the State of Israel in 1948. Many contemporary New Yorkers hold the city in special regard. Many of these do not know why, relying usually on its "world-class" identity as the "city that never sleeps." Yet New York, and no other city, is the site at which Jews from Europe, having escaped the pogroms and other historic outbreaks of extermination fever for over fifteen centuries, have come to thrive, to prosper, to "behave as Jews,"[10] and, most significantly, to create the range of religious and secular cultures that had begun developing in Europe and were overwhelmed by the Holocaust. For several decades, New York City, with its over two million Jews, was a new homeland—a place where Jews felt at home and still do. As a result, Osherow finds muses and angels in New York City— the site of ordinary people's poetry, witnessed by St. Mark,[11] but steeped in the "homely" language whose "vowels" are visible—the sounds of everyday life, freshly rendered with each new stanza.

The Yiddish language is the actual bridge to New York City and to America. It is the vehicle of an enabling culture, Jewish secularism, which added to the welcoming poem by the "Jewish" woman who welcomes all people to America. It provided the model of a vernacular *life* that corresponded with indigenous American populism—the paradise of the "common (white) man" who may now own a home, a car, and a secure livelihood. I'll mention two poems that articulated how the bridge works: Irena Klepfisz's "Der Mames Shabosim/*My Mother's Sabbath Days*" and Gerald Stern's "Adler."

Klepfisz's poem inserts transliterated Yiddish phrases and sentences to help describe how the Sabbath was kept in her mother's home. While her grandmother knew all 613 commandments given for Jews (actually, Jewish men) by the Torah and the "3 which did not bind me [a woman]," the speaker's mother was "more modern" and taught her eleven-year-old daughter to be already a "passionate socialist," *rendered in Yiddish: "kh'bin shoyn geven a brenendike sotsyalistke"* (my translation: "At 11, I was already a burning [passionate] socialist."). The poem opens with the Yiddish sentence, *"Bay undz is es geven andersh."* (My translation: "With us, it was different.") The transition from grandmother's religiously observant life to the secular life was accompanied by an education in socialism, then the established doctrine of social meliorism, the path to a just society. Traditionally this ideal was transmitted by classic Jewish messianism. But as the winds of enlightenment increased from the eighteenth century on, for many, the Yiddish language, with its roots in religious life in Europe and its vernacular status, was an ideal medium through which to become a modern, enlightened, up-to-date citizen of the United States, a free society that protected, it was believed, such processes of social transformation.

The Sabbath in the speaker's mother's home was when they ate Chinese food *out*. "Perhaps I knew it was *treyf*. She certainly did / but was not concerned." The speaker remembers New York City: the subway, her mother returning from work, the philistinism of reform Judaism: "Miss Kant   the designer   a career woman / . . . now sat brazenly chic   in a reform synagogue."

The mother's Sabbath retained the fierce independence of Jewish life in the *shtetl*, and the daughter, a poet, remembers each of those American urban details as they lead to and add up to a Chinese dinner on *erev shabes*. The upshot of this record is that *mother observed the sabbath*. "Still—she rested." Life is different in America. Her mother had to work. Observance must take on different forms—socialism, memory, the details of the transition to a secular life. But these details are presented to us in Yiddish as well as English. The fact that things are "*andersh*" and not "different" is salient. Obviously, these individual memorials to tradition and social solidarity are not themselves enough to perpetuate the thriving culture that existed in Europe before the war, and still may not be enough in the future. But they are the first steps taken by the Americanized Jews toward rebuilding a new, free culture based on as much as possible that can be drawn from the ruins of Europe and the ideals of Jewish history. This is what Dershowitz has been advocating regarding our own tasks today as Jews.

Gerald Stern's poem "Adler," about the great Yiddish actor Jacob Adler, recounts a somewhat different context and different mood about the Yiddish transfer of Jewish culture to America. This poem makes reference to the Yiddish translation of Shakespeare's *King Lear,* a play that made the rounds on Second Avenue, the Broadway of the Yiddish-speaking community until 1945. It is no coincidence that the Yiddish theater, vibrant for over fifty years, came to an abrupt halt that year. As an institution, the Yiddish theater was largely responsible for establishing Jewish culture in New York and in America. It was a popular (not a high-brow) art, and everyone went. It was like Shakespeare in his time, like film in ours.

The speaker notices that the Yiddish Lear is different from the English: "Nothing either in England / or Germany could equal his ferocity, / could equal his rage, even if the Yiddish could make you laugh" (Rubin 193). Speakers of Yiddish will understand this reference to the characteristic ambiguity of almost any Yiddish usage. When Yiddish is spoken, it is as if everything is a simultaneous reference to the present indicative situation, and to a surrounding hostile society. It is as if living Yiddish has an echo of its place among enemies—it is a dialect/echo of the language of Jews' modern-day enemies, the Germans; with its elements of Russian, Polish, and other European languages, it is an echo of other more distant enemies as well. Stern continues, "There is a famous picture / of a German soldier plucking a beard; I think / of gentle Gloucester every time I see // that picture. There is a point where even Yiddish / becomes a tragic tongue and even Adler / can make you weep." The accession of Yiddish to tragedy refers in part to its having attained literary status. For hundreds of years a second-class vernacular (even among Jews), like Black English today, Yiddish became during the enlightenment a literary language that hosted poets, novelists, and playwrights. In the theater perhaps more than in other media,

Yiddish retained its vernacular connotations, and this richness helped to perpetuate the theater as a cultural institution.

As the poem continues, the speaker describes the magnitude of the artistic figure of Adler, how admired he was by the respected of America's art world, Isadora Duncan and John Barrymore. Most of the poem contrasts the glory of his achievement as an artist with what followed that heyday—the desecration of artistic gestures by the murderers in Europe: "For the sake of art / there always was a German or Ukrainian // walking around like a dignified Albany, / or one made sad repentant noises like Kent / and one was philosophical like Edgar, / giving lectures to the burning corpses, // those with gold in their mouths, . . . " These "artists" ended the decades of ebullient success and achievement on Second Avenue. Stern contrasts the weeping in the theater with the singing and warbling in "bitterness" that put an end to the theater, and gave pause to the long movement of celebration of Jews finding a measure of cultural emancipation in America.

Although at this moment there are attempts to gather together the key literary works in Yiddish, to republish the plays in translation[12] and to honor Yiddish as a historical force, the more consequential gestures to restore a living Jewish identity and culture are taking place through the study of history, the Biblical texts, and the attempts, primarily through Jewish feminism, to recast some of the values that have compromised the strong themes of social justice in Jewish history. Jacqueline Osherow's poems discussed earlier, recalling the role of the ordinary person as the Jewish dreamer, are one of the paths to retell Jewish history. A similar move is found in Howard Schwartz's poem "Signs of the Lost Tribe," whose speaker searches through family belongings in the attic and senses that one of the ten lost tribes of Israel are there, saturating his things: "Somehow / One of the ten lost tribes / Had wandered / Out of the desert / And all of them were living / In my house." The speaker imagines them in the closets and drawers, until, he observes, "They even inhabit / My dreams / There / Above all / They are at home." The texts, tales, and ancestors of Biblical Jewish history enter, repeatedly, in the dozens of American Jewish poets, staying finally in their "dreams"—the poems we are reading. The memories of the texts that were once learned are often combined with the memory of parents, grandparents, and lifestyles that lived before now. There is a clear movement among these poets to rearticulate the history of Jews, more so with younger and second-generation poets, born in the United States and now no longer feeling the pinch of being alien, as Dershowitz describes, even enjoying freedom and leisure.

Many of the most accomplished Jewish American poets have taken up the search for gender equality as a means of removing the stigma of hypocrisy from Jewish ideals of social justice; certainly this purpose was implicit in Irena Klepfisz's description of how her socialist mother celebrated the Sabbath—

defiantly with her daughter, who greeted her as she came home from work. The feminist theme, however, has a very interesting expression. Some of these poets, like Muriel Rukeyser, Maxine Kumin, Adrienne Rich, and Alicia Ostriker (and others), were either academically trained or became academics and promoted feminism in a variety of literary forms. Different genres were needed to articulate the different angles brought to language by the feminist initiative.

A good instance of the move into varieties of genres is found in the work of Alicia Ostriker. One of her longer term projects has been to reread the Biblical texts, partly in the services of Judaism, American Judaism, poetry, literacy, and feminism, worldwide. In the beginning of one of her mixed-genre studies, *The Nakedness of the Fathers,*[13] Ostriker sets out the issue that renders the feminist Jewish poets more distant from "American poetry" and more distant from Jewish history. The variety of genres represented in this study create a reference to the ordinary status of the author—the work is a challenge to academic genres, which are often singular and narrow; to poetic genres, which, today, are mostly lyric; to prose genres, which are mostly fiction; and to autobiographical genres, which are taken to be referential. In this work, the combination of all the foregoing genres, a new and special problem is posed, one whose solution needs many genres of writing as well as fundamental change in human societies.

An early section of this work is in italic prose and reflects:

> *I am and am not a Jew. I am a Jew in the sense that every drop of blood in my veins is Jewish . . . I am a Jew because my parents are. . . . My laughter and my tears are Jewish laughter and tears. What else could they be? My ancestors are Russian-Jewish ancestors. The shtetl mud is hardly shaken from my roots. . . .*
>
> *But I'm not a Jew, I can't be a Jew, because Judaism repels me as a woman.*
>
> *To the rest of the world the Jew is marginal. But to Judaism I am marginal. Am woman, unclean. Am Eve. Or worse, am Lilith. Am illiterate. Not mine the arguments of Talmud, not mine the centuries of ecstatic study, the questions and answers twining minutely like vines around the living Word. . . . It is said: Whoever teaches his daughter Torah, teaches her obscenity.* (Ostriker, 5–7)

The project of correcting the exclusion of women from Jewish learning and rabbinic authority in twentieth-century America has been part of the work of many poets (and other scholars and teachers), from early in the century to the present. It has been a central focus of a group of lesbian poets and writers, collected by Evelyn Beck in *Nice Jewish Girls.*[14] Ostriker's work breaks traditional boundaries of genre, language, and thought. If poetry is a starting point, its generic reach is expanded; the same might be said if one's starting point is any other genre.

Ostriker addresses the Bible as a historical text, rereads it, integrating in it her own story. It becomes an English vernacular, her work playing a role that Yiddish played a generation or two before her. Her job is this:

> *My fathers, whom I intend to pursue. Their stories mine. My fathers, whose meaning I am laboring to understand, since to understand them is to understand myself. Needing to know whom I love, whom I hate, Needing to remember that I am my fathers, just as much as I am my mothers.* (Ostriker, 15)

Her retelling inserts the voices of women into the history, and God's name is changed to Being. Eve says,

> He forgets that the garden was my garden. My tree, my spiral snakes, my attributes, my happiness was that I was, oh leaf. My knowledge, my power, what a yielding fruit. And he forgets that I made him: mud mother. (Ostriker, 24)

Here, what must be obvious to those not tied to the literal accounts in Genesis, namely, that Adam came out of Eve's body, and not the reverse, is announced by Eve in this rereading of the creation story. The new text seems admissible as poetry in the American sense—an isolated, marginalized, quaint genre of writing, but in the Jewish sense of what a rereading means, it (in principle) becomes part of the Talmud, a learned commentary on the law. Such insertions are common in traditional Biblical commentary and are found routinely in the classic rereadings of Genesis by the medieval commentator Rashi. In learned circles, such rereading would be routinely discussed; suppose those study circles[15] included women? Suppose such issues were raised by a class of Jews whose interest in the law governing them were equal to the interests of the rabbis? Suppose the women providing the commentary were as learned as the men? The latter is, in fact, the case among those men and women, today, rereading the Biblical stories, songs, poems, myths, and dreams.

Frequently in Ostriker's book, a characteristic American voice is found. Describing how Joseph is trying to restore the filial bond, Ostriker has him say:

> *Feel free to use my limousine, boys. I'll send my tailor over in the morning. Charge it on my card, listen, here's the key to the liquor cabinet, Just don't worry about a thing, you'll be looked after, your children also. What can be more precious to a man than his family.* (Ostriker, 115)

The American Joseph, the corporate mogul, provides for his needy siblings. The justification? (Male) family values! Ostriker has combined Jewish and American history in this "poem," as well as prose and poetry, fantasy and reality. This is a totally new vision of American Jewish life, perhaps of how compatible, on the basis of androcentrism, this combination of Jewish and

American idealism has been. How much harsher this Joseph is than Osherow's, the dreamer! How disturbed Ostriker is of what has become of Joseph, who from the traditional standpoint is an inspiring dreamer, victim, and leader, but from the standpoint of a realistic account of history is a corporate mogul pitching the nuclear family as a way of life.

The title of a previous book of Ostriker's is *Stealing the Language*. The phrase is taken from Claudine Hermann's phrase (1979) *voleuses de langue*, which describes "female Prometheuses."[16] The role of such thieves is to "have it in our power to 'seize speech' and make it say what we mean. More: there is a desire to make female speech prevail, to penetrate male discourse, to cause the ear of man to listen" (211). Is this the work of poets? Yes, if we take the role and place of poets from Jewish history. Poets among Jews are unneeded because all speakers are poets. In trying to include women's voices, Ostriker, and many like her, are bringing an idea of poetry that is characteristically Jewish into discussion. It is a poetry that includes prose genres; a poetry that revises the sacred texts; a poetry that includes reference to the experiences of daily life in any living society; it is the poetry that is tied to established accounts of history and to the ability to change and add to those accounts. This is the "poetry" that many feel was enacted in the mere speaking of Yiddish, a double-voiced ironic language at almost every turn, yet a language combined, like English, of so many elements from other languages that they are difficult to identify.

The significance of the Yiddish bridge to America lies in part in the social kinship of Yiddish and English. To a British person, American English may also seem to be a developed slang, a cultivated way of speaking that grew from humble origins, from an insistence on cultural and economic autonomy. Those who nourish such kinships are poets, in the broader sense, the (German) *Dichter*, the writer, the reader, the "one who speaks." In this sense American Jewish poets have been and continue to be teachers, of course in their formal appointments in universities, but further, in the projected sense of teaching us to hear poetry in a way less marginalized that it has been, historically, in America. The voices we have heard briefly in this discussion—but who are copiously available on the shelves of Barnes and Noble, Amazon.com, etc.—have already been doing what Alan Dershowitz has recommended to those who don't read much poetry (people like myself, for example!), learning, learning, and teaching, teaching, and they have been doing it for more than a century. They have affirmed an inner Jewish life that can be brought into the public *without* assimilating it to everything else. They can join, teach us to join, yet teach us to be our collective selves by dreaming in new genres, stealing many languages, overtaking others' words, making old texts new, revising what has already been said, written, read, heard. Like Emma Lazarus, these poets have done for a long time what some are calling for in a context of crisis: learning about what we already have to make room for ourselves, for our own, for others, for Others.

Notes

1. Alan Dershowitz, *The Vanishing American Jew: In Search of Jewish Identity for the Next Century* (New York: Little, Brown, 1997).

2. Susanne Klingenstein, *Jews in the American Academy, 1900–1940* (New Haven, Conn.: Yale UP, 1991); see also; Klingenstein's, *Enlarging America: the Cultural Work of Jewish Literary Scholars, 1930–1990* (Syracuse: Syracuse UP, 1998); Rael Meyerowitz, *Transferring to America: Jewish Interpretations of American Dreams* (Albany: SUNY, 1995); also, perhaps, Susan Handelman, *The Slayers of Moses* (Albany: SUNY 1982).

3. Neal Gabler, *An Empire of Their Own: How the Jews Invented Hollywood* (New York: Anchor Books, 1988).

4. Hannah Arendt, *Rahel Varnhagen: The Life of a Jewish Woman*, trans. Richard and Clara Winston (1957; New York: Harcourt Brace Jovanovich, 1974).

5. Anzia Yezierska; *Bread Givers* (Garden City: Doubleday Page and Company, 1925).

6. Historically, American writers (of all genres) have been marginal figures in society, even when their works were bought and read. A good example of popular literature that had no effect on American society is utopian fiction twenty years before and after the turn of the twentieth century. American poetry was even less of a social factor; compared to the effect of industrialists, poets were "geeks." The depth of this negative status is represented, in part, by Hart Crane's father's attitude toward his gay son and toward poetry. He was not just homophobic about his son. He thought that *poetry* was not manly, not a real vocation, and so on. Poetry was feminized and marginalized (the two go together)—certainly not an occupation for the men of a nation of the ever-expanding frontier.

Some Jewish men were affected by the virus of masculine insecurity represented by Crane's father (for a full discussion of how this feeling spread among assimilated Jewish men, see Daniel Boyarin, *Unheroic Conduct: The Invention of Heterosexuality and the Rise of the Jewish Man* [U of California P, 1997]). In male contexts of assimilation, Jewish poets may become preoccupied with who is better; addressing the claims of superiority advanced by T. S. Eliot, Hyam Plutzik in his 1959 poem "For T. S. E. Only" cites Eliot's (quoted) line, "You hypocrite lecteur! Mon semblable! Mon frere!" in order both to admonish him for his bigotry and to assert absolute equality with him. But: Imagine using a lyric poem to persuade a bigot of his error.

7. By this I am referring to the need for aspiring Jewish critics wanting to teach poetry to overlook the bigotry against Jews in Western literature. My own experience in graduate school was this: I was uncomprehending, until recently, why my Jewish professor, teaching modern poetry, paid no attention to the bigotry of Eliot and Pound. Poets did not have to practice such concealment.

8. Steven Rubin's anthology *Telling and Remembering* (Boston: Beacon Press, 1997) includes two poems entitled "Kaddish" by Charles Reznikoff, and they are germane to

the present discussion. One of the poems is the "rabbi's" Kaddish, a wish for peace and safety for Israel. The second is a meditation on his dying and dead mother (like Ignatow's), and metaphorically, her returning to returning to life. At the end of the second poem, the speaker reflects on his knowledge that his mother does not mind his *not* saying Kaddish or lighting a *Yahrtzeit* candle on the anniversary of her death. He calls these rituals "trifles." However, the poem itself remains as the memorial, as does the rest of Reznikoff's poetry remain as an extended marker of transplanted Jewish life in America. Perhaps the "Kaddish," also the title of one of Leonard Bernstein's symphonies, can be read as a collective name for the death of Jewish life in Europe and its rebirth in America; its not mentioning of death or passing makes it especially eligible for this role.

9. Jacqueline Osherow, "The Yiddish Muses," in *Looking for Angels in New York* (U of Georgia P, 1988). In this poem, the speaker tells of the "unexpected" arrival of the Yiddish inspiration for her poetic singing. She wants to "catch" them but is diffident because of the vernacular status of Yiddish. Yet, to her, these muses have inspired dreaming (Joseph's kind) that represents religious and historic Jewish social idealism and aspiration. The speaker, at the end, notes that these vernacular muses are founding in the synagogue to "chuckle / As they praise the Name," and that they still build a transcendental edifice higher than even the division between men and women in the synagogue, above any religious constriction of the Jewish imagination ("any memory of its walls and domes").

10. Gerald Stern, in his poem "Behaving Like a Jew" (Rubin, 189), calls attention to the luxury of self-observation—in public—afforded by American society. This poem makes a distinction between the spontaneous involvement of Jews in living existence and the detached spirituality of American culture as represented by the anti-Semite Charles Lindbergh: The Jew will examine the dead opossum on the road actively without idle reflection, characterized by Stern as "the spirit of Lindbergh over everything, / that joy in death, that philosophical / understanding of carnage." The speaker instead touches the dead body and recalls with trembling pain its life, its "dancing feet." Such public self-acknowledgement is unknown in Europe, as suggested by the elaborate disguises of Jewish themes found, for example, in the fiction of Franz Kafka. For more on Stern's poem see also "New Jerusalems: Jewish American Poetry and the Puritan Tradition," by Jonathan Barron, in *The Calvinist Roots of the Modern Era* (University Press of New England, 1997), edited by Alicki Barnstone et al.

11. The St. Mark's Church Poetry Project has presented readings—particularly of avant-garde and performance poetry—and sponsored poetry workshops at St. Mark's Place in New York City since the 1960s.

12. Nahma Sandrow, *God, Man, and Devil* (Syracuse: Syracuse UP, 1999), five Yiddish plays in translation; also extant are cassettes of the Yiddish films of the 1930s and 1940s. There are Yiddish sections at the MLA. Still, this means that, as in essays such as this, Yiddish is being *studied as a historical phenomenon*, and outside the Hasidic world there is not much activity of, for example, young parents speaking Yiddish to their children.

13. Alicia Suskin Ostriker, *The Nakedness of the Fathers: Biblical Visions and Revisions* (New Brunswick, N.J.: Rutgers UP, 1994).

14. Evelyn Torton Beck, ed., *Nice Jewish Girls: A Lesbian Anthology* (Beacon Press, 1982, 1989). Included in this volume is Adrienne Rich's essay "Split at the Root," an autobiographical account of her different identities, Jewish and Christian, straight and lesbian. Here too there is a statement (p. 89) of how she is a Jew if she had to wear the yellow star, but also "a woman, not a Jew." A similar sense of ambivalence is described by Naomi Scheman in "Who Was That Masked Woman?" but with a different emphasis: She feels more comfortable identifying as a Jew because she is so distant from it; less comfortable as a woman, because female identity in this society is so uncertain.

15. See Samuel C. Heilman, *The People of the Book: Drama, Fellowship, and Religion* (U of Chicago P, 1983), which describes ethnographically the all-male Talmudic study circles.

16. See the English translation *The Tongue Snatchers*, trans. Nancy Kline (Lincoln: U of Nebraska P, 1991).

Essays on History: Editors' Introduction

The next two essays introduce the early history of Jewish American poetry. In "Poets of the Promised Land, 1880–1920," Steven Rubin offers us a tour of the founding generations of Jewish American poets, from Penina Moise and Emma Lazarus at the end of the nineteenth century to Charles Reznikoff and the other Jewish Objectivist poets writing in the 1930s at the height of Modernist experimentation. Rubin's essay deepens the story of Jewish American poetry found in our introduction. In so doing, it necessarily assumes a straightforward working definition of Jewish American poetry. In an essay attempting to make the unfamiliar familiar, one cannot expect the three principal terms—"poetry," "American," and even "Jewish"—to be overly complicated or troubled by internal problems of definition.

The next essay, "Diasporic Poetics," by Michael Heller, does investigate some of the problems inherent in these three terms. For, as Heller explains, the Jewish Objectivists had serious questions about the meanings of the term "Jewish" and of the term "poetry." In a combination of memoir and close reading, Heller invites us to see how the Objectivists' ability to work both within and against Jewish tradition offered his own poetry a way back to that tradition, however across or against the grain.

Poets of the Promised Land, 1800–1920

STEVEN J. RUBIN

Steven J. Rubin is Professor and Chair of the Department of English at the University of South Florida, where he also directs the Florida Center for Writers. His books include *Meyer Levin* (Twayne, 1982), *Writing Our Lives: American Jewish Autobiographies, 1890–1990* (Jewish Publication Society, 1991), and *Telling and Remembering: A Century of American Jewish Poetry* (Beacon Press, 1997).

> I have married and married the speech of strangers
> —Charles Reznikoff, "The Hebrew of Your Poets, Zion"

Jewish poetry is defined most simply as poetry that is written by Jews about Jewish subjects or themes. In the best Jewish poetry, however, there is a deeper resonance, one that is an expression of the Jewish spirit and one that embraces several diverse traditions. Jewish poetry began as early as the Bible with the Psalms and the lyrical verses of the Song of Songs. It flourished in the Middle Ages with the great Sephardic poets Solomon ibn Gabirol and Judah Halevi of Spain and thrived in the centers of Yiddish culture in Eastern Europe with the work of such writers as Morris Rosenfeld, H. Leivick, Moshe Leib Halpern, Mani Leib, and Abraham Reisen, many of whom were able to continue their careers in the New World.

American Jews began writing poetry in English as early as the beginning of the nineteenth century, although in general there was little to distinguish the literary efforts of most early Jewish authors from that of their American counterparts. It was generally true—as Sol Liptzin in his study *The Jew in American Literature* affirmed—that nineteenth- and early twentieth-century Jewish writers: "suffered from inhibitions and sought to avoid being too conspicuously Jewish" (Liptzin, 28). Many of those who did publish with some success— writers such as Horace Traubel (1858–1919), Arthur Guiterman (1871–1943), Stanton A. Coblentz (1896–?), Franklin P. Adams (1881–1960), and John Cournos (1881–1966)—were unconcerned with Jewish issues in their work.[1]

One notable exception was Penina Moise (1797–1880), the first recognized American Jewish poet to develop a body of work consistently devoted to Jewish themes. Best known for her religious verses, many of which are still included in the Reform Jewish service, she was admired by her Jewish contemporaries and received some degree of national recognition through the publication of her work in such popular nineteenth-century journals as *The Daily Times*, *The Southern Patriot*, and *Godey's Lady's Book*. The author of hundreds of poems, many of them devotional, Moise was born in Charleston, South Carolina, into a large and wealthy Jewish family. Her parents (both of Sephardic descent) had immigrated from the Caribbean several years before Moise was born. Devoutly religious, Moise refused to marry outside her faith and remained single throughout her life.

Consciously Jewish in her life and poetry, Moise wrote on a number of Jewish topics, including the persecution of Jews abroad (although not at home), and Jewish ritual, history, and religion. In 1833 Moise published *Fancy's Sketch Book*, generally acknowledged to be the first volume of American Jewish poetry. Moise also composed dozens of poems and essays for both the Jewish and general press, and almost the entire *Hymns Written for the Use of Hebrew Congregations* (1856), originally written for Temple Beth Elohim in Charleston, and the first Reform Jewish prayer book printed in the United States.

Unfortunately, Moise's poetic talent did not match her religious ardor, and her work remains mostly uninspired. Here, for example, are the opening verses from "Miriam," a poetic rendering of the story of Miriam, the mother of Moses:

> Amid the flexile reeds of Nile a lovely infant slept,
> While over the unconscious babe his mother watched and wept.
> Nor distant far another stood whose tears flowed fast and free,
> 'Twas Miriam the beautiful, the bright star of the sea.
> With breaking heart that parent bids farewell to her doomed child,
> Commending to Almighty God his spirit undefiled.
> The sister lingers yet to mourn o'er tyranny's decree,
> And bitter was thy agony, fair maiden of the sea.
>
> (Matza, 20)

As was often the case in her poetry, "Miriam" suffers from language that is at times awkward, a fairly unsophisticated rhyme scheme, and a metrical pattern that seems to contradict the poem's solemn narrative.

Somewhat more interesting is her later work decrying prejudice and anti-Semitism, "On the Persecution of the Jews of Damascus." The poem—based on the notorious 1840 "Damascus Affair," in which the Jews of Syria were accused of murdering a Capuchin Monk in order to use his blood for Passover, and which included the arrest, torture, kidnapping, and murder of hundreds of Syrian Jews—is both a plea for tolerance and a call to arms:

> Oh! For the god-like champion now, the gallant charioteer
> To rally with a brother's love, round Hebrews in despair.
> Yet woe to thee, Damascus! whose burden was rehearsed,
> When prophesy denounced thee as a city thrice accursed.
>
> (Matza, 22)

An earlier poem, "To Persecuted Foreigners," published in *The Southern Patriot* in 1820, foreshadows Emma Lazarus's famous sonnet "The New Colossus." While the language is not as eloquent and the effect less compelling, the theme and emotions expressed are similar:

> Fly from the soil whose desolating creed,
> Outraging faith, makes human victims bleed,
> Welcome! where every Muse has reared a shrine,
> The respect of wild Freedom to refine. . . .
> If thou art one of that oppressed race,
> Whose name's a proverb, and whose lot's disgrace,
> Brave the Atlantic—Hope's broad anchor weigh,
> A Western Sun will gild your future day. . . .
> Rise, then, elastic from the Oppressor's tread,
> Come and repose in Plenty's flowery bed.
> Oh! Not as Strangers shall welcome be
> Come to the homes and bosoms of the free.
>
> (Gray, 27)

In spite of her considerable poetic output and the recognition she received during her lifetime, Moise remains virtually unknown to present-day readers. Her poetry displays many of the characteristics of mediocre nineteenth-century verse: a reliance on simplified rhyme schemes and metrical patterns, a disassociation of form and content, imagery that appears forced and unrelated, and language that is too often stilted. Nevertheless, her work reflects her passionate commitment to Jewish causes, as well as a certain sincerity and energy of style. Moreover, Moise should be recognized and acknowledged for her pioneering role in the development of American Jewish poetry. She was the first—man or woman—to express openly her Jewish concerns and preoccupations in her poetry. In so doing, she became a model for several who followed, allowing them to write freely and without apology about Jewish issues and themes.

Of much greater fame and talent was Emma Lazarus (1849–1887), the first

American Jewish poet whose works reached a wide and diverse audience. Lazarus was born in New York City to a successful and mostly assimilated family that could trace their roots back to the revolution. Her mother was Ashkenazi and her father, a wealthy sugar-refiner, was of Sephardic descent. As a child, Lazarus led a privileged and sheltered existence and was thus shielded from any overt anti-Semitism. She was schooled at home by private tutors and demonstrated an early proficiency for languages and writing. At the age of eighteen, her first book of poetry and poetic translations, *Poems and Translations*, was published privately by her father. Lazarus's first commercially published collection, *Admetus and Other Poems,* appeared four years later in 1871. By 1877 she had published two collections of poetry, a novel, a verse drama, a book of translations of Heinrich Heine's poetry, and dozens of individual poems in such nationally recognized journals as *Lippincott's Magazine, Century, Scribners's Magazine, The Independent*, and *Galaxy*.

Lazarus's interest in Judaism until about 1880 was peripheral. Her translations of Heine, for example, included none of his poems on Jewish themes. Her own early work, with the notable exception of her well-known poem "In the Jewish Synagogue at Newport," was similarly devoid of Jewish content. Moreover, this poem, written in 1867 and published in 1871, was inspired not by her sense of Jewish identity, but by Longfellow's famous elegy, "The Jewish Cemetery at Newport." Like Longfellow, Lazarus depicted a vanished religion, symbolized for her by an abandoned synagogue:

> Here, where the noises of the busy town,
> The ocean's plunge and roar can enter not,
> We stand and gaze around with tearful awe,
> And muse upon the consecrated spot.
>
> No signs of life are here: the very prayers
> Inscribed around are in a language dead;
> The light of the "perpetual lamp" is spent
> That an undying radiance was to shed.
>
> (Lazarus, 23)

In spite of her respect and reverence for the past, Lazarus expressed little hope for the survival of Judaism in America, and the poem ultimately echoes Longfellow's sad conclusion that "dead nations never rise again."

The irony, of course, is that within several years Lazarus was to become one of the most fervent poetic voices for Jewish renewal and for the establishment of a Jewish homeland. In the process, her poetry became less conventional, less reliant on past models, and more imaginative and passionate.

In spite of accounts to the contrary, Lazarus's transformation was gradual and probably the result of several diverse factors. Although "In the Jewish Synagogue at Newport" evoked a sense of lost tradition, it nevertheless demonstrated Lazarus's willingness to explore Jewish subjects. A few years later—in 1876—she published another piece of Jewish interest: a translation of Heine's "Donna Clara" in the *Jewish Messenger*. The poem portrayed, somewhat ironically, the love of an anti-Semitic Spanish lady for a mysterious "knight," who turns out to be the Grand Rabbi's son. Lazarus than added two of her own poems, which, based on Heine's notes, continued the story. As in "In the Jewish Synagogue," however, Lazarus maintained a tone of objectivity and impersonality. The reality of anti-Semitism is treated with comic irony, rather than with personal outrage. Nevertheless, "Donna Clara" was an early indication of an increasing interest in and concern for issues relevant to her Judaism.

This fledgling interest was, by most accounts, motivated by two unrelated but converging events: first, her reading of George Eliot, most specifically *Daniel Deronda* (1876); and second, the czarist pogroms in Eastern Europe. Clearly, Lazarus admired Eliot's writing and was later to dedicate her 1882 verse drama "The Dance to Death" to Eliot for "elevating and ennobling the spirit of Jewish nationality," a reference to Daniel Deronda, who, at the conclusion of the novel that bears his name, voiced the dream of a Jewish homeland. A second factor that contributed to Lazarus's transformation was her growing awareness of the persecution of European Jewry. Periodic violence against the Jews in Russia existed throughout the nineteenth century, but began to increase in frequency and intensity toward the end of the 1870s and reached its climax in the early 1880s after the assassination of Czar Alexander II in March 1881—an event blamed on the Jews. Newspapers in New York began to report eyewitness accounts of organized violence and murderous mobs bent on the destruction of the Jews of Russia. Reaction and condemnation on this side of the Atlantic was soon forthcoming, and Lazarus found herself at the forefront of the attack against anti-Semitism.

In 1882 Lazarus began publishing a series of essays in the *American Hebrew* under the title "An Epistle to the Hebrews," which dealt with the history and culture of the Jews, as well as the theme of a return to Palestine. At the same time, her poetry took on a new tone, style, and purpose. Earlier, Lazarus's poetry—while competent—was hardly original or particularly noteworthy. Her subjects were conventional: nature, history, art, Greek mythology, miscellaneous musings on the trials and tribulations of men and women. When she dealt with the occasional Jewish subject (as in "In the Jewish Synagogue" and "Donna Clara"), it was in terms of historical occurrences, not current situations. Her style too was traditional: Her language was "correct" and proper, at times artificially so; her poetic forms were the accepted conventions of her time.

Lazarus's poetry during the last five years of her life (she died in 1887 from cancer at the age of thirty-eight), however, was distinctly different from what she had produced earlier. In 1882 she published *Songs of a Semite: The Dance to Death and Other Poems*, which included a verse play about a fourteenth-century pogrom in Germany, several translations of medieval Spanish Jewish poetry, and six of her own poems on current Jewish events. From that point on until her death, Lazarus's subjects and themes were determined by her commitment to Jewish causes. The style of her poems underwent a transformation as well: The tone of dispassionate intellectualism was replaced with one of personal polemic and anger. Her language became more direct and less flowery, her imagery more forceful. Here, for example, is the opening verse of "The Crowing of the Red Cock," her denunciation of the pogroms of Russia, published in *Songs of a Semite*:

> Across the Eastern sky has glowed
> The flicker of a blood-red dawn,
> Once more the clarion cock has crowed,
> Once more the sword of Christ is drawn.
> A million burning rooftops light
> The world-wide path of Israel's flight.
>
> (Lazarus, 30)

Another effective poem, "The Banner of the Jew," published in *The Critic* in 1882 and then in the same year in *Songs of a Semite*, is a final repudiation of her vision of the demise of Judaism expressed in "In the Jewish Synagogue at Newport." Here Lazarus calls for Jewish heroism, rebellion, and the rebirth of a Jewish state: "Wake, Israel, wake! Recall to-day / The glorious Maccabean rage." Instead of her depiction of Judaism as a useless "relic of days of old," she here implores her people not to give in to those who would see their race perish:

> Oh deem not dead that martial fire,
> Say not the mystic flame is spent!
> With Moses' law and David's lyre,
> Your ancient strength remains unbent.
> Let but an Ezra rise anew,
> To lift the *Banner of the Jew!*
>
> (Lazarus, 28)

By 1882 Lazarus had obviously abandoned the genteel Victorian poetic tradition and her own aspirations to follow in the footsteps of Emerson, with whom she had earlier corresponded. In "The Banner of the Jew" her tone is one of anger and urgency ("Strike! For the brave revere the brave!"), and her images are visceral ("When men have bled and women wept"). Moreover, these poems are addressed to fellow Jews; Lazarus's intended audience is her own people, not the mainstream of American readers.

In the years that followed the publication of *Songs of a Semite*, Lazarus continued to express her call for Jewish unity, her condemnation of injustice, and her indignation at the world's indifference to Jewish suffering in several essays and poems. Her last composition, published in 1887, but written several years earlier, was a series of prose poems—surprisingly modern in form and technique—entitled "By the Waters of Babylon: Little Poems in Prose." Perhaps influenced by Whitman, these free-verse poems are a culmination of the major themes that preoccupied Lazarus for the last ten years of her life: the threat of anti-Semitism, exile, and the hope for a Jewish homeland. Although experimental and not entirely successful, "By the Waters of Babylon" indicates a willingness on the part of Lazarus to reinvent her poetry, just as she had done once before.

Lazarus's most famous poem, and the one for which she will be most remembered, is her sonnet "The New Colossus," written on the occasion of the erection of the Statue of Liberty in 1883 and engraved on its pedestal. Although the poem is not without its faults (overuse of the hyphenated adjective, for instance), it is an eloquent statement of Lazarus's final affirmation of America and her recognition of the role it was to play in welcoming oppressed people:

> Not like the brazen giant of Greek fame,
> With conquering limbs astride from land to land;
> Here at our sea-washed, sunset gates shall stand
> A mighty woman with a torch, whose flame
> Is the imprisoned lightning, and her name
> Mother of Exiles. From her beacon-hand
> Glows world-wide welcome; her mild eyes command
> The air-bridged harbor that twin cities frame.
> "Keep, ancient lands, your storied pomp!" cries she
> With silent lips. "Give me your tired, your poor,
> Your huddled masses yearning to breathe free,
> The wretched refuse of your teeming shore.
> Send these, the homeless, tempest-tost to me,
> I lift my lamp beside the golden door!"
>
> (Lazarus, 40–41)

Lazarus died in 1887, just as the great wave of Jewish immigration to America was beginning to crest. That migration, which lasted from approximately 1880 to 1920, brought more than three million Eastern European Jews to the United States and profoundly changed the shape of American Jewish culture for the remainder of the twentieth century. The new immigrants brought with them a rich literary tradition, and several established Yiddish-language poets— such as Mani Leib, Chaim Grade, Jacob Glatstein, and Abraham Reisen—continued to succeed in the New World. Their poetry was much admired by their Yiddish-speaking audience. Few, however, chose to make the transformation to English.

Two immigrant poets who did write in their adopted language were Samuel Greenberg (1893–1917) and Alter Brody (1895–1979?). Both were talented and produced poems that, in spite of the impediment of writing in a language not entirely their own, were in many ways extraordinary. Unfortunately, both had truncated literary careers: Greenberg because of his early death at the age of twenty-three from tuberculosis and Brody through his own choice.

Greenberg was born in Vienna, Austria, and came to the United States in 1900. Like many newly arrived Jewish immigrants, he spent his early years on New York's lower East Side. Self-educated (he left school at the age of fifteen to help support his family) and sickly (he was stricken with tuberculosis in about 1910), Greenberg wrote poetry that reflected a scattered and tragic life. His poems are often fragmentary, his English grammar, syntax, and spelling at times incorrect or unconventional. As his work survived only in manuscript (and on the backs of postcards, discarded notes, etc.), many poems are incomplete or exist in edited form only.[2] Those that remain clearly demonstrate Greenberg's poetic abilities. Written in free verse, with precise colorful images, his poems often have a magical, visionary quality. Several show flashes of true poetic inspiration.

Greenberg's relationship to Judaism is somewhat vague and mostly unknown. His decision to write in English as opposed to his native Yiddish is surely indicative of his desire to be an "American" rather than a "Jewish" poet. His father was an Orthodox Jew, and Greenberg was undoubtedly influenced by his family's traditional Judaism. His poetry, wide-ranging in theme and subject, includes references to the Bible, investigations of Jewish history and legend, and philosophic ruminations as to the nature of faith and belief. A number of his poems are based on Biblical themes and express his obvious love of the Old Testament. The brief devotional poem "Thus Be It Heaven Heavenly," with its reference to "Samuel" (both the poet and the Biblical Samuel), resonates with a sense of reverence; yet the linking of Moses and Christ in the second verse suggests that the poet was not tied to traditional Orthodox Jewish dogma:

> In our Bible, the dream of Samuel is death,
> As the clouds consume his form and bear him to Heaven—
> The song from colored birds so lyric and sweet
> We feel ourselves no more, and pray:
>   "Thus be it Heaven Heavenly."

The tales of Christ and Moses feel sacred through their Godly power
Of beauty, angels in their discipline kept
Where the clouds are not on view; we pray:
    "Thus be it Heaven Heavenly!"

(Holden, 11)

The subjects of God, belief, and mortality dominate many of Greenberg's poems, and those, like "Thus Be It Heaven Heavenly," that succeed in integrating the themes of religion and death are his most effective. Similarly, "The Holy Ghost" begins with a dream-like "ghastly" image of death, but concludes with a shared vision of "unexplained wonder":

A dark scarlet robe covered the body,
As he lay near a monastery cellar door.
Holy spirit of death swayed o'er him,
A plaintive seen skull, features sunk,
That frightens the life in the witness—
The gauzy jet black veil. In grey, shadowed
Doorlight the extinguished form lay in dignity
Against the wall; and the low and high corners
In shadows were ghastly, adhered around the pillars
Of iron, placid skeleton thrown to the cold sand
Bottom, forgotten and unrecognizable where he lay
At midnight; strange—we often share the unexplained wonder.

(Holden, 26)

By the time he died, Greenberg had produced more than 600 poems. None were published during his lifetime. After his death, his brother turned Greenberg's manuscripts over to the well-known art critic and writer, William Murrell Fisher, who became interested in the poems and published one in *Plowshares* in 1918 and several more in 1920. After that date, none appeared until 1947, when a collected edition was published with a Preface by Allen Tate. Tate, who had already established a reputation as a noted poet and critic, praised Greenberg's work and concluded: "Poetry of the twentieth century in the United States could not be complete without the publication of the poems of Samuel Greenberg" (Holden, xiv).

Tate's judgement aside, Greenberg remains mostly a forgotten poet, although his work received some attention in the late 1960s when it was revealed that Hart Crane—who had seen the Greenberg manuscripts in the winter of 1923–24—had used several of Greenberg's poems (without identifying them) as a source for his own work.[3] Nevertheless, his role in the development of American Jewish poetry, in spite of some truly inspired work, is minimal. Had he lived, had he been exposed to some of the emerging experiments in modern poetry, he would certainly have had more of an impact. As it is, we are left with a handful of memorable poems. Here, for example, is the last poem he wrote, addressed to his brother, Daniel, entitled simply "To Dear Daniel":

> There is a loud noise of Death
> Where I lay;
> There is a loud noise of life
> Far away.
>
> From low and weary stride
> Have I flown;
> From low and weary pride
> I have grown.
>
> What does it matter now
> To you or me?
> What does it matter now
> To whom it be?
>
> Again the stain has come
> To me;
> Again the stain has come
> For thee.
>
> (Holden, 45)

Like Greenberg, Alter Brody (1895–1979) had his roots in Yiddish language and the culture of the East European *shtetl*. Born in Russia in the village of Kartúshkiya-Beróza (the title of one of his most moving poems), Brody emigrated to New York in 1903. Little is known of Brody, who wrote in obscurity most of his life and ceased to publish creative work after 1930. His literary output consists of one collection of poems (*A Family Album and Other Poems*, 1918) and a volume of four short plays about life on the lower East Side (*Lamentations: Four Folk-Plays of the American Jew*, 1928). He wrote in English, and his work invariably expresses a deep sense of loss and alienation. The poems in *A Family Album* are impressive in terms of their emotional power, lyricism, and precise images. Many are autobiographical, based either on his early memories of Kartúshkiya-Beróza or his lonely life in New York. All are written in a free-verse style that seems both surprisingly modern and well suited for the sad, nostalgic mood Brody creates, especially when describing his past life. In his poignant memory poem "Kartúshkiya-Beróza," for example, Brody's Whitmanesque repetition of ordinary images and details creates a tone of incantation and a sense of religious significance in the everyday:

Kartúshkiya-Beróza
Sweet-sounding, time-scented name—
Smelling of wide-extending marshes of hay;
Smelling of cornfields;
Smelling of apple-orchards;
Smelling of cherry-trees in full blossom;
Smelling of all the pleasant recollections of my childhood—
Smelling of Grandmother's kitchen,
Grandmother's freshly-baked dainties,
Grandmother's plum-pudding—
Kartúshkiya-Beróza!

(Brody, 13)

When Brody wrote of America, as he did in "Times Square," "Ghetto Twi-light," and "Lamentations"—three of the more effective poems in *A Family Album*—there is almost always an expression of dislocation and regret, com-paring as he does his present situation to a more joyful, innocent existence in his beloved Kartúshkiya-Beróza. In "Times Square," the busy square serves as a point of departure for a detailed evocation of a boyhood incident in his native town. As in "Kartúshkiya-Beróza," tastes, smells, sounds, and sights provoke a Proustian response that draws the narrator back to his youth:

I cross the street
And suddenly,
Crowds, stores, theatres, tall buildings,
The blare and the glare of the day
Fade. . . .
October blows through the market-place
In a town of faraway Russia—
The booths are laden with fruit. . . .
A little boy,
Snub-nosed, freckle-faced, plump,
Dressed in a newly-washed jacket,
Stolidly strolls by the booths
Clutching a coin in his fingers—

(Brody, 37)

The speaker's reverie continues until "the toot of an automobile, / Insistent, shrill," jars him back to the harsh reality of New York.

The same mood of quiet despondency and isolation pervades "Ghetto Twilight," a short poem that effectively extends the personification of "old tenements . . . massed together" throughout to create a sense of desolation, loneliness, and despair. With "infinite weariness" the ghetto tenements "eye each other across the street / Through their dim windows—/ With a sad recognizing stare." The ghetto's occupants appear only once, toward the end of the poem, as depersonalized "tired faces." Brody's technique here is close to that of the imagists that were to come into poetic favor a few years later. By blending clear, simple pictures with an emotional subtext, Brody creates poetry that is compelling and forceful.

Perhaps Brody's most remarkable poetic achievement is the long, title poem of his 1918 collection, *A Family Album*. Again, Brody's method is autobiographical; "A Family Album" is a moving, first-person narrative of the author's early life in America. The style and language are reminiscent of Whitman: long, lyrical free-verse lines, interspersed with shorter, one-line observations. The poem's framing device is the album of the title, which becomes an extended metaphor for the narrator's own life in America:

> Worn and torn by many fingers
> It stands on the bed-room dresser,
> Resting back against its single cardboard buttress,
> (There were two)
> The gilt clasp that bound it, loose and broken,
> The beautiful Madonna on its cover, faded and pencil-marked,
> And the coarse wood of its back showing through its velvet lining.
>
> (Brody, 18)

The poem is held together by the distinctive voice and vision of the narrator. Once the "heavy, cardboard pages" of the album are opened, an entire emotional universe is revealed. As in "Times Square," Brody juxtaposes two very different worlds and two disparate psychological states. Strangely, the album itself, with its picture on the cover of the Madonna ("golden-haired, grave-eyed . . . Her blue eyes . . . so much bluer and clearer, and so sweetly pensive"), is the antithesis of the author's own life—both in America and in Russia. Understandably, the narrator would rather gaze at the "glorious, golden-haired Madonna" and "the soft slope of her breast" than the gloomy pictures contained within of "Grandfathers, grandmothers, aunts, uncles, cousins, / Sisters and sisters-in-law, brothers and brothers-in-law; / Photographs of some of the many boarders that always occupied our bedrooms." "I never cared to open," laments the narrator, "the gilt clasp of the album / And look through that strange kaleidoscope of Life."

Once confronted with his past, however, the author's mind "loosens like the gilt clasp of the album," and memories begin to accumulate and crystallize: "Page after page, picture after picture, / Until the miscellaneous photographs take to themselves color and meaning." The image of the Madonna is replaced by that of Sabbath afternoons in summer in Kartúshkiya-Beróza:

They rise in my brain with mysterious insistence
The blurred images of those Sabbath walks—
Poignantly, painfully, vaguely beautiful,
Half obliterated under the cavalcade of the years,
They lurk in the wayside of my mind and ambush me unawares—
Like little children they steal behind me unawares and blindfold me with
    intangible fingers
Asking me to guess who it is.

                                                    (Brody, 22)

The narrator has no choice: he is pulled unwittingly into the world of his memories, sometimes violently: "The coarse, keen pungency of satin from some girl's new shirtwaist, / Through my nose into my brain pierces like a rapier— / And suddenly I am standing on a sunny country porch with whitewashed wooden columns, / All dressed up for a Sabbath walk."

The poem ends with a series of images of family members, each remembered with a keen eye for physical detail ("portly Uncle Zalman with his fat, red-bearded face, . . . smooth-shaven, mustached Uncle Isaac, . . . big-hearted, big-bosomed Aunt Golda"). Almost against his will, the author has embraced "that strange kaleidoscope of Life,"—if only in memory, which—of course— is the ultimate purpose of his poetic journey. The result is a poem that succeeds emotionally and stylistically.

Brody was one of the first American Jewish poets to write of Jewish themes and subjects in a style that was both unique and effective. A generation earlier, Penina Moise and Emma Lazarus were working mostly with traditional poetic forms (the sonnet, rhymed couplets, accepted metrical patterns, etc.). Several years later, the work of Charles Reznikoff was experimental in ways that were consistent with the growing modernist tendencies of twentieth-century poetry as put forth by Ezra Pound and the imagists. But Brody seems to be alone as an early American Jewish poet who was concerned with particular Jewish issues and who was able to translate that concern into a distinctively individualized poetic style.

Among other Jewish poets who were born before the turn of the century and whose work has had an impact on the development of American Jewish poetry were—in addition to Reznikoff (1894–1976)—Philip Raskin (1880–1944), Louis Untermeyer (1885–1977), and Maxwell Bodenheim (1892–1954). Raskin is mostly a forgotten poet today. Yet in his collection, *Songs of a Jew* (1914), an early volume of Jewish-centered poetry, Raskin expressed some of the same sense of alienation, loneliness, and sadness as did Brody—although most of his poetry suffers from an overly solemn and pious tone. More significantly, Raskin was the editor of the first comprehensive collection of Jewish poetry in English, *Anthology of Modern Jewish Poetry* (1927), which brought together—in addition to his own verse—poems by Lazarus, Brody, Untermeyer, and other Americans, as well as translations of Yiddish, Hebrew, German, and Russian poetry.

Untermeyer, a tremendously productive poet, essayist, editor, critic, and anthologist, was the author of more than seventy volumes of poetry, fiction, travel books, translations, and critical anthologies. He wrote books about such diverse figures as Paul Bunyan, Edgar Allen Poe, John Greenleaf Whittier, and Robert Frost. He was also one of the first literary critics to write specifically about American Jewish poetry and to attempt an early definition of the Jewish poetic "spirit." In a 1921 essay in *Menorah Journal* (the forerunner of *Midstream*), Untermeyer identified three poetic "tendencies" present in contemporary Jewish poetry: "(1) the poetry of exaltation, of mystical fervor and vision . . . the Messianic note; (2) the poetry of disillusion, of bitter irony and driving restlessness—the Jew as the Wandering Jew; (3) the poetry of exultation, of sheer physical joy and thanksgiving—the old Hebraic impulse 'to sing and give praise'" (Untermeyer, 122). Although Untermeyer's proclamations were criticized by some as too parochial (D. H. Lawrence in a letter of 1926 derisively referred to him as "Der ewige Jude"—the wandering Jew [Liptzin, 145]), his essay is still cited in discussions of what constitutes Jewish poetry. Untermeyer's own poetry, however, is often overlooked, and he remains known primarily as a critic, editor, and anthologist.

Maxwell Bodenheim is not often included in discussions of American Jewish literature, as he is generally unconcerned with Jewish subjects in his work. He was a prodigious writer, producing ten volumes of poetry and more than a dozen novels before his murder (and that of his second wife) in Greenwich Village, New York. His two earliest collections, *Minna and Myself* (1918) and *Advice: A Book of Poems* (1920), contain poems with lavish, colorful images—as well as others that are ironic and austere. Several of the poems in these two collections treat Jewish issues, at least tangentially, and suggest Bodenheim's willingness to explore his heritage and his ambiguous relationship to his cultural/religious identity. "Old Age," from *Minna and Myself*, depicts a series of carefully detailed urban images, set against the larger subjects of death and the poet's subtle link to the Jewish people:

> In me is a little painted square
> Bordered by old shops with gaudy awnings.
> And before the shops sit smoking, open-bloused old men
> Drinking sunlight.
> The old men are my thoughts;
> And I come to them each evening, in a creaking cart,
> And quietly unload supplies.
> We fill slim pipes and chat

And inhale scents from pale flowers in the center of the square. . . .
Strong men, tinkling woman, and dripping, squealing children
Stroll past us, or into the shops.
They greet the shopkeepers and touch their hats or foreheads to me . . .
Some evening I shall not return to my people.

(Bodenheim, 13)

"East Side, New York," from *Advice*, is another of Bodenheim's early Jewish-centered lyrics. An example of his emerging imagistic technique, the poem depicts an old Jewish peddler, who is seen not as part of the "huddled masses" but rather as a distinct individual: "An old Jew munches an apple, / With conquering immersion / All the thwarted longings of his life / Urge on his determined teeth." It is not an optimistic poem, for Bodenheim did not see much hope in urban life.

In 1944, when most Jewish authors had barely begun to come to grips with the reality of Auschwitz and when many of those who did realize the full extent of the horror either could not or would not write about it, Bodenheim published a vitriolic condemnation of Nazi genocide. Entitled "Poem to Gentiles," it begins with these bitterly ironic lines:

The butchering must be wholesale and the smell
Of dead Jews must be strong enough to drift,
Like vastly stifled echoes of a yell,
Before the easy, widespread protests lift.
How many of them are sincere?—the tears,
The blades of conscience do not wait, mild, slow,
Until the slaughter-house revolves for years
And business lags because supplies are low.

(Bodenheim, 180–81)

The effect is immediate and intense, beginning with the image of butchery and continuing with those of wartime slaughter. The poem's themes of the horrors of war and the evil of anti-Semitism come together to form a compelling and forceful poetic protest against the Holocaust and the world's indifference to the Nazis' systematic destruction of European Jewry.

Of all the American Jewish poets born before the new century and who wrote in English, Charles Reznikoff had perhaps the most lasting influence. Although a contemporary of Brody and Greenberg, he—unlike them—was not only able to take part in the mainstream of modern American poetry but also helped shape the path it took. Early in the century, Reznikoff joined with George Oppen, Carl Rakosi, and Louis Zukofsky, to form the Objectivist Group, whose manifestos proclaimed the primacy of the poem an "object," important and in and for itself, rather than as a representation of any inner reality. Although Judaism was nowhere discussed in their credos, all the members of the group—with the exception of William Carlos Williams, who was an early partner in the enterprise, and Lorine Niedecker, a later compatriot—were Jewish. Reznikoff, however, was the only one among them whose Jewish concerns permeated almost all his poetry—especially later in his career.

Reznikoff, the son of Russian immigrants, was born in Brooklyn, New York. He graduated from New York University Law School in 1915 and was admitted to the bar the following year. He practiced law only briefly, however, turning instead to a career of writing, editing, and translating. His first book, *Poems*, appeared in 1920, and many more volumes of poetry, fiction, and drama followed. None of his work attracted a wide audience during his lifetime, but since his death his reputation has grown significantly, and in 1976–77, Black Sparrow Press published a two-volume edition of his complete poems.

Reznikoff's sense of Jewish identity is central to his work, and Jewish themes such as Biblical history, the immigrant experience in America, and the Holocaust persist throughout his work. His "objectivist" technique gives his poetry a concrete, visual quality. His language is simple, unemotional, and direct. An "objectivist," Reznikoff explained, "does not write about his feelings but about what he sees and hears" (Dembo, 206). Yet as a "Jewish" poet, Reznikoff was able to integrate his Jewish preoccupations with his objectivist aims and techniques. Without drama or hyperbole, Reznikoff could paint an "objective" image of an everyday existence that often included the threat of anti-Semitism and violence:

> Yom Kippur Uncle went with Grandfather.
> It was night and they had not come. They should have been
>   home by twilight to break their fast.
> The boy went down to the stoop to wait.
> Grandfather was coming alone.
> "Where's Uncle?" Grandfather did not answer. In his hurry
>   upstairs he stumbled.
> He went to his chair beside the window and sat looking into
>   the night.
> Tears rolled out of his blind eyes and fell upon his hands.
> Uncle came, bare-headed, blood oozing out of his hair.
>   (*Collected Poems*, I, 46)

As in his later work, "Holocaust," an epic poem based on the Nuremberg and Eichmann trials, Reznikoff makes no attempt to create "poetry" out of terrible events. Reznikoff's style in "Holocaust," published the year before his death, is spare and dry, devoid of all but the facts—some of which were taken directly from trial records. The disparity between the emotions evoked and the "objectivity" of the telling becomes almost too great for the reader to bear:

> One of the S.S. men caught a woman with a baby in her arms.
> She began asking for mercy: if she were shot the baby should live.
> She was near a fence between the ghetto and where the Poles lived
> and behind the fence were Poles ready to catch the baby
> and she was about to hand it over when caught.
> The S.S. man took the baby from her arms and shot her twice,
> and then held the baby in his hands.
> The mother, bleeding but still alive, crawled up to his feet.
> The S.S. man laughed
> and tore the baby apart as one would tear a rag.
> Just then a stray dog passed
> and the S.S. man stooped to pat it
> and took a lump of sugar out of his pocket and gave it to the dog.
>
> (*Holocaust*, 28–29)

Reznikoff also understood (before Hitler almost succeeded in annihilating the Jews) that Jewish survival in the Diaspora was as much a cultural issue as it was physical. "We must build," Reznikoff intoned in his poem "In Memoriam: 1933," "in Babylon / another Zion / of precepts, laws, ordinances and commandments / to outlast stone or metal." Survival and endurance—both physical and ethical—were, after all, essential aspects of Jewish history:

> Let other people come as streams
> that overflow a valley
> and leave dead bodies, uprooted trees and fields of sand;
> we Jews are as the dew,
> on every blade of grass,
> trodden under foot today
> and here tomorrow morning.
>
> (*Collected Poems*, I, 141)

More than any other poet of his generation, Reznikoff was able to express in his work the duality of being a Jew and an American. His perception of himself as a diaspora Jew, alienated from his culture, adrift in the New World, permeated all aspects of his work. Although he accepted the central dichotomy of his existence, he was never at ease. Sadly, he viewed the United States as "the noisy world / not mine" and its language "the speech of strangers," ultimately incapable of fully conveying meaning:

> The Hebrew of your poets, Zion
> is like oil upon a burn,
> cool as oil;
> after work,
> the smell in the street at night
> of the hedge in flower.
> Like Solomon,
> I have married and married the speech of strangers;
> None are like you, Shulamite.
>
> (*Collected Poems*, I, 107)

There are other nineteenth- and early twentieth-century American Jewish poets one could discuss as well, interesting in their own right, but whose impact on those who followed was not significant: writers such as Jessie Sampter (1883–1938), whose Zionist poems were popular among Jewish readers of the 1920s and 1930s; and Adah Isaacs Menken (1835–1868), a convert to Judaism, whose notoriety as an actress and siren outstripped her fame as a poet, but whose volume, *Infelicia*, was published simultaneously in New York, London, and Paris in 1868 and went through eight editions (Harap, 282); and James Oppenheim (1882–1930), whom Louis Untermeyer judged to be the quintessential Jewish poet of "exaltation" in 1921, but whose poems are rarely read today. However, when one traces the thematic and technical strands of the work of such poets as Moise, Lazarus, Brody, Greenberg, and Reznikoff, one understands the rich and varied beginnings of American Jewish poetry. As the twentieth century progressed, Jewish poets such as Stanley Kunitz (b. 1905), Delmore Schwartz (1913–1966), Muriel Rukeyser (1913–1980), Karl Shapiro (b. 1913), and David Ignatow (1914–1997) not only entered the mainstream of American literature, but helped define that literature by virtue of their own contributions. Therein, of course, lies another chapter in the continuing and impressive story of American Jewish poetry.

Notes

1. For a further discussion of these and other early American Jewish writers, see Sol Liptzin, *The Jew in American Literature* (New York: Bloch, 1966), and Louis Harap, *The Image of the Jew in American Literature: From Early Republic to Mass Immigration* (Philadelphia: Jewish Publication Society, 1978).

2. For a discussion of the difficulties in editing and publishing Greenberg's poems, see Harold Holden and Jack McManis, introduction to *Poems by Samuel Greenberg* (New York: Henry Holt and Company, 1947), xv–xxiii.

3. For a discussion of Crane's use of Greenberg, see Marc Simon, *Samuel Green-*

berg, Hart Crane, and the Lost Manuscripts (Atlantic Highlands, N.J.: Humanities Press, 1978), and the introduction to *Poems of Samuel Greenberg.*

Works Cited

Bodenheim, Maxwell. *Selected Poems.* New York: Beechhurst Press, 1946.

Brody, Alter. *A Family Album and Other Poems.* New York: Huebsch, 1918.

Dembo, L. S. and Cyrena Pondrom, eds. *The Contemporary Writer, Interviews with Sixteen Poets and Novelists.* Madison: U of Wisconsin P, 1972.

Gray, Janet, ed. *She Wields a Pen: American Women Poets of the Nineteenth Century.* Iowa City: U of Iowa P, 1997.

Greenberg, Samuel. *Poems of Samuel Greenberg.* Ed. Harold Holden and Jack McManus. New York: Henry Holt and Company, 1947.

Lazarus, Emma. *Selections from Her Poetry and Prose.* Ed. Morris U. Schappes. New York: Cooperative Book League, 1944.

Liptzin, Sol. *The Jew in American Literature.* New York: Bloch, 1966.

Harap, Louis. *The Image of the Jew in American Literature: From Early Republic to Mass Immigration.* Philadelphia: Jewish Publication Society, 1974.

Matza, Diane, ed. *Sephardic-American Voices: Two Hundred Years of a Literary Legacy.* Hanover: University Press of New England, 1997.

Reznikoff, Charles. *The Complete Poems of Charles Reznikoff.* vol. 1. Ed. Seamus Cooney. Santa Barbara, Calif.: Black Sparrow P, 1976.

———. *Holocaust.* Santa Barbara, Calif.: Black Sparrow P, 1975.

Untermeyer, Louis. "The Jewish Spirit in Modern American Poetry." *The Menorah Journal,* 7.3 (August 1921): 121–32.

Diasporic Poetics

MICHAEL HELLER

Poet, teacher, and great-grandson of a revered Bialystock rabbi, Michael Heller is the author of *Conviction's Net of Branches: Essays on the Objectivist Poets and Poetry* (Southern Illinois UP, 1985) and many collections of poetry, most recently *Wordflow: New and Selected Poems* (Talisman House, 1997). He has also completed a memoir, *Living Root*, from which portions of this essay have been derived.

To begin, two questions: Who were the "Objectivist" poets? And why should we take notice of their work in a book on Jewish American poetry?

"Objectivist" was, at first, a label created by Louis Zukofsky for a number of poets influenced by Ezra Pound, William Carlos Williams, and the Imagists whose work Zukofsky was gathering for publication in the February 1931 issue of *Poetry* magazine. The editor, Harriet Monroe, after much urging by Pound, had agreed to let Zukofsky edit the issue, provided Zukofsky labeled the grouping as a movement. Zukofsky obliged by writing a brief introduction to this movement"—"Program: 'Objectivists,' 1931"—and appended the essay "Sincerity and Objectification: *With Special Reference to the Work of Charles Reznikoff*," to further explain its poetics. A revised version of these pieces, now called "An Objective," appeared in Zukofsky's collection of critical essays, *Prepositions*, published in 1968; it has come to be seen as one of the most important theoretical documents of modern and contemporary poetry.

The poets to whom the "objectivist" label stuck—in addition to those mentioned in the text, there were Lorine Niedecker and, in England, Basil Bunting—languished in obscurity until they were rediscovered in the 1950s and 1960s by younger poets such as Robert Creeley, Robert Duncan, and Cid Corman. Since then, their influence and importance to a large number of poets and scholars have grown considerably.

Zukofsky always insisted that, although there might be "Objectivists," there was no single doctrine of "Objectivism," but it is safe to say the Objectivist poets shared an abiding concern with the ethical aspects of poetic imagination. Oppen spoke of the "test of sincerity"; Zukofsky, of the duty of "thinking with the things as they exist"; and Reznikoff, drawing on his legal studies, referred readers "to the rules with respect to testimony in a court of law. Evidence, to be admissable in a trial, cannot state conclusions of fact: it must state the facts themselves. . . . The conclusions of fact are for the jury and let us add, in our case, for the reader." As I put it some years ago in *Conviction's Net of Branches*, Objectivist poetry "was not so much technique as it was honor code . . . a way of being in the world, and only in the most general sense of stylistics."

Was that "way of being in the world" particularly Jewish? Not all the Objectivists were Jews. And yet, the question of how one's poem relates to one's Jewishness is, for me, deeply inflected by my reading of those that were. As I reflect on my own poetry, I see that it was they who led me into a re-engagement with Jewishness and with the philosophical and linguistic aspects of the tradition. Their ethical concern, their love of visible objective fact, and, most significantly, their questioning relationship to a Jewish God and Jewish dogma have profoundly shaped my own sense of what writing in diaspora might mean. To think about the Objectivists as Jewish poets is, for me, to reflect on the nature of diasporic consciousness and diasporic poetics, in their work and my own.

Isaac of Acre, the 13th century Spanish kabbalist, writes: "He who is vouchsafed the entry into the mystery of adhesion to God, *devekuth*, attains to the mystery of equanimity, and he who possesses equanimity attains to loneliness, and from there he comes to the holy Spirit and to prophecy." In this passage, one can identify not only a sacred journey of the soul but also a kind of poesis, for to come "to prophecy" means ultimately to come to speech, to poetry, to utter both hope and dread. The loneliness that Isaac of Acre speaks of is thus deeply connected not only to the severity and isolation of the spiritual journey but to the often wearying aloneness from which the poetic act seems to spring.

The poets who first nurtured my growth in poetry, Charles Reznikoff, George Oppen, Carl Rakosi and Louis Zukofsky, the Jewish Objectivists, struck me as being married to their aloneness, as to a bride.[1] Little noticed by the public or the academy, they wore the public neglect of their work as prideful badges. These were the poets whose books I carried on my own *hegira*, my wanderings, as I tried to find the forms my words and acts must take and be taken for.

Reznikoff, in particular, was a Jewish *flaneur*, a diminutive figure in dark suit and tie, and yet, an isolato endlessly walking the streets of the city, milling with its crowds or divagating into the suburbanlike precincts of Flatbush and outer Queens but always sensing his apartness. "I am alone—and glad to be alone," he writes in his poem "Autobiography: New York," linking himself both with the diasporic witness of an alienated consciousness and with those moments of the Jewish mystical tradition, as expressed in Isaac of Acre's words cited earlier, that acknowledge a fundamental and unbridgeable separation of God and man, but yet allow man to glimpse God, momentarily, as it were. Perhaps Reznikoff espied God on a sidewalk in Brooklyn, espied Him sardonically as kind of modern *deus absconditas*: "This pavement barren / as the mountain / on which God spoke to Moses— / suddenly in the street / shining against my legs / the bumper of a motor car." Or possibly Reznikoff experiences the religious moment as truly fleeting, like that instant of deep love in Baudelaire's poem when the poet sees and falls rapturously for a woman who passes quickly on the street, is swallowed up by the city, never to be seen again. In Reznikoff, as in Baudelaire, what passes before one can be briefly clung to, adhered to with *devekuthic* intensity, but can never be totally embraced. Whether it be God or an individual that one cannot be united with or, in the diaspora, if it is a country or place that only begrudgingly accepts one, the nature of the relationship is that it is at least partially unrequited.

Louis Zukofsky, too, made the Jew's peculiar burden of aloneness one of his major themes. In "A-12," that beautiful weave of a father's love for his son, he asks plaintively, "Where stemmed the Jew among strangers?" And answers himself: "Speech moved to sing / To echo the stranger." Writing in American English, the language of "strangers" (his own first language was Yiddish), Zukofsky listened for echoes with a kabbalist's intuition of the power of wordplay and pun. Indeed, his work seemed to reinscribe family history, religion, philosophy and the poetic tradition as so many instances of an almost sacred sonic attentiveness, a love both for the objects of his devotion and for the weight and tone of every syllable by which it is rendered. "As I love: / My poetics," the poet defines his art in "A-12." In "A-11," his prosodic masterpiece of family life, receptivity to love is a reciprocal power: "our / love to see your love flows into / Us." Poetically, love is animating force which turns speech toward praise: "If Venus lights, your words spin, to / live our desire leads us to honor." Naturally such love and care has a religious dimension, a resonance of acting under the eye of God. "There is no one," his poem's Rabbi Pinhas says, "who is not every minute / Taught by his soul."

Zukofsky, in his major prose work, *Bottom: On Shakespeare*, formulates the poetics of Shakespeare and, implicitly, the Objectivists, as "favoring the clear physical eye over the erring brain." "Love is to reason," he proposes, "as the eyes are to the mind." In a poet like Rakosi, such a trust in sensory perception is, as in Zukofsky, at once a matter of the poet's love for what he sees and a religious imperative. In his poem "The Vow," he proclaims this trust outright: "Matter, / with this look / I wed thee." And in his haunting "Associations With a View From the House," he writes, "It is the great eye, / source of security. / Praised be thou, as the Jews say, who have engraved clarity / and delivered us to the mind."

What I felt from these poets who taught me so much was the power of perception, the happenstance of authorship, the impingement and penetration by the world into our would-be discursiveness, our self-involved chatter. The gloss of eyes across and over streets, as though the city were made of languages, inscribed in the ages and designs of buildings, in the oddities and samenesses of people one passed. . . . A collection of languages, written and rewritten. From so much utilitarian secularity, one might derive a nontheological theology of language, as if to say: thank Whomever (ironically of course) or whatever has designed this world. For I find new languages daily; I find that not all is written out, and that therefore I too am allowed to speak and write. Further, there are, in the life of the writer, those moments of being sickened with one's own work, one's very words. At such times, I have risen from my desk and hurled myself out into the city, evicted myself from the precincts of my own logorrhea, partly as break or diversion, but also to be in touch with the languages of others. Thus, to gloss, to go over, as an eye savoring the textures of the world is also to be compelled into utterance, and so to provide interlinears and commentaries.

Commentary, therefore, is first eyes before words, a searchlight of eyes on texts that invoke disturbances and consonances in the reader. Commentary, too, is never synonymous with the text; it always remains apart. And so it stands, in the idealized version of interpretation, in *devekuthic* relation to the text. The commentary adheres to the text, and—whatever its virtues as a text in its own right—never enters into mystical union (one in the other) with it. George Oppen, in his late poems, expressed such adhesions as a kind of poetic radiation. In a poem to Louis Zukfosky, whom he regarded as one of his poetic fathers, he identified the poet as a lighthouse turned back on the coast, searching out the edges of the continent, illuminating the particular commonness of Americans, and ultimately of humans, as figures of differentiation, as ways of acknowledging the fundamental conditions of apartness. This recognition of difference, a refusal of sentimental or too easy identifications at the heart of all of Oppen's work, accounts for its probity. Such a voice struck me not only as embodying a full and tested knowledge of our lives, and our way of thought, but also offered us hope that such a knowledge was our ultimate value, a value out of which not only truth but compassion could be found. Oppen, the "meditative singular man," seemed to stand, like the lighthouse image at the center of his poem, "The Lighthouses," on an isolate and prophetic vantage point in which

> . . . to say what one knows and to
> limit oneself to this
>
> knowledge is
> loneliness turning and turning
>
> lights
> of safety for the coasts

Oppen's entire poetic oeuvre was for me an endless efflorescence, a singular linguistic act of the truth of boundaries and boundedness, not only on the level of nations—where the inability to tolerate aloneness was most destructive in our time—but on the level of the singularity of individuals and on the level of consciousness relating to the nonhuman world.

The impact of reading Oppen and the other Objectivists was to reinforce my own questioning of my relationship to Jewish thought and culture. In some sense, the way had been prepared by my family history, for it was my grandfather, a rabbi from Bialystok, whose strictness drove my father from his house at age fifteen, making him, at best, an uneasy participant in Jewish life. And my mother was a professed atheist who on the High Holy Days, and only at my father's strongest pleadings, went to the Temple. Remembering my own estrangements and refusals, I wrote in "The American Jewish Clock" of my generation's rejection of suburban Jewish culture: "the synagogues swelled / with increase and were tethered like calves / on suburban lawns. And then . . . O and then, / / the young walked out, walked back / to the cities / prodigals of emptied memory. / I was among them. And the door slammed shut."

And yet, the Jewishness of the Objectivists was manifest in a variety of complex ways, in their textual practices, in their love of visible objective fact, and, most significantly, in their questioning relationship to a Jewish God and Jewish dogma. On this latter point, I remember the powerful effect of reading and taking in Zukofsky's placing of Spinoza, the excommunicated Jewish rationalist heretic, at the center of the early sections of *"A"* and of Reznikoff's skepticism, his identification, in his poem "Hanukkah," with "the rebellious Jews" who "light not one light but eight— / not to see by but to look at." Equally powerful on my consciousness were the meditations of Rakosi and Oppen on the uncertainty of the theological point of view, its transmutation in their work into a phenemonology of near-secular spirituality. Most forcefully, I was developing a growing sense of a kind of diasporic consciousness in these poets, one created by the dis-ease and difficulty with which they approached their heritage and by the cultural and poetic apartness under which they worked.

But first, let me be clear: Obviously, from the view I have espoused above, there is no such stable category as Jewishness. That is, if the commonplace of Jewishness in thought and poetry involves textuality and commentary, it is also true that the poetics of Jewishness involves the undoing of text and comment, that textuality is a kind of traveling away, of departing, of heresy. As the great Jewish scholar Gershom Scholem puts it, an enacting of a "counter-history," or, as I echoed in my own memoir writing, a "counter-memory." I would allow this trope as a very Jewish commonality, one that is best seen as an attempt to unlearn when that which one has learned imprisons like a bondage or a reflex.

The Objectivist poets to whom I am indebted wrote against history's grain, wrote their poems as a kind of counter-memory, not out of any desire to reject their pasts, but to find their own specific gravities within more general traditions, to find those stories that belonged to them. For these poets, there was that other diaspora—within the larger diaspora of America and its culture—of their own estrangement from the familiar: their sense of distance from the life around them, their need to give witness to this distance, the need, as Zukofsky put it, "to sing / To echo the stranger." The texts of America and of American Jewish life as well as those of the inherited literary traditions of their time were to be revisited in this way. This is what diaspora meant, not alienation, but a need to reengage the old texts, the old familiars and circumstances. The poet John Taggart, in his brilliant meditation "Walk-out: Rereading George Oppen," maintains that "Insofar as Oppen's work may be considered Jewish, it is a differing Jewishness or, to adopt one of Oppen's own terms, it is an antinomian Jewishness." The diaspora invokes not rejection but a rethinking, a traveling with tradition in a new, even if oppositional, way.

Thus, if it appears that in the work of the Objectivists, commentary circles back to origins (or let us admit—commentary does circle back), for these poets, it does not merely lodge with prior thought but displaces it, though never totally. This partial displacement is, perhaps, another way to imagine the *devekuthic* relation of commentary to text that I describe earlier. In any case, to be human, to be humane, is necessarily to grow by traceries, to be revisited so that we may visit, so that we may visit our own experience even as we are revisited.

Ineluctably—and perhaps this is where my relation to the Objectivists and my Jewishness intersect—I, too, participate willingly in such a return not only to origins but to the modalities and thoughts of the poets who have shaped my work. Let me follow the dynamics of such traceries through a poem that I have written, bearing in mind that the poet exegeting his own poem is, himself, involved in that act of adhesion and separation, circling back and displacement, that makes up commentary, trying to account for something not entirely of his own making. Here is the poem:

Diasporic Conundrums

—Call me not Naomi, call me Mara—

And now this man is fatherless
because he had a father,
and Israel is no more.

A line encircles
deserts beyond Jerusalem,

and he who was given a name
has lost the right to silence.

The man had a mother
because he had a mother,
and Israel never was.
Jerusalem, the golden,
city's mirage
shimmers on desert sands.

How could this be real?
Who will raise up
a name like Ruth,
put a name,
like a child, onto the air?

The dead are dead.
This is certain.
This is what was written,
why it was written.
This need not be said.

This poem was written almost unconsciously at first, as though in a haze or fever. A number of things were on my mind, all of which in one way or another entail diasporas: the story of Ruth in the Bible (the poem's epigraph is from *The Book of Ruth*, Ruth 1:20), that very postmodern idea that the word is displaced from the object it refers to, that the word is exilic, and, as I have written elsewhere, that whatever my religious inclinations, the world has labeled me a Jew (or as the poet Paul Celan puts it, the Jew has nothing that is not borrowed, least of all the name, Jew).

For me, as I'm sure for others, the essence of poetry is naming, naming in the sense that the poem is a name for a thing or state of affairs that did not previously exist. For Oppen, such naming was a "test of sincerity, the moment . . . when you believe something to be true, and you construct a meaning from those moments of conviction." In this, poetry repeats the Adamic act; it bears the force of original conjunction. The German Jewish critic Walter Benjamin, for instance, sees the name as a "primordial form of perception in which words possess their own nobility as names." Elsewhere throughout his writing Benjamin suggests that this form of perception does not simply correlate words with the things of the world but creates an immediate and powerful relation between the two, short-circuiting conceptual thought. But what about renaming or, as I've tried to suggest already, what about when we revisit naming as renaming?

I'm thinking here of what textuality and commentary, at root, actually consist of. The original Adamic field of play can be seen as namelessness, as a silent and unlettered cosmos. But if it ever did exist, this undifferentiated nameless- ness is no more. It has been replaced in the contemporary consciousness by the totality of Adam's act, by Babel—or, perhaps, as the kabbalists insist, the world and all its forms are already, albeit secretly, a form of Torah, lurking as a written out and inscribed universe hidden behind apparent phenomena. Adam, then, was the first textualist, possibly, by that, the first Jew in the Bible.

But let me refocus on the poem. First, its epigraph, which came into my head and was the seed-phrase of the piece. In the story of Ruth, Naomi has suf- fered an incomprehensible and overwhelming fate. She has lost her husband and sons, and is burdened with two step-daughters. In her anguish, she cries out, "Call me not Naomi, call me Mara, for the Almighty has dealt very bitterly with me." Naomi is here testifying, heart-wrenchingly, to the perceiving func- tion of the name. "I went away full," she exclaims, "and the Lord has brought me back empty." Given her experience, she is no longer a "Naomi" (something pleasant or good), but a "Mara," which is the Biblical word for bitterness.

We know that Ruth's "conversion," the sense that Judaism is more than a tri- bal or blood kinship religion, lies at the heart of the story, as well as its fore- shadowing of the rise of David. But what most struck me in this instance was Naomi's demand to be called by another name. In my own family, such name changes have always struck me as having particularly crucial importance. My grandfather's first name was changed when he first arrived in America, an event I wrote about in "The Jewish American Clock": "Zalman, here called Solomon! / With a new syllable to lengthen his name. In the vast / benumbed space of us, a little more sound to place him." That anglicizing, still resonanant with its Biblical and even foreign-seeming source, seemed to mark his pro- found unease and displacement in the diaspora. In my memoir, *Living Root*, I conjured my father's name change from Philip to Peter as a way of explaining the shifts in his character from idealistic youth to a bit of mild chicanery when he was a young man. One speculative flight I take up is that Philip is my father's legal name, and in that name he does things legal. Peter (etymologi- cally derived from petrus, stone) is a harder character, translatable in my father's use of it as willed ignorance or guileful bluntness, as less sensitive to certain nuances and niceties. In the Bible of course, name changes are among the most significant phenomena: Abram to Abraham, one of the most impor- tant, as well as Jacob's change of name to Israel after wrestling with the angel. Naomi's fall into ruin, her changed condition, requires this self-renaming.

Yet another way of looking at Naomi's story might be by way of the notion of sympathetic magic. That is, if we keep in mind Benjamin's phrase concern- ing naming as a "primordial form of perception," then the experience of Naomi, the bodily and emotional stuff of her coming to bitterness, that is, the nonlinguistic or opaque and hidden aspect of her suffering, is revealed to us by her name change. What has happened is neither synonymity nor mere gloss but the transformation of physicality into language. The diasporic journey, as embedded in this exemplary story, is first physical, experiential, and, yes, is signaled to the reader by physical means. In my family's history of name changes, "Zalman" does not sound like "Solomon" nor does "Philip" resemble "Pete." In the Biblical story, "Mara" cannot be pronounced as "Naomi."

In this sense, the story of Naomi's name change is a prologue to the rest of the poem. For my poem seeks to address the conundrums of inherited names as fixities and the relation of these fixities to the self, to poetry, and to nationalisms and nation-states. Each stanza expresses a linked conundrum. And the conundrums are "diasporic," quite simply I hope, because they are written from the viewpoint of someone (me) in the actual diaspora, someone who embraces the diaspora as the condition of his Jewishness and of his poetry. But as well, I've tried to intuit here, as I did in the Objectivists, a sense of the transmigratory aspect of words and names, of naming and renaming, one that floats or drifts into wandering on the polyvalence of words as though one could send a word toward a meaning it did not begin with, hence disperse it, place it in diasporic motion. The French Jewish philosopher Emmanuel Levinas calls Jewishness not a metaphor but a "category of understanding." He suggests what this understanding might be for a poet when he writes: "Is it certain a true poet occupies a place? Is the poet not that which, in the eminent sense of the term, loses its place, ceases occupation, precisely, and is thus the very opening of space, [neither the transparency nor the emptiness which (no more than night, nor the volume of beings) yet displays the bottomlessness or the excellence, the heaven that in it is possible . . .]."

Levinas's thought is not concerned with the so-called nomadic tendency of the Jew or of the Jewish poet; rather, it testifies to the dynamics of the word-experience phenomena, to the poet as transmuter of a worked-upon physiology into language, the renamer. Implicit in this line of thought is that the poet is not perceived as an experimenter with language per se, for there is nothing more confident than the experimenter in the laboratory who can objectively manipulate materials (language in this case) in a fanciful manner. On the contrary, Levinas's poet is anguished and exposed; he "loses place," "ceases occupation," that is, does not perform but is performed upon by experience, by adversity, by love and history.

Again, I sense that I am wandering. So let me return to the first stanza which is about the son ("this man") maturing toward ethicality by moving out from under the father's name (the conditions of the father's world and his social realm). The son becomes a refugee or emigrant from the name, which is, basically, a diasporic movement. To put it backward (which is what conundrums do), the son does not fulfill his own hopes or potentialities while under the father's name, a name that roots him in place and identity. But he must have a father, he must have a reference point or cause to exist, in order to become "fatherless." There is no hope of fatherlessness without there first being a father. Likewise, and recent history is very clear on this, Israel, as a project of the Jewish people, can become either simply a fixed geographical place and/or the term of an ethical process beyond conception as only a nation-state. The German Jewish philosopher Franz Rosenzweig in *The Star of Redemption* refers to the solution to such a dilemma in the separation of ethics from coercion. Coercion is state business, is about maintenance and fixity. In my mind, the existence of Israel, given the recent, tragic history of Jews, has led to a conflation of hope with unbending rigidity, of self-protection with an overzealous notion of defense, security, and opposition to compromise.[2] But Rosenzweig searches for a sense of self-restraint of power, a withholding that he, as with Levinas, is convinced is the Jewish secret of survival and eternity. When the son is fatherless, that is, when he moves out from under the father's name, he also moves out from the idea of fixity, of Israel as fixity. I'm not speaking poetry here as much as I'm suggesting the possibility of an ongoing prophecy.

I sense a parallel to this conundrum of father and fatherlessness in the Objectivist poet's relation to poetic tradition. Tradition is a kind of fathering, but also potentially a dogmatic set of rules and mind-sets. So, for the poet, there is both honoring and, in a sense, abjuring. George Oppen in "The Lighthouses," which I quoted from earlier, writes "in loyalty / / to all fathers or joy / of escape / / from all fathers," in this case not only the biological ones but also those of his literary antecedents, Ezra Pound and Louis Zukofsky. In order to write with new force and significance, the fixity of one's "tradition," of one's poetic loyalties, must be escaped from. Equally for Oppen, as Taggart points out in his essay, is the troubling complexity of one's "escape" from the ancestral Jewish fixities as represented by the state of Israel, the "that land" of his "Five Poems About Poetry."

The conundrum of the second stanza, linked to the first but also autobiographical, is that there is an obligation in having been given a name. If the name represents an authority prior to understanding, it may be questioned—indeed, question is required. One of my favorite thinkers on religion, Ludvig Holberg, wrote that if a man learns theology before he learns to be human, he will never become a human being. One could paraphrase: If one learns to be a Jew, or a fundamentalist or an avant-gardist or an Objectivist, etc. . . . The received name is dogma incarnate, not experience. Thus, the obligation is to grow, to move out from under the name, and to express that movement as a new understanding. The poet's work can be seen as an undoing or at least testing of the parent's or father's authority, for one who would aspire to poetry, to identify naming as renaming. Naomi-Mara is the paradigm of this poetics.

Now the mother of the third stanza does not give a name to the child; inherited names come by way of the father. This situation is paradoxical. The mother's love is so seductive and all-embracing for the child that to stay within its confines may be to obliterate the possibility of creating an Israel. The idea of redemption for all humans, the Jerusalem of the poem, can only be a mirage unless one accepts discomfort and struggle by foregoing the child's sense of security that the mother represents. And one supposes that this makes the poem even more of a conundrum since we all have mothers and fathers whom we love. We are always living in the dynamics of being placed between their love and compassion and our own strivings. A further conundrum is that since a mother's love does not come by way of a name or authority, it need never be abandoned. The idea of the selflessness of love, often represented as a mother's love, is just that, noncentered and free of coercion. Love and compassion, without name or reference point, are always possible, even when one is renamed. Again, the story of Naomi-Mara is instructive. It is the renamed Naomi that Ruth embraces as her mother.

The fourth and fifth stanzas are questions and admonitions put to myself about the writing of poetry, and, in a personal sense, about self-growth. The name, in the act of renaming, in poetry, is, for me, a kind of seeking. And given the above three stanzas, the fourth one, with its sense of difficulty ("Who will raise up / a name like Ruth, put a name, / like a child, onto the air?"), suggests a wish for courage or means to write, a desire, perhaps a hopelessly wishful one, for the substantiality of naming. The fifth stanza constitutes an injunction to not write like the dead, for "The dead are dead. / This is certain. / This is what was written . . . This need not be said." The implicit injunction is to avoid being involved in mere repetition, writing, as it were, under the father's dictates (sometimes mislabeled as tradition). But there is a further, less explicit consideration in this last stanza, one deeply embedded in Jewish tradition, that of remembering. As the Book of Job instructs, "inquire, I pray thee, of the former generation, and apply thyself to that which their fathers have searched out." Like oneself, the dead, one's parents and one's parent poets too, sought to understand the conundrums of hope and dispersal. So of course, we must write to the dead, but about our present and our hope for the future. The closure that is their deaths demand not only our holding them in memory but also our utterance.

The question put here is how a particular Jewishness informs a poetry—and especially, how it might inform this one particular poem. I hope some of those specifics, those interrelations between prior texts and commentary, the reflections on sources and concerns, are clear. But a deeper question might be, how is one "informed" (if that is the correct word) by Judaism? I would acknowledge that there is a powerful sociology of exposure at work in me as in everyone. And yet, though I was born into a Jewish family, I was not raised in a theocratic state (despite the efforts of my stern rabbi-grandfather). In fact, I was, by my midteens, an unbeliever.

What then, I ask myself, constitutes my unbelief? As I put what I deem my aspirations both personally and poetically, what I would rise to, under scrutiny, I maintain that certain lineaments of my life—of any life are—if not theological, at least somewhat religious. How to put this? One is surrounded by the heaven and hell of the modern city, by the intense glamour and seductiveness of its people and its shops, even by the fetus-like curls of street people asleep in doorways, by the bent and unhappy riders of subways. These things are, for good or ill, an incitement to wakefulness, even if it be merely to repel the image of the foul bum or to lust for the city's sexual beings or exotic foods. What is religious, after all, are the very things that question the boundaries of our being, which enable a traverse of psychic chasms, of difference and otherness. Thus, I find in this "awake" quality, one that provokes endless curiosity and question, the meaning of Jacob Neusner's remark that "Judaism rejoices at the invitation of the secular city." The modern city is a concentrate of what Eastern religious thought calls "attachment." And without this world, without its samsaric barb (to continue with non-Western terminologies) there is no nirvana, no wisdom without confusion. So, too, with language. Without silence there is no language, but also, without babble (Babel), we have no movement from the confused and unintelligible toward legibility and articulation.

Did the secular as a category even exist for my grandfather? Asleep, in a sense, in his assured and monotonous recitation of the Haggadah, my grandfather seemed to efface not only the exact sense of ritualistic Word but the counterpointing silence by which the ritual meaning becomes articulate. Belief, for him, was an attained realm, a certainty of being in consonance with some divine principle rather than a matter of faith to be moment by moment realized. My father's beliefs were less hard and fixed than his father's; especially when it came to prayers and rituals he took more seriously each word, tried to feel its exactness, like a solid object held in his mouth, going in fear of the god he was far less comfortable with than was my grandfather. I, who am godless, took much from my father, including this legacy, a legacy that I now sense as the heart of Objectivist poetics as well: to seek for the precise word, the secular word, that would deliver.

Gershom Scholem's questions about language come to mind: "Can the human word," he writes, "contain the word of God in its pure form, or can the word of God, if it exists, express itself within the confines of the human language?" The answer, for me, to both of these questions can only be yes. Any attempt to separate God word and human word would have no meaning or force whatsoever. This idea is one that could hold true whether one were a believer or not. Or to phrase it in Scholem's words, the Absolute is recognizable by the infinite number of interpretations that can be brought to it. The causal factor of the poem is the world, the unnameable angel who is struggled with, in order to find the blessed name, Israel, the place of God or divinity. This much I allow myself. One's own writing, then, however secular it may seem, can be looked upon as a kind of commentary on one's antecedents in much the same way that Talmud and *midrash* are commentary on the oral and written Torah.

That model of commentary (Blake would call it "not Generation but Regeneration") is what I always have in mind when writing or when reading. Furthermore, I have a strong suspicion that this model, as I learned it through the Objectivist poets, is far more than merely my idea of how one approaches the making of a poem. For in truth, we circle out, we are impelled by experience into the diaspora, and lo, we have fathered our own fatherlessness.

Notes

1. Many critical studies have been devoted to the work of the Objectivists. Among them are sections of Hugh Kenner's *A Homemade World* and *The Pound Era*, portions of the many books on contemporary poetry by Marjorie Perloff, and my own study, the first book on the Objectivists as a group, *Conviction's Net of Branches: Essays on the Objectivist Poets and Poetry*. The National Poetry Foundation's *Man and Poet/Woman and Poet* series has individual volumes on Oppen, Zukofsky, Reznikoff, Niedecker, and Rakosi. Recent important treatments of the Jewish Objectivists as specifically *Jewish* American poets can be found in Charles Bernstein's essay "Reznikoff's Nearness" (in *My Way: Speeches and Poems* [U of Chicago P, 1999]), John Taggart's "Walk Out: Rereading George Oppen" (*Chicago Review*, 1998), and Mark Scroggins's *Louis Zukofsky and the Poetry of Knowledge* (U of Alabama P, 1998), and Norman Finkelstein is currently at work (as of this writing) on a study of modern poetry and Jewish American identity that treats the Objectivists—and my own poetry—with considerable nuance and depth.

2. In another poem of mine, "Accidental Meeting With an Israeli Poet," about my encountering the Israeli poet Yehuda Amichai—during his time at New York University, our sons played soccer together on the fields before the massive Con Edison plant—I tried to picture that transformation of promise and deliverance that Israel represents into something like the way we have invested ourselves in material and military strength:

> Trampled ground, grass, sun-tinged webs of cable—
> so this is how we reckon hope, as something
> blotted up by matter that it might better
> circulate in brick, in the squared off shadows
>
> of the power plant to commingle with children
> and with games and sides, with wire and with steel
> until, lo, the helmet of a soldier has sopped it up!
> It sits there, insisting on a certain rightness.

Works Cited

Heller, Michael. *Conviction's Net of Branches*. Carbondale: U of Southern Illinois P, 1985.

——*Wordflow*: *New and Selected Poems*. Jersey City: Talisman House, 1997.

Levinas, Emmanuel. *Proper Names* Stanford: Stanford UP, 1997.

Oppen, George. *Collected Poems*. New York: New Directions, 1975.

——Interview with L. S. Dembo, in "The 'Objectivist' Poet: Four Interviews," *Contemporary Literature* 10.2 (Spring 1969).

Rakosi, Carl. *Ex Cranium Night*. Los Angeles: Black Sparrow P, 1975.

Reznikoff, Charles. *First There is the Need*. Santa Barbara: Black Sparrow P, 1977.

——*Poems 1918–1975: The Complete Poems of Charles Reznikoff*. Ed. Seamus Cooney. Santa Rosa: Black Sparrow P, 1996.

Rosenzweig, Franz. *The Star of Redemption*. South Bend: U of Notre Dame P, 1985.

Taggart, John. "Walk-out: Rereading George Oppen." *Chicago Review* 44.2 (1998).

Zukofsky, Louis. "*A*." Baltimore: John Hopkins UP, 1993.

——*Bottom: On Shakesphere*. Berkeley: U of California P, 1987.

——"An Objective," in *Prepositions: The Collected Critical Essays*. New York: Horizon, 1968. Expanded ed., Berkeley: U of California P, 1981: 12–18. Forthcoming critical ed., Wesleyan, UP of New England.

Strategies of Reading: Editors' Introduction

If the second group of essays offered a historical tour of Jewish American poetry, the group of reflections that follows offers a different kind of tour altogether. Each of the following pieces offers a method, a strategy for reading any Jewish American poem regardless of its period. Jonathan Barron's essay, "Commentary in Contemporary Jewish American Poetry," explores the way that Jewish American poetry can be read as a commentary on its cultural, literary setting. To illustrate this idea, Barron reads a poem by Maxine Kumin in the context of postwar American poetry more generally. In so doing, he shows how an apparently straightforward lyric also acts as a subtle commentary on three of the dominant poetic styles of the past fifty years. By providing a tour of Projectivist, Confessional, and Deep Image poetry, Barron shows that Jewish poets have pursued commentary in order to avoid the specifically Christian themes fundamental to those three styles. Rather than rejecting them—much of them deeply embedded in the American language itself—Jewish poets have engaged Confessional, Deep Image, and Projectivist poetics in order to open in them a space for new imaginative freedom.

The essay by Eric Murphy Selinger keeps this focus on questions of commentary, but takes readers into the realm of cultural history, and into the spiritual terrain so frequented by American poets. In "Shekhinah in America," Selinger traces the varying ways that Jewish American poets have invoked and transformed the figure of Shekhinah, that at-least-grammatically feminine figure in Jewish mysticism for the immanent Presence of God. Jewish poets have long seen this figure as intimately linked to poetry, but Selinger draws our attention back to the world of new liturgy and feminist rituals where She is found as well. Recalling hot debates within the Jewish religious community over female God-language and its (perhaps) implicit challenge to monotheism itself, this essay shows what Jewish American poetry looks like when read as part of a lively religious culture: both Jewish and American, since the Shekhinah has her partisans among Theosophists, Evangelicals, and Neo-Pagans, too.

Both Barron and Selinger offer new ways of reading Jewish American poetry. Barron focuses on commentary, while Selinger focuses on the way that poetry revives repressed or forgotten elements of Jewish culture, often "marrying" them to non-Jewish traditions in deliberately provocative or troubling ways. In the third reflection of this group, Maeera Shreiber's "A Flair for Deviation," two more strategies for reading Jewish American poetry are exhibited. Shreiber shows what happens if you bring classical Jewish sources (Torah, Talmud, the Kabbalah) and the latest in Jewish and non-Jewish cultural theory to the reading of a single contemporary Jewish American poem. As Shreiber points out, poetry has been seen by Jews for centuries as a troublemaking and suspect genre, one intimately linked with the feminine, with the blurring of cultural boundaries, and above all with the idea of Exile. In her reading of Jacqueline Osherow's "Moses in Paradise," Shreiber shows how the very features of poetry that have long made it a little suspect in Jewish culture are a valued part of an American national poetics—an opportunity for cultural trouble-making that Osherow seizes with style.

Commentary in Contemporary Jewish American poetry

JONATHAN N. BARRON

Jonathan N. Barron is Associate Professor of English at the University of Southern Mississippi and editor of *The Robert Frost Review*. He has published articles on Jewish American poetry and on such poets as William Wordsworth and Robert Frost. He has also coedited forthcoming essay collections on Robert Frost and on New Formalist poetry. He is currently at work on a book about the role of the media in contemporary American poetry.

In 1808, while on a trip far from home, Rabbi Nachman of Bratslav decided to burn one of his books. Apparently, Rabbi Nachman, convinced that this same book was linked to the deaths of his wife and child, ordered the very disciple to whom he had dictated the manuscript to return to Bratslav, find the extant copies, and burn them. This the disciple did.[1]

Reflecting on this story 178 years later, the Talmudic scholar and literary critic, Marc-Alain Ouaknin finds in it a particularly Jewish view of language. Opposed absolutely to idolatry, Judaism, says Ouaknin, teaches writers and readers not to transform words into idols. When Rabbi Nachman of Bratslav burned his book, he, like Moses destroying the ten commandments, meant to destroy their idolatrous potential; he did not mean to erase the law, or his ideas about the law. In order to ensure the law's transcendent character, he destroyed its iconic representation. According to Rabbi Nachman's own disciple, three years before the burning, in 1806, Rabbi Nachman had had portions of his book, then only in manuscript, publicly recited in a number of towns. After burning the printed versions, the book, as it were, would still live but only in an oral tradition. The book had been transformed into a series of remembered quotations recited from person to person over the course of generations.

Out of this story, Ouaknin derives this lesson: "The breaking of the Law is eminently positive; it signifies the refusal of the idol. Moses does not pass on, at first, the Law but its shattering: its impossibility of being an idol, the place of perfection, a 'total book.'"[2] Like Moses, Rabbi Nachman runs in fear of perfection, in fear of the Total Book. For what is the Total Book if not the final answer: perfection itself. The Total Book is all that we mean by the term transcendence. According to the rabbinical tradition, *transcendence*, as the very definition of God, prohibits any one person from absolute knowledge. For to claim such knowledge would put one in the mind of God as the mind of God. Nonetheless, it is in the nature of the mind to want to know. Therefore, against the human urge toward such knowledge, rabbinical Judaism developed an oral tradition of commentary and interpretation—the Talmud—that avoids the danger of totalizing, absolute, idolatrous knowledge. It sets itself always in the spoken voice of a singular individual commenting, and interpreting. Commentary, unlike a pronouncement, a law, does not replicate, make, or substitute itself for, or even challenge the transcendent Law. Rather, commentary seeks to reveal and uncover the meaning of that law, now, in the context of human time. As Ouaknin says, "The speech that fissures writing, that breaks the Tables and burns the book, is the speech of interpretation."[3] Notice that Oukanin, in keeping with the rabbinic tradition, sets speech, even when it is rendered into printed words as a dialogue or transcript, against writing. In the Jewish tradition, the only writing that matters is the Torah as God's work; only it lays claim to total knowledge, for only it is of God. By contrast, speech conceived as interpretation and commentary on the written words is the means by which the Law can be understood. The great Jewish scholar Gershom Scholem tells us that revelation occurs when one interprets the written Torah. God's words, as it were, remain silent until the speech of the rabbis interprets them through commentary. Speech, as interpretation, as commentary, makes no claim to totality because it always cedes final authority to the words of the Law.

With the onset of Christianity, however, this rabbinic distinction between speech and writing was overthrown. In the Christian tradition, Jesus, as a Christ, became the Holy Word incarnate in flesh. After Jesus, interpretation is no longer necessary. It may even be superfluous. This means that in the Christian tradition, commentary as interpretation is not the very substance of revelation: It is not an act that produces revelation itself. According to Ouaknin, then, the parable of the "burnt book," as a lens through which to read the meaning of the Jewish act of interpretation, is also a way to understand just where Judaism differs from Christianity: "The Hebrew text and its Hebrew reader realize what could be called an 'anti-Christic coup.' By introducing 'blanks,' even where there are none, he [sic] makes time enter into the word to give it the chance of remaining in the planning stage, open to possible completion."[4] According to Ouaknin, commentary as revelation ruptures the timeless, universal words of the Law. The speech of one interpreter inserts itself among them and brings their transcendence into the present time. Once the present time of living speech is introduced into this transcendent realm of the Law, the Christian insistence that we already live in a postmessianic, timeless, and universal age must be denied.

Jewish time, as opposed to Christian time, is premessianic. Jewish time does not find total knowledge on earth now; it does not accept the incarnation as completion, as a totality. For the Jew, the present world must remain only in "the planning stage, open to possible completion." If there is to be a new text, a Total Book, only the messiah will write it. Until then the interpretive voice of commentary will have to suffice.

Not only does this idea of commentary as revelation assume a different concept of time than that of the Christian believer, but it also serves a psychological purpose. Since the temptation to know is so great, one can channel that urge into the interpretive act and so resist the temptation to turn one's own speech into a new law, a new totality, an incarnation of the truth. One is able to know and help encourage the process of revelation itself even as one obeys the commandment not to make idols or profane the name of God.

When Rabbi Nachman of Bratslav took the extraordinary step of burning his book, he may have thought the book would better do its revelatory work if it remained only in the living speech of his followers. Alive today in others' mouths as they quote him, who can say if in fact he succeeded in his aims? Whatever his motives may have been, however, Rabbi Nachman's story is an apt parable for the situation of today's Jewish American poets. For, like their forebears, many Jewish American poets are unwilling to let the human word rise up and challenge the Holy Words. They do not wish to write the Total Book; they do not live in an incarnate world; they turn their desire to know into a talent for commentary and interpretation. For such poets, what more likely, more welcoming genre in a secular age could there be than the lyric poem?

The one single characteristic of the lyric that unites the various definitions we have is that it is the poetic expression of a single voice. As the preeminent literary genre for the voice, the lyric is the most paradoxical of genres. Like the Talmud, it asks us to believe that its written words are, in fact, only the transcription of some particular person's speech. But what kind of speech is this? Like the Psalms, lyrics have an unusual music, an organized rhythmic sensibility that, somehow through their unworldly sounds, calls forth the transcendent realm without claiming to know what such transcendence may be, and without attempting to render that realm in words. For the theologically inclined poet who wishes to speak of the holy, the mystical, the transcendent but who also seeks to avoid the danger of idolatry, the lyric becomes the most welcoming of literary genres: It allows the voice to speak of holy things without risking idolatry or hubris. But what of those poets who may not be so theologically inclined? Of what use is the lyric to those who have no interest in expressing the transcendent? How do we account for the many talents of non-theologically vested Jewish American poets? Of what use is the lyric to them?

When understood as the genre most suited to even a secular version of revelation through commentary, the lyric also welcomes the Jew who does not believe. If revelation is understood not in moral and theological terms but only and entirely in ethical terms as political, social, and economic pragmatic truth, it still, in a Jewish sense of the term, depends on someone's interpretation of the situation. Whether we choose to understand revelation as theological or ethical revelation in Judaism, if there is no commentary there is no revelation. For the secular Jewish American poet, the lyric, as the deepest literary expression of the singular voice, becomes the one place where such secular ethical revelations can be made.

Ironically, the American lyric tradition has been, ever since the Puritans began writing English language lyrics on these shores, a theological tradition and not a secular one. And the theological tradition begot by the Puritans, one need hardly add, depends entirely on a Christian theological understanding. Ever since Edward Taylor and Anne Bradstreet set pen to paper, the American lyric has been about the incarnate word. As a poetics of immanence, the American lyric's task was to reveal, through its words, the holy and the mystical truth of God. If Taylor, Bradstreet, and the Puritans were merely adhering to an English tradition that had come to view lyric poetry as an expression of Christian faith, then the romantics must be understood only as challenging some of their terms but not the premise of incarnation itself. If anything, romantic poetry, particularly as described in this country by Ralph Waldo Emerson, made of the lyric tradition a counter testament to the new testament but it is still a testament. Poetry, for the romantic poets like Emerson, was not only about the soul, but also about the soul as read either against or in a Christian context. The idea that such a context could be entirely avoided and ignored is not to be found in their work. In other words, the poetry is dependent on a reading of humanity as "fallen." Their poetry either depicts humanity before the Fall in an ideal Edenic state or after the Fall. Either they attempt to find in lyric poetry a prelapsarian place to reinvision a new garden and a new Adam, as did Emerson, or, they write out of essentially Christian convictions about humanity as fallen and in a state of sin in need of grace. In either case, the lyric is the genre for the holy to express itself as if the words themselves were somehow holiness incarnate. Emerson put it best (as he always does): "Words are signs of natural facts. Every natural fact is a symbol of a particular spiritual fact. Words are symbols of the spirit."[5]

Recent scholars, like Elisa New, have begun to show how the lyrics of such major poets as Whitman, Dickinson, and T. S. Eliot depend on the story of the Fall, the Incarnation, the Crucifixion, and the Second Coming. Ever since the Puritans inaugurated the formal conventions by which to tell this Christian story, American poets have continued to do so. Today we call the American lyric tradition a poetics of presence, the incarnate word, etc.[6] In American lyric poetry, then, Christ's time determines a major narrative thread. And the American lyric itself has been, ever since Emerson, tied to logos, to writing, and not to speech.

It is this theological ground made so visible by romantics like Emerson that literary theorists have, for the past thirty years, been attacking. They have been condemning the lyric poem precisely because its implicit theology asks readers to believe in, and to adhere to, its singular law—what Wordsworth called its "counter-faith." For two generations now, literary theory has taught students that the lyric voice's claim to immanence is absolute and so potentially tyrannical. Every lyric poem, it is said, insists on its singular status as the Truth, and demands that the reader approach it only through those claims. In deconstruction one is made witness to the interpretations of resisting readers unwilling to submit to the lyric's tyrannical monologue.

Whether secular or religious, the Jewish American poet of today enters into a three-hundred-year predominantly Christian tradition of revelation as immanence, as incarnate in the land or in a messiah, or Christ-like figure. Revelation in American poetry is not transcendence, commentary, or interpretation. The American tradition of poetry from the Puritans into our own day asks readers to understand poetry as a kind of incarnate Holy Text. Lyric poetry, from this perspective, is understood as the genre where "presence" speaks: where the Incarnation happens again and again.

To the believing Jew, the American lyric poem, even when it is understood as leaves of grass, looks too much like a new idol, a new incarnation, a new testament. And to the nonbelieving Jew, the American poem also looks too much like a new testament. What is all this mystical stuff, he or she too often asks? As a way around the dilemma posed by the theological interests of the American lyric, many Jewish American poets redefine the very idea of lyric poetry. In so doing, they retain their identity as Jews (either as believers in a radically transcendent God, or as non-believing non-Christians). The only way to claim one's identity as a Jew and still write a lyric poem in the American tradition of the incarnate word and the poetics of presence is to re-define the lyric itself. For the Jewish poet, the lyric is that genre where the personal voice of the poet can express its interpretive commentary. Understood in this way, a Jewish American poet can enter a lyric tradition and write about Original Sin, Grace, Redemption, the Fall, even the Second Coming without having to believe in them. Through commentary, a Jewish poet (believing or not) can use the lyric to interpret and comment on these Christian theological elements without ceding any authority to them.[7] By simply quoting from the American poetic tradition itself, Jewish American poets both secular and believing have been able to transform the American lyric from a totalizing genre of incarnate presence into a more open-ended genre of interpretive commentary where there is never any completion, where every commentary requires yet another and another.

Even in the past fifty years, the contemporary period, the American lyric poem continues to depend on a poetics of immanence. Looking at just three of the major poetic movements from the past fifty years, one finds in their spiritual

premise a latent Christian story. One finds, for example, humans as fallen crea-
tures in need of grace. According to James E. B. Breslin, Paul Breslin, Robert
Von Hallberg, and Michael Davidson, between 1945 and 1975 three poetic
movements dominated the American scene and so established the conventions
for today's poets: Projectivist verse (also known as Black Mountain Poetry),
Confessional poetry, and Deep Image poetry.[8] According to Paul Breslin, each
of these movements is beholden to the "psycho-political muse": Charles
Olson's Projectivism, Robert Lowell's Confessionalism, and James Wright's
Deep Image share a "desire to recover a self disentangled from acculturation
and its burden of guilt."[9]

Conventional lyric poetry after 1945, in other words, makes the following
assumption about the individual self: it is alienated, unhappy, despondent, in
search of psychic health. All three forms, Breslin argues, developed strategies
of recovery and all three share "a conception of poetry as engaged in the liber-
ation of human consciousness from a false consciousness imposed by soci-
ety."[10] For the Confessional poet like Lowell or Plath this meant that the poet
became a "representative victim"[11]: Already guilty, the speaking voice seeks
redemption through the grace bestowed by art itself, by the poem. In the Pro-
jectivist poem, by contrast, the "self -absorption is more naive . . . than that of
confessional poetics."[12] In other words, the poet has the ability to get to the
healthy place that the Confessional poet never quite reaches. This is in part due
to a philosophy of immanence that allows the poet to reach the blissful state of
being where there is no disease, despair, or guilt. In the Projectivists' optimis-
tic poems, a spiritual connection uniting both the external world of nature and
the inner soul of the poet is foregrounded. Deep Image poetry also structures
its forms in terms of the individual spiritual need for solace, health, grace.
Breslin explains that in Deep Image work the reader is asked "not merely occa-
sionally but continually, [to] . . . attribute an inherent significance to a recurring
symbolic vocabulary."[13] Rather than focus on poetry as such for their redemp-
tion, Deep Image poets turn to a series of isolated, external images—tropes
that act as deep psychic, emotive correlates to grace. Breslin lists such tropes as
"wings, jewels, stones, blood, oats, water, light, bones, roots, . . . sleep, dark-
ness"—he tells us that such "deep images" are common to poets like Wright,
Merwin, Kinnell, Strand, Simic, and Robert Bly.

What Breslin does not say but what Elisa New explains is that these com-
mon themes only *seem* to belong to a secular philosophical conception of the
universe or a rather benign nondenominational spirituality. In fact, they belong
to a Christian theology; they are certainly not universal, insofar as the spiritu-
ality latent in all three forms is resolutely *not* in line with traditional rabbinic
Judaism. In all three forms incarnation or immanence—the idea that spiritual-
ity and the divine exist in nature, even the idea that God can be incarnate in
people—is given foundational primacy. At once resisting such conventions and

adhering to them, and also at the same time quoting from other sources, Jewish American poets are able to resist their narrative pull.

For the Jewish American poet who wishes to retain his or her identity as Jew, whether secular or not, and still write in this mainstream lyric tradition, the only alternative is to comment, interpret, and so reveal either the latent Christianity behind these movements' tropes, or, in some way, reveal an ethical issue that is somehow able to exist outside of the Christian context in which it had been embedded. Generally, such commentary is made possible by simply quoting from other poets and allowing one's own poem to comment on those quotations. Rather than write a Confessional poem of the soul after the Fall, of the alienated, diseased, guilty speaker understood as an example of the effects of original sin, the Jewish American poet comments, in his or her lyrics, on the need for other poets to do this, often by quoting from such poets in their own poems. And rather than write poetic dramas where sinners search for redemption through grace, Jewish American poets offer interpretive commentaries about such stories by quoting them.

Through the art of quotation, then, many Jewish American poets are able to participate in the conventional language of the American lyric without adopting its system of faith. Many Jewish American poets adopt the now conventional techniques of the three movements—Projectivist, Confessional, Deep Image—without accepting those movements' theological premise of immanence, original sin, or the need for grace. Jewish American poets do use deep images, depressed, victimized, alienated speakers, anecdotes, and projectivist form; but, at the same time, through their use of quotation, they also upset the Christian narrative on which these terms so often rely. This use of quotation is a formal method by which some Jewish American poets both believing and secular question the implicit Christian meaning latent in the images and metaphors inspired by the psycho-political muse. The quotation, when it appears in the conventional rhetoric of one of these three forms, often works as an implicit commentary on those conventions. Rather than challenge, critique, or deny the utility of the technique under scrutiny, the quotation interprets the technique in such a way as to call attention to an already implicit Christian interpretation that is still said to be universal, even secular. The Jewish American poet does not ask the quotation to make the form more Jewish. Instead, the quotation, by revealing the latent Christian meaning of the form, suggests that the lyric's claim to being the universal Total Book will necessarily involve an exclusionary politics. Through the art of quotation, and a conception of the poem as an interpretive commentary, the Jewish American lyric poet does not have to forsake the need for a single organic speaker but can, at the same time, import a critique of the Christian reading of that speaker into the poem.

In Jewish textual tradition, the use of quotations is meant to seal gaps and tie together apparent holes in the fabric of meaning. Commentary, in Jewish tradition, is the art of addition because only through such commentary can revelation be achieved. Commentary depends, formally speaking, on the exact duplication of a text—the prooftext from the holy scriptures—and the exegesis of that text. Reversing this process, the Jewish American poet uses quotations—prooftexts—from the scripture of the American literary canon in order to reveal gaps and tear out the threads that would force the Jewish voice to be understood only in Christian terms. By using quotations in order to write a poetic commentary on the assumptions behind them, Jewish American poems are able to speak in the idiom of their peers without adopting a theology that would deny their own identity as Jewish. If we ask—can a Deep Image poem *be* a Deep Image poem without immanence as part of its structure? Can a Confessional poem *be* a Confessional poem without the wicked, guilty speaker as its lyric subject?—we can also, thanks to contemporary Jewish American poets, answer, "yes." These forms do not depend on these particular narratives. They lose no structural integrity by adapting them to other stories.

For many Jewish American poets, the lyric is a genre where their singular voice can participate in the theological work of revelation if revelation is understood as the act of interpretive commentary itself. Rather than enter the American lyric tradition and run the risk of having to burn their words, Jewish American poets enter as rabbis whose commentaries often question, reinterpret, and reveal surprising facets of and in the poetry.

When understood as commentary, then, Jewish American lyric poems ask readers to participate with them in their revelatory work; they do not ask readers to be silent and attend to their oracular pronouncements with awe. To explain what such poems as I have been discussing look like and illustrate how they work in more detail, I offer a close examination of but one poem from but one poet: Maxine Kumin's "Living Alone With Jesus—." In this poem, Kumin incorporates quotations as commentary into the rhetoric of all three dominant postwar styles—Projectivist, Confessional, Deep Image—and so disrupts their Christian theology. In so doing, she renders these forms not more Jewish but certainly less Christian, and, as a result, she reveals a series of ethical issues that would go otherwise unheralded.

To read Maxine Kumin's poem is to read a lyric commentary that uses the structure of Projectivist poetry, the metaphors of the Deep Image, and the apparently victimized speaker of the Confessional poem.[14] By quoting other voices in her poem, Kumin places those voices in the center of her American page and, in so doing, she places herself, and her voice, on the margins as a kind of commentary on them.[15]

Turning now to Kumin's poem, one notices that, beginning with the very first stanza, she uses the conventions of a Confessional poem. In these opening lines, Kumin identifies herself as a marginal figure, a potential victim:[16]

> Can it be
> I am the only Jew residing in Danville, Kentucky,
> looking for matzoh in the Safeway and the A & P?
> The Sears, Roebuck salesman wrapping my potato masher
> advises me to accept Christ as my personal savior
> or else when I die I'll drop straight down to hell,
> but the ladies who come knocking with their pamphlets
> say as long as I believe in God that makes us
> sisters in Christ. I thank them kindly.

In these lines, the Jewish law that commands one to eat matzoh on Passover clashes with the fundamentalist Baptist law to proselytize. Both laws figure Kumin as a Jew. The first law is internal—it is something she chooses to obey—while the second law is external—it is an identity imposed on her from without. The first law identifies Jews as those who obey the commandments, while the second law identifies Jews as those who lack Jesus. The two anecdotes of this stanza announce Kumin's marginal position as absolute: It is both internal—her adherence to the command to eat matzoh—and external—others recognize her as Jewish and seek to convert her.

Although, in these lines, she *is* a victim of misunderstanding, she is not a victim in terms of the typical Confessional narrative: She indicates no sense of her own guilt, nor do these lines speak of her sense of herself as a sinner in need of grace, or redemption. Rather than reject the marginal position into which those who seek to convert her have placed her, Kumin accepts that position.

Despite her acceptance, however, the town has defined her Jewishness as the-one-who-is-without-Jesus. In Kentucky, a Jew is not one who obeys the scriptural law but rather one who is in need of Jesus. The first stanza, then, reveals the conflict between her internal sense of self and the external identity assigned to her by her neighbors. But more than just a lyric description of this cultural clash, the first stanza is also a lyric commentary on the ethics of proselytizing. Notice that, of the two attempts to convert her, only the women are thanked kindly. This is because they refuse to relegate Kumin to a place completely outside of their moral universe. Even though their insistence that she already believe what she clearly does not believe—"We are sisters in Christ"—could be seen as an example of extreme hubris, Kumin recognizes the gesture for what it is, an act of kindness.

Like a Confessional poem, then, her anecdotes reveal inner pain, and they tell us about her emotional landscape. But, as commentary, the anecdotes, which consist of quotations from her neighbors, also instruct. The words of her neighbors tell us what Kumin thinks about the Baptist urge to proselytize. To paraphrase, she says, "If you're going to try to convert me, acknowledge my belief in God. Do not ship me off to a hell I do not even acknowledge." The rhythmic force of "I thank them kindly" is not just a wry salute to "the sisters" but it is also a strong rebuke to the salesman. And, as a rebuke, it is an interpretation of *his* words. It tells us that, according to *his* words, he does not see Kumin as fully human.

Having established her identity as Jewish—as one who believes in God and obeys the commandments—she has also established her marginal position in this community and the precarious situation such marginality implies. At the same time, by rejecting the Christian interpretation of her Jewish identity, she also has rejected the normative trajectory of the Confessional lyric. As a Jew, she will not describe herself as a sinner in need of grace; she will not define herself as the one who is without Jesus even if Jesus is but an image for any mediating agent, even natural ones.

In this first stanza, Kumin has invoked Confessional poetry. As the poem continues she will also invoke the elements of the other two dominant postwar movements as well: Projectivist and Deep Image poetry. Like Projectivist verse, the poem's structure is, to use Denise Levertov's phrase, "organic." As Charles Olson, famously quoting Robert Creeley, insisted, "form is the extension of content." The form of Kumin's poem, in other words, is an extension of her thematic need to offer a commentary. Her poem adheres to the formalist code of Projectivist verse, and, as we will see, she even quotes the doxa of that code. And, in subsequent stanzas, Kumin's poem will also resort to the rhetoric of the Deep Image poem by entering an internal imaginary space where blood, water, stones, bones, and other familiar Deep Image tropes are meant to speak to an immanent spirituality.

Despite the poem's use of these movements' conventions, it does not adhere to the Christian narrative they seem to require. And, by not adhering to that narrative, Kumin is able both to call attention to the existence of that narrative and to reveal certain ethical issues that arise from it. In her poem, in other words, one can see how a non-Christian poet can use the rhetoric of the Deep Image, the victimized speaker of the Confessional lyric, and the organic form of the Projectivist lyric without rejecting them, without resorting to new genres or inaugurating new movements.

If, in the first stanza, Kumin rejected the Christian interpretation of her Jewish identity, then, in the second stanza, she explores the consequences of such a rejection both in terms of the three dominant poetic forms and in terms of her own position in this community:

> In the country there are thirty-seven churches
> and no butcher shop. This could be taken
> as a matter of all form and no content.
> On the other hand, form can be seen as
> an extension of content, I have read that,

> up here in the sealed-off wing where my three rooms
> are threaded by outdoor steps to the downstairs world.
> In the open risers walnut trees are growing.
> Sparrows dipped in raspberry juice
> come to my one window sill. Cardinals
> are blood spots before my eyes.
> My bed is a narrow canoe with a fringy throw.
> Whenever I type it takes to the open sea
> and comes back wrong end to.
> Every morning my pillows produce tapioca.
> I gather it up for a future banquet.

In this stanza, Kumin quotes Charles Olson's now foundational essay, "Projective Verse." There, Olson, using capital letters to insist on the point, wrote: "FORM IS NEVER MORE THAN AN EXTENSION OF CONTENT."[17] According to Olson, the internal breath and speech rhythms of each individual are unique. Therefore, no poem would ever, if it were true to its author, have the same form. To write in a fixed pattern, he argued, was to deny one's own individuality. Seeing Olson's law as the Protestant reformation it was, Kumin, in this stanza, relates it to the Baptist belief that Jesus, as God incarnate, is a "*personal*" savior. To her Baptist neighbors, Jesus cannot be mediated by anyone other than the individual believer, just as, for Olson, poetry, as a personal genre, could not be mediated by other than personal forms.

At first, this stanza seems to mock the Baptists by declaring that they are all form and no substance. In the opening lines, the churches are a symbol of form while the butcher is a symbol of content. But having made this symbolic argument, Kumin realizes that, as a symbolic landscape, as text, the churches can just as easily be misread as read well. Recalling Olson's law is her own recognition that she has misread the meaning of the thirty-seven churches: "*On the other hand*, form can be seen as / an extension of content" (emphasis added). In other words, if she reads the landscape according to Olson's law—according to the law of this very poem whose own form is itself an extension of its content—then it becomes understandable *and* acceptable. A landscape of thirty-seven churches and no butcher shop is no longer alienating to Kumin because she realizes that thirty-seven churches are the formal, concrete expression of a spirituality based on radical individuality: If one does "live alone with Jesus," then no one church, no one religious community, can adequately account for what is always an intensely personal relationship.

In this second stanza, then, Kumin's quotation of Olson lays bare the form of his theory by removing its narrative of spiritual immanence. She discovers that the law, form *is* an extension of content, is a rule, not a spiritual theory. As a rule, Olson's law allows her to read the forms of a Christian landscape even as she acknowledges the fact that those forms must exclude her from that same landscape. By recalling Olson's law, Kumin is able to read her Christian neighbors on their own terms. She learns that if Jesus can only be approached individually—if, only when alone, one can accept him for what he is—then, thirty-seven churches are not only understandable but, potentially, even a modest number. An abundance of churches becomes the organic formal expression of an indigenous belief system based on radical individualism.

The stanza, however, does not end with the detached recognition of how someone else's belief system is expressed. Instead, Kumin next expresses her own personal, spiritual needs. Rather than turn to Jesus, as do her Baptist neighbors, she turns to nature—a turn in line with the conventions of both Projectivist and Deep Image poetry so dominant when this poem was written. If this were a typical Confessional, Projectivist, or Deep Image poem, the turn to nature would be not only conventional but essential. Read from the Christian perspective of salvation, these lines would symbolically represent salvation through Christ-like incarnate figures. For example, the cardinals, walnut trees growing, and "sparrows dipped in raspberry juice" would each be symbols (Deep Images) of grace: they would tell us that Kumin, despite her self-definition as Jewish, actually does learn to accept a nonrabbinic natural Judaic creed. But this is not what happens. Instead, Kumin—recalling the spirituality of the native Americans who first inhabited this place—imagines herself (typing on her bed) into a new allegorical landscape: into a canoe. The paddles, her prayer, are the text itself. Her own writing, this poem in particular, now becomes a vehicle of transport to take her to the sea of faith. Few moves could be more American, more in line with the lyric tradition after Emerson. But she does not reach her goal: The transcendent place to which her writing will take her is not found. The poem does not turn finally and fundamentally to nature. Its final lines do not make an Emersonian connection between words and nature. Instead, Kumin insists on the radical separation of nature from words. And rather than give us the transcendent place of spirituality incarnate in her words, she tells us instead to focus on her words *as words, as writing*. When Kumin, in these final lines, turns to the act of writing for her faith, she not only rejects nature as the location for revelation, but also the definition of the Jew as one who follows the 613 commandments. By this point in the poem, she no longer sees herself as one who obeys the commandments but rather as one who writes. In other words, she has now rejected both terms—Jew and Christian—and she has rejected them both on their own terms, for neither now applies to her sense of individual spirituality: the only name that can possibly speak to her identity as a spiritual being is "poet." It is to this non-Christian, nonrabbinic sense of the poet as spiritual, as one who is neither a sinner, nor lost and in need of grace, nor one who follows the commandments (the *halachic* or rabbinic definition), that her third stanza turns.

> I am leading a meatless life. I keep
> my garbage in the refrigerator. Eggshells
> potato peels and the rinds of cheeses nest
> in the empty sockets of my daily grapefruit.
> Every afternoon at five I am comforted
> by the carillons of the Baptist church next door.

In the first line of this stanza, Kumin, as a kind of monk, performs rituals that complement those of her neighbors. But this monk's rituals are intensely personal; they follow a pattern of her own design neither Jewish nor Christian. Because the first two stanzas taught her to see the intense individualism of her neighbor's spirituality, she now, in this third stanza, offers her own version of spirituality through a series of direct quotations that, at first, seem to be Deep Images—blood, lamb, rock, ground, hand. In fact, these images are a series of direct quotations from the titles to Baptist hymns. The verse pattern Kumin employs in this section—Biblical parallelism—accents the sacredness of the texts she quotes. If, however, we did not know that these images were quoted titles they would appear to be conventional Deep Images. This double meaning—Deep Images and Baptist hymns—asks us to see, in the rhetoric of the Deep Image poem, a set of Christian metaphors masking themselves as secular devices:

> I let the *rock of ages* cleave for me on Monday.
> Tuesday I am *washed in the blood of the lamb.*
> *Bringing in the sheaves* on Wednesday keeps me busy.
> Thursday's the day on Christ *the solid rock* I stand.
> The Lord lifts me *up to higher ground* on Friday so that
> Saturday I put my hands in the *nail-scarred hands.*
> Nevertheless, I stay put on the Sabbath. I let
> the whisky bottle say something scurrilous. [My emphasis]

Are we to assume that in these lines, this lyrical hymn of acceptance, the Jewish woman releases herself from her marginal position? Is this a moment of conversion—a moment called forth as much by the narrative force of a predominantly Christian poetic tradition as by her own desire? I think not, because, on the Christian Sabbath, she "stays put." Rather than go to church she lets "the whisky bottle" speak. The whiskey bottle has the last word: it becomes a metaphor for her emotional confusion. This final image of the whiskey bottle suggests that, even in the unique space provided by lyric poetry where she *can* imagine herself into a life with Jesus, she fails to solve the riddle of her marginal identity: She cannot, even metaphorically, go to church. In the end, rather than speak for herself, she lets the profane whiskey speak for her. While she may understand her neighbor's need for Jesus, she herself will not share in it.

Perhaps this failure explains why the fourth and final stanza is necessary:

> Jesus, if you are in all thirty-seven churches,
> are you not also here with me
> making it alone in my back rooms like a flagpole sitter
> slipping my peanut shells and prune pits into the Kelvinator?
> Are you not here at nightfall
> ticking in the box of the electric blanket?
> Lamb, lamb, let me give you honey on your grapefruit
> and toast for the birds to eat
> out of your damaged hands.

The final two lines of the poem, "for the birds to eat / out of your damaged hands" resonate loudest despite how quiet they are in tone. In these lines, Kumin offers Jesus, figured traditionally as a lamb, the comfort she had, in the previous stanza, sought from him. The agent of such comfort—grapefruit, honey, and toast—links the three worlds—natural, Christian, and Jewish—that compete for her attention. In the end, her meatless life in Kentucky does become a holy life but its holiness is not rabbinically Jewish (it does not conform to a certain *halachic* code of conduct), not traditionally Christian. It is, however, both holy and Jewish insofar as it maintains a core spirituality invested in words not as incarnate idols but as agents of revelation. Through her commentary on three poetic movements, through her canny ability to relate those movements to a specifically Protestant American theology, she has written a Jewish poem. Through a commentary on the devices of the three most dominant forms of postwar American poetry, Kumin reveals an implicit Christianity that is itself but one narrative possibility among many, one theme among many. By insisting that we see such devices as Christian, Kumin makes it possible for other non-Christian poets to use them without sacrificing their own spiritual identity.

In her poetic commentary on a poetic law, Baptist hymns, and the conventions of three poetic movements, Kumin may have rejected one particular definition of Judaism but she enacts another. Her poems, as commentary, reveal a set of complex ethical and spiritual problems that must be addressed. When her poem concludes with a few questions and an imagined gesture, she denies us a final answer. Instead, her final gesture, a gift of food, makes a last silent but powerful appeal for a response. And what would that response be? She must know that even our "thank you" is a commentary revealing more than we might be willing to admit, requiring more from us than we are often willing to give. Commentary upon commentary without end, that is the Jewish gift to the American lyric.

Notes

1. Marc-Alain Ouaknin, *The Burnt Book: Reading the Talmud.* Trans. Llewellyn Brown (Princeton, N.J.: Princeton UP, 1995), 264–65.

2. Ibid., 300.

3. Ibid., 300.

4. Ibid., 301.

5. Ralph Waldo Emerson, "Nature," in *Ralph Waldo Emerson: Essays and Lectures* (New York: Library of America, 1983).

6. Alisa New, *The Regenerate Lyric: Theology and Innovation in American Poetry* (Cambridge: Cambridge UP, 1993).

7. Although Jews and Christians share much of the same Bible, familiarly known as the Old Testament, they do not share the same interpretation of it. In the Book of Genesis, for example, where one finds the story of Adam, Eve, the Serpent, and the Garden, their interpretations differ dramatically. In reading of these events, rabbinic Judaism does not find either the Fall or Original Sin. Even though this Christian interpretation of the plot found in Genesis is familiar to many readers, it is not at all typical of Jewish theology.

8. Paul Breslin, *Psycho-Political Muse* (Chicago: U of Chicago P, 1987); Robert Von Hallberg, *American Poetry and Culture* (Cambridge, Mass.: Harvard UP, 1988); James E. B. Breslin, *From Modern to Contemporary* (Chicago: U of Chicago P, 1984) and Michael Davidson, *San Francisco Renaissance* (Cambridge: Cambridge UP, 1991).

9. Breslin, *Psycho-Political Muse,* 21.

10. Ibid., xiii

11. Ibid., 50.

12. Ibid., 205.

13. Ibid.,120.

14. In what follows I do not mean to suggest that Kumin necessarily *intended* the sort of commentary that I imply occurs in her poem. Rather, I mean to show that, no matter what Kumin may have iintended, the words of her poem *do* work a subtle and impressive commentary on the three poetic movements that dominated American poetry when this poem was published. Also, it should be said that Kumin's talents as a poet have long been applied to traditional poetic forms as well. One need only look at "For Anne at Passover" in this volume to see how Kumin approaches traditional, as opposed to free-verse, forms in her work.

15. To a Jewish poet, the margins are not a negative space. Ever since the Middle Ages, the rabbinic Bible and the Talmud have printed commentaries in the margins of the page and the sacred texts in the center. These commentaries themselves operate according to their own system, their own rules. The fact that commentary is part and parcel of both the written and oral law is due, in large part, to rabbinic Judaism's conception of revelation. According to nonmystical rabbinic Judaism, God is revealed not

through things but through the sacred scriptures. Revelation, as the late French Jewish philosopher Emmanuel Levinas explains, is both that which is "laid down in square letters" and that which "illuminates living faces" (Emmanuel Levinas, *Difficult Freedom: Essays on Judaism* [Baltimore: Johns Hopkins UP, 1990], 25). Jewish tradition, in other words, does not read revelation as immanence in natural things, nor does it read revelation as incarnation in Jesus. By investing words, rather than the things of nature or Jesus, with holiness, Jewish tradition makes the interpretation of the sacred words—commentary—a part and parcel of revelation itself. To interpret the law, in other words, is to make manifest and establish that same law. The great historian of Judaism Gershom Scholem explains: "Revelation needs commentary in order to be rightly understood and applied"("Tradition and Commentary as Religious Categories in Judaism," reprinted in *Understanding Jewish Theology*, ed. Jacob Neusner [New York: KTAV, 1973]). The scholar, says Scholem, "perceives revelation not as a unique and clearly delineated occurrence, but rather as a phenomenon of eternal fruitfulness to be unearthed and examined. . . . Out of the religious tradition they bring forth something entirely new, something that itself commands religious dignity: commentary" (Neusner, 47). The meaning of the text of the scriptures, in other words, must always be filtered through the interpretive act itself. If the sacred words are revealed, then the process of revelation is incomplete until those words are interpreted through commentary.

Gershom Scholem explains that in Rabbinic Judaism "tradition" refers to the revelation as it is transmuted first into speech and then into the written scriptures. Revelation, therefore, can only be "discovered" in and as text. According to Scholem, the entire system of revelation as text (both oral and written) "creates in the process a new type of religious person . . . The Biblical scholar" (Neusner, 46). The scholar, says Scholem, understands commentary as a task, as one of the means by which one learns justice. As a textual strategy, it combats both doubt and silence because to comment is to further the task of revelation in time: "Revelation needs commentary in order to be rightly understood and applied" (Neusner, 47).

16. Raised in a Jewish family in Philadelphia, Maxine Kumin grew up next to a convent. Its location was so convenient that from the ages of three to six she went to its school. Even at that young age, as she explains in an interview, the clash between her Jewish home and her Christian school was noticeable: "To a child who is looking for absolutes these two opposing views of the world are terribly confusing" (Maxine Kumin, *To Make a Prairie* [Ann Arbor: U of Michigan P, 1979], 60–61). As she grew older these confusions only became more stark, more obvious. Discussing her poem "Living Alone with Jesus—"Kumin told an interviewer that she never felt more marginal, less at home, than in Kentucky. Compared to Paris, she says, life as a writer-in-residence in Baptist Kentucky was nothing short of "exotic"—her wry word for the marginalization she felt as a Jew in the Bible belt:

Living in Kentucky in a hardshell-Baptist area where I was writer-in-residence was an exotic experience, more exotic, say, than going to live in Paris. I was more at home in Paris than I was, initially, in Kentucky. . . . There was this pervasive, Pentacostal Evangelical Baptist proselytism: 'Are you saved? Repent! Repent! Jesus is the answer!' everywhere you turned. I had never seen so much of Jesus or seen him taken so personally. I saw much more of Jesus in Kentucky, really, than I saw of Jesus in the convent. (*To Make a Prairie*, 61)

17. He then added: "(Or so it got phrased by one R. Creeley, and it makes absolute sense to me, with this possible corollary, that right form, in any given poem, is the only and exclusively possible extension of content under hand)." (*Poetry New York* No. 3, 1950; reprinted in *Postmodern American Poetry*, ed. Paul Hoover [New York: Norton, 1994], 614). With this law, Olson meant to attack the blind adoption of traditional forms that prevailed in the late 1940s, and with this law he launched a poetic version of the Protestant reformation against the Catholic orthodoxy of meter and traditional forms. According to this law, no meter and no traditional verse pattern was necessary unless warranted by the content. But, Olson went on to claim, no American and no individual would have need of such forms.

Shekhinah in America

ERIC MURPHY SELINGER

Eric Murphy Selinger is Assistant Professor of English at DePaul University. His first book, *What Is It then Between Us? Traditions of Love in American Poetry*, was published by Cornell University Press in 1998; he is now at work on *Delight in Disorder: The Theory and Practice of Pleasure in Contemporary Poetry* and a book-length version of this essay. A regular contributor to *Parnassus: Poetry in Review*, his essays and reviews have also appeared in *Agni*, the *Boston Phoenix*, *Tikkun*, and the *Washington Post Book World*.

Twenty-five years ago, Jerome Rothenberg wrote a new version of the "Hymn to Shekinah for the Feast of the Sabbath" by the sixteenth-century rabbi (and poet) Isaac Luria. A hymn to *who*? When Rothenberg reprinted the piece in *A Big Jewish Book*, the capacious, audacious anthology he composed some four years later, he added a helpful pair of definitions.[1] The first comes from Raphael Patai's book *The Hebrew Goddess*. "*Shekhina*," it explains in part,

> is the frequently used Talmudic term denoting the visible and audible manifestation of God's presence on earth. In its ultimate development as it appears in the late Midrash literature, the Shekhina concept stood for an independent, feminine divine entity prompted by her compassionate nature to argue with God in defense of man. (36)

The second passage, from Gershom Scholem's *On the Kabbalah and Its Symbolism*, observes that as Rabbi Luria and his followers used the term Shekhinah, they radically transformed its meaning—specifically, by revising the old and comforting Talmudic notion that God's Presence stays with God's people even in Exile. If the Shekhinah is in exile, they surmised, then "a part of God Himself is exiled from God"; indeed, the "exile of Shekhinah" signals a (so to speak) split within the Divine, the "separation of the masculine and feminine principles in God" (36). Properly performed *mitzvot,* or religious commandments, performed "*l'shem yichud,*" in the name of reuniting the (masculine) Holy One and His (feminine) Presence, let Jews help to heal this breach in the Godhead. And on Friday night, as observant husband and wife embrace below, the estranged heavenly couple reconcile above in the realm of God's attributes, the ten Kabbalistic *sefirot*.

I will come back to Luria's hymn of marital reunion. For now, though, let me draw your eye to an odd little note in *A Big Jewish Book* from Rothenberg himself. As he explains that the Shekhinah's evil twin—all right, her "counterpart among the *sefirot* of the left side," to be precise—is the infamous she-demon Lilith, the poet looks up from his lecture notes to fix us with a stare. The Shekhinah's "reappearance among us," he sternly announces, apropos of nothing, "is an event of contemporary *poesis, not* religion" (36).

Much of the best new writing on Jewish American poetry follows Rothenberg's lead in linking the Shekhinah to *poesis*: the broad Latin term (from the Greek *poiein*) for the creation and shaping of poems. Norman Finkelstein calls her the Jewish "mistress of presence and absence, immanence and transcendence" (93), while the poet Allen Grossman declares that "it is for knowledge of her that the people should look to the Jewish poet and the Jewish poet to his or her own nature" ("Jewish Poetry," 167). What interests me, though, isn't the deep cultural logic that underwrites this connection between the Shekhinah and poetic making—the way it stems from Jewish cultural anxieties at least five, and maybe *twenty-five,* centuries old. Rather, I want to dwell a while on the simple historical fact that, where religion was concerned, Rothenberg was dead wrong.

Since the early 1970s, the Shekhinah has staged a remarkable "reappearance" in progressive American Judaism. Once she was an esoteric figure, peeking out from the untranslated introductory *kavvanot* [prayer intentions] of, for example, the Orthodox Metsudah prayerbook. (If you can read the Hebrew, you'll spot the "*l'shem yichud*" formula of reunification right at the start of the book [2, 4]; if you can't read the Hebrew, you probably shouldn't know it's there.) Now, however, the Shekhinah has become as commonplace a term as her political cousin *tikkun olam*, or repair of the world.[2] The new Sabbath prayerbook of the Reconstructionist movement, the smallest and arguably most American of Jewish denominations, now gives the "*l'shem yichud*" formula a page of its own just before the Sabbath morning prayers: "For the sake of the union of the blessed Holy One with the Shekhinah," it reads, "I stand here, ready in body and mind, to take upon myself the mitzvah, 'You shall love your fellow human being as yourself,' and by this merit may I open up my mouth" (*Kol Haneshama,* 150). As a not-just-grammatically feminine name for God, the Shekhinah shows up in reworded blessings, in feminist rituals, and even in religious popular culture. Recent recordings by the Reform Jewish songwriter Debbie Friedman feature Shekhinah songs; you can find them by rabbis from Shlomo Carlebach (Orthodox) to Geela Rayzel Raphael (Reconstructionist) and Shefa Gold (Jewish Renewal). Even the thoroughly secular band the Klezmatics tips its cap to her in the woozy "Mizmor Shir Lehanef (Reefer Song)."

"A funfe *hayst af yidish / Vos af english* rifer *hayst,*" they sing, *"Un makht di shkhine shruye, / A tikn farn gayst.* [*Funfe* is the Yiddish word / For what's called a *reefer* in English. /. . . . / It causes the Shekhinah to be spread out / Upon whoever's smoking, / It's a tikkun for the spirit.]" As for books, a quick scan of my own bookshelves finds her in Rabbi Lynn Gottlieb's *She Who Dwells Within*, Rabbi Wayne Dosick's *Dancing With God*, Rabbi Arthur Waskow's *Down to Earth Judaism: Food, Money, Sex, and the Rest of Life*, Rabbi Marcia Prager's *The Path of Blessing*, Rabbi Tirzah Firestone's *With Roots in Heaven,* the poet Rodger Kamenetz's *Stalking Elijah*, Judy Petsonk's *Taking Judaism Personally: Creating a Meaningful Spiritual Life*, and more.

There's a rangy omnivorous book to be written on the strange career of Shekhinah in America: one that takes on everything from summer camp song-books to scholarly texts, with a sprinkle of Neo-Pagan and evangelical Chris-tian material for seasoning. (We say She*khee*nah, they say She*cki*na, the name of a prison ministry, a gospel record label, and a Minneapolis-based Christian rock and roll band.) A down payment on that larger project, this essay will stick to poetry—or, rather, to two or three poetries, all invoking this figure. The first grows out of the kabbalistic counterculture of the 1950s, 1960s and 1970s, and is mostly written by men. The second, which comes of age a little later and has lasted rather longer, is a specifically *feminist* recasting of this figure, often with a progressive communal and spiritual agenda in mind. The third, and least cat-egorizable, takes us back to the question of America. What happens when the "exile of Shekhinah" takes her to the land of Shekina Glory Records and Shek-hinah Mountainwater, the author of several books on feminist-Dianic Wiccan rites? In a country where religious borrowing has always stirred up the cultural roux, and in a poetic tradition where even the Muse is, in Whitman's words, an "illustrious émigré," this figure of exile may turn out to be right at home.[3]

God the Bachelor, Meet Naomi Garbo (1961–1962)

The story of Shekhinah in America ought, by rights, to start with Emma Laz-arus, that post-hoc founding figure of the Jewish American poetry tradition. And in her most famous work, "The New Colossus," Lazarus offers a place to begin. As the poet and liturgist Marcia Falk reminds us, this sonnet renames the figure of "Liberty Lighting Up the World" (its sculptor's long-forgotten original title) as the "Mother of Exiles": a fitting name for the Presence who goes into exile with Her people and who, like Rachel, weeps for her children.[4] Well before Lazarus, however, Herman Melville may have brought Shekhinah to American literature, in *Moby-Dick*. "Apparently Melville, in his study of comparative religions, had come across this notion of Immanence," the poet Eleanor Wilner explains, "an indwelling . . . and merciful side of the Biblical

divinity, what suffers with us." We find Her "in 'the measureless sobbing that
stole out of the center of the serenity around' when the cruel stepmother world
becomes, for a moment, motherly, and Ahab, just once, weeps and almost re-
lents, almost calls off his mad revenge." She reappears at the novel's close "in
the form of *Rachel*, the ship whose mourning captain has lost his son and
which picks up Ishmael, the orphan of history" (Wilner, "Wrestling," 319).

These are tempting leads, and—in the case of the Melville—refreshingly
counterintuitive. The story I want to tell, however, begins more recently, with
the generous, prescient review of Allen Ginsberg's poem "Kaddish" (1961) by
the thirty-year-old poet Allen Grossman in *Judaism*. "The Jew, like the Irish-
man," Grossman begins, "presents himself as a type of the sufferer in history."
Just as the Irish burst onto the international literary horizon in the 1890s, so
"the Jewish poet in America today . . . is emerging from parochialism into the
mainstream of writing in English, and he is bringing with him a cultural mys-
tery arising out of his centrality in history as a sufferer, and also out of his rela-
tion to a vast body of literature in another language"—works like the
thirteenth-century *Zohar*, the Spanish-Jewish classic of Kabbalah (102).

Now Grossman makes no claims to find Kabbalah encoded in the text.
Rather, in a subtle critical move, he hones in on the way that Ginsberg presents
his mother to us as, in effect, two contrasting archetypes. The first is a victim of
history: "an old woman, haunted by the image of Hitler" who imagines being
"hunted by friend and family alike, by her own mother, by her husband, by
Roosevelt, Hitler, by Doctor Isaac, by history itself," whose twentieth-century
horrors are inscribed on her broken body and mind (105). As for the second,
more redemptive Naomi we spot from time to time—a "Communist beauty . . .
married in the summer among daisies, promised happiness at hand—," the
"glorious muse . . . from whose pained head I first took Vision," and even the
"beautiful Garbo of my Karma" (shades of *Ninotchka*!)—well, when Ginsberg
turns his mother into Greta Garbo or a muse, he surely twists her free of any
particular *Jewish* historical burden (223). In the process, paradoxically, he re-
veals the poem's kabbalistic core. "The mysticism of Ginsberg," Grossman
writes, "is peculiarly Jewish in the same sense that the *Zohar* is Jewish," since
both "Kaddish" and that older text mark "the attempt of the Jewish mind to re-
constitute itself outside of history." Naomi's death thus "represents the death of
parochial culture," and the poem shows the need "to lament that loss and to re-
found the sense of identity on more essential and less time-limited images," in-
cluding the image his mother most resembles, the Shekhinah (105–9).

Do we have any evidence that Ginsberg *knows* he's up to this mystical pro-
ject? He might have: texts by Martin Buber and the translated Soncino edition
of the *Zohar*, among others, might have given him leads to follow and sources
to draw on. But nothing in Ginsberg's published "Kaddish"-era journals sug-
gests that he found this figure of any particular interest. (There's an entry for

"Shit" in their index, but not for Shekhinah.) Still, to reread "Kaddish" with Kabbalah in mind is a remarkable experience—and, indeed, makes you wonder why Grossman was so circumspect. Consider this passage from the second part of the poem, where Naomi tells her college-age son about some of the "beautiful thoughts" she thinks all day:

> "Yesterday I saw God. What did he look like? Well, in the afternoon I climbed up a ladder—he has a cheap cabin in the country, like Monroe, N.Y. the chicken farms in the wood. He was a lonely old man with a white beard.
> "I cooked supper for him. I made him a nice supper—lentil soup, vegetables, bread & buttermiltz—he sat down at the table and ate, he was sad.
> "I told him, Look at all those fightings and killings down there, What's the matter? Why don't you put a stop to it?
> "I try, he said—That's all he could do, he looked tired. He's a bachelor so long, and he likes lentil soup. (219)

This vision of a lonely bachelor God, needing a nice supper and some wifely love and care, begs to be read as the Holy One Blessed Be He who needs the help of His exiled Shekhinah. The infamous exchange that follows between Naomi and her son would then serve as the exilic counterpart of this. She serves him "a plate of cold fish—chopped raw cabbage dript with tapwater—smelly tomatoes—week-old health food—grated beets & carrots with leaky juice, warm" and then seems perhaps to be "trying to make me come lay her—flirting to herself at sink—lay back on huge bed that filled most of the room, dress up round her hips—" (219). A horrifying parody of the tender care she takes of God, this come-on prompts the poet to break into Aramaic, reciting the first line of the Kaddish prayer, as though at once to escape and to set things right through the one scrap of religious observance he can recall.

The Ice Queen, Shirley, and My Wife (1964–1972)

Whether or not Ginsberg meant his mother to be a figure for Shekhinah, then, she turns out to be one—as, in fact, Grossman's essay-review turns out to have been, by accident or design, a manifesto for the next wave of Shekhinah poetry. What, after "Kaddish," remains to be done? Grossman's conclusion is both learned and brash. "Judaism is an ahistorical religion," he flatly declares. Its poets dare not be hobbled by a "perverse commitment to history" (109). This commitment can only result in a parochial, merely ethnic poetics: the poetry of being immigrants' children, perhaps, or of writing as an American Jew fourteen years after Israel's founding, and not yet twenty years after the Holocaust. Instead, he advises, take and read the *Zohar*, the works of Gershom Scholem, and other texts that make every Jewish age simultaneous—as they are, for example, in the Talmud, where rabbis debate across the centuries with each other and us. (Grossman does not mention this last association, but his readers in *Judaism* would surely know it.)

Might such a poem sound something like this?

> A young editor wants me to write on Kabbalah for his magazine.
> What do I know of the left and the right, of the Shekinah, of the
>   Metatron?
> It is an old book lying on the velvet cloth, the color of olive
>   under-leaf and plumstain in the velvet;
> it is a romance of pain and relief from pain, a tale told of the
>   Lord of the Hour of Midnight,
> the changing over that is a going down into Day from the Mountain.
>
> Ah! the seed that lies in the sweetness of the Kabbalah
> is the thought of those rabbis rejoicing in their common devotions,
> of the thousand threads of their threnodies, praises, wisdoms, shared loves
>
> There are terrible things in the design they weave, fair and unfair
>   establisht in one.
> How all righteousness is founded upon Jacob's cheat upon cheat, and
>   the devout
> pray continually for the humiliation and defeat of Esau,
>   for everlasting terror and pain to eat at the nephilim.
> . . . .
> It is an old book of stories, the Bible is an old book of stories
> —a mirror made by goblins for that Ice Queen, the Shekinah—
> a likelihood of our hearts withheld from healing.
>
> A young editor wants me to write on Kabbalah for his magazine . . .

(3–4)

What does this poet know of the Kabbalah? A fair amount, apparently. His poem is on easy terms with the "vast body of literature in another language," including the *Zohar*, that Grossman recommended. He knows enough to hear odd echoes and take familiar liberties. The stories of Kabbalah find a soul mate here, for example, in Hans Christian Anderson's fairy tale "The Ice Queen." The Jewish sparks of holiness spilled at Creation's Breaking of the Vessels look just like the shards of the distorting mirror made (in Anderson) for the Ice Queen, which made everything look stunted and ugly and small—and it turns out that the uglifying goblin mirror is the normative Bible itself! Such syncretism certainly forgoes the "cultural and linguistic parochialism" that Grossman chastizes, and it's free of a "perverse commitment to history," as well. If the poet does his job, the "old book" of the Kabbalah and the "young editor" and his magazine turn out to be contemporaneous, annulling time. And as he frees the heterodox "Ice Queen" Shekhinah from Jewish ethnocentrism, annulling history, the poet can set free his readers, too.

The author of this poem isn't, of course, a Jew. It's a piece by Robert Duncan, "What Do I Know of the Old Lore?," written sometime in 1959 or 1960 and included at the start of *Roots and Branches* (1964). Perhaps alone among American poets of his generation, Duncan had read in the Kabbalah from his early childhood. He grew up, biographer Ekbert Faas explains, in a Theosophist family where "the knowledge of shaman rites amongst the Indians mingled with the occult practices of American spiritualism" (23, 28) and Rosicrucian translations of the *Zohar* and the *Sefer Yetsira* were part of the family's regular studies. Duncan's ease with the Shekhinah leads him to treat her as a half-forgotten, richly syncretic, quite ambivalent figure. On the one hand, she is "She in whom / the Jew has his communion," a figure for the links between Jewish and non-Jewish visions of female spark and divinity ("The Maiden," *Opening*, 27). On the other hand, however, she remains in part a frigid "Ice Queen," trapped in the Jewish failure to escape belief in itself as (in Duncan's words) "the incomparable nation or race" and thus envision a true "symposium of the whole" ("Rites," 327).[5]

Throughout the late 1950s, Duncan buttonholed fellow poets and artists, especially but not exclusively Jews, telling them to brush up their *Zohar*, their Scholem, and their symbolic repertoire. One who took him up on this challenge was the visual artist Wallace Berman, whose work often juxtaposed images of sexual or pop-cultural domesticity with mysterious arrays of Hebrew letters, especially a talismanic Aleph. (He had one on his motorcycle helmet, too.) Inspired by his marriage to the non-Jewish Shirley Morand—an act of quite literal intermarriage, but one with ample symbolic resonance—Berman made his art a place where things could align and, as Duncan would say, have their communion: "A Rose. Shekinah. Music. Shirley" (Meltzer, "Door of Heaven," 100–1). The poet David Meltzer, too responded to Duncan's urgings. He read deeply and widely in the Kabbalah, and the domestic mysticism of his early work, like that of Berman's art, plays twentieth-century changes on the sixteenth-century practices that identified "the *Shekhinah* not only with the Queen of the Sabbath, but also with every Jewish housewife who celebrates the Sabbath." No wonder Meltzer opens "Letters and Numbers" with a scene of the poet walking "down the path to help my wife / (in green and gold light) carry / groceries back to our tree house." They're living in, or living out, a "Paradise *Pardes*" (Tens, 109).

In the middle 1960s, when Meltzer came of age as a poet, two books appeared that seemed to corroborate Duncan's vision of the Shekhinah: *On the Kabbalah and its Symbolism* by Gershom Scholem (1965) and Raphael Patai's

The Hebrew Goddess (1967). Between them, these books offer a vision of what one might call (following Greil Marcus) "the old, weird Judaism." Sex magic at the heart of Shabbos dinner? A Shekhinah who turns out to be "by function and position, a direct heir to such ancient Hebrew goddesses of Canaanite origin as Asherah and Anath" (Patai, 137; quoted in Rothenberg, *Exiled*, 36)? A Goddess, Asherah, whose statue was worshipped "for no less than 236 years" at Solomon's Temple, her worship "part of the legitimate religion approved and led by the king, the court and the priesthood" (Patai, 50, 52; Rothenberg, *Exiled*, 109)? A Heavenly King who becomes, with Shekhinah in exile, "no longer King, nor great, nor potent," and who lets the arch-demoness Lilith "take the place of his true queen" (Patai, 196–97; Rothenberg, *Exiled*, 129)? As Duncan had told Berman, Meltzer, Rothenberg, and anyone else who would listen, Jewish culture was always "comprised [of] heterodox variants" alongside, or even within, the bounds of "'official' Judaism" (Patai, 20; Rothenberg, *Exiled*, 106). Where an earlier generation abandoned such "archaic" or "primative" material in the name of assimilation, Jews of the American counterculture could be part of a broad national movement precisely by conjuring its return.

For Meltzer and the other California kabbalists, the Shekhinah offers a part-for-whole figure for the occluded, unorthodox, and above all *poetic* undercurrents in Jewish culture: currents repressed by normative traditions from Biblical times ("thou shalt not suffer a shaman to live," as Rothenberg renders the line) well into the American 1950s. "No minor channel, it is the poetic *mainstream* that he [the poet] finds here," Rothenberg insists, connecting "magic, myth & dream; earth, nature, orgy, love" with "the female presence the Jewish poets named Shekhinah" (*Exiled*, 5). What does this "mainstream" poetry look like?

A longer version of this story would turn, at this point, to accounts of any number of texts. There's the "Shekhinah" issue of Meltzer's journal *Tree* (vol. 3, 1972), which incorporates work by, among others, Jerome Rothenberg, Jack Hirschman, Isidore Isou (the French *lettriste*), Deena Metzger, Howard Schwartz, Rabbi Moses Cordovero, a Christian kabbalist named "Frater Achad," and the first American translation of *The Book of Questions,* by the Egyptian-French writer Edmond Jabes. (Note to publishers: A *Tree* reprint or anthology is long overdue.) The year 1973 brought Meltzer's sly and under-stated *Hero/Lil* from Black Sparrow Press; another issue of *Tree* followed shortly thereafter (Lenny Bruce meets the poet Paul Celan, with the Hasidic master Nachman of Bratslav presiding) and in 1975 New Directions released the complete *Lyrics for the Bride of God*, by the ethnopoet Nathaniel Tarn. For the sake of brevity, however, I will focus on only one book from this cultural moment: Jerome Rothenberg's *Poland/1931*.

The first installments of *Poland/1931* were published in 1969, shadowed by assassinations, riots, and the Vietnam war. "If America meant anything to me it was in some nineteenth-century sense, as a meeting place of the nations," the poet would later recall. ("A meeting place of the nations" and "She / in whom the Jew has his communion" are commensurate ideas, as we shall see.) "What America had developed into," however, "was something that at that point I felt to be repulsive, and I wanted to, in some very violent, for me, sense, dissociate myself from this. And it seemed to me no longer worth very specifically *not* being Jewish or not being what I was ancestrally to have a share in the American present" ("Interview," 114). Returning like Ginsberg to the past of a previous generation, Rothenberg's book is steeped in European and immigrant Jewish experience, and it features pictures of the poet himself in peddler garb (on the cover) and the poet's mother, Esther, as a young woman in a theatrical pose. But it casts its net far more widely, in space and time and Judaic material, than any book of Jewish American poetry before it. It includes untranslated amulets, photos of family postcards, found poems extracted from the classic restatement of Jewish law, the *Shulkhan Aruch*, and accounts of ritual acts that turn, out of context, into surreal "Events." Annulling space, Rothenberg imagines the founder of Hasidism, the Baal Shem Tov, born into a tragicomic Wild West, where his broad-rimmed Polish *shtreimel* makes him look like a cowboy. (He gets the nickname "Cokboy," more on which in a moment.) As for time, the book takes place in what the final poem calls "kabbalistic time / that brings all men together": another version of America as the "meeting place of nations" that the nation ought to be. If the book ends on a despairing note, in an "America disaster / America disaster / America disaster / America disaster," it is in large part because of the hopes it has raised, in form and content, all along (143, 151).

One figure for those hopes, their persistence and their vulnerability, is the Shekhinah. You don't have to look far in *Poland/1931* to find her. The fourth poem, "Satan in Goray," names her in English: "Something is Presence," it announces in a solitary, enigmatic line (9). A few pages later, in the troubling mix of rape and hope, vision and vulgarity called "The Bride," she takes center stage. "O Shekinah o thou my defeated flower," it begins:

> trampled my Bessarabian daisy by the boots of strangers
> cossacks have struck their cocks on thee
> on thy thighs have slept generations of tartars
> what bitter exiles have brought thee to this bed
> to leathern blankets aflake in Polish air
> contamination of lungs o my Slavic moongirl
> my bride where hast thou gone then
> & wherefore wherefore hast thou left thy milk bottles behind
>
> (26)

The pseudo-Shakespearean diction here stands in sharp contrast to the vulgarity of those brutalizing "cocks," suggesting at least for the moment that the poem will draw a bright line between the Shekhinah's husband (the poet) and those who have assaulted her in exile (Cossacks, Tartars, and so on). As the poem continues, however, the line begins to blur. It's the poet who pledges to squeeze her "tits" for wisdom, who hymns her as "o Hole" as well as "Holy Mother," and who dreams of her as a "daughter spread on table / with red & yellow drops thy cunt doth come undone." As he describes these assaults on her his own voice rises with involuntary excitement: "gone the forced nights in Polish brothels the whip of the delighted nobles / on thy ass brought low brought to thy knees in sucking homage / o cunt of God o Goddess o thou egg thou albumen / thou eye thou semen spurt thou lip thou whisper of rising into scream / thou my SHEKINAH . . ." (26–27).

The risk, the *dare* of "The Bride" lies in Rothenberg's desire to make his own poetic persona part of the Shekhinah's problem. He may not take part in the physical assaults on her, those marks of her exile, but the language he uses implicates him in it. For all that the book delights in ribaldry, the exuberantly lewd—"let's put the Id back in Yid," it seems to cry, like Philip Roth's Portnoy—Rothenberg also understands the cost of all this male release. In a world ruled by the God that Rothenberg names "O / El / O / Him"—a pun on the traditional Hebrew God-terms *El* and *Elohim*—there's as much danger as exuberance in the strut of a Jewish Cokboy lighting out for the territory, "jaunty with cock slung over shoulder," ready to take on the world (150, 149). The book knows this—and at several points it silently hints at an alternative. One comes in the pair of generation-old pictures of the poet's mother, Esther, as the elusive, self-reliant "Esther K," a. k. a. "Mrs. L. L.," a. k. a. "Mme. Shekinah, Jewish Soul Healer and Adviser." The other I find in the photograph of Rothenberg performing the mitzvah of *teffilin*, wrapping his arm and head in the leather phylacteries of traditional practice, which steadies the reader just after "The Bride" (28). Or, to be more accurate, the poet has the *teffilin* laid upon him, the black straps held by a mysterious female figure. It's clearly a staged, performative gesture: not the *mitzvah* per se, done in the name of the unification of the Holy One and His Shekhinah, but a poet's decidedly heterodox and aesthetic invocation of that act. Yet there is nothing stagy or kitchy or forced about it. Quite the contrary—its mix of stony, hieratic stillness (on the man's part) and a steady, almost wound-binding attentiveness (on hers, whoever she is) offers a still center to the book's otherwise unsettling verse.

Along with Rothenberg's new translation of Rabbi Isaac Luria's hymn to the Shekhinah, the piece I described at the start of this essay, this picture of the poet in *teffilin* tethers *Poland/1931* to an image of both moral and marital seriousness. (I say "marital" because as one puts on *teffilin*, one recites the lovely lines of betrothal from the prophet Hosea: "I will betroth you to me forever, I will betroth you to me in righteousness and in justice and in lovingkindness and in mercy, I will betroth you to me in faithfulness, and you will know

YHVH.") Unlike Luria's hymn, however, which celebrates reunion, the picture suggests a continuing split between male and female principles even as the betrothal rite of *teffilin* is enacted. This iconic couple (the poet and his muse, the Holy One and his Shekhinah) don't even so much as *look* at each other. And from the lighting, the expressions on the faces, and the local context of the image—just after "The Bride," with its imagery of rape and exploitation—you can't help but feel that he, not she, is to blame.

At first glance, then, the "America disaster" where *Poland/1931* ends is the result of racism, war, and political sterility at the end of the Nixon presidency: another exile for the Shekhinah to wander in and mourn. At heart, though, the book suggests another, equally culpable cause: the Jewish dis-aster, or dissing of the aster / Ishtar / Eshter K. / Shekhinah figure of the book by her male counterpart. She's been exiled, we can see, in his masculine imagination: an exile that only some change in human and American gender relations will be able to cure. The mutable, beleaguered Shekhinah that Rothenberg invokes may still hope mostly for something like domestic tranquility, on a national or intimate scale. But she raises questions about that very ideal—and about the Jewish culture that sponsors it—which other writers, mostly women, would use the Shekhinah to press in the decade to come.

"It is all many / It is all one" (1971–1987)

Looking back on the first renaissance of Shekhinah in America, then, two things are clear. First, it's an arrival of this "illustrious émigré" that produces remarkably thorny, resistant, or slippery poetry: work that doesn't give a damn about communal practice or liturgical reconstruction. You can't use Rothenberg's translation of the Luria hymn as a hymn; there's little or nothing in any of these volumes that you can borrow for a prayerbook. Rothenberg himself describes the reappearance of Shekhinah as part of the "Great Subculture" coming home to roost, a resurgence of "a long subterranean tradition of resistance to the twin authorities of state and organized religion," not as a first step toward Jewish Renewal ("Pre-Face," xii).

And yet, the arrival of Shekhinah in 1970s America marks a period of remarkable change and possibility on other fronts as well. The same years that give rise to *Tree* produce the founding organization of modern Jewish feminism, Ezrat Nashim, and Rabbi Lynn Gottlieb's feminist Bat Kol performance ensemble, and the first American services using female God-language, and the participatory *havurah* [religious fellowship] movement, and the do-it-yourself *Jewish Catalogue*. The overlapping is often fortuitous: 1976 was the year not only of David Meltzer's *Secret Garden*, an anthology of the Kabbalah, but of the first issue of *Lilith*—a Jewish feminist magazine, edited by Aviva

Cantor, with rather wider readership than the esoteric *Tree*. The same year (1978) that Rothenberg insists that Shekhinah belongs to *"poesis, not* religion" brings the anthology *Womanspirit Rising*, edited by Carol Christ and Judith Plaskow, and E. M. Broner's novel *A Weave of Women*, books where the feminist investigation and reconstruction of patriarchal religion is itself a form of *poesis*, but a *poesis* whose "making" aims to shape a broader communal and spiritual life.

Unlike the Shekhinah poetry that I have traced so far, the work of explicitly feminist liturgists, poets, and theologians makes a bid to reconstruct the Jewish world in its own image. It thus sparks considerable communal debate. In 1979, for example, an article in *Lilith* by Cynthia Ozick blasted the use of female God-language for prayers. "What?" she demands. "Millenia after the cleansing purity of Abraham's vision of the One Creator, a return to Astarte, Hera, Juno, Venus, and all their proliferating sisterhood? Sex goddesses, fertility goddesses, mother goddesses?" Even the use of Shekhinah, "the female shadow or emanation of the Godhead," turns out to be "an assault on monotheism" (121). (Liturgical poems like Rabbi Lynn Gottlieb's 1980 "Psalm" illuminate one source of her concern—it is, after all, an ancient hymn to Ishtar touched up for Jewish liturgical use. Duncan would have approved.) For Arthur Green, by contrast, Skekhinah language and imagery mark a way for women to begin constructing "a truly feminine, and truly Jewish, spirituality"—a project, he tells the women of the Women's Rabbinical Alliance, that is "one of the urgent tasks of our age," but whose *"proper* point of origin" will be "the encounter of contemporary Jewish women with those symbols of the sacred feminine given us by our tradition" (259, my emphasis). The tension between these two responses, one hewing to purity, the other open to offers, but anxious to keep Jewish feminism "Jewish," marks the context for the next two poets I want to examine, Eleanor Wilner and Marge Piercy.

In 1984, the University of Chicago Press published Eleanor Wilner's second collection of poems, one simply called *Shekhinah*. The book opens with four epigraphs: the first on its own page, from Raphael Patai, describing "The Withdrawal of the Shekhinah from Her Home in the Temple"; the other three grouped together, one classical (from June Rachuy Brindel's *Ariadne*), one American Romantic (from *Moby-Dick*), and one Inuit (an Eskimo shaman quoted by Joseph Campbell), each drawing our attention to a consoling female presence we are asked to imagine as a *voice*. The juxtaposition is worthy of Duncan—and, indeed, Wilner shares Duncan's wariness about what happens when one believes in "the incomparable nation or race, the incomparable Jehovah in the shape of a man, the incomparable species," and so on ("Rites," 327). After reading these epigraphs one reads every compassionate, suffering, or antipatriarchal figure in the book a version of the Shekhinah—and, in turn, to read the Jewish figure *not* as the Presence of God but simply as one local expression of the cross-cultural longing to feel at home in what Melville called "the stepmother world."

I'm tempted at this point simply to walk you through the first few poems of *Shekhinah*, to show you how the book makes "Mary Taylor who went off to Australia / and set up shop with a woman friend" one version of Shekhinah ("Emigration"), only to pivot and recast her a moment later as a medieval woman, secretly pagan, weaving a ritual basket while the lord of the castle goes to hunt or to war ("Without Regret"), only to spot her, a moment later, in the German mother Marianne Bachmeier, who, a headnote informs us, "walked into a Lubeck courtroom, fired six shots and killed Klaus Grabowski, 35, accused of molesting and strangling her 7-year-old daughter" ("Eleusis"). The book can be read, that is to say, as a grand exegetical challenge to us readers—a chance to revise and complicate our sense of the Shekhinah as we go. What we find is, as in Rothenberg, a figure of resistance to the Great Lies of Church and State—but she is not, on the whole, a figure of "magic, myth & dream; earth, nature, orgy" (although she still is a figure of "love"). Her central attributes seem now to be compassion, disobedience, and care, with these qualities, as Wilner explains elsewhere, "inextricably linked" ("Wrestling," 319).

If Wilner's project in *Shekhinah* poses a challenge to readers, it challenges the poet as well. For if the female figure this book centers on is known to us, as the epigraphs explain, primarily as a *voice*, then it's up to Wilner to create a voice we hear her in. Not simply a character, however complex, the Shekhinah comes to life in our minds as Wilner's own style, her distinctive poetics: musing, thoughtful, sympathetic, sometimes "loving-angry" (as Mary Taylor often was with her dear friend Charlotte Bronte), always deeply skeptical of such aesthetic extremes as The Masterpiece (too inhumanly perfect), The Difficult Avant-Garde Work (too self-congratulatory in its "ear- / splitting syntactical tricks"), and above all The Confessional Poem (narcissistic and banal, too comfortable with its pretense to tell us "the true / grit, the way it is," and other bluff cliches).

The poem I'm quoting, "Ars Poetica," poses one long satirical stanza of disdain against one that enacts, as well as describes, the poet's more supple aesthetic ideal. Here's how the latter sounds:

> And all the time, the shy and shapely
> mind, like some Eurydice, wanders—
> darkened by veils, a shade
> with measured footsteps. So many things are gone
> and the end of the world looms
> like a shark's fin on the flats of our horizon.
> Fatigue sets in, and the wind rises.
> The door is swinging on its hinges—the room
> pried open, the one upstairs in Bluebeard's castle.

> They have been hanging there a long time
> in their bridal dresses, from hooks,
> by their own long hair.
> The wind that makes them sway until
> they seem almost alive
> is like the rush of our compassion.
> Yes, now we remember them all
> and the sea with its unchanging heaving—a grief
> as deep and dactylic as the voice of Homer,
> and, as we turn another way, we lay the past out
> on Achilles' shield, abandon it to earth,
> our common ground—the bridal hope, its murder,
> the old, old story, perpetual
> as caring; the scant human store
> that is so strangely self-restoring
> and whose sufficiency
> is our continual surprise.

(Reversing, 242)

In a meditative adagio, the poem itself "wanders" through a series of allusions: to Eurydice (the lost wife of Orpheus), to Bluebeard's castle (where a test of one wife's curiosity leads her to the corpses of those who failed the test before her), to Achilles' shield, from the *Illiad*. To make such stories come alive, Wilner suggests, we have to care about them, to fill their lungs with the "rush of our compassion." That wind of compassion, in turn, takes us out of ourselves and our own exhaustion. It reminds us of "the scant human store" (of stories, of longings, of sadness, of hope) whose very commonality seems to restore us, to refresh us, to bring us back to the chance of surprise. To care about such stories is, after all, to feel in ourselves the shapely, shaping, mental and physical "rush" of empathy and spirit that other poems in the book, notably "See-Saw," identify with the "healing sorrow" of the Shekhinah. And here the difference between Wilner's Shekhinah and those of a Rothenberg or Duncan becomes sharply clear. For in this book, we don't simply read *about* her, we get to *be* her, however provisionally, so long as that voice is in our ears, and in our mouths.

As the classical and fairy-tale allusions of "Ars Poetica" suggest, Wilner is not terribly concerned to keep her Shekhinah "Jewish." Other poems by her, notably the title poem of her third book, *Sarah's Choice*, reinforce how skeptical she is of making such distinctions (Jew / Gentile, True God / False Idol, Self / Other, etc.), which she sees as central to any number of moral and political horrors. This skepticism allies her with any number of recent American poets, from Robert Duncan to Muriel Rukeyser. It also places her in a long line of Jews uncomfortable with Jewish particularism, including such modern Jewish thinkers as the Israeli (and Orthodox) professor Ze'ev Falk and the American founder of Reconstructionist Judaism, Mordechai Kaplan. But given how crucial the making of distinctions is in Jewish thought and culture, theologians perhaps cannot afford to be as broadly syncretic or skeptical as poets. And poets who write work for liturgical use, or even whose poems find themselves adopted for prayer, face a slightly different set of challenges from those Wilner handles so expertly in *Shekhinah* and elsewhere.

Consider, for example, the work of Marge Piercy, whose poetry has been borrowed—indeed, often *offers* itself for use—in Jewish communal practice. Deeply involved with Reconstructionist Judaism, as well as with the worlds of feminist poetry and fiction, Piercy has always had a broad audience in mind for her work—and, indeed, has found one. Her poetry, in particular, finds a place on the shelves of those who are not, by profession or habit, readers of poetry: readers who want to learn, as the title of one collection has it, *The Art of Blessing the Day*. The style and voice of her poem "Wellfleet Sabbath," a "reading" offered to worshippers by the Reconstructionist *Kol Haneshama* prayerbook, are perfectly suited for this sort of cultural work:

> The hawk eye of the sun slowly shuts.
> The breast of the bay is softly feathered
> dove grey. The sky is barred like the sand
> when the tide trickles out.
>
> The great doors of the Sabbath are swinging
> open over the ocean, loosing the moon
> floating up slow   distorted   vast, a copper
> balloon just sailing free.
>
> The wind slides over the waves, patting
> them with its giant hand, and the sea
> stretches its muscles in the deep,
> purrs and rolls over.
>
> The sweet beeswax candles flicker
> and sigh, standing between the phlox
> and the roast chicken. The wine shines
> its red lantern of joy.
>
> Here on this piney sandspit, the Shekinah
> comes on the short strong wings of the seaside
> sparrow raising her song and bringing
> down the fresh clean night.
>
> (*Kol Haneshama,* 737)

Read this poem just after a piece by Rothenberg, or even by Wilner, and you're instantly aware of just how relaxed and *available* it is to the reader. Anyone can find its pleasures: the way that bird motif runs through the stanzas, linking the hawk-eyed sun and the feather-breasted bay at the poem's start to the "phlox" (smile when you say that) and roast chicken near the middle to the "seaside / sparrow" of the Shekinah raising her song at the close. The "I" of the piece, like that of a psalm or *piyyut*, the traditional Jewish liturgical poem, is deliberately unspecified, open, inviting us to take it for our own. One of Piercy's finest New American *Piyyutim*, this is the sort of poem that I, a student and teacher of avant-garde writers, am not *supposed* to like. Perhaps that's why it seems like such a fitting Sabbath poem to me: I read it out of school, when work is done, on the day when restful and sanctified sensuous pleasure finds its proper home.

When the work week starts again, of course, I look at the poem somewhat more skeptically—in search, I'll confess, of the paradoxes or difficulties that professional critics so love. Formally the poem seems straightforward enough. And theologically speaking, there's not much in "Wellfleet Sabbath" that even a strict or conservative reader—say, for example, Cynthia Ozick—could object to. But in her essay elsewhere in this collection, Maeera Shreiber argues that even the most orthodox of liturgical poems were seen by some rabbis, centuries ago, as a threat to the sanctity of the prayer service. And indeed, when you return the poem to a slightly broader context, both in Piercy's work and in its Jewish American cultural moment, some delightful complexities indeed come to light.

Well before its use in the Reconstructionist Kol Haneshama prayerbook, "Wellfleet Sabbath" appeared in Piercy's collection *Available Light,* published in 1988. Turn the page after reading it and you find I Saw Her Dancing": a piece that invokes, not the Shekhinah, but the Voudoun goddess Yemanja. The poem's scenario is simple. The speaker has been to a *santeria* ceremony in Cuba and seen Yemanja come to possess, or "ride," one of her worshipers. Piercy knows, as a poet, what this sort of possession is like; indeed, she claims, not only all artists but all women know what it is like to be used in this way, as the vehicle for something that longs to be created, made manifest, or born. Hence the confident, uncompromising declaration that opens the poem's third section, where Piercy, as a Jew, not only says she saw the goddess come but that she "worshiped," too. For, as in the Kabbalah, with its multiplication of named divine attributes (including the Presence, or the Shekhinah), in this poem strict monotheism yields to a vision of deity that is (or threatens to be) remarkably polymorphous. After all, Piercy insists, ostensibly singular parts of the physical world turn out to be, on inspection, internally multiple and various. (Consider an egg, the poem suggests, or the seed of a plant, or a fire.) And, just as important, the many parts also add up to a single whole. (Consider your own body, the poem invites its readers.) The American motto *e pluribus unum* thus turns out to apply to the divine. The One is manifold, irreducibly plural, while the many are "all one."

In the context of a Sabbath service, then, Shekhinah of "Wellfleet Sabbath" is a multiply comforting and quite traditional figure. (Jews have long prayed to find rest "under the wings" of God's Presence, for example—hence the bird imagery of Piercy's closing stanza.) But reread with "I Saw Her Dancing" in mind, this Shekhinah can seem as much a figure of connection between Jewish and non-Jewish, even pagan or polytheistic beliefs, as those found in Wilner or Duncan. Is there no risk or tension in placing her in a *siddur*—and thus, perhaps, of calling to mind the broadly syncretic figure of Goddess that the theologian Judith Plaskow describes as "Asherah, Ishtar, Isis, Afrekete, Oyo, Ezuli, Mary, and Shekhinah" (144–45)? In the world of Reconstructionist Judaism, with which Piercy has deep ties, these are not simply academic questions. In 1986, after all, a woman student at the Reconstructionist Rabbinical College, Jane Litman, was publically accused of idolatry for making statues of Asherah: part of an effort, as Litman explained, to "dig up women's spiritual practices from the past and see what resonates" (see Zaidman, 58). Even the sympathetic Arthur Green, by then the head of the RRC, found this too much to accept. "Let Jewish feminism clearly proclaim itself as spiritually and linguistically Jewish, cutting itself off clearly from any attempt at new-paganism or the revival of witchcraft, however wrapped it may be in quasi-Jewish garb," he urged in *Sh'ma: A Journal of Jewish Responsibility* the following year (35; see Zaidman 59).

Mother of Psyche, Love's Mother-in-Law (1987–1997)

Over the last twenty years, then, the figure of Shekhinah has found its way by steady trickles both into American Judaism—not without resistance, and perhaps rightly so—and into Jewish American poetry. To invoke her in either context seems to make all of Jewish culture simultaneous, from the Biblical and mythic past to the postmodern American present, even as she conjures up a metaphysical context for marital (or at least sexual) harmony and mystery. She stands as a counterpart or antidote within Jewish culture to the oppressively patriarchal God and forefathers that one finds—it is said—in the Hebrew Bible. The God who tells Abraham to bind Isaac for sacrifice *can't* be the only story, Alicia Ostriker thus insists, any more than the Biblical patriarchs could be the only begetters of the gentle Jewish men, "men who were tender as butter," that were her own grandfathers (*Nakedness*, 64). She bodies forth the repressed and heterodox elements in Jewish tradidit on, especially its "half-erased traces of paganism" and a repressed or occluded fascination with the feminine (*Nakedness*, xii). As a consequence the Shekhinah also presides over cultural communion or interchange, softening the stern traditional boundaries between Jew and Gentile (among other borders) without entirely obliterating them, making them in fact a space for imaginative play. As Allen Grossman has recently observed, the Jewish poet who writes under the sign of the Shekhinah owes it to Her to construct a metaphorical "place" where "the People and the peoples" are equally at home." ("Jewish Poetry," 166).

What is this welcoming "place" the Jewish poet must construct? Traditionally the people and peoples will be at home, eventually, in the redeemed Zion to which God's Presence, His Shekhinah, has returned. "Their burnt offerings and their sacrifices shall be accepted on my altar," God promises in Isaiah 56:7, "for my house shall be called a house of prayer for all people." For Jewish American poets, however, the place where the People and the peoples meet as equals often turns out not to be Zion, but that other chosen land, America. When Marcia Falk rewrites the Sabbath service in her remarkable new prayerbook, *The Book of Blessings*, she thus turns the traditional prayer that God should restore His Presence to Zion into a suite of poems and blessings centered on the famous Statue of Liberty sonnet by Emma Lazarus, "The New Colossus." And in his wonderful recent poem "Wig," C. K. Williams shows what even an implicit identification of America with the meeting place of nations, presided over by the Mother of Exiles, can do for one's poetry.

"Wig" is the fifth poem in a sequence called "Symbols," and in it, Williams begins by looking out at a dreary winter afternoon and attributing symbolic resonance, however playfully, to the figures he sees:

> The bus that won't arrive this freezing, bleak, pre-Sabbath afternoon
> must be Messiah;
> the bewigged woman, pacing the sidewalk, furious, seething, can be
> only the mystic Shekinah,
> the presence of God torn from Godhead, chagrined, abandoned,
> longing to rejoin, reunite.

Although he draws on two Jewish myths of absence or loss—the long-awaited Messiah who keeps not coming and the exiled Shekhinah—Williams clearly takes pleasure in making these attributions, delighting in the sudden twist his poem takes from a bus to Messiah and from a fully human woman, "furious, seething" and "bewigged" (and thus quite observant, but it's a funny word) to the mystic pathos of the Shekhinah. (That he calls the Shekhinah "chagrined" in the last line shown gives Her a fully human attribute as well—and the "grined" of "chagrined" echoes the hard "g" and short "i" of "bewigged" to give it, too, a slightly comic touch.)

Now, since the (feminine) Shekhinah traditionally longs to reunite with the (masculine) Holy One Blessed Be He, the logic of the myth suggests that this woman's husband, if she has one, will be assigned the role of God Himself. Instead, Williams shifts the focus of the poem from the fine romance Above to the more earthly cares of marriage Below—and, in the process, changes the myth: The husband, we next see, bearded, his head covered, turns out not to be God but "the human spirit," doggedly following the "obviously self-absorbed" Presence of God through "degrading tracts of slush and street-filth," longing for Her to redeem our passage. And in the third and final stanza, having given us a wife and a husband who pushes their stroller, Williams gives the myth one last twist. "And the child," he writes, "asleep, serene, uncaring in the crank and roar of traffic, his cheeks afire, / ladders of snowy light leaping and swirling about him. . . ." Yes? Yes? For the first time we have to wait nearly two full lines for a symbolic attribution, as though the poet were so captivated by what he sees that he hasn't decided yet. When it comes at last, the poem can close, for the child

> . . . is what else but psyche, holy psyche,
> always only now just born, always now just waking, to the ancient truths
>   of knowledge, suffering, loss.
>
> (41)

The tenderness of these lines, their ease with abstraction (and benediction), is typical of Williams's work. Their willingness to link "knowledge" to "suffering, loss" is characteristic as well—and also suggests that "Wig" lives up to Allen Grossman's proviso that the Jewish poet who invokes the Shekhinah must construct a metaphorical "place" for the nations to meet, but also one where "the intelligibility of experience" can be affirmed: a "place of holiness . . . where loss is given back as meaning" (166). And indeed, when Williams names the child in the poem "psyche, holy psyche," he makes these two projects one.

Who, after all, is "psyche"? Etymologically, the word means "soul"—but in classical mythology, as you may recall, Psyche is also a god—or, rather, a goddess (this poem has changed his / her sex), and divine not by birth but by marriage. She is most famous for her much-vexed marriage with Cupid (or Eros), the son of Venus, a godling of Love, in which she was forbidden by her mother-in-law from ever seeing her husband. This story, like that of God and the Shekhinah, starts out as a tale of loss. But although Psyche loses her beloved at first—spurred by the jealousy of her sisters, she takes a lamp to see her invisible husband as he sleeps, and he must flee—after many trials, she regains him, wins the approval of Venus, and eventually gives birth to a child.

Williams's poem doesn't strut or fret about this slip from Jewish to classical mythology. Rather, it simply assumes that in the American mind of its speaker, both resources are equally present, equally possible, ready and willing to meet.

Williams's poem turns out to be just the sort of "meeting place of the nations" that Rothenberg dreamed and despaired of in *Poland/1931*, that the epigraphs to Wilner's *Shekhinah* embody, and that Robert Duncan (another poet of Cupid and Psyche) described as a "symposium of the whole" where "all things have come into their comparisons" ("Rites," 327). What happens when they do? The poem gives no obvious or deliberate answer; but then, as we've seen in Ginsberg and elsewhere, poems don't *have* to. No, no, whatever Williams wanted his verses to suggest, the logic of "Wig" means that the thoroughly Orthodox "presence of God torn from Godhead" is destined to become not only the mother-in-law of the Roman god of Love (!) but also the grandmother of a new character, a daughter named Pleasure. And whatever the statistics suggest, I'm willing to bet that her mother—or is it her father?—will raise baby Pleasure as a Jew.

As my own grandmother would put it, "Only in America!"

Notes

1. Rothenberg has since turned *A Big Jewish Book* into *Exiled in the Word*, a slimmer volume published in 1989 and still in print. All page references are to *Exiled*.

2. The Internet listserv H-JUDAIC recently featured a thread of inquiries and discussion wondering when "tikkun olam"—once an esoteric doctrine associated with the healing of the Godhead—acquired the liberal political connotations it now has. The "politics of meaning" sponsored by the magazine *Tikkun* got much of the credit, but this use evidently dates back to the mid 1970s, making it contemporary with the rediscovery and reinterpretation of Shekhinah.

3. Readers who wish to explore a range of other poems that invoke the Shekhinah yet fit neither of the catergories I have set here—many quite ambitious, and quite wonderful—should turn to John Hollander's *Spectral Emanations*, Allan Mandelbaum's *Chelmaxioms*, poems such as "In My Observatory Withdrawn" and "The Law" by Allen Grossman, Norman Finkelstein's "Braids," and Jacqueline Osherow's "Moses in Paradise." Enjoy.

4. Falk includes "The New Colossus" in the "Restoring Shekhinah, Reclaiming Home" portion of a revised Shabbat *Shaharit Amidah*, in her rewriting of the Jewish prayerbook, *The Book of Blessings*. Shreiber treats Emma Lazarus at length in *Dwelling and Displacement: The Genres of Jewish American Poetry*, forthcoming (as of this writing) from Stanford University Press. For more on the link between Shekhinah and Rachel, see the thirteenth-century *Gates of Light* by Joseph Gikatillia. "In the time of Abraham our father, of blessed memory," he explains, "the Shekhinah was called Sarah. In the time of Isaac our father, she was called Rebecca. In the time of Jacob our father, she was called Rachel" (quoted in Green, "Bride, Spouse, Daughter," 258).

5. "The Jewish community [in the *Zohar*] can't believe in the human reality of other human beings," Duncan tells Rodger Kamenetz in a 1984 interview, "and yet the

"pan-Arabic" background of the *Zohar* suggests that this very particularism is above all an attempt to "disown the Diaspora," a nervous effort to obscure the cultural exogamy always present even within "The Tradition" itself. See "Realms of Being" (12).

Works Cited

The Complete Metsudah Siddur: Weekday/Sabbath/Festival. Trans. and commentary Avrohom Davis. New York: Metsudah Publications, 1990.

Duncan, Robert. *The Opening of the Field*. New York: Evergreen, 1960.

———."Realms of Being: An Interview with Robert Duncan." *The Southern Review* 22, no. 1 (1985).

———. "Rites of Participation." In *Symposium of the Whole: A Range of Discourse Toward an Ethnopoetics*. Ed. Jerome Rothenberg and Diane Rothenberg. Berkeley: U of California P, 1983. 327–336.

———. *Roots and Branches*. New York: Charles Scribner's Sons, 1964.

Faas, Ekbert. *Young Robert Duncan: Portrait of the Poet As Homosexual in Society*. Santa Barbara, Calif.: Black Sparrow P, 1984.

Falk, Marcia. *The Book of Blessings: New Jewish Prayers for Daily Life, the Sabbath, and the New Moon Festival*. San Franciso: Harper San Francisco, 1996.

Finkelstein, Norman. *The Ritual of New Creation: Jewish Tradition and Contemporary Literature*, Albany: SUNY P, 1992.

Ginsberg, Allen. *Collected Poems, 1947–1980*. New York: Harper & Row, 1984.

Gottlieb, Lynn. "Psalm." In *Women Speak to God: The Prayers and Poems of Jewish Women*. Ed. Marcia Cohn Spiegel and Deborah Lipton Kremsdorf. San Diego: Women's Institute for Continuing Jewish Education, 1987. 79.

Green, Arthur. "Bride, Spouse, Daughter: Images of the Feminine in Classical Jewish Sources." In *On Being a Jewish Feminist*. Ed. Susannah Heschel, New York: Schocken, 1983.

Grossman, Allen. "The Jew as an American Poet: The Instance of Ginsberg." In *On the Poetry of Allen Ginsberg*, Ed. Lewis Hyde, Ann Harbor: U of Michigan P, 1984. 102–10. Reprinted, with small but significant revisions, in *The Long Schoolroom*, Ann Arbor: U of Michigan P, 1997: 150–58. Originally published in *Judaism* (Fall 1962).

———. "Jewish Poetry Considered as a Theophoric Project." In *The Long Schoolroom*, Ann Arbor: U of Michigan P, 1997: 159–67.

The Klezmatics, "Mizmor Shir Lehanef (Reefer Song)." On *Possessed*. Xenophile 4050, Green Linnet Records, 1997, track 5.

Kol Haneshama: Shabbat Vehagim. Wyncote, Pa.: Reconstructionist P, 1994.

Meltzer, David. "The Door of Heaven, the Path of Letters." In *Wallace Berman Retrospective*. Los Angeles: Fellows of Contemporary Art, 1978. 92–101.

———. *Tens: Selected Poems, 1961–1971*. Santa Barbara, Calif.: Black Sparrow P, 1972.

Ostriker, Alicia. *The Nakedness of the Fathers: Biblical Visions and Re-Visions*. New Brunswick, N.J.: Rutgers UP, 1994.

Ozick, Cynthia. "Notes Towards Finding the Right Question." In *On Being a Jewish Feminist*, Ed. Susannah Heschel, New York: Schocken, 1983. 120–51.

Patai, Raphael. *The Hebrew Goddess*. New York: KTAV Publishing House, 1967.

Petsonk, Judy. *Taking Judaism Personally: Creating a Meaningful Spiritual Life*. New York: Free Press, 1996.

Piercy, Marge. *Available Light*. Knopf, 1988.

Plaskow, *Standing Again at Sinai: Judaism From a Feminist Perspective*. San Francisco: Harper San Francisco, 1990.

Rothenberg, Jerome, ed., with Harris Lenowitz. *Exiled in the Word: Poems and Visions of the Jews from Tribal Times to Present*. Port Townsend, Wash.: Copper Canyon P, 1989.

———. "An Interview [with Barry Alpert]." *Vort* 7 (1975): 93–118.

———. *Poland /1931*. New York: New Directions, 1974.

———. "Pre-Face." In *Symposium of the Whole of the Whole: A Range of Discourse Toward an Ethnopoetics*. Ed. Jerome Rothenberg and Diane Rothenberg, Berkeley: U of California P, 1983. xi–xiii.

Scholem, Gershom. "Kabbalistic Ritual and the Bride of God." In *Symposium of the Whole*, 303–10. This essay is an excerpt from *On the Kabbalah and Its Symbolism*.

———. *On the Kabbalah and Its Symbolism*. Trans. Ralph Manheim, New York: Schocken, 1965.

Smith, Richard Candida. *Utopia and Dissent: Art, Poetry, and Politics in California*. Berkeley: U of California P, 1995.

Tarn, Nathaniel. *Lyrics for the Bride of God*. New York: New Directions, 1975.

Williams, C. K. *The Vigil*. New York: Farrar, Straus, and Giroux, 1997.

Wilner, Eleanor. *Reversing the Spell: New and Selected Poems*. Port Townsend, Wash.: Copper Canyon P, 1998.

———. "Wrestling the Angel of Inscription." In *Dwelling in Possibility: Women Poets and Critics on Poetry*. Ed. Yopie Prins and Maeera Shreiber. Ithaca, N.Y.: Cornell UP, 1997. 318–26.

Zaidman, Nurit. "Variations of Jewish Feminism: The Traditional, Modern, and Postmodern Approaches." *Modern Judaism* 16, no. 1 (1996): 47–65.

A Flair for Deviation: The Troublesome Potential of Jewish Poetics

Maeera Shreiber is Assistant Professor of English at the University of Utah. She is currently completing a book on Jewish American poetry, forthcoming from Stanford UP, and is the author of numerous articles on modern poetry. She is also the coeditor of two volumes of essays, *Dwelling in Possibility: Women Poets and Critics on Poetry* with Yopie Prins (Cornell UP, 1997), and *Mina Loy: Woman and Poet* with Keith Tuma (National Poetry Foundation, 1998).

While one might locate an inaugural moment or rationale for Jewish poetry, it is nevertheless tellingly difficult to determine precisely when "poetry" emerges as a genre in the history of Jewish discursive forms. Looking at the entry under "Hebrew Poetry," an ordinary subset of "Jewish poetry," as provided by the *New Princeton Encyclopedia of Poetry and Poetics*, one gets the impression of a long, unbroken tradition, beginning with Biblical texts clear through to contemporary Israeli achievements. Such mappings have the effect of smoothing out what was in some quarters a lively, fissured, and sometimes contentious set of developments. Consider, for example, James Kugel's calculatedly extravagant argument in *The Idea of Biblical Poetry*, in which he protests the very *idea* of "poetry" as a Biblical genre. What I find especially interesting is how Kugel's argument works to identify "poetry" as an alien and potentially problematic, or troublesome, enterprise. Picking up where Kugel leaves off, Adele Berlin (in *Biblical Poetry Through Medieval Eyes*) notes that in Hebrew literary theory there is a sharp distinction to be made between prophetic and poetic speech—two kinds of discourse that are often viewed as related in Western literature. Prophecy was the word of God, while poetry belonged to the human. Simply put, according to Berlin, "God does not compose poetry" (48). To speak of poetry, then, in Jewish discourse, is to speak of what is human, malleable—at a necessary distance from the divine.

The humanness of the poetic is important to keep in mind when considering how poetry, to use an evolutionary rather than a creationary metaphor, crawls out of the sea of Hebrew discursive forms. Formally, prayer rather than prophecy is poetry's closest kin—most specifically the *piyyut* or the liturgical poem, which began as a supplement to the fixed or statutory prayer service. The history of this literature is enormously interesting—well suited to contemporary sorts of cross-cultural inquiry. Turning, for example, to noted liturgical historian Ismar Elbogin's description of the period, one discovers a striking drama that speaks to poet-critic Charles Bernstein's formulation: "Poetry is turbulent thought." Early in his account Elbogin explains that liturgical poetry served as an "escape"—a way of relieving the tedium of the fixed synagogue service (221). But taken as a whole, his account suggests a considerably less benign function, for he frequently likens poetry to an epidemic—a "contagious disease" that is beyond restraint (225). Poetry is figured as a colonizing or "conquering" force that works to violate or trouble the integrity of the synagogue ritual, the dominant religious institution; interruption becomes disruption: once restricted to festivals and special Sabbaths, "it also took control of the minor festivals and fast days" (225).[1] His description thus contains the possibility of reading liturgical poetry as a potential way of speaking back at dogmatic and institutional discourses.

These liturgical innovations, and their attendant potential for disruption, were variously received depending on the community. In Palestine, for example, where issues of exile were perhaps felt less acutely, prayer-poems were tolerated rather easily, even encouraged. But in Babylonia, where anxiety about God's enabling presence reached an absolute fever pitch, it was altogether another matter. Viewed as a "foreign" and hence dangerous element, *piyyutim* were subject to serious opposition. The extent to which these poems represented a subversive presence is evident in a brief Talmudic fragment, which begins with the well-known claim, "From the day that the Temple was destroyed, the Holy one of Blessing has no place but the four cubits of Halacha" [the Law] (B. Berachot 8a); in other words, God dwells only in the Law, not in aesthetic productions such as prayer-poems. This Talmudic fragment continues with rabbis Asi and Ami responding to this claim, determining that "even though there were thirteen synagogues in Tiberias" (presumably where they lived), they would pray only "in between the pillars where they studied," shunning the synagogues where prayer-poems occur.[2] Having been contaminated by the poetic, synagogues are thus figured as transgressive spaces to be studiously avoided.

As time goes on and the genre becomes more distinct and its practitioners more accomplished, the antagonism toward the poetic as problematic or troublesome becomes that much more pronounced.[3] Of particular note are the theoretical implications of the various aesthetic innovations that characterize the period—most notably the emergence of metrical verse, as an instance of what I would call aesthetic intermarriage or miscegenation. In terms of Hebrew aesthetics, meter and rhyme are construed as foreign imports, learned or borrowed primarily from Arabic writings, and hence frequently targeted for sharp critique. According to one school of Hebrew poets writing in the eleventh century, meter, as a mark of exile, indicated an irrecoverable loss of origin:

> for each and every people has its own rhythmic structure and grammar, but ours was lost to us because of our many sins and hidden from us for our great transgressions ever since we were exiled; what had been of such breadth was now diminished and hidden and become lost. (Kugel, *Idea,* 190)

The implication for Jewish aesthetics is not only that its origins are irrecoverable, but that the notion of a Jewish poetic practice was, from very early on, already Other. Not only is metered poetry contaminated, it is contaminating, diluting the "native integrity" of Hebrew, the holy tongue. The great poet Yehudah Halevi, who infamously once repented of having ever written in the Arabic meters for which he was known, inspired one of his students to write: "But surely it was after our exile that we saw the Arabs making rhymes and metered poems and we began to do like them and caused our Holy Tongue to go astray and enter into a place where it ought not to go" (Kugel, *Idea,* 191).

Throughout the Middle Ages such debates about origins, purity, and authenticity, as well as attendant questions about Judaism's shifting status as culture and/or religion, bubble and churn—debates that are strikingly resonant with many of the sometimes hand-wringing discussions characteristic of American Jewry's ongoing concern with its own identity and future.

In my own readings, however, I mean to attend not only to points of contiguity or continuity, but also those of difference, discontinuity. Indeed, particularly significant for my purposes is the contrast between the medieval position and that of contemporary Jewish *American* aesthetics—in which exile becomes not the contaminating mark of the *loss* of identity, but indeed, the cherished grounds of identity construction itself. The condition of exile and alienation gets naturalized as the mark of the modern Jewish self; loss is reclaimed as meaning, separation and distance become enabling conditions.

This reclamation gets consolidated with the emergence of the Shekhinah—the kabbalistic term for the feminine aspect of the Godhead—as a shaping aesthetic force. According to normative rabbinic Judaism, the Shekhinah is a relatively minor figure. But in contemporary Jewish American poetic practice, the Shekhinah has been celebrated and embraced by a whole range of writers as different as Jerome Rothenberg, Allen Grossman, Eleanor Wilner, Nathaniel Tarn, Adrienne Rich, and Alicia Ostriker.[4] For some the focus has been on her gendered status, while for others the interest lies with her exilic position. For not only is the Shekhinah a feminized presence, but—since she dwells with the people of Israel in exile, which is to say in the very condition of a diasporic identity—she also emerges as the founding principle of poetic creation, a Muse-figure that demarcates the discursive space of poetry.[5] With the Shekhinah comes the recognition that gender is the third term by which poetry and exile are linked; just as poetry has been long represented as a feminized position, so it is with exile.[6] So, the arising of this figure again calls attention to the gendered narrative deeply embedded in American poetics, for the Shekhinah may be understood as an ethnically/theologically inflected incarnation of that steady presence in American literary culture, which poet Susan Howe has taught us to call the "antinomianism" or "Lawlessness" that is "at first feminized and then restricted or banished" (1).

One might regard such arisings as an instance of what historian Yosef Yerushalmi calls collective *anamnesis*, or recollection. While memory (*mneme*) serves to maintain or preserve that which is "essentially unbroken," anamnesis entails retrieving what has been lost or forgotten. More importantly, this retrieval is not simply a wholesale recovery of the past as intact and unchanged; on the contrary, it effects a metamorphosis—a cultural/theologic transformation:

> Every "renaissance," every "reformation," reaches back into the often distant past to recover forgotten or neglected elements with which there is a sudden sympathetic vibration, a sense of empathy, of recognition. Inevitably, every such anamnesis also transforms the recovered past into something new. (Yerushalmi 113)

American Jewish poetic practice is therefore engaged in such an act of anamnesis, recognizing the fundamental mutability of this figure (the Shekhinah possesses a profoundly unfixed nature) as deeply resonant with its own moment (Tishby, 371). The Shekhinah may be understood as correlative to, but importantly different from, the Greek/Western Muse, thereby expanding our notion of the poetic function (Grossman, 163). For while the Greek muse Mnemosyne signifies poetry's function as the site of memory (preserving culture), the Shekhinah signifies a poetics that is about a culture in flux, under negotiation.[7] The Shekhinah makes her presence known along culture's fault lines and she speaks to poetry's subversive capacities. The poetry that interests me does more than chronicle the loss of founding institutions; it actively participates in making a shambles of them, leveling the ground so that something new may "spring forth"—which is, after all, the Latinate definition of *exilio*.

With such abstract claims in place, some fleshing out is in order. To this end, I want now to turn to Jacqueline Osherow's award-winning poem "Moses in Paradise"—a bit of high exegetical fun that provides one strong example of poetry's capacity for radical subversion. Focusing on the controversial questions surrounding the status of God's sexuality, this dramatic monologue, written under the sign of the Shekinah, calls attention to the role poetry plays in the feminizing of the masculine—a construction that cultural critics from Sander Gilman to Daniel Boyarin have understood as historically central to accounts of Jewish identity.

Osherow's "Moses in Paradise" can perhaps be most easily classified as an example of midrashic verse—a poem that performs an act of Biblical interpretation, a speculative response to, or an interrogation of a fissure, a gap, or a soft spot in the precursor text. In this instance, the point of entry is one of the more extravagantly unintelligible verses in the Hebrew Bible, one of the first reports of a theophany—a "God sighting" from the Book of Exodus:

> And they saw the God of Israel and underneath
> His foot it was like a brickwork of sapphire
> and the sky itself for purity
>
>   (Exodus 24:10)

What is striking about this particular vision, especially for my purposes, is the focus on God's feet—a figure for divine revelation that rabbinic writings have imaged as the *ragle shekhinah*, that is, the feet of the Shekhinah or the Presence (Wolfson, "Feet," 146). Osherow's revisionary treatment amplifies how such an immanence may license a certain amount of trouble, beginning with Moses's opening lines: "You'll laugh when I tell you how I spend my time here.//. . . I read poetry: Ezekiel's, David's, Isaiah's." Poetry, and the body of God that it takes as its subject, is an occasion of laughter. It breaks through prohibition, introducing a countertext rich with multiple transgressions, beginning with the radical reclassification of prophecy (the texts of Ezekiel, Isaiah, and David) as poetry.[8] As Osherow would have it, poetry—which is generated by a desire to know of the divine and to say the unsayable—is the mark of full-blown intimacy. At its core, the poem makes a critique of God as remote—a critique that begins with the speaker (Moses) calling attention to terza rima as the meter of choice:

> . . . I remember an Italian one we made a lot of—
> It's a pity I'm too old to learn to speak
>
> But it was enough to hear those smooth vowels move
> In and out of cadences, like muffled chimes.
> Still, I suspect they dwelt too much on love
>
> Which is not—despite those clever triple rhymes—
> Take it from me—really a divine motive.

> God doesn't much go in for simple themes
>
> And I don't think He ever bothers to give
> Particular thought to how a person feels,
> For example, what it might be like to leave
>
> Whatever it is you know: . . .
>
> (78–79)

The lines suggest that those medieval rabbinic commentators, whose fears of foreign forms and influences I discussed earlier, indeed had something to worry about: Strange meters make for strange stories. The terza rima belongs, of course, to Dante—the prototypical poet of the West—an association that speaks immediately to the ongoing conversation about Jewishness as a "fit" subject for ethnic studies, since it raises thorny questions about Judaism's status as an Eastern import or a "native" Western construct. But the trouble does not end here; Dante is not simply a Western poet, he is also Catholic. In positing an affinity between the Italian patriarch and the Hebraic one, Osherow's poem suggests that Jewishness may pose a particular kind of challenge to American (post-Protestant) poetics, which, with its own doctrine of antiformalism, may register as aesthetically, if not ritually, impoverished.

The strongest critique, however, is not national, but theological. Dante devised the terza rima, a triplet form based on the Holy Trinity, for his *Divine Comedy*, a poem that concludes with a spectacularly luminous return to God's love (*Agape*), mediated by Lady Beatrice. Christian *agape*, courtly love, the Trinity: What could be more *treif*, more forbidden, to a Jewish patriarch? And what could be more alien to the sometimes wrathful, wholly inscrutable (male) God of the Book of Exodus—Who Is What He Is?[9] It is precisely this distance between a wrathful, unknowable God and human longing for intimacy that seems to activate Moses's own poetic longings, upon which he proceeds to act, explaining that "I was never very good at taking dictation" anyway. These poetic longings are realized, not in the Song of the Sea nor in the blessing of Deuteronomy 32, which are traditionally ascribed to Moses, but in the poetic rendering of the theophany that serves as the epigraph. In Osherow's revisionary text, it is Moses who interrupts the divine narrative thus:

> It was after the strangest thing I heard him dictate
> *And they saw the God of Israel* He then went on
>
> With something else entirely and I blurted out
> But surely you won't just leave it hanging there?
> Then I looked up *and underneath His foot*

> *It was like a brickwork of sapphire*
> *And the sky itself for purity . . .* and God
> Humored me and murmured in my ear
>
> You like that? Write it down. Go ahead.
> My eight words in Exodus. My poem . . .

                                                        (78–79)

So Moses composed the foot-sighting.

What needs to be stressed here is that poetry is represented as the exception rather than the rule; it interrupts the dominant discourse (God's own word, no less); it represents a deviation from the norm. The poetic here is not strictly a matter of divine inspiration; it belongs to that which is wholly human, for each word portends change, bringing with it what Moses terms "a flair for deviation." (Here Osherow provides a strong example of how Jewish American poetry can trouble—much more extravagantly than the *piyyutim*—and even displace the sacred and canonical, even the Book of Exodus.) This "flair" makes for a singularly social, even chatty text—an effect achieved through slant rhymes and a heavy use of enjambment. The poem is also characterized by a stylistic heterogeneity, an interweaving of different voices and dictions. Moses's own garrulousness is particularly remarkable in light of his traditional reputation as a disabled speaker—a leader who, at the outset of his career, is denied the power of efficacious speech (Exodus 4:14–16). Indeed, according to rabbinic tradition, Moses is a chronic stutterer, suffering thus from a disability that, as I have argued, signifies a poetic predisposition.

Poetry can entail crossing all kinds of boundaries including those of language, of culture, of institutions, and of gender. Such traversings and transgressions are put into motion when the poet—Osherow—shows her hand, as Moses's "slightly bumbling scribe," when the patriarch recounts how it is that his "poem" came to light:

> It's a pity you can't know them all without the scars
>
> Of my slightly bumbling scribe's English translation.
> . . . .
> I found her working out the cantillation
>
> She's stopped at my eight words, overthrown,
> So I had to use her, though her Hebrew's imprecise . . .

                                                        (80)

Translation is a "scar"—a gash in the textual body that locates itself at the site of an aesthetic/theologic disturbance, only to aggravate it further. The question becomes who indeed is "using" whom, as translation turns out to be transgendered and in the service of Osherow's own purposes (after all, she writes herself into the text). In the ensuing gap between poet and persona, upon which Osherow insists, resides the notion of poetry as a feminized and feminizing enterprise. Historically, translation has long provided women with a strategy through which a reading subject, one who works "out the cantillation," becomes a writing one (Simon, 39). In this instance the emphasis is on translation as an act of creative transmission, a relational exchange through which the translator-poet seeks to understand and make audible the very mind of the "other," even of the divine (Simon, 83; Galli, 329).

Linking poetry to translation, Osherow suggests how writing under the sign of the Shekhinah may mean claiming allegiance to a model of poetic production other than the one that literary critic Jed Rasula, in his own recent inquiry into the gendering of poetry, has rather chillingly described as the "confidential insinuation of another's voice into the poet's own mouth" (160). The Shekhinah thus interrupts the dominant narrative of poetry as the colonizing breath of divine inspiration, offering in its stead a model based on a desire to acquire intimate knowledge of the "other," to know the other reciprocally—"face to face."[10] It is a model narratively embedded in that part of the Bible where the profound intimacy between God and Moses is represented as a "face-to-face encounter" where the one addresses the other as "a man speaks to his friend" (Exodus 33:11). Yet this countermodel, and the intimacy it presumes, can only be contained—in a dominant rabbinic, heterosocial order—by reading Moses as feminine; Jewish cultural theorist Howard Eilberg-Schwartz puts it bluntly: "Because of his intimacy with God, Moses's masculinity is put in question" (*Phallus*, 142). As we will see, this is a question to which Osherow's poem gives full rein, contributing to what is arguably a significant source of anxiety in American literary culture.[11]

The poem's close finds Moses off to perform at David's concert series— "He's got something booked for every evening"—hoping perhaps that his poem will draw God closer. Here one learns a bit more about the transgressive nature of the kind of knowledge to which poetry aspires:

> Did I tell you? David's asked for me tonight
>
> And, well, really, what have I got to lose?
> He's promised to accompany me on the lyre.
>
> . . . .
>
> You never know—do you—who might come
> I was hoping I might catch a glimpse of sapphire
> Beneath a tapping foot, keeping time . . .

(83)

The focus on God's feet is a detail that is neither simply whimsical nor predictably fetishistic; instead, it is a matter of serious theology. In rabbinic writings, God's feet—as a figure for divine revelation—are imaged as the *ragle shekhinah*, the feet of the Shekhinah or the Presence. So to speak of God's feet is to invoke the Shekhinah—the Presence of God—who is generally construed as feminine. As it turns out, however, these feet complicate the sexual status of God's body, compromising the positions of both orthodox scholarship and revisionary feminism, making for a poetics of gender that is even more satisfyingly ambiguous. Although the Shekhinah is widely figured as feminine, there is a significant tradition within kabbalistic literature where the feet function symbolically as a euphemism for the phallus (Wolfson, "Feet," 164). The implications are rather wild, both theoretically as well as theologically. To begin with, the idea of a God whose gender is fluid has potentially critical consequences for whatever illusions one may harbor about the fixedness of human sexuality. (This is particularly true for Shekhinah: The feet are "bipolar," sometimes marking masculinity, and sometimes femininity [Wolfson, "Feet" 164].) In other words, the Shekhinah marks an instability that is in its own right purposively destabilizing, as are the texts it engenders. Reading, for example, Osherow's "Moses" within the matrix of Jewish mystical thought, at least two interpretive possibilities emerge: If one codes Moses as male, then the operative model of relations in the poem (vis-à-vis God) could be construed as homoerotic. But one can also read the poem within a heterosocial frame—a reading sanctioned not so much by dominant ideology (heterosexuality is the primary model of relation in Jewish discourse), but because the poet insistently writes herself into the poem, demanding that she be recognized as more than just a mediating presence, thereby short-circuiting the now familiar model of homosocial desire that is mediated either through women or "female" texts.[12] In such a reading (which privileges the partnership between the poet and Moses), his desire to gaze upon God's feet would seem to put Moses in a feminized position—a possibility already allowed for by virtue of his "poetic" inclinations (and the attendant affiliation with the Shekhinah). Either prospect is bound to stir up a certain amount of cultural anxiety, all brought to you by way of the poetic.

Focusing on God's sexuality, Osherow's "Moses" calls attention to the role poetry plays in the feminizing of the masculine—a construction that has been recognized as historically central to accounts of Jewish identity. In its emphasis on this gendered association, and on the anxiety it potentially provokes, the poem takes us that much further in understanding poetry's marginalized status in the history of Jewish American writing. Further, by boldly insisting on this linking, Osherow's poem interrupts that trend in Jewish cultural discourse to read the "feminized Jew" either in the negative context of anti-Semitism; or, as a "positive attribute" to be recovered and cherished, as an antidote to the dominant discourse's endorsement of "muscular masculinity"—for in either instance women are only rarely heard to speak. In Osherow's "Moses in Paradise," that is to say, gender and poetry are mutually and fruitfully implicated in making trouble for Jewish culture.

Notes

1. Stefan Reiff also uses colonizing language to describe the development of *piyyutim*: "The spread of the piyyutic genre was so successful that it invaded almost every aspect of Jewish liturgical expression, establishing its presence and threatening to dominate the whole environment of prayer" (145).

2. I am indebted to Aryeh Cohen for his reading of this passage. See his "Reading, Exile, and Redemption: A Meditation on the Talmudic Project" for a fuller treatment of this text.

3. This is a much condensed summary of a more detailed argument I make in my forthcoming book.

4. See the essay by Eric Selinger in this volume.

5. In addition to the poets named in the text, which is only a partial list of writers for whom the Shekhinah figures large, the journal *Tree* devoted two issues to the subject (winter 1972, 1974).

6. There is much evidence for this claim, beginning with the association between the Shekhinah and the Biblical matriarch Rachel, who is said to weep with the people of Israel in exile. See also Amy-Jill Levine's essay on "Diaspora as Metaphor," in which she writes, "Woman is in effect in perpetual diaspora; her location is never her own, but is contingent on that of her father, husband, or sons" (110).

7. It is also possible to think about the relation between the Greek/Western Muse and the Jewish Shekhinah as complementary rather than oppositional; in this way, she shows us something about the cultural work of poetry that most discussions that have taken the Muse as their point of origin tend to miss. Traditionally, to summon the Muse means to invoke an agent of otherness, a strange or demonic presence, who reaffirms the radical or fundamental *difference* between the human and the divine; think, for example, of Hesiod's founding encounter in the *Theogony*: "Daughters of Zeus, I greet you; add passion to my song, and tell of the sacred race of gods who are forever . . . Relate these things to me, Muses whose home is Olympus." By thinking, however, of the Shekhinah as a conceptual variation on the Muse, one begins to intuit a countermove in poetics, which, as I will argue, seeks to put this difference in question. Jewish American poetry thus intersects with and contributes toward to a revisionary account of American poetic practice that might begin with Whitman's revolutionary commitment to substituting a grammar of inclusion for one of difference: "And what I assume you shall assume"; "it avails not, time nor place—distance avails not." Such a discussion would lead, necessarily, to one of the thorniest problems for American poetry (not to mention policy)—the fact of such irresolvable differences as race and gender. See my essay on Adrienne Rich, where this issue is taken up more fully.

8. On the subject of poetry as prophecy, James Kugel writes, "It certainly would not

be impossible for Jewish homilists in early centuries to compare the activities of Isaiah or Jeremiah or other prophets to the occupation of poet; yet nowhere is this done . . . So, were the prophets 'poets?' Heaven forfend!" ("Poets and Prophets: An Overview," 12).

9. One strong portrait of divine wrath may be found in Jack Miles's chapter on the Book of Exodus in his "biography" of God.

10. This alternate model is, of course, hardly the exclusive property of Jewish American writers. Rather, it is a countermodel within the larger tradition of Anglo-American writing. One could compose a diverse and extensive list of poets and poems that speak to this counterposition. Such a list might include Keats, Dickinson, Clare, Stein, and so-called "language poets" like Charles Bernstein and Ron Silliman, as well as artists engaged in exploring the relation between poetics and the visual, such as Joanna Drucker. Theoretically, of course, it is Levinas who has made the locution "face-to-face" central to an ethical, perhaps even aesthetic, argument.

11. Daniel Boyarin's most recent study, *Unheroic Conduct: The Rise of Heterosexuality and the Invention of the Jewish Man*, makes an analysis of the strengths and limitations of that strain in the rabbinic tradition that seeks to contain, if not accommodate, homoeroticism.

12. Again see Boyarin, who draws upon both Eve Sedgwick and Wayne Koestenbaum in his analysis of rabbinic models of homosocial desire, especially the chapter in *Unheroic Conduct* entitled "Rabbis and Their Pals: Rabbinic Homosociality and the Lives of Women."

Works Cited

Berlin, Adele. *Biblical Poetry Through Medieval Jewish Eyes*. Bloomington: Indiana UP, 1991.

Bernstein, Charles. "What's Art Got to Do with It? The Status of the Subject of the Humanities in the Age of Cultural Studies." *The American Literary History Reader*. Ed. Gordon Hunter. New York: Oxford UP, 1995. 370–388.

Blasing, Mutlu Konuk. *American Poetry: The Rhetoric of Its Forms*. New Haven, Conn.: Yale UP, 1987.

Boyarin, Daniel. *Unheroic Conduct: The Rise of Heterosexuality and the Invention of the Jewish Man*. Berkeley: U of California P, 1997.

Cohen, Aryeh. "Reading, Exile and Redemption: A Meditation on the Talmudic Project." *The Reconstructionist: A Journal of Contemporary Jewish Thought and Practice* 61, no. 2 (fall 1996). 32–40.

Eilberg-Schwartz, Howard. *God's Phallus and Other Problems for Man and Monotheism*. Boston: Beacon P, 1994.

Elbogin, Ismar. *Jewish Liturgy: A Comprehensive History*. Trans. Raymond P. Scheindlin. New York: Jewish Publication Society, 1993.

Ezrachi, DeKoven Sidra. "Our Homeland, the Text . . . Our Text the Homeland: Exile and the Homecoming in the Modern Jewish Imagination." *Michigan Quarterly Review* XXXI, No. 4 (fall 1992: 463–97.

Galli, Barbara Ellen. *Franz Rosenzweig and Jehuda Halevi: Translating, Translations, and Translators.* Montreal: McGill UP, 1995.

Grossman, Allen. "Jewish Poetry Considered as a Theophoric Project." *The Long Schoolroom: Lessons in the Bitter Logic of the Poetic Principle.* Ann Arbor: U of Michigan P, 1997. 159–68.

———. "The Passion of Laocoon, or the Warfare of the Religious Against the Poetic Institution." Unpublished manuscript.

Howe, Susan. *The Birthmark: Unsettling the Wilderness in American Literary History.* Hanover, N.H.: Wesleyan UP, 1993.

Kugel, James L. *The Idea of Biblical Poetry: Parallelism and its History.* New Haven, Conn.: Yale UP, 1981.

———. "Poets and Prophets: An Overview" In *Poetry and Prophecy.* Ed. James L. Kugel. Ithaca, N.Y.: Cornell UP, 1990. 1–25.

Levine, Amy-Jill. "Diaspora as Metaphor: Bodies and Boundaries in the Book of Tobit." In *Diaspora Jews and Judaism: Essays in Honor of, and in Dialogue with, A. Thomas Krabel.* Ed. J. Andrew Overman and Robert S. MacLennan. Tampa U of South Florida P, 1992. 105–117.

Miles, Jack. *God: A Biography.* New York: Alfred A. Knopf, 1995.

Osherow, Jacqueline. *With a Moon in Transit.* New York: Grove P, 1996.

Rasula, Jed. "Gendering the Muse." *Sulfur* 35 (fall 1994): 159–75.

Reif, Stefan C. *Judaism and Hebrew Prayer: New Perspectives on Jewish Liturgical History.* Cambridge: Cambridge UP, 1993.

Scheindlin, Raymond P. *The Gazelle: Medieval Hebrew Poems on God, Israel, and the Soul.* New York: Jewish Publication Society, 1991.

Shreiber, Maeera. "'Where Are We Moored?': Adrienne Rich, Women's Mourning, and the Limits of Lament." In *Dwelling in Possibility: Women Poets and Critics on Poetry.* Ed. Yopie Prins and Maeera Shreiber. Ithaca: Cornell UP, 1997. 301–17.

Simon, Sherry. *Gender in Translation: Cultural Identity and the Politics of Transmission.* New York: Routledge, 1996.

Tishby, Isaiah and Fishel Lachower. *The Wisdom of the Zohar.* Trans. David Goldstein. Vol. I. Oxford: Oxford UP, 1989.

Wolfson, Elliot R. "Images of God's Feet: Some Observations on the Divine Body in Judaism." In *People of the Body: Jews and Judaism from an Embodied Perspective.* Ed. Howard Eilberg-Schwartz. Albany: SUNY P, 1992. 143–81.

———. "Woman—The Feminine as Other in Theosophic Kabbalah: Some Philosophical Observations on the Divine Androgyne." In *The Other in Jewish Thought and History: Constructions of Jewish Culture and Identity.* Ed. Laurence J. Silberstein and Robert L. Cohn. New York: New York UP, 1994. 166–204.

Yerushalmi, Yosef Haim. *Zahor: Jewish History and Jewish Memory.* Seattle: U of Washington P, 1982.

The Diversity of Jewish American Poetry: Editors' Introduction

This final set of reflections, unlike the previous three, opens doors onto the internal diversity, the internal multiculturalism, of Jewish American poetry. Janet Kaufman's essay, for example, introduces and analyzes the achievement of Jewish American women poets. In so doing, she finds both a wide diversity in projects, concerns, and poetics and a shared, exemplary ability to integrate the stereotypically disparate elements of Jewish American identity. "Woman, American, and Jew," she quotes from Muriel Rukeyser, "three guardians watch over you." At our invitation, Kaufman focuses on nine women not in Part I, including Adrienne Rich, Jane Shore, Shirley Kaufman, Robin Becker, Grace Paley, and the Yiddish-American poet Malka Heifetz Tussman. Her essay gives readers new ways to read the women poets of Part I, and it looks outward, into new reading and new pleasures that no single anthology can contain.

Meanwhile, the urge to read Jewish culture solely or simplistically in terms of the Ashkenazi experience is questioned by the final three essays. Diane Matza, for example, shows how the term "Jewish American" has too often and for too long been read only through the lens of Eastern European and German Jewish, predominantly Yiddish experience. In fact, as she shows us, Jewish American poetry embraces the wide array of Sephardi culture. She explains how any account of Jewish American writing that neglects these riches is as sorely impoverished as one that leaves out women—or, for that matter, one that leaves out poetry.

Following Matza, we print: "*Di feder fun harts*/The Pen of the Heart: *Tsveyshprakhikayt*/Bilingualism and American Jewish Poetry," by Irena Klepfisz. Klepfisz's work in bilingual Yiddish/English poetry—a project she has pursued, then abandoned, and now returned to again—raises searching questions about the politics of nostalgia, the aesthetics of cultural revival, and the dangers of turning Yiddish into a set of jokey catch-phrases or a pious cultural icon. As she complicates the picture of Yiddish American culture, she asks readers to recall that culture's poetry as a grand, neglected part of the American literary inheritance—a resource that even in translation could become an integral part of our imaginative lives.

Our final essay, John Felstiner's "Jews Translating Jews," picks up where Klepfisz leaves off. Meditating on the whole question of translation, this master translator sees the bringing of poems from language to language as, at heart, an act of cultural renewal. Felstiner takes us back to the Bible, to the Talmud, to the medieval Spanish poets, and to more recent writers (Chaim Bialik, George Steiner, Walter Benjamin) to show how the act of translation has been bound up in Jewish culture since the return from Babylonian Exile. With his attention to the translations of Emma Lazarus—her first efforts to define herself as a Jewish Poet—and with his broad theoretical outlook, Felstiner takes one back with new eyes and to the poets of Part I, notably Chana Bloch and Marcia Falk, as well. (Most of the poets have, in fact, translated work from a variety of languages.) Raising more questions than it answers, Felstiner's essay makes a fitting conclusion to this volume.

Life, Freedom, and Memory: The Poetry of Jewish American Women

JANET KAUFMAN

Janet Kaufman is Assistant Professor of English at the University of Utah. Her work focuses on Education and Women's Poetry. She is coeditor of *"How Shall We Tell Each Other of the Poet?" The Life and Writing of Muriel Rukeyser* (St. Martin's P, 1999).

> The themes and the use I have made of them have depended on my life as a poet, as a woman, as an American and as a Jew. I do not know what part of that is Jewish; I know I have tried to integrate these four aspects, and to solve my work and my personality in terms of all four. . . . To live as poet, woman, American, and Jew—this chalks in my position. If the four come together in one person, each strengthens the others.
>
> (*Under Forty,* 9)

The poet Muriel Rukeyser declared these words in 1944, at the age of thirty-one, and they resonate with the work of contemporary American Jewish women poets because it is impossible—and unnecessary—to measure out the degree of Americanness or Jewishness or femaleness in each. Not caught in the traditionally male position of rabbi or prophet, not easily classified as poets of social resistance or Holocaust poets or poets of exile, their writing, as Robin Becker puts it in her poem "The New Year," creates and speaks from "new borders and the undefended life." With these poets, primarily from the last half of this century, entirely new possibilities emerge for integrating "the four aspects" of identity—poet, American, Jew, female. The Jew in these poems no longer has to be the victim but can speak for the Other because she knows what it is to be Other; the American does not have to defend her Americanness—America is home (as much as any poet can be at home); the woman does not have to couch her womanhood but instead brings voice and power to her poetry through her roles as writer, activist, mother, daughter, and lover. Rather than defending or hiding their lives or identities, these poets show multiple aspects of identity to be inherent in and inseparable from the way they make sense of the world. At times these writers are prophets against injustice; at other times

287

they are purveyors of the individual life, documenters of history, negotiators of relationship and war, redactors of grief. Their poetry traverses vast terrain historically and autobiographically as well as formally and experimentally.

Assuming, as Rukeyser does, that each aspect of their identities offers strength and distinct vantage points, these poets redefine what it is to be American, Jew, woman, poet. Whether they rail against injustice or investigate war, they do so not as the Other, but with the intimate knowledge of what it means and feels like to be Other. The power of their voices comes from having this knowledge yet claiming their own belonging, bringing us to a moral center. Blessed with the problem of too many poets to discuss in this essay, I will explore some of those whose work has not been addressed elsewhere in this book and hope that this will lead readers to further discovery. The poets I will discuss—Muriel Rukeyser, Adrienne Rich, Ruth Whitman, Jane Shore, Linda Zisquit, Shirley Kaufman, Robin Becker, Grace Paley, and Malka Heifetz Tussman—have very diverse projects and concerns; their poetry looks quite different on the page from one another. Yet we can make some distinctions among those such as Rukeyser and Rich, who insist on the intersections of seemingly contradictory aspects of identity and on relationship—meeting the Other—as an ethic for personal and political change; as Shore and Whitman, whose poetry is markedly different but who document history, tracing individual lives and creating autobiography and biography in verse; as Zisquit and Kaufman, whose poetry takes shape in the context of their lives as immigrants in Israel; as Robin Becker, whose Jewishness becomes a resource for grappling with family and sexual identity, for moving beyond her felt exile and accepting herself; as Paley, whose poetry documents the mesh of trauma and joy in everyday life and in acts of political resistance; as Malka Heifetz Tussman, one of our major Yiddish-American poets, whose poetry celebrates and accounts for the ironies of sensuousness and sadness of life in the old world and the new.

The author of twenty-five books of poetry, novels, biographies, and children's books, Rukeyser has been called "the mother of us all" by writers Erica Jong and Anne Sexton. Between the publication of her first book published in 1935, when she was twenty-one years old, and her last book, which appeared only two years before her death in 1980, Rukeyser became one of the great American poets of the twentieth century. Always driven by an ethical impulse to care about those society least cared about, and by the impulse to experiment with language—to find ways of using language as both action and art—Rukeyser said once in an interview, "It isn't that one brings life together—it's that one will not allow it to be torn apart. And not only the wars but the thing that wars are images of, the tearing apart of life entire in ourselves and in our relations with each other" (Packard, 132). Rukeyser was one of the first twentieth-century American Jewish poets writing in English to write explicitly and affirmingly as a Jew, proclaiming the ethical and spiritual value of Judaism and recognizing its centrality to her identity and poetry.

In 1944, amidst the European genocide of the Jews, she wrote a sonnet that begins: "To be a Jew in the twentieth century / Is to be offered a gift." It was a strange yet crucial time to make such an assertion, to find dignity and strength in being Jewish, as the sestet of her sonnet claims:

> The gift is torment. Not alone the still
> Torture, isolation; or torture of the flesh.
> That may come also. But the accepting wish,
> The whole and fertile spirit as guarantee
> For every human freedom, suffering to be free,
> Daring to live for the impossible.
>
> (Out of Silence, 65)

What makes the gift of being Jewish and the "accepting wish" into "torment," even beyond the history of oppression that Rukeyser invokes in her poem? Throughout her poems, even those without overtly Jewish content, Rukeyser posits the idea that accepting one's Jewishness dares one to resist injustice and pursue justice, to take risks for the sake of possibility. She evokes the language of the covenant between God and the Israelites at Mt. Sinai. When Moses says to the people, "Not with our fathers did the Lord make this covenant, but with us, even us, who are all here alive today" (Deuteronomy 5:3), the people respond: "We will hear it and do it" (5:24). To accept the gift of being Jewish, then, is to accept a binding responsibility to speak and act such that we make the seemingly impossible possible. The idea of the covenant courses through Rukeyser's poetry: the gift of Judaism is a binding relation to God, history, and the future.

In Adrienne Rich—the author of more than fifteen volumes of poetry and four prose works, the recipient of such honors as the MacArthur Fellowship, and one of our strongest political, poetic voices in the second half of the century—we see a writer who seems a literary daughter to Rukeyser. Not only in the content and scope of her poems but also in her lines, spacing, and punctuation, we see Rich seeking out relations among seemingly unrelated elements, such as the freedom and power to love women and the freedom to use her identity as an American to capture the "country's moment" and "this unbound land." Throughout her poetry is her determination to claim the Jewish part of her identity and to use it, like the lines on a topographical map, to locate her relation to history and the present. In autobiographical lines, she recounts the silence about Judaism in her home while she was growing up. Apparently speaking to her father, she writes in *Sources*, "For years all the arguments I carried on in my head were with you." Although a daughter, she felt herself "raised as a son," taught that authorship and inquiry were themselves holy activities. I saw the power and arrogance of the male as your "true watermark," Rich muses, and missed "the suffering of the Jew, the alien stamp you bore, because you had deliberately arranged that it should be invisible to me" (9). In a 1982 essay, "Split at the Root," when she first wrote about the Jewish part of her identity in prose—a "dangerous" act, "filled with fear and shame"—Rich explains her southern family's taboo of her father's Jewishness: Her father "did not speak the word [Jew]"; she admits that even to explore her identity in writing feels like a betrayal of her father and her mother, "who must have trained [her] in the messages; of [her] caste and class; of [her] whiteness itself" (104). As with Rukeyser, making the invisible visible is always central to Rich's task; in her poetry and prose, Rich sees the simultaneous suppression of herself as both female and Jew.

A sequence poem called "Eastern War Time" from her recent collection, *An Atlas of the Difficult World*, helps us imagine possible explanations for Rich's father's inclination to make his Jewishness invisible to his daughter. Imagining the horrifying youth of children across Eastern Europe—a girl who "knows she is young and meant to live / taken on the closed journey" and a girl and boy walking hand in hand through the Vilna forests together who, under the guise of romance, are "watching the woods / for signs of the secret bases lines / converging toward the resistance" where weapons or aid might be found (39–40) —Rich also asks, imagining or remembering the voice of American adults during the war: "What the grown-ups can't speak of would you push / onto children? . . . how do you say *unfold, my flower, shine, my star* / and *we are hated, being what we are?*" (38). However, even with compassion for the shame and horror felt by American Jews during the war, Rich remains incisive. Her poems seem to extend the responses to the questions that Rukeyser asks and responds to throughout her poetry: "What do we see? What do we not see?" Part of Rich's response involves wrestling with the silence and shame passed down to her from her own parents about her father's Jewishness. Linking her identity as a woman to that of herself as a Jew, Rich concludes in the poem addressing her father: "It is only now, under a powerful, womanly lens, that I can decipher your suffering and deny no part of my own" (9). In poems imagining the loss and suffering in the Holocaust, responding in language when language is inevitably unequal to the task of response, Rich makes poetry into a place of both memorial and memory, always in the service of intensifying the relation to history and to the present.

So much of her poetry attempts to put forth, directly and in unsparing terms, the difference that geography, that physical location in the world—as well as time, as well as gender and race and sexuality—makes to us. Hence, in her *Atlas of the Difficult World*, her poems carry us back and forth, from our own homes and history to those on the other side of the globe—and on the other side of town. In the closing poem of the sequence "Eastern War Time," Rich imagines "Memory" as the voice of a man accused of blood-libel, as the Seder table "set with room for the Stranger," as an immigrant tailor, as "a woman standing in line for gasmasks," and as a figure standing "on a road in Ramallah." While the history of anti-Semitism and the Holocaust are the driving force in this poem, Rich shows at the end that Memory—and Jewish memories—as a haunting voice connects her, and us, to the struggle for American civil rights, to the Gulf War with its gas masks, to the Intifadeh with individuals stranded in Ramallah and Israeli women who became known as "Women in Black" staging their weekly protests—other Eastern wars. Without naming any of these outright, the character of Memory asserts their presence. Then, at the very end of the poem, having brought herself to a critical vantage point for internalizing these contemporary terrors and atrocities through Memory's voice, Memory announces: "I am standing here in your poem unsatisfied / lifting my smoky mirror." As the poet, Rich allows Memory in to stand in her midst—and implicitly in ours, to hold up a mirror of our world for us. Even if the poet feels powerless in the presence of the intrusive Memory, it is still the poet allowing Memory in to use it.

While Rich addresses us through both long and short poems, with an intensely intimate voice linked to a highly political one, two poets I wish to discuss here, Ruth Whitman and Jane Shore—while clearly different from one another—have crafted book-length biography and autobiography in verse that wrestle with the question of memory and our place in it. Ruth Whitman, in her book *The Testing of Hanna Senesh* (1986), creates the journal she imagines the young Zionist pioneer and parachutist Hanna Senesh wrote before being executed. Whitman, the author of eight books of poems and three important translations of Yiddish poetry, has been vast in her probing of history and of Jewish life and culture in both long poems and the lyric. In addition to writing about Hanna Senesh, Whitman has written long and book-length poems about other women in history—Lizzie Borden, the nineteenth-century Massachusetts alleged murderer; the nineteenth-century American pioneer Tamsen Donner; the dancers Anna Pavlova and Isadora Duncan; and Queen Hatshepsut, the only known woman pharaoh in Egyptian history—because, she has written, she wanted to transform her perceptions of women's lives in the second half of the twentieth century, including those of repression and vulnerability in the 1950s, rebellion in the 1960s, self-empowerment in the 1970s, and confrontation with loss and aging in the 1990s—by speaking in other's voices (*Laughing Gas,* 17–18).

Her subject Hanna Senesh, herself a poet, joined the Haganah and parachuted into Hungary to save Hungarian Jews—among them her own family—in 1944. Captured by the Hungarians, she was imprisoned and then executed; though a few of her poems made their way out of the prison, Senesh's actual diary was confiscated by Hungarian prison guards and never released. Whitman, having researched the details of her life, imagines Senesh's voice, feelings, fears, and the torture that Senesh sustained:

> After the first shock
> it's like letting a wave of flame singe your hand:
> first a sharp sensation, then no feeling.
> I watch myself like a person in a dream
> while they invent devices to break me down.

Invoking the courage and imagination that helped Senesh sustain the torture, Whitman turns to Zion:

> think of that hill in Jerusalem,
> the little lights shining in the villages,
> breathe the aromatic Judean air,
> watch the sun set over the Old City,
> the shadows creeping up the towers,
> pulling the bruised light behind them:

> you see: I feel nothing.
>
> (*Testing,* 28)

Having experienced increased anti-Semitism in her youth, particularly in her high school, Senesh became increasingly politicized as a teenager. In 1938, at age seventeen, she wrote in her diary: "I am a Zionist. That word conveys a lot. I am more aware now of my Jewishness and sense it with all my heart. I am proud of being Jewish and I hope to go to Eretz Israel to help in building up the country" (*Testing,* 16). Zion for Senesh—and the refuge and hope attached to it—was no metaphoric vision. In imagining Senesh's diary, Whitman makes herself a witness to Senesh's history—which is also Jewish history and women's history—thus enabling us to be witnesses as well. When Rukeyser writes about Akiba, the great rabbi of the second century, she asks, "Who is the witness?" And then she answers: "The witness is myself. / And you." Witnessing a life becomes a way of making relation with it and being transformed by it. About her biographies in verse, Whitman has written that they have been metaphors for her most basic concerns: "refusing to be a victim, learning endurance, learning the skills of survival" (*Hatshepsut,* 12). Her book *The Testing of Hanna Senesh*, read as a book of personal and historical witness, becomes a testing of us as readers, testing how we will take history into the present.

A glance at the titles of Whitman's lyrics in her other volumes of poetry reveals the active and natural integration of Jewish life and history into her vision. We see, for instance, two poems about hair juxtaposed against each other. In "A Daughter Cuts Her Hair," we see a "cat princess" who, wanting to grow up, "cuts off her golden hair" and loses her babyhood (64). In the very next poem, "Cutting the Jewish Bride's Hair," Whitman asserts, "It's to possess more than the skin / that those old world Jews / exacted the hair of their brides." Concluding and telling us just how dramatic and how high the stakes of this ritual are, she writes, "but this little amputation / will shift the balance of the universe" (65). Writing of real or imagined moments in the Touro synagogue, in a Jerusalem bakery, at a reading in Nazareth with an Arab poet, Whitman's poems seek the gestures, rituals, and strokes of language that do shift the balance of the universe, reminding us of how we can shift it and of who we are.

Jane Shore, in her third volume of poetry, *Music Minus One*, traces her own life story in narrative verse with calm precision and incisiveness. Her poems begin in her New Jersey childhood, growing up Jewish above her parents' clothing store; they move to her adult life in Vermont, her own motherhood, and the deaths of her parents. Being Jewish is part of the scene of Shore's life, inseparable from the presence of her parents' store, her childhood games, or the marking of time. It defines yet it is not defining. As Shore traces her life story, creating a version of home—what home means and how it evolves over the course of a life—her Jewishness signals that she is both at home and not at home above the store in New Jersey, that to be at home means to have markers of loss and the presence—or invasion—of history and ritual. The first line of her book locates us in the post-war era: "When I was twelve, I read *The Diary of Anne Frank*" (3). We learn that the poem's title, "Washing the Streets of Holland," comes from the game she made up as a twelve-year-old, responding to her family's admiration of the Dutch for hiding Jews during the war and, as her mother said, for keeping their streets immaculate. The power of the poet, or of the child making such a game, is to have some control over the stories and comments overheard in the family conversation, "blurring the words / and washing them away."

Throughout these poems, Jewish images serve as references for memory. In a poem called "The Sunroom," Shore remembers playing in the sunroom Easter morning during a bout with the chicken pox, which leads her to remember "playing in the sunroom the whole week before / during Passover" (16). The holiday marks her sense of time and, with that memory leading to the next, she remembers the way her mother koshered chickens, and then imagines the first Passover, when the Angel of Death went in search of the Egyptian firstborns. In the poem "Last Breath" she remembers "Larry Cohen's mother / impaled by a flying beach umbrella in Asbury Park / the windy summer before his bar mitzvah" and, with her understated, irreverent humor, remembers the rabbi's comment: "'The will of God'" (40). Much in the same vein, in the title poem memorializing her father, a big-band musician, Shore tells us: "You had to imagine his life before the war. / At fifteen, on the Lower East Side, he played weddings and bar mitzvahs. . . . / You had to imagine him before he changed his name from Joseph Sharfglass / to George Shore" (58). It is the Bar Mitzvahs, the holidays, the mysteries of spelling "*G-d*" with "the missing *o* dashing into its hole" that locate us in these poems, that remind us of the world Shore is in as she negotiates family relations.

In "The Sunroom," Shore makes the connection to the Angel of Death intimate, and with the immediacy of a child itching from pox, she writes, "I was the first born. My body was covered with signs." Ultimately she returns to fantasies of lovely Easter dresses and colors, imagining the pink Easter ham "stuck all over with cloves," but the cloves were "like the burning scabs [she] scratched" (17–18). This was a complicated world: the Jewish part of it filled with ritual, superstition, and frightening stories, and the gentile world full of danger. In "The Holiday Season" she recalls, "The electric eye of the mezuzah / guarded our apartment over the store / as innocent of Christmas / as heaven, where God lived . . ." and the poem goes on to wrestle with childhood questions of theology: how does the Jewish child reconcile singing Christmas carols and letting the word *Christ* slip out? "It was an accident!" (24–25). And in a poem remembering the onset of menstruation, "The Slap," Shore remembers the ritual slap Jewish mothers gave to their daughters for generations. While she expected a kiss and a blessing, instead her mother "laughed, tears in her eyes, / and yelled, 'Mazel Tov! Now you are a woman! Welcome to the club!' // and slapped me across the face—/ for the first and last time ever—// '*This* should be the worst pain you ever know' (45–46). In these poems, Jewishness has a bittersweetness precisely because it is in the family, where joy and anger, shame and grief, love and loss are bound up together. Nonetheless, this Jewishness is an inextricable part of what it means for Shore to have grown up an American girl in New Jersey.

If Jane Shore crafts a poetic history of growing up Jewish and female in America, defining her stories partly by their Jewishness without defining Judaism, Linda Zisquit and Shirley Kaufman are two American poets who complicate the question of home by choosing to live in and write from Jerusalem. In lines as spare as the Judean desert and intense as its sun, Zisquit's themes ring familiar: the intricacies of being wife, mother, poet, lover, and the shifting of one's balance between private and public lives. The Jewishness in these poems is pervasive, as the geography and history of Israel—the people and the land—are part of the tenor of daily life. We see here that part of what it means to be a Jewish poet in Israel is to work out the questions of a life with a Jewish vocabulary, on Jewish ground. In her poem "Mt. Ardon," Zisquit writes:

From the start I saw borders break—
my way into speech,
to cleave. Like these folds,
this tectonic shift
awaiting movement
a thousand years.
Till one day
a creature comes
and a fissure
unknown to the mountain
cracks open.

(*Ritual,* 50)

Intensely observing the breaks and fissures of private life in the neighborhoods of Jerusalem, in the Judean desert, in the separations from family in America, in the war she has witnessed, and in the acute encounters and pain of love, Zisquit's speech in her poetry is like the tectonic shift she writes about, like the creature who surprises the mountain, cracking it open. In the title poem of her first book, "Ritual Bath," she writes:

My body contains a foreign tongue,
words becoming pure
only if you open, allow me
to free the fiery syllables,
translate the dreams.

(57)

We do not know who the "you" is—perhaps a lover or God—but the ritual bath seems as much an immersion in language for purification as the *mikveh* itself could ever be. In that language, Zisquit keeps turning and returning to Biblical and historical figures, to the Hebrew language and calendar, and to the Talmud, as the vantage points for making sense of a life.

As she makes these turns, she finds much to argue with, to resist, and to claim on her own terms. In "Ritual Bath" it is Beruria, the wife of Rabbi Akiva, who is "the clear one"—not the rabbi himself—who left a "trace" the poet can follow, "who burns in me as she burned in the desert" (57). In "Ethics of the Fathers," invoking the wisdom of diet and emotion in *Pirkei Avot*—"Eat a third, drink a third, and leave a third for anger"—Zisquit writes, "Shaking off sand and dread, / our bodies rise and learn to speak again" (15). She understands that, with help from the wisdom of the *Pirkei Avot* who advise rising slowly after waking or lovemaking, or despite their wisdom, we ourselves must rise and learn to speak. It cannot be done for us. Zisquit's words resonate and sear, achingly familiar. But always they are, themselves, an immersion in the depths of experience for the sake of transformation. In "Blue Distance," the concluding poem of her second book, *Unopened Letters*, Zisquit writes,

> She knew what is over
> is over only after
> it has been transformed.
>   (86)

Language creates that ability to transform—to end something and thereby to begin again. It is this poet's task, Zisquit's poems seem to say, not only to have the courage to open the unopened letters, but first to write them.

"What lets us be who we most are?" Shirley Kaufman asks in her poem "Lemon Sponge." The author of six collections of poetry, three translations of Hebrew poetry and one of Dutch, and the winner of many awards, including the Poetry Society of America's Shelley Award, Kaufman's poetry spans twenty-five years and the distance between San Francisco and Jerusalem, where she went "From One Life to Another." How do roots survive transplanting? How do they thrive in new soil, or without soil? Writing about the Bengal ficus tree, whose roots dangle in the air, Kaufman writes:

> Sure of which way is down
> but unable to get there,
> one tree makes a hundred
> out of the steaming soil it comes from,
> replanting itself.
>   (128)

So much of this poetry is about transplanting—from one continent to another, and from relative safety to danger. Kaufman reflects in "Meeting in Ramallah," "I might have stayed / on my own side where it's common / to say the wrong things / and be forgiven" (126). But her poems keep moving, courageously and daringly, to the other side, where they realize that any safety is illusion. In Kaufman's poetry, rootlessness results from choice; it is not the exile imposed upon the Jews since the destruction of the First Temple, but the privilege of choice to leave home in America for home in Israel, which ironically becomes a new kind of exile. However, even with roots hanging in the air, the roots are still there hanging, to be seen from a different angle but not cut off.

This ability to move between worlds and to discover the notion of an ideal Jewish "home" as an illusion distinguishes Kaufman as a poet of the late twentieth century. When, before, has a Jewish poet been able to move in the world like this? Witnessing firsthand the destruction and devastation of war in Israel,

Kaufman writes, in the "Decisions" section of her poem "Intifada," of a woman resigning herself to the ruins around her—not just the "ancient eroded / vineyards in the Judean hills," but also "The boy with his leg blown off. The dutiful children." The woman in this poem vacillates while choosing which flavor of ice cream to order and is told,

> Decide. Decide. As if her life
> were the life she'd chosen. As if anyone's life
>
> (143)

The poem ends like that, without punctuation, leaving us to complete the line. In her more recent poems, Kaufman leaves more ends open, showing the inability to completely define an experience or draw a stable conclusion. But while these poems understand the force of the potential resignation in the ability to fully grasp or define experience, they do not give in to it. She finds physical metaphors for feelings of powerlessness in the land itself; for instance, in the poem "The Road out of Poland," Kaufman writes, "When I stand on this ridge, / the earth slides helpless / in two directions"(108). However, in "Starting Over," she admonishes:

> the world is full of chances
> to miss
>
> . . . .
>
> this is where you
>   begin
> (76)

Poetry, after all, is where chances can be taken, and, for that reason perhaps, poetry is the safest place for learning and sustaining a new life. Remembering someone once saying, "You can't learn two / landscapes in one / life," Kaufman challenges this assertion, even if it means that her roots stay in the air. In her poem "For Dear Life," she writes about a lizard on a path:

> We both breathe
> as softly as we can to keep it
> from moving, to keep this minute
> from slipping into the next.
> (204)

One may not be able to master two landscapes, but one can learn to live in them, and move between them, these poems seem to say. While fully expressing the despair of war in Israel, the ancientness of family strife and political conflict going back to Abraham and Sarah, Hagar and Ishmael, Kaufman's poems seem driven by the desire both to acknowledge the pain of the shifting terrain of life and to celebrate it. Indeed, this sensibility is evident even in the title of her first book, *The Floor Keeps Turning*. Wherever she is, she finds roots and makes them. It is, perhaps, the work of the American Jewish poet in the late twentieth century not to mourn the exile from Zion—because, as Kaufman's life and poetry show, one can return to the land. What remains to mourn, though, is the knowledge that there is no mythical Zion, no pure home or even a vision of one. Instead, the poet's work is to discover the expansion of roots and home as they move across continents and into the air, and to insist that they are hers, and ours, to claim.

In Robin Becker's work, too, we see questions of exile addressed, though dramatically differently from Kaufman's. In poems such as "The Crypto-Jews" and "Too Jewish," Becker investigates the history of exile and its impact, particularly in the context of tracking her evolution as a woman and lesbian. Jewish history and culture offer a lens through which to see the felt exile of other aspects of herself. In "The Crypto-Jews," Becker remembers learning the history of the Jews of Spain and writes, "I love the sad proud history / of expulsion and wandering . . . persistence of study and text" (5). The idea of the Jew as the evicted wanderer becomes a point of reference in this poetry—almost a treasure, were it not so tragic—for the individual trying to reconcile and create her place in the world. Among poems such as "Peter Pan in North America," which recalls the persona in childhood seeing the play with friends, the poems examining Jewish life suggest a model for survival, persistence, and the insistence on claiming one's identity—even, or especially, through struggle. In "Peter Pan," in response to their mothers' question about whether she and her friends liked the play, Becker writes, "We dangled from the hook // of their question, the answer as overdetermined as Hook's / effeminate ways. Being a boy was best." And then she explains: "After all, Mary Martin could fly, take a drag / from a pipe, dance with her shadow, reject predictable versions // of femaleness. Call it chutzpah or perversion / we imagined ourselves: breasts bound, hooked / to guy wires, smartly dressed in roguish drag" (31).

Becker's poems have tremendous *chutzpah*; indeed, her book *All-American Girl* seems a project in challenging the image of the "all-American girl," redefining that girl. Her Jewishness lends support to this project. In "Too Jewish," Becker recalls her Bubbie's efforts to persuade her to fix her too-Jewish nose and remembers her own resistance: "*You'll be more yourself,* my Bubbie argued. / *I already am myself,* I shouted." Invoking the shame that her grandmother felt for her Jewishness, Becker makes her grandmother's felt choices perfectly clear: as a Jew, one could either remain in exile or risk being "too Jewish." Reflecting on her sister's still imperfect nose after the surgery and the

childhood lessons she learned from it, she writes: "I believed I could fix a prob-
lem / by cutting it away. In the name of love / we draw a blade across the
beloved's face" (35). The violence and betrayal in this image resonates
throughout Becker's poems because so many of them are about loss—the loss
of lovers, the loss of her sister by suicide—and the ability to move beyond
grief. By writing, Becker creates the possibility that drawing the blade is no
longer the only possibility. Then the lingering question remains: how to move
beyond exile? That is perhaps the penultimate Jewish question, even as the
task—as it is in Becker's poetry—is to remember exile.

If Robin Becker's persona is yelling back at her Bubbie that she already *is*
herself, Grace Paley's is the voice cheering her on. Paley, in the tradition of
Jewish resisters, agitators, and peace-makers, and in a folk voice that could be
equally at home railing in the *shtetl* as it is in the countryside of Vermont and
New York City, has been giving her readers courage and inspiration for over
forty years. The author of three books of short fiction and three collections of
poetry, a former State Author of New York, a teacher and winner of many pre-
stigious poetry awards, Paley has been documenting—with fierce determina-
tion, joy, and a profound appreciation for the connection between the intimacy
of family, friendships, and relationships in world affairs—the personal and
political life in writing. Her poetry, like her active involvement in the antiwar
and feminist movements—including in organizations such as War Resister's
League, Resist, and the Women's Pentagon Action—comes to us as yet an-
other way of her acting in the world, for the world. In her book of poems of
both prose and verse, *Long Walks and Intimate Talks*, which is a collaboration
with the artist Vera Williams, Paley introduces the reader to the aspirations for
their art: "We hoped that our work would, by its happiness and sadness, dem-
onstrate against militarists, racists, earth poisoners, women haters, all those
destroyers of days. One common purpose would be to celebrate the day,
which is its own reason for peace, to praise and offer to its inherent beauty and
reality our work as daily movement people and artists." Indeed, Paley's work
is, consistently, a demonstration, one that demonstrates for joy as much as it
does against destruction.

The Jewishness of Paley's work feels palpable. *Long Walks* opens with a
story, or prose poem, "Midrash on Happiness," as if to prepare her readers that
the entirety of her work is *midrash*, commentary on what is sacred. Immedi-
ately the conversational rhythm of her language greets us, as the *midrash* be-
gins: "What she meant by happiness, she said, was the following: she meant
having (or having had) (or continuing to have) everything": a list including
children, an adult partner, three or four women friends, long walks and inti-
mate talks about "every personal fact," as well as "the economy, the constant,
unbeatable, cruel war economy, . . . the complicity of male people in the whole
structure . . ." Then she ups the ante:

For happiness, she also required work to do in this world and bread on the
table. By work to do she included the important work of raising children right-
eously up. By righteously she meant that along with being useful and speaking
truth to the community, they must do no harm. By harm she meant not only per-
sonal injury to the friend the lover the coworker the parent (the city the nation)
but also the stranger. (N.p.)

Then Paley returns to the Exodus story for rationale: "because we were strang-
ers in Egypt." *Because we were strangers in Egypt*: Paley's poems never forget
that; her poems take us to the Mothers of the Disappeared from San Salvador,
the Tonkin Bay, the "Contra of Uncle Sam" which ironically, brutally defeated
the contra dance of villagers in Jinoteca. Always these poems remember and
honor the lives of individuals, common life, family, and children. In a poem
called "If you have acquired a taste for happiness," Paley gives us "another ex-
ample of ordinary joy":

> the gathering together of comrades
> in disagreement and resolution
> followed by determined action

which, for her, must be accompanied by

> dances in the schoolrooms and kitchens
> and sometimes
> love
>
> (*New,* 113)

Her poems about her family let us know, in no uncertain terms, the trauma suf-
fered by generations for being Jewish. In "My Father at 89," she gives us her
father with his "brain simplified," on the road home from the Czar's prison,
"lonesome / and singing" (*New* 94). In "People in My Family," she tells us the
difference between the people who were eighty-two and those who were
ninety-two:

> The eighty-two year old people grew up
> it was 1914
> this is what they knew
> War World War War
>
> . . . .
>
> The ninety-two year old people remember

it was the year 1905
they went to prison
they went into exile
they said ah soon

Now, when they speak to the grandchild, they are sure there will be revolution and "the earth itself / will turn" but this time, they both promise and direct:

then you   my little bud
must flower and save it.
(*New*, 125)

Paley has taken that injunction and gives it back to her readers. So much her own, her voice still has a familiar quality, as if it could be ours. With her poetry we are at home and, therefore, challenged to venture out far beyond home as she has.

In her poem about the German artist Käthe Kollwitz, Muriel Rukeyser wrote lines that have since been oft quoted by women writers: "What would happen if one woman told the truth about her life? / The world would split open." This exploration of American Jewish women's poetry cannot conclude without a discussion of Malka Heifetz Tussman, the Yiddish poet of whom, writes translator Marcia Falk, "one may honestly say" that her "legacy was the world split open" (30). Born in 1896 on a farm in the Southwest Ukraine, she immigrated to the United States when she was sixteen and left us six volumes of poetry and an unpublished manuscript at her death in 1987 in Berkeley. Tussman's poetry appeared in Yiddish journals worldwide, and she was awarded the Manger Prize for Yiddish Letters in 1981. (I take these facts from Falk's invaluable introduction to *With Teeth in the Earth: Selected Poems of Malka Heifetz Tussman.*) Tussman's searing honesty, her adoration of the natural world, her running commentary in verse on Jewish women in history and the Bible, her musicality and playfulness with language, her love poems that always contain the sorrow of love, her creation of a Yiddish American life in verse (see Falk 11–34)—all this is part of the world Tussman splits open, geode-like, for us to see.

In the volume that Falk gives us—a gift for those who can at least in translation gather a sense of Tussman's enormous spirit—Tussman's poetry seems like an ongoing conversation between herself and her multitude of subjects. Many of her poems, in fact, read like dialogue, and it is through the dialogue that she pushes herself to keep seeing the world anew. Perhaps, for this reason, the great Yiddish poet Abraham Sutzkever wrote this of Tussman's long life as a poet: "The older she grew, the younger her poetry became. There is not a trace of old age in the lines written with twisted fingers and dimmed eyes of ninety. They are ecstatic affirmation (qtd. in Falk, 22)." In Tussman's poem "Walls," when an acquaintance asks her "'What's new in the world?'" she replies, "'I don't know,' I say, / 'I haven't been there yet.'" And then she tells her acquaintance, when asked, that she's got words in the sack she's carrying: "'radishes, onions, / matches . . .'" (122). Though connected to the things of the world, as she is in this poem, she affirms and insists throughout her work that the way we attach language to those things affects our relationship to them. Even at her most playful, her poetry seems an effort to dismantle rigidity of vision; with language, she makes the world malleable. Concluding the poem "Walls" with humility and then determination, she writes:

> I, the big know-nothing,
> have gathered and stored
> a whole treasure of words,
> hoping with word-lights
> to look for the world.
>
> Now they've surrounded me,
> they've become my walls.
>
> Like a fetus with eyes still shut
> inside mama's belly
>
> I kick in the walls,
> I storm them from within,
> my word-walls.

(122–23)

With her acute sensitivity to how we use language and to how it, in turn, affects us, she also recognizes how often we turn language—one of the great abstractions—into *thing* and, in doing so, obstruct its power. Writing and poetry return us to the power of language by making it new. In her poem "Under Your Sign," the persona of the poem could be Moses talking to God: "When I am under your sign, / can I run away? / Or should I shield myself in you?" But it could equally be the poet writing about the signs that constitute language: "How can I hide from you / when everywhere / I am under your sign?" (135). The poems consistently show that, while she may ask this question, she never hides.

Thus the poems are full of joy as well as fear, a fullness of experience. From her first volume of poetry in 1949, Tussman foregrounded matters of identity for Jewish women, which we see in the poem "I Am Woman." As a list, the poem encompasses a vast range of women:

I am the exalted Rachel
whose love lit the way for Rabbi Akiba.

I am the small, bashful village girl
. . . .
I am the pious girl

(50)

"I" is "the obedient bride," "the rabbi's daughter," "the woman of valor," "the mother," "the Hassid's daughter," "the barrier-breaker," "the pampered girl," and more. The poem's final declaration—"And everywhere, always, I am woman."—recognizes and accepts the range of women's roles, experiences, and politics. Don't even try to classify and compartmentalize "woman," Tussman seems to say. Throughout the poems in Falk's volume, we see the "I" of the woman and the poet constantly transformed by emotion as well as by the roles she plays. In "Anguish," the poet addresses God intimately as she often does in her poems; anticipating her own transformation into music, she imagines not just harmony but an intense music broken off from itself—anguish, as the poem's title describes: "My step is slow / but my sigh—oh God!— / my sigh is unbridled fire. . . . In a moment I'll be / a torn tone from Brahms' 2nd" (63). In "Taste of Tears," however, she returns to the feeling of the self made whole: "My joy / has the taste / of tears. . . . When you / make me happy, / it's as if // you feed my longing for myself—// for my finest self" (105). While she speaks directly to "you" here in the end, she returns to her own self. Her poems are like a dance between the world and her self, and the "I" in them becomes stronger and more celebratory with the steps out into the world and the steps back in.

In her poem "The Boundary," again addressing "you," Tussman writes, "I meet you at the very border. / You are the boundary / that allows me / to go further. // I go" (165). American Jewish women poets, at the end of the twentieth century, are crossing over every possible boundary, refusing to be bound in, assuming their right to be who they are with all the complexity of their experience. They insist, as Rukeyser would say, upon "breaking open." Unfortunately, there has not been the space to discuss the poetry of Gail Mazur, Linda Pastan, Judith Baumel, Myra Sklarew, and others whose poetry engages, responds to, and shapes questions of both Jewishness and art. The poets discussed here, though, as the others do, share a significant aspect in their work: the inherent place of their Jewishness in their poetry, its expression as an integral part of who they are and, therefore, of what the poetry is. In expressions of exile in this poetry, it is not Judaism particularly that causes the exile, but it is often Judaism that lights the way out or enables the necessary arguments with history, the resistance to oppression, the reckoning with God. With their

identities as Jews and as women integrated into the wholeness of their iden-
tities, we cannot measure what part of these poets is Jewish, what part Ameri-
can. We can see, though, that with language these poets define and redefine the
experience of being Jewish, American, female, and poet. In moving between
the conscious and the unconscious, the past and the present, family and culture,
languages and continents, they bring American Jewish poetry at the end of the
twentieth century, and Jewish women's poetry in particular, to the heartening
project of making a home with language, *in* language, but also in the world.
Linked to the history of Jewish letters and to the future, these poets live up to
the demand Rukeyser heard from the "angel of the century" in "Bubble of Air,"
a poem from 1941:

> The angel of the century
> stood on the night and would be heard;
> turned to my dream of tears and sang:
> Woman, American, and Jew,
> three guardians watch over you,
> three lions of heritage
> resist the evil of your age:
> life, freedom, and memory.
> And all the dreams cried from the camps
> and all the steel of torture rang.
> The angel of the century
> stood on the night and cried the great
> notes Give Create and Fight—
> while war
> runs through your veins, while life
> a bubble of air stands in your throat,
> answer the silence of the weak:
> Speak!

Works Cited

Becker, Robin. *All-American Girl*. Pittsburgh: U of Pittsburgh P, 1986.
Falk, Marcia. "Translator's Introduction." In *With Teeth in the Earth: Selected Poems of Malka Heifetz Tussman*. Trans. Marcia Falk. Detroit, Mich.: Wayne State UP, 1992. 11–34.
Kaufman, Shirley. *Roots in the Air*. Port Townsend, Wash.: Copper Canyon P, 1996.
Paley, Grace, and Vera Williams. *Long Walks and Intimate Talks*. New York: Feminist P, 1991.
———. *New and Collected Poems*. Gardiner, Maine: Tilbury House, 1992.

Rich, Adrienne. *An Atlas of the Difficult World*. New York: W. W. Norton, 1991.

————. "Split at the Root." *Blood, Bread, and Poetry*. New York: W. W. Norton, 1986.

————. *Sources*. Woodside, Calif.: Heyeck P, 1983.

Rukeyser, Muriel. *Out of Silence*. Evanston, Ill.: Triquarterly Books, 1992.

————. "Under Forty: A Symposium of American Literature and the Younger Genera-
tion of American Jews." *Contemporary Jewish Record* 7, no. 1 (February 1944):
3–36. Reprint in *Bridges* 1, no. 1 (spring 1990/5750): 26–29.

Shore, Jane. *Music Minus One*. New York: Picador USA, 1996.

Tussman, Malka Heifetz. *With Teeth in the Earth*. Trans. Marcia Falk. Detroit, Mich.:
Wayne State UP, 1992.

Whitman, Ruth. *Hatshepsut Speaks to Me*. Detroit, Mich.: Wayne State UP, 1992.

————. *Laughing Gas*. Detroit, Mich.: Wayne State UP, 1990.

————. *The Testing of Hannah Senesh*. Detroit, Mich.: Wayne State UP, 1986.

Zisquit, Linda. *Ritual Bath*. Seattle, Wash.: Broken Moon P, 1993.

————. *Unopened Letters*. Riverdale-on-Hudson, N.Y.: Sheep Meadow P, 1996.

Heritage as Detail and Design in Sephardi American Poetry

D I A N E   M A T Z A

Diane Matza is Professor of English at Utica College, and author of numerous essays on Sephardim and American culture. She is the editor of the groundbreaking collection *Sephardic-American Voices: Two Hundred Years of a Literary Legacy* (Brandeis UP/UP of New England, 1997).

Shortly after I knew I was to prepare a piece for this book, I received a letter from the poet Vicki Angel. She wrote, "when I read your anthology, *Sephardic-American Voices*, I didn't know there was such a thing as a Sephardic-American poet. I suppose I am one." What are we to make of this new category of Sephardic poetry? Does it help us to understand American experience or Jewish experience in a way we did not before? Is this distinction merely a response to the latest literary emphasis on ethnicity? Is this really an ethnic literature and how does "Jewishness" shape its sensibility? Is Sephardic poetry infused with the spirit of a particular cultural landscape or history? Does it have its own language and themes and subjects? Do Sephardi poets speak to and for a particular audience? The emphasis on such questions today lies in the history of American and American Jewish literature.

In discussing Sephardi American literature, the problem of definition is particularly acute because, as I've commented elsewhere, such literature questions a too narrow definition of what Jewish literature is supposed to be. For decades American Jewish writing has meant "Yiddish-inflected speech, irony, urban angst and alienation, wisecracking humor, social radicalism, tension between assimilation and tradition, and Jewishly colored humanistic values" (Matza 2). In 1990, *Studies in American Jewish Literature*'s special poetry volume echoed these views. Here is the critic David Zucker on the poetry of Delmore Schwartz: "The earnestness itself is moving. And terribly Jewish. The immigration saga, anti-Semitism, self-doubt and differentness, class consciousness, language awareness, endless detail of lower-middle-class wretchedness and aggressiveness are all here" (157). But can this apt description of Schwartz's

"Jewishness" help us to understand the "Jewish" qualities in Lawrence Spingarn's ironic poem "Keeping Kosher," whose cosmopolitan characters share nothing but a very distant common ancestry with Eastern European immigrants or their descendants? Or in Ruth Behar's "Nameless Daughter," whose passion is a plaintive attachment to landscape and language that are not Eastern European and Yiddish?[1]

American Jewish literature must face its multicultural nature because the Jewish voice has never been singular, not in America and not in the ancient Jewish communities where debate and difference characterized rabbinic commentary. Expanding definitions, however, solves only one of the problems with the entire enterprise of assigning distinctiveness. The other problem concerns our tendency to term "Jewish" traits based in historical, social, and cultural experience. Only occasionally, as in Howard Schwartz's "Miriam's Well: A Personal Account of Drawing Upon Jewish Myths and Legends," do specifically Jewish beliefs or values derived from Jewish texts inform our literary criticism. More typically, one reads in the *Studies in Jewish American Literature* issue devoted to poetry that "Baby Villon" is a Jewish poem because "it [was] a celebration of courage and integrity and the difficulty of life wherever it takes place" (200). And in another article in the same collection, we read that "the Jew is identified . . . as a strenuous witness to something unquenchable about the human spirit" and that Jewishness means "keeping up humane battle even when notions of humanity sheer off toward fanaticism among some and supine passivity among others" (239). In my anthology, *Sephardic American Voices*, I sidestepped the issue by focusing on national rather than religious background, claiming for writing by Sephardi Jews a certain cosmopolitanism or a willingness to question patriarchal traditions. These traits may be part of a *Jewish* habit of mind, but we can hardly claim these propensities only for the Jews or for every Jew.

One critic and poet who challenges the emphasis on broad humanistic traits as defining of Jewish writing is Gary Pacernik. In his *Memory and Fire: Ten American Jewish Poets*, he suggests a role for more explicitly religious yearnings. He says,

> much of the religious dynamism and energy of contemporary Judaism is maintained by poets who act as voices and exemplars of Jewish moral and spiritual rectitude and justice. While some impetus for this advocacy may come from such secular movements as socialism, communism, and anarchism, the essential poetic source is the strong ethical and moral cry of the Hebrew prophets for a people in the image of God. (7)

Yet Pacernik's view is complicated by its application to several poets who are alienated from the ritual and practice of Judaism. Also, his assertion that David

Ignatow's Jewishness is "his belief in suffering as a source of meaning and 'grace'"(151) is unsettling, first because it doesn't differ from a Christian view of suffering, and second because the Holocaust dramatically challenges any equation between suffering and meaning.

Meanwhile, renewed attention to the Sephardi voice in American Jewish literature is fraught with its own problems. In my own case, a prominent Sephardi rabbi objected to my book on the grounds that its sense of the Sephardi experience was not sufficiently religious. He said that the vast majority of Sephardi writers I identified are "removed from the wellsprings of Sephardic life," that almost all of them are "Jews who are relatively inactive in American Jewish life and who consciously and willingly choose to live separated from the institutions of American Jewry." Thus, in his view, the book, while well-intentioned, is merely a "collection of nostalgia." Finally, the rabbi claimed, the book "strikes me as a work that has some interest, but which very consciously seems to want to exclude those who are actually living within a Sephardic context."

At first, the criticism seemed to me outrageous; we are, after all, living in America, where the attractions of secular life and a culture of materialism have pushed religious faith for most Jews toward the periphery of life. Yet, these comments deserve a more sensitive response as I once again try to make some generalizations about Sephardi writing.

The rabbi who responded to my book was motivated by awareness that the authentic religious Jewish communities in the United States keep Judaism alive and are embattled. In these isolated pockets of activity, a vibrant daily texture of religious life exists in customs and rituals, synagogue liturgy, musical traditions, and rabbis working as commentators or historians. Elsewhere, Jewish observance, Jewish education, and Jewish intellectual activity about things Jewish seem woefully inadequate. Because creative artists in America have long chafed under religious restrictions, they have often traded devotion to Jewish texts for a love of secular writing. Indeed, this classic scenario is upheld as an example of the American Dream fulfilled.

Of course the religious person must despair that such voices, bound together in a book such as mine, may be seen by the larger American community to represent the totality of Jewish reality in the United States. Certainly, they do not. Perhaps trying to resolve the issue is impossible; our job as critics must be to see its complexity. I find that despite my uneasiness with some of Gary Pacernik's depictions of Jewishness, I am sympathetic to his unwillingness to reject humanistic expressions of Jewish identity. In fact, Pacernik's final comments apply equally to Ashkenazi and Sephardi writers, who "celebrate their bond and/or their empathy with the Jewish tradition by depicting the lives of their ancestors and by creating prophetic poems of condemnation and praise." (229)

Who are the Sephardi poets? Some have achieved substantial fame; others are less well known. Among them are Ammiel Alcalay, Ruth Behar, Richard Kostelanetz, Rosaly De Maios Roffman, Brenda Serotte, Rebecca Fromer, Stephen Levy, David Altabe, Vicki Angel, Ivanov Yehudi Reyez, Lawrence Spingarn, Sarah Fresco, Emile Luria, Linda Ashear, David Del Bourgo, Jack Marshall. Nearly all of these writers have written heritage poems, whose details are the languages, foods, and historical experiences of their national and religious background. Each writer has also written poetry without any obvious ethnic content. When Stephen Levy first answered my invitation to submit poetry to my anthology, he wrote, "Here are all of my poems which are in some way or other Jewish. (I have other poems too . . . They are not Jewish? The truth is, I find that question deeply intriguing and exceedingly difficult to answer fast or clearly.)" I am guided by Stephen Levy's words in what follows.

Notable Sephardi themes are memory, religion, cultural heritage, and what I call "witnessing." In what follows I look at a few Sephardi poets in order to show how these themes inform their work. One of the best known of the Sephardi poets is Michael Castro. He founded the poetry organization River Styx, and is author of four books of poetry and a work of criticism, *Interpreting the Indian: Twentieth Century Poets and the Native American*. Castro's poems of memory focus primarily on the immigrant generation, the Holocaust, and historical figures as different as Moise Gadol and Maimonides. This poetry distills decades of experience and historical fact into carefully compressed lines that leave the reader—to quote Castro's poem, "Vigil"—"mesmerized / by a sense of the eternal / up and down motion of life."[2] This sentiment is beautifully echoed in three of Castro's poems, "La America," "Grandfathers," and "Stella's Story."[3]

"La America" tells the story of the great Sephardic newspaperman and community activist, Moise Gadol. Gadol, also memorialized in the book-length manuscript by Rabbi Marc D. Angel that inspired Castro, was already middle-aged when he came to America from Bulgaria. Imbued with messianic-like zeal, Gadol devoted enormous energy and money to an enterprise most likely doomed to failure from the beginning. His goal? To unite a tiny yet diverse community, whose poverty and clannishness insulated its members from Gadol's dreams of social power and cultural preservation. Conflict between the "warrior for truth" and the wary immigrants is inevitable. Consonance in the opening lines establishes a hard, driving rhythm to represent Gadol's discipline and will:

> armed only with pen,
> press, & knowledge
> that language is power
> the powerless don't know
> they possess . . .

Castro admires and sympathizes with this "Ghetto Moe," whose tireless campaign was met with "abuse & ridicule." The staccato rhythm and the propulsive onrush of words get Gadol's passion and daily tensions just right:
In the beginning

> was the Word, Moise, & in *La America*
> you/we begin again. Touch
> each new arrival, every
> > neighborhood group. Watch
>
> > your watch, pause, think, drink
> > coffee, eat okra at a cheap café;
> > plot, scheme
> how to pay the bills; write notes:
> this lunch
> is research, remember
> to mention the need for better food
> in these Turkish corner joints in the next edition
> (if you can get it out).

Details of action and place convey much of the time's social reality, the "cheap cafés," derided as gambling dens by the tonier Sephardic community but havens for immigrants seeking an employment connection or a familiar face, and the unrelenting strain on Gadol's own finances.

Castro's suggestive language, his easy American slang ("joints"), reinforces what is earthy and contemporary in Gadol's struggle to take hold of a new land and realize its opportunities and so make it relevant to us, today. Reinforced by *La America*'s multiple meanings—name of poem, newspaper, and nation—he underscores both the powerful link and powerful disjunction between dream and reality.

Toward the end of the poem, Castro's realistic picture of Gadol's death in obscurity shows him remembered by a few only as a "loco-meshugge." Still, at the poem's end the message is upbeat, the language colloquial, the tense present, a hymn for Gadol as a model for us even now: "not knuckling under, discovering / yet another home, opening/ *La America*."

Castro faces the twentieth century's instabilities unflinchingly, with unflagging energy and even humor, infusing our reading with pleasure. Nowhere does he achieve this more than in "Grandfathers," a chronicle of five generations, including grandfathers he can only imagine. In Castro's essay for this volume, "The Grandparent Poems: Self-Reflections in a Smoky Mirror," he explains, "I instinctively found images of smoke to suggest the haziness of my impressions, the tenuousness of the connection to that older world, that source of who I am." The figurative and the literal here cannot be separated: Real smoke constantly surrounds these family members. They chain-smoke, sweep up butts, open cigar stores. Beyond such details of personal behavior, however, the smoke motif mirrors the individual's impotence before history's advance. Castro comments ironically on the British troops' role in Salonika's Great Fire of 1917. Callously setting fire to the Jewish quarter,

> They preferred to destroy the city
> than to let the Germans have it.
> People jumped into the harbor
> to escape the conflagration.
>
> All that smoke.

As in "La America," Castro's essential optimism rises from the last lines of the poem. Not only can he imagine his own "grandsons in the hazy future," but smoke itself is transformed into a symbol for the creative impulse:

> lit a candle, a joint,
> watched the smoke rise;
> it lingered into thin air,
> except for what remained
> inside him

Castro's "Stella's Story," a Holocaust poem, is based on a factual account by Rebecca Camhi Fromer. Except for four lines, the entire poem is narrated in a survivor's controlled and unsentimental present tense. This is not memory but re-creation:

> First they round us up
> in the town square, on Rhodes, then ship
> us like freight to Greece—
> the lucky ones they drown—

Here, and in the rest of the two opening stanzas, the narrator is witness and the power of witness is the immediacy of her telling: Smells, sights, sounds, physical actions, interrupted only occasionally with word of the detainees "smothering in terror," or with two predictable but poignant questions: "where are you going? / would we ever return?"

At the end of the second stanza, Castro deftly plucks out the distance separating narrator and reader, first by introducing a figure familiar to us, and second by allowing the narrator to tell her personal story against the backdrop of the generalized horror she has already established. Stella's telling, sharp and precise, with dramatic emphasis on verbs and the contrast between the long and short line, collapses the distinction between past and present:

> Waldheim looks away, inhales tightlipped rage
> & looks around at us, at my mother
> at the gold wedding ring he notices on her finger.
> He erupts
> a torrent of abuse.
> She understands & yet she doesn't.
> She pulls,
> but mama's fingers are swollen & moist,
> & the ring will not budge.

After the two daughters help the mother remove the ring, Waldheim takes it and leaves. But the trauma has only just begun; much worse will follow, as we learn from the remarkably restrained final comment:

> This was but a minor incident,
> a few moments in a pitstop
> en route to Auschwitz.
> My family's last moments
> together, in Greece

But what is minor in the history of the period is the most wrenching of Stella's life. This is the compelling story of a last instance of family solidarity, one Stella repeats to the interviewer of the poem and one she lives with each day. The quiet reserve of the last stanza undercuts any attempt to invest the experience with meaning; we are left with the raw emotion and the deeply unsettling knowledge that nothing can erase the survivor's personal pain.

In each of these poems, emphasis on the dignity and significance of the ordinary person creates a direct dialogue to the larger culture's celebration of the prominent and famous. Several other poems by Sephardi writers issue a similar challenge. One of my favorites is Jack Marshall's "Grace," a tender and lyrical poem about his mother contemplating an old photograph of Grace and her new husband: The son, Jack Marshall, expresses his mother's life of uprootedness and disappointment in elegiac lines such as these:

> . . . holding a groom with what appears like love
>
> but was not, or was and then not, or was
> over by God so quickly—

> looks charm choice
> gone . . .[4]

The poet's sadness is obvious and deep but does not overwhelm the poem, for its opening lines reach beyond these realities to stamp his mother's life with wonder and singularity:

> My mother who cannot read or write
> her name is Garaz in Arabic
>
> I used to hear as a boy and to this day still
> prefer hearing that way: two warm *a*'s glowing
>
> apple-red between consonants, and *z*'s
> lightning-flash spurring air
>
> to sparkle and freshening sight,
> the way her roses did;. . .

A sustained, generously descriptive language commemorates his mother's powerful essence. Her roses become "perennials to come grown to of nothing / bigger than a few wrinkled berries," her hair is "over one shoulder, long / thick piled brown hair you can feel," and her swimming is "flying / through an opening in the waves." Marshall refuses to allow his mother's life to disappear into nothingness.

Rejecting the elegiac mode for an almost shocking aggressiveness is Vicki Angel's "From the Other Side of the Nile."[5] The poem juxtaposes the corrosive resentment of a young Sephardi girl who wants nothing more than to pattern herself after a real American and the adult's profound sense of loss. The girl's desire to hide is thwarted by the language, food, and smells of her heritage, captured through a powerful alliterative style:

> I thought I could disguise it, but the Jew in me
> oozed through like grease stains
> that soaked into my shameful lunch sacks
> filled with fried fish cakes and panezicos
> bilebizes and spinach pie.

And later,

> . . . But the kitchen reeked
> of feta and cashcaval and the cupboards

rained down rose petal jam even thicker
than my father's foreign tongue.
And parked out front the pink-finned Ford
gleamed in the sun, stank from the garlic
that swung from the rearview mirror
where there should've been a cross.

The poem's message and tone are softened by the opening and closing stanzas. A "Lord knows" on the first line lets us in on the poet's distance from the bitterness she expresses in the three middle stanzas. At the start she is looking backward, and so we expect her to close the poem by reviewing the past, though we are not fully prepared for the depth of her regret, so powerfully expressed by the three words in Ladino. She reinforces her complicity in the death of her culture with a reference to the Biblical story of Jacob and Esau:

How was I to know when I demanded,
when I raged and locked my arms across my chest,
Grandmother speak to me
solo in Ingles that she would listen?
and I'd be left with this mouth full
of swear words, selling birthrights
for this goddamned bowl of beans.

David Del Bourgo's use of heritage details in "Sunday Visits" creates a completely different effect.[6] The poem uses memory not to comment on to past but the capture the vivid, sensory experience of a young boy who wants to keep forever a moment of pleasure and possibility. Surrounded by his peripatetic Sephardi family's food and worldly goods, the "Chinese love seat / embroidered with gold thread / blue silk worn pale as the thin sky," "a dish of Spanish rice," and "the sweet smell of roasted chicken and raisins," the boy wants nothing to change. The California of "Park La Brea Towers" and "Papa / with a tweed sport coat & bold black glasses / the fashion back in '52 / for small men with sharp dreams" hint at a palpable tension between the evocative beauty of the scene and the world's reality. But Del Bourgo is less interested in social comment than in the image, the spark to the creative imagination, which the poem evokes at its end as the boy's thoughts become "buoyant in the onrushing light."

Del Bourgo is interested in outward manifestations of the internal experience, and so is Stephen Levy, but Levy's focus is the individual's relationship to religious experience.[7] None of Levy's "Jewish" poems is more than half a page long, and several of them begin similarly, with participial phrases modifying a personal pronoun. Levy creates a miniaturist tableau in which he expresses the binding of private spirituality with the individual's attitude and action. For example, one prepares oneself for prayer in "Singing for Saturday Morning," which is short enough to quote in its entirety:

> Unhurried,
> we will come to tall trees
> all abloom, then
> with ease we will sway in the wind, and hum
> as one

This rigorous simplicity underscores the mystery of religious feeling in several other poems also. In the lovely "Teacher in Bayside," Rabbi Rackovsky's passion bursts forth in the "waning sunlight gleaming into" his small classroom. Levy celebrates such intensity of feeling again in the first line of stanza three, "children resoundingly singing," and a third time at the close when the rabbi's physical being reaches out to the children, his "hands, / his whole arms, leading us."

Spirituality also infuses many of the poems of Rosaly DeMaios Roffman.[8] Her poems, some haunted by "the eyes of Auschwitz children," her translations of poetry from and into Ladino, her travels to the Greece of her ancestors, and her role as witness in the larger international community (twice she has been invited to speak at the World Congress of Poets) remind us that Judaism, the spiritual achievement of a coherent, historical community, emphasizes *tikkun olam*, repair of the world. An acute observer of obstacles to peace and health, Roffman remains remarkably free of pessimism or fear. Instead, her deeply generous sensibility repeatedly affirms her belief in the healing power of art. "Entertaining Strangers," full of the materials of everyday life but no obviously Jewish or Sephardi images, might be said to be Roffman's self-portrait:

> Come to my hospitality table—
> I will feed you from every pot—
> I will allow you to wear my clothes,
> my blue kimono, my black hat.
>
> I will call my brother out
> and make him sing comfort songs
> to help with months of longing.
>
> I will ask my sister to dance over the bear's hill, a lodestar
> to sail you to your destination.
>
> If your body sits in a room
> and your reptile brain gets restless

> I will ask my broom to sweep away
> all the dust that settled in your heart . . .
>
> And when you move
> with the quick rhythm of the red cedar
> you will remind us—
> we may entertain angels unawares.

The value of engagement with the things and people of the world is the sentiment of another Roffman poem that skewers stereotypes of Jews. This is the opening of "Sometimes People Think:"

> I'm not a Jew
> because my name is DeMaios
> and I always got the jobs I wanted
> and I went to Japan
> just like those daughters
> of missionaries and generals
> And I sing at Church
> with my friend on Sundays
> and read Ezra Pound
> and I'm not savvy about money
>
> But then I read books
> on Polish villages
> that don't exist any more
> and count the eyes of Auschwitz children
> and see pictures of heaps of bones

This is Roffman's history, both the one she has lived and the one that has shaped her moral consciousness. The depth of her identification with both means she situates herself at the center of human activity, whether bleak or joyous. The poem's final stanza is typical Roffman in its identification of poetry with healing:

> Every time a child is abused or an old man
> is found shrieking in the streets,
> I conjure up my 3,000 year old face
> and sit at table with all of the missing
> Every piece of bread I give to *you*.

A poet with a similar devotion to world affairs is Ammiel Alcalay. Alcalay concentrates specifically on transforming our discourse about Jewish identity, offering a radical critique of Jewish intellectual and literary history in his *Beyond Jews and Arabs, Remaking Levantine Culture*. Alcalay rejects as incomplete the Western tradition's definition of the Jew as quintessential outsider, finding a more complex picture in the history of fruitful Sephardi and Mizrahi encounters with the Arab world. Alcalay emphasizes shared Semitic traditions and cross-cultural influence as part of a political program to narrow the deep divide between Arabs and Jews in the Middle East. He knows that intransigent problems (the Palestinian-Israeli conflict) remain intransigent partly because habit and expectation constrain our discourse about them. Willingness to take risks must, then, accompany any effort to alter the terms of debate. For Alcalay this means not only adding his voice to scholarship in the field, but using his moral, political, and aesthetic consciousness to shape the artistic sensibility of his prose poem collection, *the cairo notebooks*.[9]

One of the compelling poems in this collection, "'I Had Thought of Writing a Play Based on the Following Facts:'" relies on historical facts, listed one following the other without coordination or subordination to convey Alcalay's essential message. Thirty-seven facts are stated; here are facts 6–11:

6. The villagers of Sheikh Badr used to pray at the mosque that's now on Strauss, in back of the Edison Theater.

7. The Edison Theater was built in 1932 by M. Y. Mizrahi and Sons.

8. I have a great aunt who lives in Istanbul but now she spends half the year in Athens with her daughter's family since being evicted by a developer. We've never met.

9. A relative on my mother's side, Shlomo Almuli, published a book called *The Interpretation of Dreams* in Constantinople in 1530 which was first quoted by Freud in 1899.

10. Another great aunt, whom I know well, was a patient of Freud's for a brief period after being sent from Belgrade to study in Vienna.

11. Sheikh Badr, who had a feud with Sheikh Jarrah and was sanctified for his power of answering prayers for rain, is buried under the Hilton, to the right of the graveyard.

In just these half-dozen facts, Alcalay challenges our notions about the compartmentalization of history and of identity. Lives intersect, cultures overlap; memory, identity, and history ignore their boundaries. Cultural influence must be expansively defined and searched out, for our contemporary numbness to connections between the past and present hardens living political options into deadly ideologies. *the cairo notebooks* is thoroughly personal, political, poetic, and moving.

Some, no doubt, will find this poetry too personal, too fragmented, too quick to shift from one time frame or landscape to another. But try reading it *as if* you understood each reference to person, place, or event. Then the poems' uncomfortable closeness, broken wholes, and disconnected scenes become meditations on the beauty and tragedy of the Middle East. Alcalay confronts us with facts of searing clarity and honesty, daring us to allow his sometimes startling juxtapositions to reshape our own vision.

As I close this discussion of the Sephardi poets, I find the question of what is Jewish and what is ethnic in their work to be even more difficult to resolve. After all, this group of writers is singularly varied, even idiosyncratic, in sound, image, viewpoint, and subject. Is this—the individuality, the creativity, the distinctiveness, the "startling juxtapositions"—the point, one that makes the tenuous recurrent pull of memory and moral seriousness seem all the more pervasive? For these poets an insistence on and commitment to an utterly free use of all the materials within their reach rules out an ethnic poetry narrowly defined by subject matter, attitude, or political stance. For the Sephardi poets this means remaining fully alive to the many artistic possibilities found in individual confrontation within a diverse cultural and religious heritage. Such confrontations, as we have seen, prod memory, enrich experience, and fire the imagination. Attending to their visions will urge us toward more flexible rather than more narrow interpretations and appreciations of what is Jewish, American, and poetic.

Notes

1. "Keeping Kosher" by Lawrence P. Spingarn was accepted by *European Judaism* in late 1988, and "Nameless Daughter" by Ruth Behar can be found in *Sephardic American Voices*, p. 306.

2. "Vigil" was published in *Sagarin Review*.

3. "La America" can be found on p. 151 in *Sephardic American Voices*, "Grandfathers" on p. 153, and "Stella's Story" on p. 232.

4. "Grace" appears on p. 162 in *Sephardic American Voices*.

5. "From the Other Side of the Nile" was originally published in *Seattle Review* 18 (fall 1995/winter 1996) under the title "Falling in Line."

6. "Sunday Visits" appears on p. 160 in *Sephardic American Voices*.

7. Stephen Levy's poems can be found on pp. 313–15 in *Sephardic American Voices*.

8. "Sometimes People Think" appears on p. 299 in *Sephardic American Voices*, and "Entertaining Strangers" was first published in the late 1980s by the *Dorothy Day Catholic Worker* and in 1992 was used as part of a collaborative piece called VESSELS at a women's composers' conference.

9. Ammiel Alcalay's "I Had Thought About Writing a Play Based on the Following Facts:" appears on p. 291 in *Sephardic American Voices*.

Works Cited

Brenner, Rachel Reldhay. "A. M. Klein's 'The Hitleriad': Against the Silence of the Apocalypse." *Studies in American Jewish Literature* 9 (fall 1990): 228–41.

Chess, Richard. "The Tradition of American Jewish Poetry: Philip Levine's "'Turning.'" *Studies in American Jewish Literature* 9 (fall 1990): 197–214.

Matza, Diane, ed. *Sephardic-American Voices: 200 Years of a Literary Legacy*. Hanover: University Press of New England, 1997.

Pacernik, Gary. *Memory and Fire: Ten American Jewish Poets*. New York: Peter Lang, 1989.

Zucker, David. "'Alien to Myself': Jewishness in the Poetry of Delmore Schwartz," *Studies in American Jewish Literature* 9 (fall 1990): 151–62.

Di feder fun harts / The Pen of the Heart: Tsveyshprakhikayt / Bilingualism and American Jewish Poetry[1]

I R E N A   K L E P F I S Z

Irena Klepfisz was born in 1941 in Warsaw, Poland, and emigrated to the United States in 1949. The author of A Few Words in the Mother Tongue: Poems Selected and New (1971–1990) (Eighth Mountain Press, 1990) and Dreams of an Insomniac: Jewish Feminist Essays, Speeches, and Diatribes (Eighth Mountain Press, 1990), she teaches Jewish Women's Studies at Barnard College. She is a recipient of an NEA poetry fellowship and is currently translating the fiction and poetry of Yiddish women writers. She serves as the editorial consultant for Yiddish and Yiddish culture on the Jewish feminist journal Bridges.

Twentieth-century American literature of Ashkenazi Jews has a history of a specific kind of bilingualism, one markedly different from that produced more recently by Latino or Asian writers. Anzia Yezierska, Tillie Olsen, and Grace Paley have used Yiddish sentence structure and intonation in their English fiction to evoke the "sound" of Yiddish, the language that their Jewish immigrant characters spoke to each other and that also shaped their spoken English. These writers achieved their effects almost exclusively without naming the language or using Yiddish words. Henry Roth was also conscious of Jewish bilingualism, except that he overtly paid tribute to the poetic nature of Yiddish; but he too barely used any Yiddish words in Call It Sleep (though, interestingly, he transliterated large portions of the Hebrew religious texts that David reads). Roth's strategy was to assume Yiddish as his characters' linguistic norm and to translate their lyrical Yiddish speech and thoughts into a parallel lyrical English—an English with hardly any Yiddish vocabulary, sentence structure, or intonation. In fact, if the narrator didn't identify the language, the reader would have no way of knowing that the characters were speaking Yiddish. To further emphasize that Yiddish "*iz di feder fun harts*/is the pen of the heart,"[2] Roth contrasted this Yiddish-via-English lyricism with the characters' crude, truncated English. The latter he transliterated phonetically as if *it* were the alien language requiring decoding and imaginative reconstruction.

Roth, Yezierska, Olsen, and Paley force us to think about Yiddish, Yinglish, and broken English. And they do so brilliantly in very different ways. But what is remarkable about all four writers' work is the lack of Yiddish itself. I point this out as a curiosity, rather than a failure, for there is nothing lacking in the artistic craft of any of these writers. But it is something to dwell on and consider. Why *is* the Yiddish language so visibly absent among writers so conscious of it? Does it have to do with each of the writers' particular talent, sensibility, knowledge of Yiddish, Jewish background, American attitudes toward assimilation, American literary criticism and readership?

The answers are complex and probably specific to each writer. But at least in part, they must stem from the time periods during which each writer began to shape him/herself as an artist, periods when Yiddish—perhaps erroneously—was still being taken for granted, was still assumed to be a living language with a secure future. When these assumptions shifted, the literary approach to Yiddish would inevitably shift as well. At least that is how I account for the difference in my own involvement with this linguistic issue.

I first began to consider Yiddish as a literary medium when it was already publicly being declared dead or, at best hanging on by a thread.[3] This was also a time when advocates of multiculturalism and opponents of the melting pot were first becoming vocal, and writers, among others, began to think about the importance of languages in the United States other than English. Style, intonation, accents were never the issue. The heart of the matter was always language itself: its words, grammar and culture.

In the early 1980s, my response to these ideas was to begin an experiment, which, over the past fifteen years, I have repeatedly abandoned and returned to. That experiment involved a decision to try to incorporate Yiddish into my creative work. When I first considered the idea, I had already been writing poetry for more than twenty years and publishing for about half that time. During those same twenty years, I had studied Yiddish literature as an undergraduate with Professor Max Weinreich at City College, a decade later completed postdoctoral work in Yiddish Studies at Max Weinreich Center of YIVO, Institute for Jewish Research, and had taught for a number of summers in YIVO's intensive Yiddish language program at Columbia University. Yet during this entire time when I considered myself a serious poet, had devoted much time to thinking about poetic language, and had produced writing with recognizable "Jewish content," it had never occurred to me that Yiddish or Yiddish culture was something that could or should inform my poetry. Only in the late 1970s and early 1980s did I become increasingly focused on Yiddish and Jewish languages and their relationship to English. I have written elsewhere about how I managed for so long *not* to think about (what appear to me now) such obvious linguistic and cultural issues and have analyzed some of the process of my assimilation and acculturation in this country, my own needs as an immigrant to master and root myself in mainstream English.[4]

What I want to explore in this essay is why and how I was moved to experiment linguistically with Yiddish. In the course of the discussion, I hope to reflect on some of the aesthetic and political implications of shifting my poetry in this direction and to explore why this path has proven to be so problematic.

Yiddish as Reclamation

Much of the impetus came directly from the women's movement. I became active in the multistranded feminist and lesbian/feminist movement in the mid 1970s. At that time, identity politics with its implicit multiculturalism pushed many of us to strengthen our ties to our cultures of origin and to search for our specific women's history, our cultural foremothers and role models. Since I had been raised in a secular Jewish environment, a community of Polish-Jewish survivors most of whom were active before the war in the Jewish Labor Bund, I naturally turned a feminist lens on my Yiddish socialist background and—not surprisingly—like many women from other cultures, discovered that Yiddish women's history and artistic and intellectual achievements were barely known. This seemed particularly depressing since in the mid 1800s Eastern European Jewish life had begun to experience a Jewish secular revolution, with the result that Jewish women had become, for the first time, active in the public arena. Especially in the last 100 years in Eastern Europe and in U.S. Yiddish-speaking centers, women had taken on an important role in (re)shaping and building the Jewish *svive*/environment. Supporting this public emergence of women as artists, political and community leaders, doctors and nurses, and teachers was a variety of progressive movements (Bundist socialist, communist, Zionist, and anarchist) that expressed a commitment to women's equality and encouraged women's participation in the Jewish future.[5]

In the late 1970s and early 1980s, I instinctively knew there was much to know, yet was unable to furnish very many details. In fact, when pressed, I could hardly name a woman in any field that touched upon Yiddish. For example, though I had received a solid Yiddish education, I was unable to cite a single Yiddish woman historical figure or writer, Kadya Molodowsky being the lonely exception. At this time, Jewish feminist scholarship was just beginning to emerge with the publication in 1976 of *The Jewish Woman in America* by Charlotte Baum, Sonya Michel, and Paula Hyman and later with the scholarship of Norma Fain Pratt. So initially there was little out there to help me in my particular field of interest. The lack of information coupled with my awareness that women had been excluded from Eastern European political and cultural history naturally made me more preoccupied with the field of Yiddish and eager to learn, at the very least, something about its women literary figures. The problem was very clear. My role in contributing to its solution was not.

Two encounters intensified my reexamination and interest in Yiddish. The first was contact with many Latina feminists who used Spanish in their writing and who were creating a substantial body of bilingual work. Their creative uses of bilingualism made me reflect on my own cultural *yerushe*/legacy and I suddenly found myself self-conscious about my seemingly total indifference to Yiddish: On the one hand, I had devoted a great deal of time and energy to Yiddish; on the other, I had never given it a role in my art. An occasional use of a word—like *rebetsin* (rabbi's wife) or *bashert* (predestined or inevitable)—was all the Yiddish reflected in twenty years of poetry writing. I was becoming aware of a disjunction.

The second event occurred in July 1983 when I accompanied my mother to Poland for our first visit since we had left in 1946 and for my first view of that country as an adult. During this seven-day trip, I found myself constantly returning to Warsaw's mammoth Jewish Cemetery, whose half-buried, broken tombstones provided me with my first concrete knowledge of the richness and complexity of Jewish life before the war. Perhaps because my feminist commitment had already been pointing me in that direction, perhaps because of my heightened awareness of bilingualism in Latina literature—I returned from that trip determined that somehow I would be more involved with the preservation of Yiddish and Yiddish culture. I wondered: Why haven't I used Yiddish? Why can't I start now? What's stopping me?

And I was stopped. I was stymied. Yiddish as it appears in the cultural mainstream is not exactly a language to embrace. The popular American (public) view of Yiddish is that it is inherently comic or obscene because that is the Yiddish promoted by Hollywood and by comedians on late-night TV. This view trivializes Yiddish culture and Jewish history, treats the language itself as a joke. *That* Yiddish embarrassed and enraged me. Only someone rooted in the Yiddish-speaking world can understand how demeaning these free-floating fragments of Yiddish are. I knew that if I were to use Yiddish, it had to be in a way that did not feed into popular vulgarisms.

But there were other obstacles. I knew, from the outset, that I wanted to maintain English as my primary language. I had no interest (never mind ability) in becoming a Yiddish poet. I had struggled too long to acquire linguistic control of English. I was also aware that as a Jew, I had a very different relationship to Yiddish than Latina writers had to Spanish. Spanish was their mother tongue, and their spoken English often had an identifiable accent. Equally important: The United States has a huge population that understands

Spanish and its variations and mixtures with English. So when a Latina chooses to write bilingually, she is not cutting herself off from her audience. She is, in fact, replicating the linguistic reality of millions.

I, on the other hand, had never spoken Yiddish with my mother (Polish had been my first language), nor had it ever been my everyday language, though it was all around me when I was growing up. And, though I could converse comfortably in Yiddish, could teach it, I have never felt totally at home with it. So trying to incorporate Yiddish into my writing felt somewhat artificial and strained. Complicating matters even more was the lack of a significant Yiddish-speaking, Jewish secular audience that could understand a bilingual poem or story. To the overwhelming majority of American Ashkenazi Jews, Yiddish is the language that parents or grandparents continued to speak so that *di kinder zoln nisht farshteyn*/the children would not understand what they were saying. The last thing I wanted to do in my own writing was to duplicate that experience and maintain Yiddish as the language of secrets.

Still, the idea of using Yiddish remained challenging. I wanted to see if poetry could serve as a path back to a language that repeatedly was pronounced dead or in intensive care. I wanted it alive. And I wanted it accessible.

Other obstacles: how to highlight women without caving in to nostalgia. I wanted to use Yiddish in ways that would reflect my feminist political visions. I wanted to look at Yiddish and Yiddish culture lovingly, but critically, and—when relevant—to acknowledge their sexist and patriarchal assumptions and stereotypes. All these various needs and impulses—though at the time I'm not sure I would have been able to articulate them—were behind my first attempt at bilingual poetry—my poem "*Etlekhe verter oyf mame-loshn*/A few words in the mother tongue."

To make it intelligible to non-Yiddish speakers, I interpolated and translated—as rhythmically as I could—all the Yiddish in it. But at a certain moment in the poem I allowed the Yiddish to take over. Using repetitions much like in the tradition of much of the sweatshop oral Yiddish poetry I had learned in my secular *shule,* I felt confident I would not lose my listener or reader and, toward the end of the poem, simply abandoned English all together.

Etlekhe verter oyf mame-loshn
A Few Words in the Mother Tongue[6]

lemoshl: for example

di kurve the whore
a woman who acknowledges her passions

di yidene the Jewess the Jewish woman
ignorant overbearing
let's face it: every woman is one

di yente the gossip the busybody
who knows what's what
and is never caught off guard

di lezbianke the one with
a roommate though we never used the word

dos vaybl the wife
or the little woman

   . . .

in der heym at home
where she does everything to keep
yidishkayt alive

yidishkayt a way of being
Jewish always arguable

in mark where she buys
di kartofl un khalah
(yes, potatoes and challah)

di kartofl the material counter-
part of *yidishkayt*

mit tsibeles with onions
that bring *trern tsu di oygn*
tears to her eyes when she sees
how little it all is
veyniker un veyniker
less and less

di khalah braided
vi ir hor far der khasene
like her hair before the wedding
when she was *aza sheyn meydl*
such a pretty girl

di lange shvartse hor
the long black hair
di lange shvartse hor
·   ·   ·

a froy kholmt a woman
dreams *ir ort oyf der velt*
her place in this world
un zi hot moyre and she is afraid
so afraid of the words

kurve
yidene
yente
lezbianke
vaybl

zi kholmt she dreams
un zi hot moyre and she is afraid
ir ort
di velt
di heym
der mark

a meydl kholmt
a kurve kholmt
a yidene kholmt
a yente kholmt
a lezbianke kholmt

a vaybl kholmt
di kartofl
di khalah

yidishkayt

zi kholmt
di hor
di lange shvartse hor

zi kholmt
zi kholmt
zi kholmt

What did I gain by writing in this way? By making Yiddish itself the subject and the vehicle of contemporary poetic expression, I hoped to reclaim a small part of the language for myself (and perhaps for others). The act of writing partly in Yiddish also allowed me to place myself somewhat closer to my Yiddish literary ancestors. But one unforeseen consequence was that the closer proximity accentuated the major differences between us. In the past, Yiddish poets praised the range of Yiddish expression, its nuances, its richness *in Yiddish* to an audience that understood and appreciated their poetic passions and linguistic ingenuity. For example, in 1918 in New York City, Rachelle Vaprinski could write:

> *O mayn shprakh*
> *du bist zilberik bloy—*
> *du bist likhtiker gold . . .* [7]

> Oh my language
> You are silvery blue—
> You are bright gold . . .
> > (translation mine)

Vaprinski expected her readers to judge whether her poem's characterization of Yiddish paralleled their own experience and, thereby, also judge and engage with the poem itself. Today, however, I could never expect the majority of readers to engage with Yiddish in the same way—at least not without translation. In "*Etlekhe verter*," I was simply trying to maintain an awareness of Yiddish's continued existence, of its continued meaningfulness to an audience, that at most, understands (and then only in the context of the poem) a minimum of selected words and phrases.

This technique inevitably highlights our present impoverishment in relationship to our past richness. It emphasizes that, to most of us, Yiddish is not a language, but an aroma of cooking in an aged relative's kitchen, a stomach cramp when overhearing a raging argument whose words we cannot make out, a song whose lyrics we no longer remember and when recited cannot understand. Yiddish: a smell, an ache, a melody, a longing. Everything but words, sentences, poetry.

A bisl yidish/A little Yiddish

A few months ago I received an e-mail with the subject heading "*A bisl yidish*/A little Yiddish." Someone wanted to know what "*Favos vil tu yidish?*" means. It was one of those sentences ("What want de Yiddish?") people always hand me, which, over time and expanding amnesia, has eroded into an incomprehensible string of sounds that our tongues and throats can barely pronounce. Incomprehensible because consonants, vowels, syllables, whole words and phrases have been lost so that all that is left are echoes of echoes of echoes of Yiddish.

On the day of the e-mail, I happened to turn on the news and heard that survivors and heirs of survivors had reached a settlement of millions of dollars with Switzerland. When the news broke for a commercial, I watched for the first time, a campaign ad for New York's Senator Alphonse D'Amato. It featured a very old survivor ("Sen. D'Amato helped me get my father's money," she said in heavily Yiddish-accented English) and footage of concentration camp inmates and corpses. Now the dead are out campaigning in our elections, I thought. But in what language?

So I returned to the e-mail, which had the following omissions: the "r" in "*farvos*" (why) and, more important, the relationship via verb between the "*tu*"—actually "*du*/you" (ourselves) and the object of the query: Yiddish. This e-mail led to my taking the following notes:

Kashes vegn yidish / Questions About the Status of Yiddish Today
> [Some notes for evaluating the present attitudes towards Yiddish]

Farvos vilstu gedenken yidish? / Why do you want to remember Yiddish?

Farvos vilstu bahaltn yidish? / Why do you want to hide Yiddish?

Farvos vilstu avekgebn yidish? / Why do you want to give away Yiddish?

Farvos vilstu redn yidish? / Why do you want to speak Yiddish?

Farvos vilstu borgn yidish? / Why do you want to borrow Yiddish?

Farvos vilstu analizirn yidish? / Why do you want to analyze Yiddish?

Farvos vilstu shlingen yidish? / Why do you want to swallow Yiddish?

Farvos vilstu fargesn yidish? / Why do you want to forget
Yiddish?

Farvos vilstu bagrobn yidish? / Why do you want to bury
Yiddish?

Farvos vilstu lernen yidish? / Why do you want to study
Yiddish?

*Farvos vilstu aroysvarfn, avekvarfn, untervarfn, kokhn, shmekn, trinken, esn,
farflantsn, tsehakn, derhargenen, brenen, farleshn unzer mame-loshn, yidish?* /
Why do you want to throw out, throw away, abandon, cook, smell, drink, eat,
plant, chop up, murder, burn, put out our mother-tongue, Yiddish?

To Yiddish or Not to Yiddish

The use of a fragmentary Yiddish in my poetry was (and remains) a minuscule
step towards reclamation—but a step nevertheless. I have no illusions that any-
one will learn Yiddish from the words or phrases found in my poetry, but I have
some reasonable hope that for a moment readers may be able to center them-
selves in a poetic world in which Yiddish is a true reference point, rather than
one where it is relegated to a glossary line or footnote, and that the experience
of that centering will perhaps move them to take another small step. My ex-
tended bilingual poem "*Di rayze aheym*/The journey home," about my trip to
Poland in 1983, followed the method of "*Etlekhe verter*." Looking back at it
now, I realize that I wanted the repetitions and simultaneous translations to
serve as skimpy linguistic bridges in the readers' crossings of oceans and ce-
metery walls; in the process, I hoped they would recognize that Yiddish is the
means and the object of the journey they may be envisioning for themselves as
well as their ghostly companion. In short, I wanted Yiddish to be simultane-
ously memory and guide so that subject and form and language would be in-
separable. At least that is what I was groping toward.

In other writing—poetry, essays, and fictional parables—I used Yiddish
sometimes less, sometimes more prominently. At times, I would introduce a
Yiddish phrase because it seemed appropriate at a specific point in the piece—
a feeling or idea I associated with the Yiddish conversations of my childhood
or with my later readings. Other times I featured a certain word, like in the par-
able "*Di yerushe*/The Legacy" because the legacy I was referring to was a Yid-
dish one.[8] In "Rhythm + Jews," a parable that served as liner notes for the
Klezmatics' CD of the same name, I created a column down the center of the
page with the entire Latin alphabet, each letter serving as a line that reads both
right to left and left to right as a way of physically illustrating the simultaneous
presence of Yiddish and English culture in our consciousness.

But there were instances when I felt I was being arbitrary and simply intrusively inserting Yiddish. It is this feeling of arbitrariness and the knowledge that I was severely limited in how much Yiddish the English text could bear that has made me question what I was doing. How *do* I decide what will be rendered bilingually in Yiddish and English and what will be stated in just English? The following poem (still unfinished) makes me particularly conscious of this issue.

Ir harts/Her heart

Men vet mikh gedenken
    I'll be remembered
for my worst sin—my forgetfulness—
For I intend to forget it all
to leave it all behind.

Dos vel ikh ober yo gedenken
and it will stick: My mother's voice
"*'Khken nisht* I can't" as she took
a seat on the bench in Van Cortland Park
(Medem strolled here before his death
when *sotsyalizm* was still the future)
the incline of the hill all that gravity
tsi shver far ir harts
too heavy for her heart.

Yes, I'll always remember *ir midkayt*
her exhaustion *ir harts*
as I turned my back
to the park to the building
to the block and
dreamed of space
on grenetsn without boundaries
lender lands *geshikhte* history.
How I will dance to think
that history cannot be nailed into my winter boots.

Vos ikh vel ale mol gedenken
if anything remains at all
it will be the weight of the hill
as we walked a hill
tsi shver far ir harts.

The Yiddish in this poem is sometimes translated, other times contextualized with the assumption that the reader will be able to figure it out. But I am not sure whether I could justify why the Yiddish (with the exception perhaps of "*ir harts*") appears where it does in this particular version. Its placement seems to lack the sense of inevitability which, I believe, some of my other poems have. And I worry if the poem strains with too much (self) conscious intent, too many grammatical leaps just for the sake of making Yiddish present.

The issue of arbitrariness leads to other questions: Does Yiddish belong only in "Jewish work"? If so, am I not ghettoizing the language? Distorting it? Am I not implying that Yiddish is a language that is limited, that it can only convey ideas about Jewishness? Since that can't possibly be true, why haven't I tried using it in writing without "Jewish content"? I write about many things. What's the relation between these "non-Jewish" subjects and Yiddish?

These questions, of course, do not stem from an inherent incompatibility of Yiddish with non-Jewish subjects. Yiddish speakers and writers have never made such distinctions via language—they speak and write about everything in Yiddish, whether it touches upon Jewish themes or not. I am only conscious of these "problems" because my audience does not know Yiddish; because I learned my poetic craft in English and English is where I remain grounded; and because, inevitably, the use of Yiddish in a fragmentary way involves selection and issues of placement. The result is that it "feels" as if Yiddish belongs only in a poem with Jewish content.

Put another way: Unlike writers whose sole, and therefore *neutral*, medium was Yiddish and who linguistically never distinguished between Jewish or non-Jewish content, I find nothing neutral or casual about introducing a Jewish linguistic element into a non-Jewish language. Inevitably the use of Yiddish alters something about the speaker in the poem, about her point of view. I think—I'm not sure. It may be that if I did this often enough in my poetry and fiction, then Yiddish would seem naturally (and neutrally) to belong everywhere. But then what would be the point, since Yiddish would lose its special Jewish quality and become a kind of linguistic quirk? And that, of course, would defeat the entire purpose of my experiment.

Yiddish as Denial

Between 1988 and 1991, I was very active in women and peace work in New York City in an effort to support the Israeli Women in Black. As part of my activism I gave speeches and published essays in feminist and Jewish journals. I also published some poetry on this subject. Sometime around 1989 or 1990, Karen, a woman running a poetry series in Massachusetts, wanted to create an event that would "bridge" audiences in her community—Jewish and non-

Jewish, feminist, gay/lesbian and straight—and invited me to participate in a program together with a local academic and poet. This man, I was told, was a "fan" and included my bilingual and "Holocaust" poetry in his syllabus for Jewish literature and Holocaust courses.

When approached by Karen, however, my "fan," apparently aware that I supported a two-state solution and negotiations with PLO "terrorists," informed her he would read with me only if I agreed not to mention Israel during the event. Karen, a non-Jew and not knowledgeable about the various splits Israel caused in the U.S. Jewish community, was bewildered when she passed on his response. Hoping to salvage the event, I sent him everything I had written since the start of the *intifada* and suggested we engage in a private dialogue. But even this was apparently beyond him and he never answered. I, of course, refused his condition and ended up reading alone. This man—who also identified as a poet—seemed to approve of me as *a lebn-geblibene dikhterin*/survivor poetess, but not as an engaged Jew with political opinions which differed from his own. Today, ten years later, the episode seems absurd. Arafat administers the West Bank and Gaza and will soon declare these areas a Palestinian State.

And yet I cannot totally dismiss that incident as something belonging only to the past. It is, I believe, representative, of an underlying censorship among some Jewish critic/academics—and sometimes even artists—who believe that the function of Jewish art is to support Jewish (religious?) survival and to affirm acceptable (to the Conference of Presidents?) political positions. The Jewish artist who touches on the future of Jerusalem, the settlements in the Occupied Territories, gay marriages, affirmative action, Black/Jewish relations in Crown Heights is often in peril from the Jewish literary establishment (academics, reviewers, cultural leaders) if s/he fails to endorse mainstream views.

I have been frequently told that my Holocaust and my Yiddish/English writing is my most powerful work. I am not in the habit of ranking my writing nor, for that matter, the writing of others. Still, how can anyone make such a judgment when certain "Jewish writing" is considered taboo? In this case poetry and prose about Israelis and Palestinians is read and judged through the lens of a specific, rigid political position. Theoretically, of course, any artist—Jewish or otherwise—is free to create whatever s/he wants. But, for example, could a novel, in which a Jewish woman who marries a non-Jew and decides (while the narrator remains neutral) it is better for her to raise her children as Christians, ever receive a good review in *The Jewish Week*, much less win the Jewish Book Award for fiction? It's unlikely. It would be criticized, not for its literary qualities, but for its tribal disloyalty. Communal Jewish prizes (and praise) support Jewish unity, survival, continuity. They would perhaps be self-destructive if they didn't. Nevertheless, such validation of a specific kind of Jewish literature inevitably censors or discourages another.

This unstated censorship, this tacit assumption that Jewish artists must create art that "is good for the Jews" is relevant to this discussion of Yiddish and bilingual poetry. Certainly, I am not interested in catering to preapproved political positions. This does not mean that I am automatically at odds with the community. Quite the contrary. I think often our interests coincide. Certainly my involvement with Yiddish has evoked very supportive responses. But I wonder to what degree that response would be tempered were I to move Yiddish into areas more controversial than some of the work I have already published in bilingual form.

Recently I found an unpublished poem that I wrote at the end of the 1980s, sometime during the *intifada*.

Der soyne / The Enemy: An Interview in Gaza

i.

I live here with my family.
The Jews come. I throw rocks.
I yell out: *Heil Hitler!*
My friend is shot with a rubber bullet.
They take him to the hospital. He will
live but he's a cripple.
My mother weeps: When will it end?
Me? I'm happy school is closed.
Who needs to study?
I like to see them hide
behind the walls. Down with the Jews!
Long live Palestine!

ii.

Ikh voyn do mit der mishpokhe.
Di yidn kumen. Ikh varf shteyner.
Ikh shray: Heil Hitler!
A fraynd vert geshosn mit a gumener koyl.
Men nemt im in shpitol. Er vet
lebn ober er vet zayn a kalike.
Di mame veynt: ven vet es zikh endikn?
Ikh? Ikh bin tsefridn az di shul iz farmakht.

Vos darf ikh lernen?
'Sgefelt mir ven zey bahaltn zikh
unter di vent. Nider mit di yidn!
Zol lebn palestine!

I wrote this poem in this way—a different form of the experiment—specifically to test what would happen when only the language differed. I wanted to see how a language associated with Jewish powerlessness sounded in the mouth of someone who was oppressed by Jewish power. The entire piece was *one* poem in two parts in which neither the English nor the Yiddish dominated. Did the use of Yiddish transform the content/meaning of this poem?[8]

I remember once during a peace rally, I was engaged in a rather hostile debate with an elderly couple. When I realized they spoke Yiddish, I started using it also. But the woman immediately snapped: "*Ze nor, zi tut mir a toyve. Zi nitst yidish!*/She thinks she's doing me a favor. She's using Yiddish!" By extension, in the case of "*Der soyne,*" I can hear her say: Why didn't she write the poem from the point of view of the Israeli soldiers? Why is she always siding with the Palestinians? And what does it matter that she's writing in Yiddish?

I believe the Massachusetts academic-poet was a supporter of my bilingual work because it makes Yiddish more visible. I also believe that he has placed on this support, perhaps unconsciously, rigid boundaries: He does not envision Yiddish embracing the present. In other words, his kind of attachment to Yiddish is a screen that blocks and protects us from embarrassing and painful realities. So one danger in our growing passion for Yiddish is a desire to reconnect with Jewish innocence, with a time when we were a people without national power: pre-Israel, pre-middle-class America. If that is our motive, then our use of Yiddish is fantasy, nostalgia, escapism, an attempt to turn back the clock. Yiddish as denial.

We diminish Yiddish if we use it to deny the present, if we see it only in terms of a fixed past, unrelated to our current problems. We trivialize the language that so many used to express the best and worst of Jewish life, to debate all issues—political, moral, aesthetic. No topic, position, perspective, idea, passion, or viewpoint should be excluded from Yiddish expression. In fact, only if we enfold within this language our contemporary lives and crises will Yiddish have any chance of surviving, becoming revitalized, and breathing those elements that will make it modern.

Yiddish: The Pen of the Heart

Language may be the heart of the matter, but without context it can never be enough. As a poet, even when I use Yiddish, I cannot act as if the language had never been used by anyone else before me. There is a complex, rich Yiddish cultural tradition with which, if we want to reconnect with Yiddish, we must also engage. Paradoxically, for most Jews this engagement can only take place in English—through translation. This is a shame, but not a cause for despair. Quite the opposite. Translations keeps Yiddish alive by making us aware of the achievement of secular *yidishkayt* and by whetting our appetites for the original. I am not naive enough to think that translations will make every reader immediately begin studying and reclaiming Yiddish. But I do think that English translations are the only entrance for most Jews and that for some they may prove, in fact, to be the first open door leading to their becoming committed Yiddishists.

Because of this, it is important for us as readers and as writers to internalize this translated work, to make it as much a part of our internal literary landscape as are the poetry of Emily Dickinson and fiction of Herman Melville. I am amazed that there is so much American Jewish poetry and creative writing today—especially among feminists—that uses Biblical texts as its starting point. The creation of feminist *midrashim* based on Torah is a rich development in American Jewish secular and religious literature.

Yet it is almost impossible to find Jewish writing in English that refers back to the Yiddish texts of the nineteenth and twentieth century. We need poems and stories that make these texts and authors—Molodowsky, Heller, Schnirer, Dropkin, Korn, Schtok—part of our daily consciousness. We should internalize them, make them a significant reference point in our writing. Only then will the Yiddishist tradition become an integral part of our work by manifesting itself through citations, epigraphs, allusions, subject matter, themes. Such a visible presence of that tradition will reflect our own awareness of the work and figures who wrote in Yiddish; our content will become recognizably Yiddish, even when our language is not.

This approach linked with some modest steps toward *tsveyshprakhikayt/* bilingualism in our poetry will, I believe, keep the Yiddish literary tradition alive for those who may one day want to embrace it in its original. So, creating bilingual Yiddish/English American poetry—linguistically and culturally—is something I will probably continue to consider and experiment with. Like my other poetry, it is often frustrating and difficult to evaluate—but for different reasons. I sometimes find it hard to move quickly enough from one language to another, hard to know which language to use when and how to ease the strain between them. But it is precisely this strain that feels creative for it raises questions about me as an American Jewish poet—about my languages, my literary legacy, and my cultural roots. And these are questions I want to try to answer in whatever bilingual form presents itself.

Notes

1. This essay draws on my lecture "Yiddish and the Contemporary Jewish Woman Writer," presented as part of the Rennert Jewish Feminist Lecture Series at Barnard College, November 22, 1998.

2. Used by Sore Schnirer in 1938 in her essay *"Yidishkayt un yidish/*Jewishness and Yiddish" in *Never Say Die! A Thousand Years of Yiddish in Jewish Life and Letters*, ed. Joshua A. Fishman (The Hague: Mouton, 1981), 175. Schnirer was a passionate Yiddishist and founder of the *Beys yakov* movement for religious education for girls.

3. I am aware I am generalizing and, in doing so, mean no disrespect to those for whom Yiddish is a living language. I realize: (a) that Yiddish is the daily language of thousands of Khassidim wherever they live; and (b) that there is currently, at the very least, a mini-revival of Yiddish (often led by ardent lifelong Yiddishists) among many Ashkenazi Jews who are studying it in order to reclaim it. Still, the reality is that Yiddish as a *literary medium* is very precarious, almost nonexistent. There are not only fewer and fewer Yiddish writers and poets; proportionately, there are probably even fewer readers. The Khassidim shun secular Yiddish texts, and the fledgling generation of Yiddishists committed to those texts is extremely small. For the vast majority of Ashkenazi Jews, Yiddish culture remains completely inaccessible in the original.

4. I address these issues in "Secular Jewish Identity: *Yidishkayt* in America" and "Forging a Link in *di goldene keyt*: Some Possibilities for Jewish American Poetry" in my collection *Dreams of an Insomniac: Jewish Feminist Essays, Speeches and Diatribes* (Portland, Ore.: Eighth Mountain P, 1990), 143–66 and 167–74.

5. See my essays "Feminism, *Yidishkayt*, and the Politics of Memory" in *Bridges* 4, no. 1 (1994), 12–47, and "Queens of Contradiction: A Feminist Introduction to Yiddish Women Writers," in *Found Treasures: Stories by Yiddish Women Writers*, ed. Frieda Forman et al. (Toronto: Second Story, 1994), 15–62.

6. In Irena Klepfisz, *A Few Words in the Mother Tongue: Poems Selected and New* (Portland, Ore.: Eighth Mountain P, 1990), 225–27.

7. Rachelle Vaprinski (1895–?), *"O, mayn shprakh"* in *Yidishe dikhterin antologye* [Jewish Poetesses Anthology], ed. E. Korman (Chicago: Farlag L. M. Shteyn, 1928), 172–73.

8. *"Di yerushe/*The Legacy: A Parable About History and *Bobe-mayses, Barszcz and Borsht* and the Future of the Jewish Past," in *The Prairie Schooner Anthology of Contemporary Jewish American Writing*, ed. Hilda Raz (Lincoln: U of Nebraska P, 1998), 7–12.

9. *"Der soyne"* would probably have its own resonance to Yiddish speakers and readers, who would expect any topic to be addressed in Yiddish. But I think the effect is a different one for non-Yiddish speakers, precisely because of the nostalgic associations most have with the language.

Jews Translating Jews

JOHN FELSTINER

John Felstiner is Professor of English at Stanford University and author of the critical biography *Paul Celan: Poet, Survivor, Jew* (Yale, 1995), which won a number of distinguished national and international awards in 1995. He has translated works by Enrique Lihn (*The Dark Room*), Pablo Neruda (*Translating Neruda: The Way to Macchu Picchu*), Paul Celan, and many others.

Whenever any poet translates another, an act of furtherance and renewal takes place. If the translator is an American Jew, and the other language is Hebrew or Yiddish or indeed any tongue spoken elsewhere by Jews, then possibly that act pushes forward a little the ever-deferred hope ingrained in Judaism.

Kol omer davar b'shem omro mevia geula l'olam. The Hebrew (here transliterated) of the Babylonian Talmud tells us: "Whoever speaks a word in the name of its speaker, brings redemption to the world." This saying, from Megilla 15a, is taken to hold for translation. Specifically, it refers to Queen Esther bringing news from Mordechai to Ahasuerus that averts the King's assassination, whereupon she reveals her Jewishness and saves her people. (Esther 2:22). So an act of translation may carry redemptive force. Except sometimes. A more recent source, the Yiddish and first modern Hebrew poet Chaim Nachman Bialik (1873–1934), claimed that reading a translation is like kissing a bride through the veil.

Bialik is famously seconded by Robert Frost: "Poetry is what gets lost in translation." And by the Italian *traduttore/traditore*, "translator/traitor"—or more rhythmically and idiomatically, "render/bender." And by countless other gainsayers. Yet this chutzpah goes on, from generation to generation. "You translate poems?—isn't that dreadfully difficult?" To which one would respond like the Seabees in World War II, those dogged Construction Battalions laying pontoon bridges over the Rhine: "The difficult we do immediately, the impossible takes a little longer."

From time immemorial the matter of translation has preoccupied Jews. Babel's hubris and disaster, a myth found in many cultures, was crystallized for the Judeo-Christian West in Genesis (11:1–9). Once "the whole earth was of

337

one language." Then the people built a city and a tower to reach unto heaven, "And the Lord said, behold, the people is one, and they have all one language," now there'll be no stopping them. So the Lord confounded their language and did "scatter them abroad upon the face of all the earth." Hence we speak thousands of tongues: multilingual, multinationed, richly disunited. Hebrew calls that city Babel, akin to Babylon the Israelites' place of exile–which is to say that Jewishly, exile implies the need for translation. "Trans-late": "Carry-across." The word "Hebrew" itself denotes a "crossing-over" people: Abraham out of Ur to Canaan, Moses through the Red Sea to Sinai, Joshua across the Jordan into the Promised Land, the Israelites back from Babylon to Zion, Spain's Jews fleeing the Inquisition, Europe's seeking America.

"After Babel," George Steiner called his 1975 tour de force on the philosophical, linguistic, and literary elements of translation. And after Babel, translation tracks the steps of a people persisting in Diaspora, for whom language— whether mother tongue or holy tongue—often forms their only homeland. Even in postexilic Eretz Yisrael, as the common people gradually ceased understanding Hebrew, translation and interpretation came into play. We have this magnificent Biblical moment, after the return from Babylonian captivity to Jerusalem:

> And all the people gathered themselves together as one man into the street that was before the water gate; and they spake unto Ezra the scribe to bring the book of the law of Moses, which the Lord had commanded to Israel. And Ezra the priest brought the law before the congregation both of men and women, and all that could hear with understanding, upon the first day of the seventh month. And he read therein before the street that was before the water gate from the morning until midday, before the men and the women, and those that could understand; and the ears of all the people were attentive unto the book of the law. And Ezra the scribe stood upon a pulpit of wood, which they had made for the purpose. And Ezra opened the book in the sight of all the people; (for he was above all the people;) and when he opened it, all the people stood up: And Ezra blessed the Lord, the great God. And all the people answered Amen, Amen, with lifting up their hands: and they bowed their heads, and worshiped the Lord with their faces to the ground. So they read in the book in the law of God distinctly, and gave the sense, and caused them to understand the reading. And Nehemiah . . . and Ezra the priest, the scribe, and the Levites that taught the people, said unto all the people, This day is holy unto the Lord your God; mourn not, nor weep. For all the people wept, when they heard the words of the law. . . .And all the people went their way to eat, and to drink, and to send portions, and to make great mirth, because they had understood the words that were declared unto them (Nehemiah 8:1–12).

In a later period, at the weekly Torah or prophetic lesson, a *Targeman* or *Meturgeman* would stand next to the reading desk and immediately translate orally into vernacular Aramaic, often weaving commentary around the original text. Notably, those early Jewish translators were enjoined not to lean against the desk but to stand deferentially off; not to look into the Torah as if the *targum* were *there*; not to speak louder than the reader but to declaim in the same pitch. And we have a rabbinic dictum about the targumists who made written versions of Scripture: "He who translates quite literally is a liar, while he who adds anything is a blasphemer." This might well baffle modern translators!

According to legend, Ptolemy in the third century B.C.E. brought seventy-two elders of Israel, six from each tribe, to Alexandria to translate the Pentateuch into Greek. This plus later Biblical books became known as the Septuagint, having huge influence on Jewry's Hellenistic diaspora (as well as serving Christian churches). And the medieval period, in Spain and elsewhere, saw immense production of translations from Arabic and also Latin into Hebrew: theology, philosophy, grammar, mathematics, medicine, and other sciences. Jews during Spain's Muslim (and then Christian) centuries lived with some tolerance, comfort, strength, but also grave insecurity—which helps explain an epigram by Judah Al-Harizi (1170–1235), a Hebrew-language poet who wandered from his native Spain:

> The broadest land's too tight a squeeze
> To give two foes an ample space,
> Meantime a very narrow place
> Can hold a thousand friends with ease.

Al-Harizi translated Maimonides' *Guide of the Perplexed* into Hebrew, and also secular Arabic poetry. Samuel HaNagid, Ibn Gabirol, Moses Ibn Ezra, Judah Halevi, and Abraham Ibn Ezra, besides occasionally translating from Arabic, all "translated" Arabic and Spanish poetic forms into Hebrew verse. On the threshold of the Italian Renaissance, Immanuel of Rome translated Dante and composed Petrarchan sonnets in Hebrew. The story is proverbial: When in Diaspora, do as your hosts do, but with a Jewish bent—and then some. Spain's medieval Jewish poets do write of war, love, and wine, but they also explore Judaic lore and yearn for Zion.

In the modern Diaspora, as in Alexandria, translation does not move out of but into the vernacular. Take the special case of Bible translation (a field that itself occupies a vast dimension). Moses Mendelssohn, leader of eighteenth century German Jewry (and grandfather of the composer Felix Mendelssohn), translated the Torah into High German—an act of Jewish Enlightenment—and published this text in Hebrew characters, as distinct from Martin Luther's hegemonic German Bible. After World War I Martin Buber and Franz Rosenzweig, again translating the Bible, attempted to convey its Hebraic voice through innovative, renovative German diction, syntax, rhythm. With Nazism's takeover, Schocken Publishers doughtily began a series of slim volumes (1933–1938) promoting Jewish culture: first Buber and Rosenzweig's rendering of Isaiah 40–55, entitled "The Consolation of Israel," then Rosenzweig's version of Judah Halevi's Songs to Zion, Buber's Hasidic tales in German, and the Hebrew author S. Y. Agnon's stories, translated by Gershom Scholem and Nahum Glatzer. All this to infuse Hebraic spirit into the body of German Jewry and into their mother tongue. After the Shoah, however, and the end of any German-Jewish symbiosis, Scholem could only tell Buber that his Bible translation (from Hebrew to German) formed "the tombstone of a relationship that was extinguished in unspeakable horror."

The philosopher Franz Rosenzweig (1886–1929), who wrote *The Star of Redemption* and led the first Jewish Lehrhaus or study institute, remained acutely conscious of the dynamics between translation and Diaspora Jewishness. On his wedding trip he translated the Hebrew "Grace After Meals," but he would hide it from a guest who knew any Hebrew, because "the least comprehended Hebrew word yields more than the finest translation." Rosenzweig calls Diaspora Jewry's need to translate Hebrew sources into the native tongue "our predicament" and accepts it: "We cannot avoid this path that again and again leads us out of what is alien and into our own." Thus Jewish spirituality abides in Hebrew per se, yet the Hebrew may have to pass through our vernacular. Perhaps this paradox resolves if translation, as Rosenzweig says, points us back toward the source.

While it's true that Judaic essentials inhere within Hebrew and Yiddish sources, it's also true that Bible, theology, and liturgy do not occupy the whole domain of translation. Rosenzweig's sense of "our predicament," of the bending path "into our own," also has much to do with non-religious literary translation from any language. Why then might a Jewish writer—Emma Lazarus, Cynthia Ozick, Franz Rosenzweig, Paul Celan—want to bring another Jewish writer into English or into German? In most times and places, Jews have not felt completely *zu Hause*, at home. Frequently marked if not actually demonized as the "other," they might well want to prove that difference, to test and contemplate it, by voicing some "other" writer's work in their own tongue, especially as their birthright to that tongue has, at various times and places, been called into question.

Migrant or marginal as they have tended to be, for better and worse, Jewish writers often move inevitably between languages. Celan, for instance, learning German at home, Romanian at school, and Russian under occupation, translated the German-speaking Czech Jew Franz Kafka into Romanian and the Russian Jew Osip Mandelshtam into German—Kafka and Mandelshtam being his chief presiding spirits, as much for their hedged and nuanced Jewishness as for their brilliant writing. "I consider translating Mandelshtam into German to be as important a task as my own verses," Celan once said. In his case, that task meant transfusing something new, some cleansing strangeness, into a German language recently corrupted by Nazi-Deutsch such as *Endlösung* ("Final Solution"), *judenrein* ("Jew-free"), *Sonderehandlung* ("Special Treatment"). Nothing so drastic bears on the at-homeness of Jewish writers within American English. Yet in translating, they may feel themselves (literally) endorsing a strangeness, a Judaic otherness that nonetheless reroots them, reconnects an affiliation.

Incidentally, two major fields of translation do not figure in these considerations: prose, and the Bible—not for lack of significance, but because a brief survey can more pointedly explore the options and effects involved in translating poems.

Emma Lazarus (1849–1887) first made translations of Heinrich Heine (and Victor Hugo) in her teens, but these were melancholy Romantic lyrics, harmonizing with her own sentiment, not the German Jew's poetry of bitterness and anger, such as his "Rabbi of Bacharach" or "To Edom." The same held true when Lazarus years later published a full collection, *Poems and Ballads* (1881). But in contrast to the poetry inside, her introduction to that collection stresses Heine's "ineradicable sympathy with things Jewish," calling him "an enthusiast for the rights of the Jews" who "buried himself with fervid zeal in the love of his race" and died "a poor fatally-ill Jew." Then in *Songs of a Semite* (1882), which betrays her outrage at recent pogroms in Russia and Germany, Lazarus does include some imitations of Heine depicting anti-Semitism with keen irony. And soon afterward, in an article on him, she identifies his Jewish "sympathy of race, not of creed," quoting his tribute that Jews have remained *Menschen,* human beings, "in spite of eighteen centuries of persecution and misery." So Emma Lazarus ended up confirming her own Jewish autonomy in endorsing Heine's. During the 1880s, she was also speaking out indignantly for a Jewish homeland, a revival of Zion. She had already translated (via German) Ibn Gabirol, Moses Ibn Ezra, and Judah Halevi, especially Halevi's "Longing for Jerusalem." In 1883, having rendered a fervent poem by Judah Al-Harizi on renewing God's Covenant, she noted something new: "I have translated this from the original Hebrew—& so am very proud of it as my first effort!"

Until well after World War II, it is hard to find any other American Jewish poet translating a fellow Jew—anyone like Joseph Leftwich, whose *Yisroel* (1933) and *Golden Peacock* (1939) introduced Yiddish literature in England, or A. M. Klein, who translated [Chaim Nachman] Bialik and others in Canada. Some such work did appear, mainly from Hebrew, but seldom by distinguished writers. Charles Reznikoff above all was fruitfully open to Hebrew poetry, whence his deft version of Halevi's Songs to Zion. And doubtless other instances exist that have not come to light. In 1953 Saul Bellow and Isaac Rosenfeld first translated stories by Isaac Bashevis Singer; this may mark a new American awareness, an access to secular Jewish tradition by way of first-rate literary translation. Marie Syrkin, Robert Friend, Sarah Zweig Betsky, and Aaron Kramer were among the earliest to translate from Hebrew and Yiddish.

During the 1960s the pace picked up, as it did for translation at large, with journals such as *Modern Poetry in Translation* in England and *Delos* in the United States. In *The Modern Hebrew Poem Itself* (1965), admirably edited by Stanley Burnshaw, T. Carmi, and Ezra Spicehandler, writers from Bialik to Dahlia Ravikovitch were "discussed into English." Irving Howe and Eliezer Greenberg's *Treasury of Yiddish Poetry* (1969), a sequel to their 1954 anthology of Yiddish stories, joined leading American with Yiddish poets: John Hollander with Moyshe Leib Halpern, Mani Leib, Abraham Reisen, Itzik Feffer; Cynthia Ozick with David Einhorn, Halper Leivick, Chaim Grade; Adrienne Rich with Celia Dropkin, Kadya Molodowsky, Dvorah Fogel; Armand Schwerner with Peretz Markish; Jerome Rothenberg with Melech Rawitch; Carolyn Kizer with Rachel Korn; Stanley Kunitz with Israel Emiot; Irving Feldman with Isaiah Spiegel (some of these appear elsewhere in this anthology). Through such matchmaking, various voices otherwise inaudible— women, exiles, immigrants, innovators, victims of Stalin and Hitler—were heard in an increasingly monolingual country.

Eventually more poets reached out elsewhere and to other languages. Not every one would echo Robert Mezey's sense that his translations (of Uri Zvi Greenberg) were "my best work." But perhaps they all felt a "shock of recognition" such as Melville experienced in reading Hawthorne: "genius, all over the world, stands hand in hand, and one shock of recognitions runs the whole circle round." Carl Rakosi finds a kindred voice for Ibn Gabirol and "the earth / which expands my thought." Shirley Kaufman, transplanting her life to Israel, brings alive in English the partisan-poet Abba Kovner's Vilna and Sinai, the Ukrainian-born Amir Gilboa's traumatic revision of Abraham and Isaac, the woman's sensibility of Dutch poet Judith Herzberg. Ruth Feldman transmits Primo Levi's blasphemous 1946 "Shema." Cynthia Ozick and C. K. Williams gravitate to Avraham Sutzkever, whose Yiddish lyric voice persists after the Vilna ghetto for more than fifty years. Ruth Whitman makes herself responsible for a virtual survivor: Born in Poland but coming to America in 1914, Jacob Glatstein suffers the *Churbn* "as if," and calls his first postwar book *Radiant Jews*. Chana Bloch takes on the Bible-haunted Ravikovitch, a Sabra, and also catches the idiomatic humor and passion of Yehuda Amichai, who fled Germany for Palestine in 1936. Joachim Neugroschel brings Gertrud Kolmar within earshot, who could not flee Germany. Steve Berg, helped by a native Hungarian, translates Miklós Radnóti, whose wife found him in a mass grave, poems in his overcoat pocket. Peter Cole evokes the courtly, battle-tried, fatherly presence of Samuel HaNagid perfecting Hebrew within a Muslim nation. And I myself try for the quotidian, reiterated deathcamp rhythm of Celan's "Deathfugue" (1944–45), which exposes Nazism's orchestrated genocide.

If poetry is not, or not merely, what gets lost in translation but what gets gained, then what is it that gets gained in these translations? Naturally, American Jewish poets have not turned only to coreligionists: Louis Zukofsky's Catullus, Stanley Kunitz's Voznesensky and Akhmatova, Richard Howard's Baudelaire, Anthony Hecht's Aeschylus and Sophocles, Muriel Rukeyser's and Eliot Weinberger's Octavio Paz, Allen Mandelbaum's and Robert Pinsky's Dante, just to mention a few. But when they have, why have they? What have they stood to gain?—besides, of course, the elation that inheres in this exacting craft, in getting something right, as well as the primary cognitive gain: "I myself understand a poem," Rosenzweig remarked, "only when I have translated it." Several motives come to mind, coinciding variously, and they all might take the motto that Walter Benjamin prized from Karl Kraus: *Ursprung ist das Ziel*, "Origin is the goal"—a motto that holds as well for the practice of translation itself.

Perhaps foremost, in opting for poets who by reason of time or circumstance stand closer to Scripture, translators have brought themselves and their readers into touch with the Bible and Judaic tradition. *Schreiben als Form des Gebetes*, Kafka once jotted in his notebook, "Writing as a form of prayer." For many Jewish writers, translating becomes a form of—and often takes the place of—prayer.

Israel, no less than Holy Writ, compellingly draws American Jews. They need to know what it feels like to live in a country where Jews predominate, Hebrew fills the streets, and enemies daily threaten. So Miriyam Glazer renders a Yona Wallach poem about what emerges from Hebrew's gendered nouns and verbs. Or in a time of crisis and loss, it may matter to align oneself with Amichai's lines on the Six-Day War:

> *et hayeled hachai tsrichim*
> *lenakot b'shuvo mimischak*
> it's the living child we need
> to scrub when he's back from play

Finding a cadence here and a syntax and line break can mean growing answerable, responsive, participant.

To translate poets who survived or did not survive the European Jewish catastrophe asks for acute attentiveness and keeps current the atrocious loss. If the Romanian-born Israeli Dan Pagis took twenty-five years after the Shoah before writing his quintessential vignette, "Katuv b'iparon bakaron hechatum" (Written in Pencil in a Sealed Railway Car), those lines should probably be urged upon people whose families were not equally at risk:

> *kan bamishloach hazeh*
> *ani chava*
> *im hevel b'ni*
> *im tiru et b'ni hagadol*

kayin ben adam
tagidulo sh'ani
here in this transport
I Eve
with Abel my son
if you see my older son
Cain son of Adam
tell him that I

Possibly the human family feels as drastically ruptured in English as in He-
brew, since it stems from the one myth, the founding text long common to Di-
aspora and Zion alike. But the plural addressee of Pagis's *tagidulo* gets lost:
"tell [ye] him." That is to say, English cannot inflect the verb to show that Eve
has something to tell a great many people, even unto the present generation,
about her son's murder. And does the silence cutting short her last words *tagi-
dulo sh'ani*, do our questions suspended in that silence after "tell him that I,"
resound the same in English as in Hebrew?

As for the East European and immigrant dimension of Jewish experience:
Even if it seems to have relapsed as a source and recourse, as the vital stuff of
contemporary literary creation, nevertheless American translators since the
war have regained more and more of their inheritance. Some years ago the New
York Yiddish poet Glatstein complained: "I have to be aware of Auden, but
Auden need never have heard of me." And Cynthia Ozick's story "Envy; or,
Yiddish in America" rings with the cry of a Glatstein-like poet to a young
American woman: "Translate me!" Yet those scales may be balancing. The
translation of Singer's writings, in itself a cottage industry, led to the Nobel
Prize. The efforts of numerous other translators and scholars, the ingathering
and redisseminating of crumbling Yiddish books, the songfests and theater, the
proliferating Klezmer bands and camps, the guided tours to Manhattan's
Lower East Side and to eastern Europe, the *shtetl* on CD-ROM: Does all this
bespeak mere nostalgia or a kind of restitution? Maybe it will always be too
soon to disentangle such things.

Whatever else may be said for American Jewish poets and other translators,
they have brought striking new voices and a salutary strangeness into this
country's literary bloodstream, at times into its mainstream. They have helped
dissolve a little the dominant Christian strain in modern American poetry, from
Eliot, Auden, and Stevens to Lowell and Frost. Or rather, the admixture of
Judah Halevi and Samuel HaNagid, Halpern and Glatstein, Mandelshtam and
Celan, has moved toward a deep common ground. Witness Walter Benjamin,
who himself died before crossing the border to freedom in 1940, in his essay
"The Task of the Translator": "Translation kindles from the endless renewal of
languages as they grow to the messianic end of their history."